A CLOISTER
IN THE WORLD

To the Holy Cross Brothers in Chile
wishing you every blessing from
the Lord
Patrick Barry OSB

A CLOISTER
IN THE
WORLD

The Story of the
Manquehue Apostolic Movement
A Benedictine Movement of the Laity
& its Work in Chile

Patrick Barry OSB
former Abbot of Ampleforth Abbey

Published from
THE ABBEY OF SAINT MARY AND SAINT LOUIS

Quotations from Scripture have been taken from
the New Jerusalem Bible 1985
Darton Longman & Todd Ltd
& Doubleday & Company Inc
or from
The Revised Standard Edition, Catholic Version 1966
Division of Christian Education of the National
Council of the Churches of Christ in the
United States of America
Quotations from the Rule of St Benedict are from
RB80 translation – Liturgical Press or from
Translation by Patrick Barry – Hidden Spring

A CLOISTER IN THE WORLD
Copyright © by Patrick Barry
500 South Mason Road, St Louis MO 63141

Outskirts Press
http://www.outskirtspress.com

ISBN-10: 1-59800-085-3
ISBN-13: 978- 1-59800-085-6

The Abbey of Saint Mary and Saint Louis
500 South Mason Road
St Louis MO

Cover Photograph of Manquehue Mountain
by Paula Gross

Library of Congress Control Number: 2005930522

Outskirts Press and the "OP" logo are trademarks belonging to
Outskirts Press, Inc.

Printed in the United States of America

CONTENTS

+

This book is dedicated to

Our Lady of Guadalupe

Patroness of the Americas

and through her to

José Manuel Eguiguren Guzmán

Ignacio Eguiguren Cosmelli

all the family and all the Oblates

and members of the

Manquehue Apostolic Movement

℞

Introduction
by
José Manuel Eguiguren Guzmán

The idea of writing a book about the Manquehue Movement arose during some conversations I had with Abbot Patrick Barry in the year 1999. I wanted someone to introduce us in writing to the Benedictines and asked Abbot Patrick if he could do this. I felt that this might be necessary because six years earlier, in 1993, our Catholic lay Movement had been requested by Cardinal Pironio, then President of the Pontifical Council for the Laity in Rome, to develop and deepen its contact with Benedictine monasteries. This contact had begun in many quite surprising ways, but it was necessary to follow it up with some sort of explanation as to who we are. We came up with the idea of a book and *A Cloister in the World* is the result. It is the fruit of much laborious gathering and digesting of a large amount of source material, almost entirely in Spanish, all of which has placed huge demands on Abbot Patrick's reserves of patience, strength and energy. I am thoroughly indebted to him for his painstaking work in bringing this book to the light of day virtually single-handedly, and to his monastery, the Benedictine Abbey of St. Laurence at Ampleforth, of whose constant support and friendship this work is but an example.

A Cloister in the World tells the story of the first twenty-five years of the Manquehue Movement. It has been written by someone who has, in many ways, come to know us better than we know ourselves. Indeed, Abbot Patrick has made numerous trips to visit us in Chile and has lived with us for long periods of time on several occasions since the mid 1980's when, as Abbot of Ampleforth, he first began to take an interest in what we were doing here. He knows us well and I cannot help feeling that he has acted as a charitable and benevolent Abbot in choosing not to dwell in what he has written on our many frailties and weaknesses. The story does, of course, involve many people and countless different situations and Abbot Patrick has enabled us to reflect on what has happened from the perspective of his own vast experience and profound spiritual vision. We have learnt much from the insights and reflections he offers in these pages and I am sure they will be helpful to many who read this book.

On a more personal level, *A Cloister in the World* has led me to focus on the essence of what we have lived to-date as a young Movement in the Church. Indeed, if I had to sum up our experience in one word I would say that what we have experienced is friendship. I would say that friendship is, in fact, the foundation upon which everything in the Manquehue Movement has been built: friendship with Christ; friendship with others in Christ; and friendship for Christ.

Friendship with Christ. We have seen in our Movement how Jesus Christ addresses people personally in Holy Scripture, offering unconditional love, for God is love. "In this is love, not that we loved God but that he loved us and sent his Son to be the atoning sacrifice for our sins."[1] We have seen how He makes people aware through His Word of the fact that He is calling them, offering them a joy and fulfillment that comes from the discovery that they are loved by Him "because God's love has been poured into our hearts through the Holy Spirit that has been given to us"[2], filling them with a desire to love others. Christ befriends them in a dialogue of friendship in Scripture. He speaks to them in His Word revealed in Holy Scripture and they respond to Him with their prayer. Christ addresses each person as a friend. "I have called you friends", He says "because I have made known to you everything that I have heard from my Father"[3].

We have seen how this personal encounter has had a far-reaching impact in the lives of many people. Conversion takes place: a change of heart, transformation in our deepest self, at our spiritual center, a change of direction, a shifting of priorities, an about-turn in the deepest dimension of the heart, a *metanoia*, bringing about a new way of seeing the world and people, a new way of life. It is precisely this inner revolution, that comes through daily listening to the Word, that St. Benedict calls for in his Prologue when he says "Let us get up then, at long last, for the Scriptures rouse us when they say:[4] 'It is high time for us to arise from sleep.'[5] Let us open our eyes to the light that comes from God, and our ears to the voice from heaven that every day calls out this charge: 'If you hear his voice today, do not harden your hearts'.[6]And again: 'You that have ears to hear, listen to what the Spirit says to the churches'.[7] And what does he say? 'Come and listen to me, sons; I will teach you the fear of the Lord'[8]." God's voice in the Bible awakens a person to the reality of God's presence and daily sets them on a path back to the Lord. The Risen Christ reveals himself as Love, as a friend, inviting them to see things as He sees them, to recognize Him as Lord and King. It is a life changing experience that needs to be lived day-in day-out.

Friendship in Christ. We have also seen how strong and binding friendships between people emerge from this personal encounter with the Lord in Holy Scripture. A person makes space in their heart and mind for another, 'wastes' time on them, listens with patience to them and also communicates to the other their own personal experience of the Risen Christ. When the other reciprocates this giving of self and sharing of experience, and there is mutual acceptance, friendship begins to grow. It is a different sort of friendship. It is neither unnatural, nor is it forced, nor affected, nor over earnest. It is profound, rooted in the presence of the Lord and nourished through a constant dialogue with Him. It requires time. It does not shy away from mutual correction, nor from praying together. It looks to share with and serve the other for "No one has greater love than this, to lay down one's life for one's friends."[9] This friendship, as St. Aelred says, is born, grows and reaches fulfillment in Christ.[10]

At the very beginnings of our Movement, when we were a small, young and inexperienced group trying to organize ourselves in response to the Lord's call to do something in the Church, we were clear in stating that 'the basic characteristic of this Movement can be summed up in one word – friendship – Christian friendship – Christian love. "God is love and, if we find our nourishment in this love and pass it on to our brothers (and sisters) we shall be satisfied and our desire to give will increase. We are young and we will keep the doors open to this development. We shall now make a start in giving to others what we have to give, but, however small it may be, it must manifest our friendship."[11]

Friendship for Christ. The single, most important way that this friendship has been manifested down the years in the Movement, through this 'giving to others', is the way people have felt the need to live and build community. We have seen from our experience how friendship in Christ leads to a friendship lived for Christ, whereby friends work together in a common sense of mission. St. Benedict uses the language of military service when he urges people "to give up your own will" and "do battle for the true King, Christ the Lord"[12]. This sense of selfless idealism, of desiring to serve a cause, Christ's cause, is something that emerges quite naturally from friendship. Indeed, the first and most important mission that we have seen and encouraged amongst Manquehue members is the mission of creating community.

The Rule of St. Benedict has proved invaluable in this process. The Lord has placed the Rule in our hands as a sure guide in the task of building community and allowing the Spirit to strengthen lay men and women in their search for God and their desire to work together in a common cause, that of God's Kingdom. The Rule enables us to orientate our lives towards the Gospel with others. It gathers us around the Word of God and makes us bring the Word to bear upon the life and culture of the society in which we live. It teaches us to celebrate that same Word in the Liturgy and acknowledge it as the source and origin of our community life. Moreover, as Cardinal Basil Hume said, the Rule "makes it possible for ordinary folk to live lives of extraordinary value"[13], and when this happens something revolutionary occurs: the gap between the Faith people profess and the way they live their lives is narrowed. The divorce between Faith and life, Faith and culture, so characteristic of our age begins to disappear, so that "God may be glorified in everything"[14]. God's love poured into our hearts enables us to "set nothing before the love of Christ"[15] and to love others in community with Christ's love in the hope that He may "bring us all together to eternal life".[16] What we have come to call an 'alternative society' emerges, or what in the Church is referred to as the 'small community', or 'la comunidad ecclesial de base'[17], which in turn has a transforming effect upon human society at large, irradiating outward as something contagious, expanding the Kingdom.

The Manquehue Movement is one small community among countless groups and associations throughout the Church and it is a wonderful thing to be part of this. United in prayer with all the many expressions of the life of the Church in our Diocese - with our own Bishop and all the Bishops of the whole Church - together with all its different charisms and states of life - with the Holy Father who presides in charity from the Church in Rome[18] - united also with the whole People of God and all those related to it in various ways[19]- wishing to remain in communion with all of them in the construction of the 'Civilization of Love'[20], we ask for the intercession of the Most Holy Mother of God that we might, as one of the those many communities in the Church, continue to journey along the path that the Lord has granted us. For "what is not possible to us by nature, let us ask the Lord to supply by the help of his grace"[21].

Once more I thank Abbot Patrick for his generosity and the friendship he has shown us in writing this book. I hope that it will help others as much as it has helped me.

José Manuel Eguiguren Guzmán
Santiago, Chile. Monday of Holy Week
Anniversary of the Passing of St. Benedict, Abbot
21ˢᵗ March, 2005

ଔ

Notes for the Introduction

[1]   1 John 4, 10
[2]   Romans 5,5
[3]   John 15, 15
[4]   Rule of St. Benedict, Prologue 8-11 (RB 80)
[5]   Rom 13,11
[6]   Ps 94(95),8
[7]   Rev 2,7
[8]   Ps 33(34),12
[9]   John 15,13
[10] cf 'On Spiritual Friendship' Book 1, v 10
[11] Statement made by the founding members of the Manquehue Movement, Santiago, 28th May, 1977.
[12] Rule of St. Benedict, Prologue, v 3 (RB 80)
[13] In Praise of St. Benedict, Basil Hume OSB, Archbishop of Westminster. Talk given at Ealing Abbey, London, 21 March 1980.
[14] Rule of St. Benedict, chapter 57; 1 Peter 4, 11
[15] Rule of St. Benedict, chapter 4, v 21 (Parry)
[16] Rule of St. Benedict, chapter 72 (Patrick Barry)
[17] Evangelii Nuntiandi 58, Apostolic Exhortation of His Holiness Paul VI 1975
[18] c.f. St. Ignatius of Antioch, Letter to the Romans, 1
[19] c.f. Dogmatic Constitution of the Church, Lumen Gentium 16
[20] His Holiness Paul VI defined Christian civilization as the 'Civilization of Love'. His Holiness John Paul II has often used this expression in his teaching.
[21] Rule of St. Benedict, Prologue, 41 (RB 80)

Chapter 1 ~ PROLOGUE

This is the story of a lay Movement, called the Manquehue[1] Apostolic Movement, which started from very small beginnings in 1977 in the Church of Santiago in Chile. The questions and problems, however, with which this Movement was concerned as well as the vision which inspired their response belong to everyone. They are universal in their scope and inspiration. All the members of the Movement, both men and women, are from the Catholic laity. They include no priests or deacons. They live and work, however, in close communion with the Archbishop and the Church in Santiago. The Archbishop has approved their Statutes. These Statutes establish the Movement as a self governing Private Association of Lay Faithful under canon and civil law. The Movement has also received the approval (*laudatio*) of the Pontifical Council for the Laity in Rome. The membership includes both celibate and married members and all live in close association through the prayer, the listening to the word of scripture and solidarity in the Benedictine way of life they have adopted as laity.

The immediate inspiration of their way of life is the word of God in scripture and Saint Benedict's Rule, which they take as a guide to their lives as ordinary lay men and women working in the world. At the request of a former Archbishop Cardinal Raúl Silva Henriquez, the chief work of the Movement is evangelization, especially of the young, in the context of education. They have founded and manage three large schools - one of them in a very poor area of Santiago. This latter school also provides pastoral and medical help for the local families and offers courses in education for adults who have been deprived of schooling. In all their educational work they are primarily devoted to the evangelization of the young and aim to pass on to the younger generation their own lay and Benedictine spirituality. It is a spirituality both traditional and new. It is firmly rooted in the sacred word of the scriptures, in the sacraments of the Catholic Church and in the 'wholeness' of Saint Benedict's Rule.

1

Yet it is a spirituality which is radically lay - in line with the new vision of laity in Vatican II.

Although education in schools is a large part of their commitment, they carry their message of evangelization also to adults in the universities and in all walks of lay life. They have founded a house for looking after the homeless in Santiago. They work in diocesan projects. They have recently been invited by the Rector of the Seminary in Santiago to teach *lectio divina* to the seminarians. In all that they do their fundamental aim is to make the word of the gospel alive in the world of today.

The founder, José Manuel Eguiguren Guzmán, as a young man at university went through an experience of spiritual desolation which mirrored the political and social and religious darkness in his country during the 1970's. With the guidance of a Benedictine monk he discovered through *lectio divina*, which is the ancient Benedictine way of reading the scriptures, that the word of God is still alive and active even in the difficult circumstances of modern lay life. He spent three years visiting daily the monastery in Santiago to devote himself to intensive *lectio divina*. This experience changed his life and enabled him later to transform the lives of young men and women who came under his influence. He was led on to found three schools with a holistic educational system in which the word of God is cherished as "a pure and lasting fount of spiritual life"[2] both in the classroom and out of it. With the aid of the young people, who had now joined him to form the Movement, he sought to treat all the pupils of his schools individually with loving welcome and so 'rescue them from anonymity'[3] and enable them to realize a loving relationship with the risen Christ, who can transform their lives.

In addition to their schools these lay men and women have founded two houses in a remote area of Chilean Patagonia which are devoted to the Christian formation of young men and women (mostly from the universities of Santiago). These unique lay foundations are recognized and welcomed by the local bishop in Patagonia and they assist the clergy by forming a pastoral unit which is able to give help and support in the local wild and scattered parish. It is an area of great beauty but also of great poverty - both material and spiritual. For the young, who go there for up to six months to live a life of great simplicity, these houses provide a unique opportunity for coming to terms with themselves through *lectio divina* in the scriptures, the Divine Office, community life, the wisdom of Saint Benedict's Rule and the gospel-inspired Christian formation offered by the resident lay Oblates[4] of the Movement. They live there without distraction the spiritual life of the Movement to which this book is an introduction.

The founder's marriage, just at the time when the Movement was growing around him, made a strong connection for all the members to family life and ensured that the family spirit should inspire the members, who now amount to nearly a thousand. These members are gathered round the center in concentric circles corresponding to different degrees of commitment. In the center are the Oblates, some married and some celibate, who have made a full commitment to the Movement and its works. José Manuel's wife, Luz Cosmelli, had suffered from the aftermath of a terrible road accident which left her in a state nearing despair. She was rescued spiritually from that negativity by members of another Catholic Movement - the Neo Catechumenate. In their marriage José Manuel and Luz have both been faithful to their different lay vocations in a spirit of profound mutual understanding and together they have raised a family of five children, two of whom are handicapped. All the children have been integrated joyfully into the life of the Movement.

The early chapters of this book give an account of the founding of the Manquehue Movement in the difficult circumstances of Chile in the late seventies and early eighties. It briefly follows the course of its extraordinary and rapid growth and the gradual development of its way of life and work. The later chapters deal with its relationship to the teaching of the Church, both in the Council and in more recent years. Then there is an explanation of its close relationship with the Benedictines. Finally some of the members of all ages in the Movement give their own testimonies about their spiritual experience in the small communities in which the Movement consists. Many other testimonies of great depth and relevance were available, but a selection had to be made. One page of personal witness is worth a whole book of description by a third person, so that these chapters at the end - and many quotations of personal testimony during the course of the narrative

- are truly the heart of this book written by those who actually live the life.

This account of the Manquehue Apostolic Movement was written at the request of the founder, José Manuel Eguiguren Guzmán. I would like to record my deep gratitude to him for this invitation and for the wonderful welcome I have received from him and his family and the Manquehue Oblates and for all the assistance they have given me in this task over many visits during twenty years. Even more, I am grateful for the inspiration I have received through working with members of the Movement on this project. One is not left unchanged by close encounters with the Manquehue Movement. It has been a wonderful time of learning new things and old, which defies description. It has enabled me to understand what happens to so many of the young who visit the Movement - because it can happen to the elderly as well. Above all it has made me anxious to share the relevance of this Chilean experience to the dark waves of secularist negativity which threaten the young in so many different ways throughout the world.

There are others also whom I need to mention. I owe and gladly record my gratitude, over the years during which I have been working on this book, to the Abbot and Community of Saint Louis Abbey for their kindness and tolerance. Their Benedictine prayer and community life has been the framework and inspiration of my work, and by their generous tolerance they have assisted me in more ways than I can easily describe. I am thankful to Mr Lee Hawes for many hours which he spent on keeping my computer going and keeping me up to date on its technology. I am grateful for the help of Mrs Julie Constantino, Director of Development of Saint Louis Abbey and Priory School for her help in preparing this edition, and to her assistant, Mrs. Terri Wood, for her generous work and computer skills in formatting the text. I gladly acknowledge also a very special debt of gratitude to Mrs Katharine Le Mée, who with great generosity in a busy life has read everything for me and given me her knowledgeable advice. Her comments and encouragement were vital to me and indispensable in the early shaping of this work. Finally, I owe a very special debt of gratitude to Jonathan Perry, General Secretary of the Manquehue Movement for valuable and indispensable help in the final revision of this text and to José Manuel Eguiguren himself for the unique authority of his comments and suggestions.

ℭℛ

Notes for Prologue
[1] Pronounced 'Man-kay-way. It is the name of a mountain overlooking a district of Santiago which is named after it. The name is used also for other activities and institutes within the district.

[2] Vatican II - Dei Verbum n.21

[3] This is José Manuel's own, often repeated, expression of his intention or 'mission'.

[4] The Oblates are the members of the Movement, both men and women, who have made a formal commitment and are, as will be explained, at the center of the Movement. They form the Council who support and advise José Manuel in the government of the Movement.

Chapter 2 ~ The Wisdom of
Cardinal Silva Henriquez

A New lay Movement arises in Chile at a time of darkness and confusion
The Manquehue Apostolic Movement was founded by lay Catholics in
Chile towards the end of the twentieth century.[1] It started among young
people, but now it embraces all age groups. It grew up within the
Catholic Church and remains faithful to it, preserving always its
communion with the Archbishop and Church of Santiago in Chile and
with Rome. It was first inspired by the impact of the word of God in
scripture on the young Chilean, José Manuel Eguiguren, who founded it.
This happened when he gave three years of his life to *lectio divina*[2] under
the guidance of a Benedictine monk. He then taught his followers so
that reading the word in scripture became a regular practice in the
ordinary lay lives of those young people. The word of scripture and the
Church's sacramental and prayer life still sustain the members of the
Movement in their spiritual life and work.

There is another source, closely connected with *lectio,* which also
guides the Movement. This is Saint Benedict's Rule which, through its
timeless Christian wisdom, gave them the inspiration they needed about
how those devoted to Christ may live together in community. The Rule
has helped them to understand the spiritual roots which lie hidden in
scripture and which in any age are needed to achieve and maintain the
ideals of community and harmony and reconciliation and peace, which
everyone wants and few in the world today know how to achieve.

The Movement has found its mission through first of all learning the
gospel message of conversion to the rock who is Christ and then through
seeking to communicate that message to any others who are open to
hearing it and to accepting its inspiration in their personal lives. The
earliest mission of the Movement was to the young and this brought
them into the world of education (in the broadest sense of that word)
both in school and out of it, among children and among young adults.

Their method of educating the young, in a way that would encourage personal commitment to God, grew from the first out of their own personal experience of continuing conversion through the word of scripture in the light of the basic teaching of St Benedict's Rule. They sought simply to convey to the young the vision they had received of Christ as truly in everyday life: The Way the Truth and the Life[3].

It was a difficult time in Chile when the Movement came into being. It was in the seventies of last century, when Chile was going through a time of exceptional confusion and division. This was true not only on the political scene itself but also in the hearts of Catholics, who form the majority of the country, as they sought a balance between their Catholic faith and the harsh social and political realities of their lives. Chile is exceptional in South America because it is a democracy of long standing, but that did not save it from some of the wild social and cultural changes and fantasies that were current in the 60's and 70's. Apart from all that, as a strongly traditional Catholic country, it was vulnerable to the often disturbing and soul-searching innovations among Catholics that came partly from the teaching of Vatican II and partly from less authentic claimants to the role of prophet.

Politically for Chile the seventies began with the accession to power on a minority vote in 1970 of a controversial left-wing government under Salvador Allende. Allende was elected by an alliance of socialists, communists and members of the Christian left. The extremists came gradually to dominate political policy. It was a time when prophets of change in most aspects of human life were in the ascendancy everywhere and expectations ran high. There was talk all over the world of a new generation battering on the doors of established order and established government with a view to taking over and transforming the world so that everything would be new and everything would, of course, be better in every way.

In 1968 the student movement in France had brought the threat of violent political change into the heart of Europe. In South America - and not only in South America - Che Guevara of Cuba had become a cult figure among the young, and Castro with his left-wing, one party government tied to Moscow seemed to many to have shown the way

8

July 3

Don,

    I found this book in my collection. I do not need it.

    You may have it or I will put it out on the General Table

            Bill

20 COUNT WITH MESSAGE

forward. He had strong influence on the policies of the Allende regime in Chile and paid a long visit to Chile to reinforce his influence.

There was another factor with strong influence on the people of Chile. Within the Catholic Church in South America the self-examination which followed the Council was led by a strong Bishops' Conference. It sought to respond energetically to the urgent needs of the Continent. The Conferences of CELAM[4] met at Medellin in Columbia 1968 and at Puebla in Mexico in 1979 and called for radical Catholic action to deal with the gap between rich and poor and to revive in the modern world the gospel perspective on poverty. The CELAM bishops' called specifically for a *preferential option for the poor*. In itself that call was no more startling nor revolutionary than many of the words of Christ himself in the gospel, but in the context of the time they were disturbing to many Catholics in Chile.

At the same time Liberation theology[5] was gaining ground as a way of addressing the same subjects by using fundamental critiques of all the existing structures of western society. Some Catholic intellectuals looked to the extreme left - and even to Marxist theory and practice - as an instrument for the development of what they proclaimed would be a new form of Christianity. There were others among Catholics who with equally fierce dedication resisted change and in response to the ruthless violence of the left looked towards the equally ruthless authoritarian military power of the right in the hope that it would counteract 'disruptive influences' and provide what they claimed was the only way of escape for the West from the threatening embrace of Soviet communistic imperialism.

It was against this background and as a result of the confrontations it aroused that in 1973 there was a violent military take-over in Chile led by the navy, army and air force. A military government was established under a *Junta* led by General Pinochet. It was seen by some in Chile as the overthrow of legitimate government by a violent right-wing intervention with the ruthless suppression of opponents and cruel denial of human rights. Others in Chile saw it as the timely and necessary salvation of good order and strong government at a time of economic collapse and general disorder aggravated by the menace of international communism.

At the time the Church in Chile was led by Cardinal Raúl Silva Henriquez. He was personally inspired by the forward looking vision of Vatican II and the social teaching of Pope John XXIII, whose strong but humble orthodoxy he personally shared. He was a man of strength, understanding and vision, remembered at his death years later as a friend of the poor[6] who had always sought to mitigate violence, to defend human rights and bring about reconciliation. He was pastoral in his care for the people of Santiago and committed to the initiatives of the Council. He tried to avoid rigid barriers and was open to talks with both sides of the political divide. However, it was not possible at that time to count on unqualified support for either Vatican II or the Church's social teaching among many of the traditional Catholics of Chile. The vast continent of South America was everywhere the scene of internecine struggles between right and left, between rich and poor, between religion and irreligion. These struggles were concerned with real problems in the grip of which the people were suffering without prospect of peace and security so that their lives were torn and distracted by conflicting ideals. Debate and discussion were always liable to degenerate on both sides into passionate confrontation and the use of violence in the struggle for power.

Quite apart from immediate political and class struggles the Catholics in South America had their own problems and disagreements - simply as Catholics of that time. The specifically Catholic problems had taken shape as a result of the Second Vatican Council of 1962 - 1965. These problems did not arise from politics but they were sometimes related to the desperate human problems of South America and so encountered politics everywhere which increased the confusion. In the Church it was a time when some familiar landmarks in liturgy and other things as well were fading from sight. Like all ecumenical Councils since the Council of Jerusalem in the Acts of the Apostles[7] the Vatican Council had introduced some developments and changes in teaching and practice. There were other agents of change, however, which mingled with and were often confused with the initiatives of the Council. Among these were the growth of technology with its accelerating pace of change in everything throughout the world. There were also widespread social effects - in Chile as elsewhere - of an emerging consumer-oriented society under-pinned by western capitalism. The effect on ordinary Catholics was disturbing.

Moreover, for Catholics everywhere some of the cherished assumptions of the past, which had seemed secure, were being questioned or attacked. It was difficult enough that many valid changes and new initiatives which stemmed from the teaching of Vatican II were the source of either hope or anxiety to different generations of the faithful. But that was not all. There were writers in a prophetical vein who claimed the Council's authority for their own questionable interpretations of what must be done on one side or the other of the political and ideological and theological divides. They claimed the authority of the Council for their own solutions of present problems and their own predictions of the future of the Church, but there was no cohesion or unity about what they recommended. Some were of the right, some of the left. Many were equally extreme on both sides of the divide. Ordinary Catholics were deeply affected by the conflicting currents of change, political, religious and cultural in the tide-race of the times.

In Chilean society the Catholic Church was in a traditionally strong position, but it was not - it could not be - immune from the doubts and disagreements which resulted from world-wide currents of turbulence and uncertainty - of hope and fear. The Cardinal sought a balanced course of fidelity to the faith and above all reconciliation between opposing factions political and ecclesiastic, but his task was difficult and thankless at such a time. There were other voices within the Catholic community seeking to promote confrontation rather than reconciliation[8.]

The heart-searchings of loyal Catholics had begun before the advent of the Allende government in 1970. In the aftermath of the Council and before radical political change had struck with the election of Allende as President in 1970 democratic Chile had already embarked on some serious social changes. Land-reform had become a burning issue and the government was under constant economic pressure from the IMF and the US government for land reform. Chile was dependent on both for vital assistance towards developing its frail economy. This led to some very strong measures of land reform under President Frei's Christian Democrat government. As a result there were established land-owning families of impeccable loyalty to the faith and firmness in their belief in democracy, who under a democratic government had seen their land taken from them for distribution to the ordinary farm-workers. Their personal loss was great and its value to the country doubtful. It was an open question whether either the workers or the land or the economy of the country were any better for the change. It was loyal Catholics who were chiefly affected and to many of them, who suffered serious loss from the changes, the Church seemed silent or even supportive of policies which they themselves saw as not only unjust but also futile and ineffective.

From 1970 under a communist-inspired government the changes suddenly became more radical and far-reaching. Then after 1973 under the military regime new anxieties of a different nature supervened. Everything became subject to iron control and there was little room for disagreement with government policy, while political opposition was savagely neutralized by exile or 'disappearance'. By the time of the military *coup* the economy had got to a very low ebb. The future was full of uncertainty and menace. The instinct for violence was contained under ruthless military rigor but it had not disappeared from the minds and hearts of activists. It was ever present in the rhetoric of the times. How to live as a Catholic in Chile was an acute and inescapable question for those with no formal political affiliation as well as for the politically active.

Such times bring a temptation to rejection of the restraining demands of faith and the gospel; instead, they encourage violence and extreme solutions. Both the activists and those who longed only for peace and quiet, whether their inclination was towards the left or the right, could find plenty to complain of in the Cardinal's honesty about the uncertainties of the time, his clarity in proclaiming the gospel, his call for social justice, his defense of moderation and his constant call for reconciliation in the face of division and violence. He was fearless and outspoken in the defense of human rights. His was the only voice heard in Chile at that time in defense of those rights. At this stage he was not a popular figure among Catholics of the 'establishment' although he was always loved by the poor and the persecuted, whose cause he espoused publicly and with great courage.

Young people looking for a role in the Church

It was in 1976 that José Manuel Eguiguren Guzmán[9] was facing the effects of all this confusion in the minds and hearts of some of the young people he was working with. He had helped a group of young men through their confirmation at the end of their school life and had then stayed on in the school as director of religious teaching and pastoral work among the pupils. They had kept closely in touch with him after the confirmation class and after leaving school and starting at University in Santiago. Their association with him changed imperceptibly but strongly into a lasting friendship through which they were becoming ever more committed to the ideals of the gospel, which they had learnt from him to make their own. As time went on from among these young men and some others who had joined them a group of eight finally wanted to stay with him and give their lives to work in spreading the gospel among both rich and poor.

So it came about that they decided to stay together and work with him in some form of evangelization. They were strong in their commitment to the vision they had learnt from José Manuel, but it was not yet clear what exactly their role would turn out to be in the Church and they had begun to search with determination and confidence to find a way.

This was the group of young people who formed the very first nucleus of the Movement which José Manuel was forming. However, there was a big problem at the very beginning. This was José Manuel's conviction, which he shared with St Ignatius of Antioch[10] and two thousand years of Catholic saints and theologians, that to remain in full communion with the local Catholic Bishop and through him with the Bishop of Rome was a fundamental necessity for the Catholic success of anything they might undertake. He spoke of this conviction with the young followers. That was fine in theory but when he told them that it was his idea to work with the Church in close communion with the Cardinal and made it clear that he could not follow any other course, they began to see obstacles in their way. From their family standpoint they had in the recent years of confusion become accustomed to think of the Cardinal as left-wing and therefore unsound. This came about because of his defense of human rights and concern about the fate of political victims of whatever shade of opinion. They were inclined to question his leadership and were reluctant to commit themselves to follow his guidance about how their little project might develop.

José Manuel had helped them to a new perception of their lives as baptized Catholics. They wanted to stay with him and follow his vision and guidance in the service of others. But they came from traditional Catholic families. Although they were now firm in their faith and commitment to the gospel, they were suspicious about the implications of the Cardinal's commitment to Catholic social teaching and his apparent sympathy with ideas which they were inclined to reject outright as left-wing and sinister. They felt that there were other traditional concerns which were being overlooked and that a one-sided policy was not a truly Catholic policy.

So these first followers of José Manuel's vision for the laity were inclined to draw back from too close a commitment to the established Church as represented by the Cardinal. After all, it was at that time becoming quite fashionable everywhere to think that you could follow Christ as a Catholic and at the same time distance yourself from the 'institutional Church'. It looked as though the little group might fall apart before it had really started.

The meeting with Cardinal Raúl Silva Henríquez

José Manuel was always ready to listen and always ready to learn from the young as well as from the old. There were aspects of the criticisms he heard from the young and their families with which, from his own family background and experience, he could readily empathize. There were some things, however, which for him were not negotiable. To recognize the teaching of Christ in the teaching of the Church was by this time one of his fundamental principles which he sought to fulfill by remaining always in full communion with the local Catholic Church. Alejandro Allende, one of the original group from the confirmation class, remembers:

> If there was one thing which from the beginning onwards was clear to me it was the fidelity, which José Manuel always transmitted to us towards the Bishop and pastors and the Pope, whoever they

were......This was a factor which among some members of the Movement caused great division. The divisions arose because not everyone was in agreement with what the Church was saying.... Why should the Church be concerned with some people rather than with others? Why was it so concerned with the poor and not with the higher classes? We thought that there was quite a socialist tendency in the Church... This led us to want to speak with the bishop so that he could explain to us the role that the Church was playing at the time.[11]

The problem was a very real and dangerous one because these young peoples' problems were not artificial. They truly reflected the tensions in Chilean society which could easily also tear the Church in Chile apart. Somehow the Cardinal himself became aware of José Manuel's difficulties with his young followers and was anxious to help. It is a measure of his greatness of heart that he took the initiative and invited José Manuel and his little group to meet him and put to him their questions openly. He showed a truly Salesian[12] concern for the young and an understanding of their importance. He invited them all to his house and the meeting lasted for three hours.

Their encounter with the Cardinal was frank and uninhibited. It led those who heard him to a change of heart. José Manuel's own account shows how skillfully the Cardinal handled this vital meeting and how important it was for the future of the Movement:

There were some of them (the young founders of the Movement) who had very big political problems with the Cardinal. It was under the military system and the Church was very devoted to human rights so there were political problems in the first community of the Movement - and there were many other things. We wanted to know where we stood and the problems could only be dealt with by the bishop. The Cardinal - probably through Fr Puelma[13] - knew about this and he invited us to tea. We had two or three hours with him speaking of many things. He said that we must continue with the work we had undertaken. He did not mind that some of the young did not think exactly with him. The important thing was that we must have the same faith. He gave us a quotation from St

Augustine: 'to have unity in essentials, diversity in other things and charity in all things.[14]

It is difficult now to recapture the implications of that meeting in the acute tensions of the time. Now everything has moved forward a long way in politics, in the Church, in the lives of those young men and their many successors in the Movement which José Manuel was founding. It is especially difficult to capture the personal contribution of José Manuel and of Cardinal Raúl. They both seem to have taken these eight young men very seriously indeed. They gave them precious time to listen with tolerance and they both opened their hearts to them with no evasions. Alejandro Allende was one of the young men present at the meeting and he remembers the impression made by the Cardinal:

> My first impression was of his open-ness with people. I had always had an image of the Church that gave orders and one was a poor individual that had to listen, and if one wasn't in agreement one didn't obey. The Cardinal was a person who showed us much respect and much love....He made it clear to us that we had to understand the love which must exist within the Church and within ourselves. In spite of being quite divided before the meeting with the Cardinal we came out of that meeting united. He showed us the aspect of the Church which involves mutual understanding and sometimes having to do things because they are part of the gospel.[15]

The Cardinal in words he also used publicly of himself in 1973 told them that he spoke "not as a theologian but rather as a good shepherd." He faced honestly the problems which lay between them. For instance, when President Allende invited Castro to Chile, Castro had asked to see the Cardinal and the Cardinal had agreed. His willingness to do so had outraged traditional Catholics, who thought he should have snubbed Castro so as to base the strength of his position on non-communication. The memory of that visit was brought up at the meeting as an illustration of their objections to the Cardinal. The Cardinal was understanding but pointed out that he was following in the footsteps of Pope John who had personally received Khrushchev's son in law on a visit to Rome...And he told them something which had not come out at the time. He told them that, when Castro sought an interview, the Cardinal had discounted the propaganda that might be made of it, just as Pope John had done, and agreed because of the opportunity of doing good. He had in fact, he told them, also exacted a price. He had obtained Castro's agreement, and had seen that it was carried out, to allow 10,000 Bibles to be imported into Cuba and distributed to the people.

Later in that same year of his meeting with José Manuel and the first members of the Movement the Cardinal preached in the Cathedral of Santiago and left no doubt about where he stood. This sermon must be very much in the spirit of his words to José Manuel and those young men:

> We need to believe in love. Love - let us say here that it has justly its time and place in human life - it is not utopia, it is not naive, it is not an admission of inferiority. It achieves what force is not capable of achieving. It has no quarrel with the need to be watchful or to exercise just discipline. On the contrary, they are the conditions on which it subsists. Lord, grant that we may believe that love is more powerful than hate. That love unites in a way that cannot be achieved by fear. That love creates while hate destroys and fear paralyses. Take from our lips, Lord, words which cause offence and division. Open our hands to share our bread and our work, the good things which come from the one earth which you have given to everyone. Make us cease to judge one another without any pity and without readiness to forget. Enable us to believe in each other and to love; because it is only one who loves who is able to achieve justice.[16]

The later development of the Movement and its mission was wholly in accord with that vision of the Cardinal. That is one measure of the importance of the meeting in 1976. The members of the Movement put aside both controversial divisions within the Church and political factions in the world outside. Instead they turned to their commitment to Christ-centered on brotherhood with each other - and to their mission of evangelization within the Church and in communion with the bishop. Whatever their personal feelings and convictions they were not to be distracted by them from the main aim of their new commitment.

From this early stage the Movement was set on a course which is non-political but open to all and ready to listen to all. Instead of taking sides in conflict it invites everyone to listen to the word of God in scripture and the teaching of the Church. It is committed to love and reconciliation and opposed to division and hatred. The meeting with the Cardinal was important in helping to set José Manuel and his earliest followers on this course. There can be no doubt that Cardinal Silva Henriquez had personally an important formative influence on the beginnings and early growth of the Movement. There was a bond of understanding between the Cardinal and José Manuel which gave important strength to the beginnings of the Movement.

How it all began for José Manuel himself
That crucial three hour meeting of the Cardinal with the eight founding members of the Manquehue Movement at a time of doubt and division in the Church of Santiago had drawn them together and given them courage to go ahead. At this stage none of them had any real idea of where they were going except that they would stay with José Manuel in his search for God and for what God wanted for him and for them. In human terms it was a tenuous beginning and no one at the time could have predicted how it would turn out.

To understand what led them to that beginning we must go back and recall what had brought that little group together in the first place. The beginning of the whole story cannot be understood except through recalling José Manuel's own unique spiritual journey - how it came about, its significance in his own personal life and how it led him to his positive relationship with younger people. All that was to follow in his work for the young flowed directly from his own spiritual experience of conversion and renewal.

José Manuel's experience had been typical of what so many have suffered in our times. He had been torn to pieces and the deep inner choices that confront us all, but are so often disguised, had been laid bare for him. They are the real background of most religious problems today. They are often pushed aside behind the unreal masks of politics, social convention, ambition and the pretences of 'political correctness'. The life-choices that confront us, when stripped bare of all those artificial coverings, are always the same. They are: to accept the unvarnished reality of our condition as creatures, to turn to our creator and the source

18

of our being, to believe or not to believe, to obey or not to obey, to love or to destroy ourselves through the self-centered refusal of love. José Manuel had himself been through it and had come out and found peace in belief, obedience and love. It was because of that spiritual journey of his that he had so much to give to the young who instinctively gathered round him as he emerged from his own trial. We must follow the course of his spiritual journey in order to understand his achievement in the Manquehue Movement in the years ahead.

<hr>

Notes Chapter 2

[1] A 'Movement' in the Church is a group of the faithful who come together in a spirit of mutual encouragement and support either to strengthen and develop their own spirituality or to pursue some practical mission for the Church or to do both. The members may all be lay or they may be a mixture of clergy and laity. When they are given approval for their Rule or way of life by the bishop of their local diocese, this binds them into the local Church and makes the Movement 'ecclesial'. They may go on to seek wider approval from Rome either retaining their status as 'Movement' or they may become an 'Institute of Consecrated Life'. The Manquehue Movement has retained its status as a Private Association of Lay Faithful with the formal approval of the Diocese of Santiago and the encouragement and *laudatio* of the *Council for the Laity* in Rome.

[2] *Lectio divina* is a phrase familiar in Catholic spirituality in all ages. It may be translated by such concepts as 'sacred reading', 'holy reading', 'spiritual reading'. It has been strongly current, especially in monastic circles, since it was used in Chapter 48 of The Rule of St Benedict in the sixth century. St Benedict directs in that chapter that a monk's day should be divided between work and *lectio divina*. In the monasteries that followed his Rule this 'holy reading' first concentrated on the Psalms, which were the instruments of monastic prayer, and on the whole of Scripture. Scripture always came first but *lectio* was also extended to the reading of the Fathers of the Church. Long hours were spent on this and the monks' reading was always slow and meditative so that *lectio* could easily develop or lead into meditation, prayer and contemplation. *Lectio*, therefore was more than a way of acquiring information or learning. It was a means of spiritual formation in the word of God. The re-discovery of this approach to Scripture has been an inspiration to many of the laity, including the Manquehue Movement, in the post-Vatican II era.

[3] Jn. 14,6

[4] *Conferencia Episcopal Latino-Americano* - Conference of Bishops of Latin America

[5] A loose, but much used, description of the writing of certain theologians of the time, mostly from Latin America. The description covers a wide range of theological opinion and socio-religious practical programs for action, so that the use of the term can itself be misleading and likely to give rise to conflicting prejudices rather than understanding.   Gospel concern for and consequent positive option in favor of the poor was a strong element in its inspiration but there were other aspects less acceptable to the Church. Some of these theorists,

for instance, sought to bring Marxist analysis not only into politics but even into the heart of Christian theology while there were some who would favor - or at least tolerate - the use of physical violence on the grounds that it was necessary and therefore legitimate to liberate the poor from the trap of structural economic dependence

[6] On the day of his funeral in 1998 all the leading figures of every shade of opinion gathered to honor him in the Cathedral while on the back of some of the buses in Santiago a legend appeared reading: *Good-bye to the Cardinal of the poor.*

[7] Acts of the Apostles. ch. 15

[8] José Manuel Eguiguren remembers a Catholic meeting during this long crisis at which the Vicar General recalled all that the Archbishop had attempted and asked what more they wanted from him. A nun who was present responded stridently with a single word: DYNAMITE.

[9] It is the custom in Chile that men retain as a second surname their mother's family name. Thus Eguiguren is José Manuel's father's family name and Guzmán his mother's. The addition of the second surname in ordinary use is optional. A married woman will not normally take her husband's family name on marriage and will retain her parent's family names. Thus José Manuel's wife was still known as Luz Cosmelli after her marriage.

[10] Ignatius was Bishop of Antioch and may well have been a disciple of St John. When taken by Roman soldiers to be fed as a Christian to beasts in the Coliseum for the entertainment of the Roman populace, he wrote letters to various Churches in Asia Minor in which, among other points of Catholic doctrine, he underlines strongly the importance of being in full communion with the bishop of the local church.

[11] Interview with Alejandro Allende

[12] Cardinal Silva was a member of the Salesian Order, founded by St John Bosco in Milan in the late 19th century. St John Bosco was friend, protector and guide of the impoverished young in Milan

[13] Fr Puelma was the Headmaster of the school where José Manuel was at that time a teacher.

[14] Interview with José Manuel

[15] Interview with Alejandro Allende

[16] From *El Cardinal nos ha dicho* p. 257-

Chapter 3 ~ Confusion & Conversion
in a young life

Home, School, University

Chile stretches down the western coast of South America between the huge range of the Andes mountains and the Pacific ocean. In climate it is like a reversed cross-section of Europe and North Africa from mountains, forests, lakes of Finland to the sand of the Sahara but with no Mediterranean sea to divide the arid from the fertile zone. In the north there is a desert as forbidding as the Sahara. The far south is a region of lakes and mountains with glaciers from the high Andes feeling their way down a steep course to the Pacific ocean. The center is a fertile Mediterranean land rich in olives, fruit of all kinds, vineyards which produce the finest of wines. In one area or another you are reminded of southern France, Italy, Greece. Near the center of this long, long country the capital Santiago nestles among the foothills which stretch out from the Andes. It is the strongest center of population, commerce, culture and politics, although in recent years the Parliament itself has been moved to the great port of Valparaiso.

Chile has a long tradition of democracy since its struggle for independence from Spanish rule in the early 19th century which triumphed finally under the improbable leadership of a man of Irish descent, Bernardo O'Higgins, who is honored as Liberator of the country. Despite this democratic tradition Chile was disturbed and threatened by extremist influences both of the left and the right during the events of the 1970's and 80's. Finally there was a return to democracy when a plebiscite was held in 1988 which opened the way to the election of a new President in 1989. The grip of the military dictatorship of General Pinochet was gradually loosened and a new era of democratic independence began. This democratic revival has in recent years been strengthened by economic growth. But it was before this revival of democracy, while the power of the army was still supreme, that in the capital, Santiago José Manuel Eguiguren began his work and developed his vision. It came into being during some of the worst of times for Chile and blossomed into fullness of life as the return of democracy brought back both liberty and prosperity.

His own life began on the 4th June 1948 and he was given his father's name. He was the sixth in succession to bear it. His father was a lawyer in Santiago and his mother came from a farming family. He was the eldest of the family and in time had one sister and two brothers. The family lived in Santiago but they spent time also in the country among the hills not far from the sea at Leyda where his grandparents' farm was situated. The whole of this story is set between Santiago, Leyda and at a later stage a remote farmstead in Chilean Patagonia. José Manuel loved to be at Leyda on the farm spending his time among the families who worked on it and in the old Chilean family house which was the center of the local farming community. It was a deeply traditional Catholic family of strong faith and he was baptized on the day after he was born by an uncle, who was a priest, on 5th June, the Feast day of St Boniface. As an infant he was unconscious of the true spiritual meaning of baptism, but he understood it later. In fact there would come a time in his life when the inner significance of the sacrament would become a dominant inspiration for his life and mission. At the time the spiritual change in him was real but hidden.

As he grew up he was familiar with an ambience of strong Catholic faith. His father as a lawyer of sincere Catholic conviction worked for several Religious Congregations. His grandmother was a strong influence and he remembers her going daily to Mass. Hers was a loved and reassuring presence. His memories of catechism classes with the Capuchin fathers on their yearly visit, of an unforgettable image of Christ on the walls of the farm, of the great ceremony of his first communion in a chapel in Santiago filled by his extended family - all these and many other God centered images of his Catholic life nourished a faith which became for him part of normality as he grew up partly in Santiago and partly in the country on the farm at Leyda.

The old farmhouse at Leyda belonged to his grandparents and was a family center except when they had to be in Santiago for school and other things. It is remembered with affection by family and also by members of the Movement who in the early days often visited and made retreats there. It had a chapel which was always open to everyone in the country round about. As you enter the grounds by the driveway and approach the buildings the Chapel faces you near the house and at right angles to it. It is old and strong in understated Chilean baroque with a strong Catholic atmosphere of pre-Vatican II piety and devotion. But it has not slept through the last decades. The table of the altar slides discreetly forward for Mass facing the people, without interfering with the unity and prayerful tranquility of the old design.

The family house nearby is quite different. It is less impressive at first view. It is a large but unpretentious two-storied building which belongs contentedly to its Chilean environment. It follows the old design of houses in the country. There is an open veranda which is roomy and airy - called in Spanish *el corredor* - going round the outside. The roof of lovely, mature Roman tiles overhangs the *corredor* and is held up by wooden pillars whose slender design adds to the sense of light and air. The rooms all open onto it. It provides easy communication and added space for meeting, for relaxation, for conversation, whether in separate groups or all together. The family all remember their grandmother walking the *corredor* saying her rosary each day. Hers was a formative example that impressed itself deeply on José Manuel's memory. The rooms of the house are large and substantial and the furnishings built to last for generations. Surrounding the house on one side is the farmyard, on the other a garden cascading down through flowers and shrubs and trees of all kinds. The garden is on the cool side of the house, which in the southern hemisphere is the south, inviting all to walk in the shade of the impressive trees.

José Manuel went to a primary School in Santiago and from there to St George's School run by the North American Holy Cross Fathers, with which his family had connections. His father sent him there to deepen his faith and to learn English. He was happy in his school life and had a good relationship with the Holy Cross Fathers. However, by the time he was fourteen his schooling was disrupted by the need for medical treatment. From the time of his birth he had suffered from a severe handicap. There is a lesion in his back causing lameness in both legs. It involved severe limitation for a growing boy. From the first, however, he accepted this handicap cheerfully, as his mother remembers:

> He loved the country - the farm, the horses. He could get involved with anything. Because of his physical handicap he learnt to amuse himself and because he couldn't walk he had to drag himself to places and he learnt to be happy with anything.....He never said anything about his lameness. He never asked why do I have this. It seems that he always accepted it. He was never jealous or envious of his brothers. On the contrary he was very proud of them and very happy to go out with his brother anywhere. Maybe he should have been envious but he wasn't and that was very good.[1]

From the time when he was five years old he was sent two or three times for treatment to the United States. When he was fourteen surgery and special treatment began and that meant that he had to leave home and stay in the United States for nearly a year. He lived there, in Salt Lake City in Utah. He stayed with a Chilean family who lived there but it was a part of the United States which was strikingly different from Chile. Despite the warm welcome he received from the Eyzaguirre family, he experienced the strangeness of what was unfamiliar and alien to the way of life he had known.

Soon, however, he recovered from his first distress and got on very well with the people he met in the United States. There was a Catholic nurse there and a Catholic cleaner who were good to him and helped him to come to terms with his new environment. There was a school in the hospital and they offered to teach him there, but he refused because he said that he had come to the United States to be cured not to go to school.

None of the kindness he met with could take away the pain for him of being away from home. It was an exile and he felt it as such. In the early stages of his exile José Manuel learnt the lessons not only of loneliness and alienation but also of suffering. There was added disappointment when he was told by the doctors that his physical disability could not be cured. It would be with him all his life, although the surgery and treatment he received certainly helped a lot and he was grateful for that. As time went on he became very appreciative of all that was done for him there. He was left with a power of movement - even though it was with a pronounced limp - which made it possible for him to meet the demands of physical activity and travel, which his future vocation would impose on him.

On José Manuel's return to Santiago his father generously let him choose what school he would like to join to complete the last three years of his formal education. Things had changed for him. Even his way of walking was different. The change was enough to make him want a new environment and he opted for the Manquehue School[2] run by the French Fathers of the Sacred Hearts of Jesus & Mary (known often as the Picpus Fathers). He went there for three years and he remembers it as a really wonderful time bringing him new and formative experiences. His friendly nature blossomed in the companionship he found there and his mind was opened to new and challenging thought through the curriculum and the books to which he was introduced. It was, in fact, a time of new perspectives and challenges in life for all the Catholics in Chile because it was not only José Manuel who had changed. The year was 1964 when the Council ended and the impact of the Council's decisions had begun to create both problems and opportunities all over the Catholic world.

Somehow the priests who ran the school made the changes introduced by the Council entirely positive for him so that he began to see his faith in a new way. "I discovered there is another view of the faith which was very much human." He formed a good relationship with the priests. After his exile it was a time not only of homecoming but also of new growth and new strength. His three years at the Manquehue School were important for his general development. It was a time during which he matured, left boyhood behind him and became a young man who loved to mix with his contemporaries and with adults and to discuss everything with them. He was not a great worker at the academic curriculum but was a voracious reader of everything that came his way.[3] This love of books was more important than examinations to him and perhaps a richer factor in his education. He retained the habit of reading throughout his life. He was well accepted by the other boys in the school. He became known and loved as a 'character' who was always friendly and entertaining. He had come to terms cheerfully with his handicap and it never prevented him from entering fully into the life around him and making many friends.

José Manuel left school in 1966. Instead of going straight to University he decided first to pursue some private study of his own choosing. The study he chose was on Chilean social and family history for which he immersed himself in the archives of the National Library. This was an unusual way of bridging the gap between school and University. It diverted him for the moment from some of the pressures to which his generation in Chile were exposed at the time. In the sealed atmosphere of the National Library he gave himself to research on past history which was a serious introduction to the disciplines of study.

Disturbance & Violence on the campus
After this he began his University career. That is how it came about that it was in 1968 that he entered University, at the end of a year for him of quiet and scholarly study of the past. Things were different in the University. It was the year of student revolt which spread through the Universities of the world like wild fire. The contrast to the somber silence and musty peace of the archives in the National Library could not have been more marked. Quite apart from the unrest of the student world it was a time of change in the politics and social life of Chile which led on during the next few years to radical upheaval in which all that had seemed to him safe and assured was threatened. It was also a time of change and development in the Church after Vatican II which challenged many of the apparently safe assumptions of Catholicism in Chile.

Student life itself and student protest was not any longer focused simply on the affairs of the campus. Student protest had at this time throughout the western world assumed a high profile of political and social action with claimed to dictate the agenda for society. Suddenly José Manuel found himself in an unfamiliar world of conflict, confrontation and violence. The University in the center of Santiago was a forum for every sort of ideological campaign. Following the example of their contemporaries in Western Europe and the United States the students sought to make their views felt outside the University campus. They were not the only ones in Chile with a grievance. The economy was in a terrible state and getting worse. Foreign pressures were strong

28

and obtrusive - from Cuba and the Soviet Union in support of the left and from the United States under Nixon in opposition to everything that was favored by the left. There were many in the University and in the country at large who experienced disillusionment and insecurity in a world which seemed dedicated to confrontation and restless change.

It is not surprising that as a University student, José Manuel, was affected by this confusion of voices. He did not attempt to stand back. He threw himself into University life. He was himself quite deeply affected by the conflicts and opposing theories and the human problems which seemed to make up the agenda of student life at the time. He felt personally involved in the problems and dreams and doubts of his friends. Perhaps it was one of his problems that he had many friends of many shades of opinion and their problems became his problems. His mother remembers those days:

> He changed a lot and became terrible. I don't know if it was that he got into university at a moment of terrible political problems or maybe it was a crisis from his legs; I don't know. He was very much into politics and he was always changing. One day he was for Che Guevara; then he was a socialist. It seemed for a while that he even ceased to be a Catholic. That was what José Manuel was like at that time.[4]

His own course of study in the University was Philosophy and Literature. He was never a loner by temperament. He made friends - both from among those with whom he agreed and those with whom he disagreed. Thus he had friends on both sides of the current political divide. The University in those days was a place where friendship, which came so naturally to him, and ideology could easily conflict with each other.

But there were other things besides politics. At one point he found a counter-balance to the unsettling confusion of present problems through his study of literature which gave him a moment of support and inspiration. There were inspiring moments like the occasion when one lecturer - a layman[5] - was speaking on Spanish writing of the 16th /17th centuries and turned to St Teresa of Avila and St John of the Cross. It made an impression on him. It was a memory to cherish, but the crosscurrents of politics and the exposed, ambivalent position of the Church in South America were at the time more immediate and more powerful than the peace and wisdom of those great Spanish mystics. That lecture, nevertheless, was never forgotten. It was a tranquil moment of inspiration, but it was not typical.

More vigorous and more inescapable were the lurid frescos of students throwing stones at everyone which appeared on the walls around the campus of the University – just to encourage them to action. And there was the stream of political and social theory which flooded into the student body. Political ideas were at that time a strong part of José Manuel's make-up. It had started early in life, for by the time he was 15 he had joined the Partido Conservador, which attracted the traditional Catholic right wing. Its leaders dissolved the party in 1965. Now at University it was a time for José Manuel of profound disharmony and disillusionment, as he remembers himself.

The University was a very militant and emotional place and that caused many questions for me: first because people like me, who were from private schools, made companions of others from different social backgrounds; secondly the teachers were very partisan. All this caused different ways of looking at things. I had to enter this confused situation and I made friends there.... In the first or second year I was cultivated by the party of the right in student relations in the university. I didn't want that and a big change was coming on me, as I moved away from the right. I began to live a liberal life. I stopped going to Mass etc, although I never formally left the Church. I never, in fact, considered leaving the Church, although I was in a lot of confusion because of the different parties in the Church and because the Church seemed to me at the time to be falling apart. There was a lot of idealism at that time. My own position was changing and I was very influenced by Marxist thinking - in everything I would say - except on what had to do with faith itself. I started thinking like a Marxist in many ways and the same thing also happened to priests who studied with me. But Marxism was not really good enough. I wanted an answer deeper than Marxism could give. I thought there must be some strong points in the theories of the marxist society, but it had no answer to what happened after this life was over. I joined groups and we tried to do things politically, but really we achieved nothing. This was my state by 1970 when President Allende was elected and his policy involved very big changes throughout the country. Personally by that time I had already withdrawn completely from everything. I was not involved in politics any more. I could see no hope in politics and I belonged to no political alignment any more.[6]

In spite of all this alienation there was one thing which he cherished from his past - his own copy of the Bible. He had bought it at about the age of 15 with money given him by his grandmother.

She was dying and I made her very happy by saying to her that I had bought a Bible for myself. I read it now at University to search for an answer, but I did not understand it. I searched for answers to justify my political positions - first for the right and then for the left. And I bought little Bibles in which I underlined things. I was influenced by a church Movement which was for the young and by other Movements here in Santiago and I followed other Latin American leaders. But I didn't find an answer. So, little by little, I turned aside to other ways and started studying other religions - not so as to change myself but because I wanted to know more. I was very afraid of life. I had a fear that God would turn out to be not a person but a disinterested spiritual force. My mother, when she saw what was happening, gave me a book.[7] She wanted to give me the answer within the Catholic faith. So I read the book and wrote to the author. I discovered that there was an answer there but I could not make it my own. Thus I got into a big crisis. I concluded that there was no sense in life; one was born, lived, worked and died and it meant nothing.

This mood of misery in which José Manuel could find no sense in human life was not unusual among young students at that time. He was personally going through the experience of a generation. This existential angst leading to no answer has been a constant threat to the young in student life of the later twentieth century. In José Manuel's time as a student it seemed almost to be institutionalized throughout the West.

31

You might have found it on any campus at the time in repetitive stereotypes. It was not whispered in corners. It was proclaimed on every platform. In the late sixties it spread through the world of students in every country like instant wildfire. Although essentially an inner experience it was made visible by one or other of two typical responses; the violent protest of the student revolutionary or the passive rejection of the despairing 'drop out'. Those for whom violence became the catalyst of this personal confusion looked for a solution in the overthrow of the existing 'establishment' very often under the inspiration of Moscow. The drop-outs on the other hand sought escape from the angst and tension in such ways as 'alternative' hippy communes or in eastern regimes for changing individual 'consciousness' through meditation and drugs. The student culture of Santiago at the time seems to have included all these strands that the world made so readily available to disoriented young in their agony.

José Manuel was as vulnerable as any of his generation. He wanted to know why he was here and where he was going. To be static was impossible. Life without any purpose was terrifying for him. He was deep in a crisis of faith, although for him it was a question not of whether to believe but of what to believe. He never doubted that there is life after death but there was darkness and confusion about what it might be, what it might mean, what to do about it. That he was not alone made the experience stronger. This questioning about the ultimate meaning of life - of their own lives - was at the very center of student talking and thinking at the time. The real agony was that there were no answers.

They were always discussing and reading new books and everyone was searching for something. There was a strong sense of life - as always among the young in universities - but it was now instinctively revolutionary. Violence was no longer a remote possibility. It had to be brought into their actual lives. There was violence outside and inside the university. At times on several days a week the university was closed because of disturbances. The students, men and women together, would set fire to tires in the streets to bring traffic to a halt, and there were very big riots against the police. Sometimes there was violence inside the university between different factions. Some disturbances were linked to Chilean politics at the time and some were more general. Rioting for whatever reason was becoming part of student life. There were riots in Santiago against the Soviet invasion of Czechoslovakia and over the war in Vietnam and about other countries of Latin America. For José Manuel life itself in the end became an intolerable burden as every thought was sucked into the agony of doubt:

> It would be true to say that it was an existential crisis because for me life made no sense. I now see that the Lord sent me little lights. There was a book also of Thomas Merton which helped, but the problem was very deep and very painful. I remembered that when I was in the US I had very strong physical pain and I thought that I would prefer that physical pain to the pain I was having in this crisis. I woke in the morning to hear the birds singing and I hated to hear them because I thought how terrible it was to face another day. I preferred to be asleep. My father saw that I was in a very bad state and he wanted to help, but no-one could help because there was no-one to answer the questions I had - neither a doctor nor anyone else. There was no answer, but I felt that perhaps it would come. Someone said to me at that time that the Lord would answer me when he wanted, and I believed that - a little bit.[8]

His father urged him to travel - to visit Europe in the hope that by traveling he might find relief through new interests, but it was no help because, in spite of the sympathy he received, his inner state of mind assured him that there were no answers to be found. In such a state all the wisdom of the world, all the advice and experience that can be offered by man is useless. There comes a time when such a sufferer cannot hear any more. The inner man becomes inaccessibly enfolded in misery. Many things were said to him. He received advice and sympathy from many on the way. He was not without friends, but their voices could no longer penetrate to his inner desolation. In the midst of friends and family who wished him well and longed to help he was utterly alone in his agony.

Meeting with Father Gabriel Guarda

José Manuel's father was so anxious to help that gave his son carte blanche to do anything he wanted to do. But that was the trouble.

There wasn't anything he wanted to do. Within his own heart he had come to a full stop. However he was anxious to respond to his father's kindness and remembered the national archives in the National Library. It was something to do, or at least something he could seem to be doing. He returned to the quiet of the reading room. He began to read old wills and testaments that were stored there. That itself brought a new shock. He had thought he would be safe among the dead, but what immediately struck him as he read those old documents was the faith, the belief, the affirmation about life that stared at him in the records of the dead. Although dead, they threw his problem back at him and emphasized the spiritual poverty this crisis had uncovered in him. The Library brought him no escape from his agony. It revived it and renewed his suffering.

One day he was there as usual in the Library when Fr Gabriel Guarda a monk from the Holy Trinity monastery[9] in Las Condes, entered the reading room. José Manuel is rather vague but thinks they had met once before on something to do with History but, if he did know Fr Gabriel at that time, it was not at all well. There was no social need, as he caught sight of Fr Gabriel entering the Library, for José Manuel to acknowledge him or say anything. Nevertheless, on a sudden impulse which later he could not quite understand, he got up from his seat and went over to greet him. Then, without giving Fr Gabriel a chance of answering his greeting, he quickly added that he must speak with him 'but not about History'. Fr Gabriel was gracious and welcoming and at once invited him to come up to the monastery where they could talk. For the moment they left it at that and parted.

José Manuel was delighted at the invitation and eager to go up to the monastery but in spite of that for some reason he did not rush to the meeting. He waited a few days. The meeting in the Library with Fr Gabriel had been on a Friday evening in 1974 during the tense and frightening period after the military take-over the year before. Many of José Manuel's friends had left the country. He had friends on both sides of the political divide and he felt torn by that also. One of these friends had taught him Latin American History in the Manquehue School and at this time he was in trouble for his opinions. José Manuel helped him to escape the country. It was his only direct involvement in the consequences of the squalid politics of the time. Later he received a wonderful letter of gratitude and friendship from his former teacher. Now for himself he did not just want to escape. The invitation to the monastery hung over him. It seemed attractive, but what did it mean in the maelstrom of his inner agony.

He waited until Monday and then curiously in spite of his anxiety he let Monday slip by. At last on Tuesday he climbed up the hill to the monastery. The monastery is a conspicuous landmark - its squat, white shape, small but inescapable on the shoulder of the mountain looking out over the valley. It stands there quietly above the city like a spiritual fortress speaking of vision and strength and confidence and security. There was a strong wind that day like the Spirit tearing away the clouds to let in light. There to greet José Manuel was Fr Gabriel looking like a timeless figure that has just stepped out of an El Greco painting in his black Benedictine habit with his neat grizzled beard and steady gaze of eyes that are gentle and calm but also penetrating.

Father Gabriel led the way into the Guest Room and listened calmly to the whole story, which José Manuel poured out in great detail. Whatever he had expected of Fr Gabriel the response he received was different and not immediately reassuring to José Manuel. Fr Gabriel said that they should begin by asking the help of the Holy Spirit. José Manuel thought of the wind which he could still hear tearing round the mountain and felt rather scared of that prospect. What might a power like that unleash? He knew all the Catholic teaching about the Holy Spirit, but only at a safe theoretical distance. This was different - actually to involve the Holy Spirit directly in his own problems. That would be a big step and it seemed to him to be a dangerous one. However, this was a day for facing up to things and he accepted this new opening to a new way of looking at his life. They prayed together to the Holy Spirit.

After that Fr Gabriel said that it was important to understand first of all that there are some things in life we can change but others that we cannot change and must learn to accept. That comment was reassuring to José Manuel. For some reason it gave him a sense of peace as he suddenly and unexpectedly began to perceive that there are indeed things which cannot be changed and how self-destructive it is to fight against them.

Lectio Divina

What happened next was the beginning of something new which would have far-reaching effects in José Manuel's life and the lives of many other people - young and old - who would in time come under his influence. Fr Gabriel began to answer his existential problems not by intellectual analysis, not in his own words, not from his own experience of life, but by referring everything to the word of God in scripture. The way it was done, moreover, made José Manuel feel at once that he was accepted by Fr Gabriel - just as he was with all his doubts and problems. There was no fear of disapproval or judgment or criticism. That meant a lot to him in his time of wretchedness.

As to the solution of his agony and the answer to his problems, Fr Gabriel offered no answers of his own. There were no precepts, no moral warnings, no inquisitions. The whole focus of these meetings was on the word of God in scripture and the truth it would bring home to José Manuel in this moment of his spiritual journey, if he received that word openly, honestly, humbly. It was not his own vision of the meaning of scriptural passages that Fr Gabriel put forward as solutions. He did not demand acceptance of his own understanding. What mattered was José Manuel's own personal encounter with the word of God. He was to receive the word as it spoke to him personally because the word did speak to him, José Manuel himself, directly, personally, lovingly. That word alone, thus encountered, and not the interpretation of others, would lead him to the resolution of his inner doubt and agony. It was his first lesson in *Lectio Divina*.

There must be, as Fr Gabriel taught him, no question of bending scripture to his own convenience to mean what he wanted. He had to confront the true meaning of each passage following the notes in the Jerusalem Bible, but they did not spend time on general intellectual and exegetic questions appropriate to formal Bible study. All that mattered was the actual meaning of particular passages. Within the literal meaning there is a meaning of personal importance for each of us to be found in scripture, if we approach it with faith and an open heart. It is a meaning which is immediate, personal and concerned with our present needs in our journey to God. On the road to Emmaus, when the risen Christ opened the scripture to the two unbelieving disciples, who thought they knew it all already, they found their hearts burning within them. It is so with the sort of reading of the word to which Fr Gabriel introduced José Manuel.

He used the Jerusalem Bible, with its invaluable notes about the meaning of the text, and started with the Book of Job and God's answer to the apparently meaningless pain and loss Job had endured. Immediately it seemed relevant to José Manual's own sense of pain and confusion and, as he read, he began to feel less alone and to say with Job: "I believe now not from hearsay but I have seen you with my own eyes."[10]

As they searched the scriptures the most baffling problems came up. There was the problem of pain and suffering and the agonizing questions about the justice and injustice of life. As hope began to return to José Manuel that question of justice also seemed urgent to his condition and his own personal sense of being abandoned. He faced the mood of misery and self-pity so common today in the face of suffering: 'why me?' In an age of intense individualism it is common to demand always a reason, but often there were no reasons. In a moment of acute pain and confusion it suddenly becomes clear that nothing can be justified in a purely rational way - neither pain nor hope. That was what José Manuel felt about his life at the time. There was an important moment when Fr Gabriel turned to Exodus and to God's response to Moses: "I will be gracious to whom I will be gracious and have mercy on whom I will have mercy."[11] It was for him a release from the absurdity of a human being seeking cosmic control for himself - or for mankind. Against that came the clear vision that everything is in the hands of the Creator of all - everything is His gift, and the reasons for His gifts are mysterious to us, impenetrable in our present life. They cannot even be evaluated by a creature.

There was another text which came to mean a lot to him at this time: "You have not chosen me but I have chosen you"[12] and one from the Apocalypse: "I correct those whom I love."[13] Such texts, when he reflected on their meaning, began to throw a strange new light on his own experience. They gradually changed the mood in which he was immersed from a querulous concentration on self to a more profound and broader perception. This made it possible to see both suffering and hope in a new light of God's creative love revealed in Jesus Christ.

37

After an introduction to the word on those lines Fr Gabriel turned to Hebrews 11 with its eloquent insistence on faith as the only possible key to a relationship between man and his creator. The whole of salvation history rested on the faith which consists in free and loving acts of acceptance and trust. The rich list of examples in Hebrews from the Old Testament was all the more impressive for José Manuel because the faith of Abraham and the patriarchs remained unfulfilled but still unshaken during their lifetimes: "all these, though well attested by their faith, did not receive what was promised, since God had foreseen something better for us." [14] This at least opened the door to the realization that what we see as hardship, suffering, pain may well be an expression of God's love because it brings greater depth and spiritual maturity to our lives. It is a way of weaning us from the superficiality of what seems to be real and lasting, when in truth it is illusory and fragile.

All this was on the first day and was only an introduction to a new and formative experience of learning that the word of God in scripture is essential for our daily spiritual nourishment. A summary like this is essentially inadequate because the reality of what was happening cannot be summarized in words. There is a real sense in which the word of God in scripture cannot be talked or written about. To come alive it must be experienced in personal confrontation. That was the essential experience of José Manuel in the monastery of Las Condes.

To read the word of scripture in this way is to accept it personally as the word of God for me in this moment of my life and to perceive in it a message which is meant not just to console me but to change me. Consolation can come only after the inner change. It is a tradition of Scripture reading derived from the New Testament which was a normal aspect of monastic life from the earliest ages. [15]

That was just what José Manuel was discovering under the guidance of Fr Gabriel. The Word of God in scripture became, under Fr Gabriel's gentle guidance, no longer a formal, detached point of reference coming into his life from a remote outside. He had found that, when he opened his mind and heart in the reading of the word, it spoke to him personally and relevantly. It was a new experience or the beginning of a new experience, which would change everything for him and many others.

Through *lectio* he realized that his whole approach to the Bible before that meeting with Fr Gabriel had been inadequate. He had valued the Bible, perhaps more than most, but he had not realized exactly what the Bible was or what it was for. He had used it rationally as one tool among others. Now it was different. He was becoming involved personally in the meaning of the word here and now for him. It was a new sort of experience.

Usually when they met Fr Gabriel listened to him. Then he chose readings from the Bible which they read together in this new way which he was learning to make his own. As he read he was daily becoming more secure in his understanding of the spiritual reality of the word of scripture. That led to sharing and conversing together, but the word of God led the way and spoke to his understanding and to his heart. All this began on the first day but its potential was so rich that it took three years of close encounter with the Word of God under the daily guidance of Father Gabriel before José Manuel was ready to turn back towards the world which had plunged him into such dark confusion. When he did so, it was with a newly found sense of purpose and strength together with a profound conviction that the source of both was the word of God in scripture.

And so for three years it continued. Nearly every morning he went up to the monastery and every day was a day of growth. Normally when they met José Manuel would bring out some aspect of his angst. Fr Gabriel would then choose a scriptural reading. They would read it listening for the impact of this word on his condition here and now expressing some hidden aspect of God's love and healing. Then they would discuss further together.

The beginning had come quickly, but the growth took time. This was not an attempt at instant religion and time was needed for depth and maturity. Time is always needed for our time-kept minds to be drawn into the eternal wisdom of God. As the days and weeks went by, he experienced more and more the liberation described in Hebrews where Christ is said: "to deliver all those who, through fear of death, were subject to lifelong bondage."[16] José Manuel experienced in himself freedom from the slavery under which he personally had been held through the fear of death. Nothing was hurried and Fr Gabriel encouraged him to take his time - or rather God's time.

There was no pressure about returning to Catholic practice and the Sacraments. At first José Manuel remembers that he was defensive about all that and said that he did not really want to make his confession. Fr Gabriel gave him a great sense of peace and security by replying that there was no hurry and he should wait until God wanted him to do that. It was not the sacraments at this stage, it was the word of God in scripture that Father Gabriel insisted on. He insisted that José Manuel should read the Bible every day. "The day that you do not read a verse of the gospel", he said, "that day you should not eat. Why let your soul starve and feed your body?" After that he was never without a Bible, wherever he went and his followers in the Movement were the same. They carried their Bibles everywhere and used them in fulfilling their mission.

Then in the end, when he was ready, he made his confession and received holy communion again in the monastery chapel. It took time, but the time was right when it came. Fr Gabriel's patience was fully rewarded and indeed his patience had been tried. For Fr Gabriel this whole process of listening day after day and then responding by beginning a dialogue based on the Bible was a severe test and at times he needed all the patience he could muster. Often he wondered how he could himself go on with it as he found that José Manuel's intensity sometimes drove him almost to distraction. Looking back he did not really know how he had persevered day after day for so long. Yet it was important and it was a triumph that he succeeded. Everything in those three years turned on Fr Gabriel's patient and tenacious availability.

It was a lesson and an example that was later not forgotten in the developing Movement. Time and again with those, both young and old, whose lives had been plunged into an agony of doubt and darkness, it was patient availability and gentle insistence on the Word in scripture through which the Manquehue Oblates led others to discover "strength for their faith, food for their souls and a pure and lasting fount of spiritual life."[17] It was Father Gabriel Guarda's persistence in faithful availability that had led the way and his Benedictine example lived on in the Movement.

St Benedict's Rule

One day during those three years Fr Gabriel referred to the Benedictine vow of Stability[18] and explained its spiritual meaning. Fr Gabriel had earlier given him a copy of the Rule but at first he did not understand it. Now, however, when Fr Gabriel spoke about stability in the Rule he began to understand that what matters is inner stability through which monks can persevere through all difficulties. He also understood that monks were essentially not clergy but laity unless, as often happens today, they received ordination to the priesthood in addition to their monastic vocation. The real meaning of that monastic vocation itself was still far from clear. In this first initiation with Fr Gabriel a seed was planted in his mind which blossomed later. When that happened the Rule became for him what it originally was - a document about the Catholic faith-life of ordinary lay people with all its perplexities and challenges and joys in their search for God.

First Teaching job & how the Movement began

The time came when the life of work had to start again. José Manuel had left the University and had no wish to return there. The National Library was no longer the answer. He needed now to find a career in life or at least a job and his first instinct was to work for poor children, but things moved rapidly and his own efforts to control and direct them were ineffective. Circumstances - or the Holy Spirit - began to carry him along he knew not where. He had learnt up at the monastery to yield to the Spirit and be shaped by his promptings. From now on his life was guided and molded by yielding in this way. He himself tells the story of how it began:

> I decided to go and work in a school for poor people where my father was a governor and the Headmaster was my old Headmaster, Fr Schneider. But before going there I attended a meeting at another school. It was my old school and my younger brother Vicente was there. It was the Manquehue School, but it was no longer run by the Fathers of the Sacred Hearts. While there for the meeting, I offered myself to the new Headmaster.[19] And he asked what I would like to

do there and I suggested history or something like that. He said he would think about it and when I returned he said I should be in charge of the Confirmation class. I was horrified because I did not know what was involved so I said I would think about it. I went to Fr Gabriel and he said: "Well, you are not prepared for that work." Thus he gave me a reason for refusing. But I went to another friend, Jorge Bulnes, and he said perhaps I was prepared for it, because I had been confirmed by the Holy Spirit. I then went back to the Manquehue School and by that time I had decided to say 'no'. There was a deacon who was in charge of this work to whom I had to say that I had decided not to accept the post. So we met and then went towards his office, but we never arrived at his office. As we were walking he stopped and said: "Excuse me a moment." He went into a classroom and I was behind him and he said to the boys in the classroom: "Well boys, this is Mr Eguiguren who will prepare you for confirmation." After that I could not say no. I went to Fr Gabriel at the monastery and told him what had happened and he said: "You must take this as the will of God and accept it."[20]

That is how José Manuel found himself in a classroom of 18 year old boys who were coming to the end of their school life and expecting to be confirmed. They were expecting to be confirmed for largely social reasons and not from a decision arising from personal conviction. They were going along with accepted convention which expected confirmation. It was expected because they would want to get married some time, and for that a certificate that they had been confirmed would be needed. That was the extent of their interest in the proceedings. José Manuel recalls his side of that first experience of bringing young people to come to terms with God.

And so I started there in the year 1976 and my brother and about 22 others formed the confirmation class - all 18 years old and all in their last year at school. It was very difficult to start with. They wanted to be confirmed partly because that was the normal accepted thing. I realized all that and I suddenly started speaking to them about what had happened to me - but I did so with the Bible. One of them came to me and said it had been very helpful and he told me about his own experience. And from that little by little the community started. I changed the normal preparation laid down in the texts they had been given and instead I read to them from the Bible. I used two periods in the week speaking on these lines to them all, the rest of the time I spent speaking to each one individually. In these talks they felt that they were being listened to and they could ask me and I would answer. I had discarded all that I believed before and now the only thing I believed was the word of God and so my answer was always the word of God. That is how I came to the end of this year and really I didn't want to finish because I was very happy in this work. The confirmation was at the end of November. They were confirmed and I was very happy.[21]

One of that first confirmation class, who was present and is still an active member of the Movement, looks back to that earliest meeting when this stranger was suddenly introduced to them as teacher. His memory of the occasion is still vivid:

José Manuel was a brother of one of the form members and he came to prepare us for confirmation. He was a person to whom I liked very much to listen at a time when the people who spoke about religion were very seldom listened to. I did like to listen to him, because what he said to me in one way or another made me think and meditate interiorly. It was for me a process of listening to a person who made an impression on me, although I did not at the time understand the importance of his message nor where it would lead. He came across as someone who was natural and unaffected and courageous. He was brave enough as a layman to speak to this group of young people whom he did not know - to speak to us about God in the preparation for confirmation. It was something which was unusual among lay people at that time. It was uncommon and it made me aware of a great emptiness inside myself. That is what made me listen to him.

During the first three years, including our confirmation, I did not speak. I was completely silent in the meetings. Just to listen to this person was very striking for me, but there was something that went further and led me to want actually to stay with him. This feeling was so strong that after the confirmation in the following year I did something unexpected, and even today I do not know why I did it, but I believe it came from God. I summoned up the courage to call him on the telephone and to say to him. 'You have been with us through our confirmation and the truth is I want to be with you. I want to be part of this group you are forming.' This was the result of listening to him. He transmitted something. It is difficult to describe but he transmitted something which in my case made me think - made me meditate. It made me see the reality of that time and the generalized emptiness of that time and to want to do something about my personal vision of things.

It had all started when José Manuel first came to our form - a group of about twenty or thirty young people still at school. He came to speak to us and he was very open with us. I would say that from the first moment he opened himself up to us in spite of how difficult that was. He opened himself up in the sense that he gave us a lot of himself. It was obvious that he liked what he did with us - the meditations, the preparation for the confirmation. Besides that, he was a person who transmitted a lot of love, a lot of friendship. He was a person who was capable of maintaining among us in the group a very great friendship. Now I think back, he was a person who liked to show his friendship - not just his own friendship towards people - but also the growing friendship between the members of the group. He caused friendship to arise and encouraged it. He made us meditate. He made us participate. He made us speak. He sought to encourage a love that went beyond the confirmation among the members of the group.[22]

Friendship & St John the Apostle

The formative influence of José Manuel on the young whom he came to teach continued after the meeting with the Cardinal and continues today. It was not a theory nor part of a program of teaching. It was the personal influence of one who gave himself to them in their real lives and did so in a way that made it possible for him to share their difficulties and problems. Some years later an Oblate of the Movement who came from

England, Jonathan Perry, emphasizes the same unique quality which broke through traditional rigid barriers of age, nationality and culture:

> He caused, he provoked, friendship. This characteristic is very significant. I have always been impressed by how careful he is to create spaces for friendship and indeed to inspire friendship with good doses of humor when needed. We have all seen how he makes a point of bringing people together for celebrating *convivencias* at the weekends and holidays - creating spaces for community. And we have all seen how his humor and sense of fun contribute to this building of community and friendship.[23]

Thus friendship was a key element from the beginning in the creation and building up of the new community. The mutual friendship that grew among them at that time was consciously and deliberately founded strongly on the word of God in the gospel of St John. St John's teaching about love in his gospel and in his first letter was so formative and so important that it led them to focus in a special way on the new commandment of love which Christ gave the disciples during the Last Supper.

> A new commandment I give to you, that you love one another even as I have loved you, that you also love one another. By this all men will know that you are my disciples, if you have love for one another.[24]

So important was this aspect of Christ's teaching in the gospel for José Manuel and the young who followed in his way, that from a very early stage Christ's words about his new commandment in John 13 became a primary inspiration of the life they forged together and of their mission to others. It was right at the beginning that they adopted St John the Apostle as the patron of the Movement.

Guided by the Holy Spirit

José Manuel could hardly fail to discern the breath of the Holy Spirit in what had happened to him since those dark days in the University when the whole meaning of life drained away from him. All that had happened had about it the supra-rational unpredictability of the Spirit. There was the meeting (was it by chance?) with Fr Gabriel. There was the new world of the word of God which he opened to him - a world given to mankind in the scriptures, which he thought he understood and, up to a point, valued, but which he now discovered again as something utterly new. There was the unaccountable decision of the priest-Headmaster to entrust his leaving confirmation class to an untried, layman with no desire to attempt it and no training to enable him to do it well. There was the strange experience, when he went to the school to refuse the job, of finding himself unceremoniously hijacked into it without a chance even of protest. And finally there was the wonderful blessing, that all could and did enter into, of the joy shared by the originally reluctant young candidates and their surprised families in that celebration of the sacrament of the Holy Spirit.

And now, when he thought it was over, he found that it had only begun. His first effort at teaching had gone better than he could ever have expected. But now what he thought was the completion of a job well done turned out to be itself a new beginning. There was more to be done. A group of the boys he had guided in their very real preparation for the sacrament came back to him and said that they wanted to continue to be together and to follow the way they had discovered under his guidance. José Manuel had the beginnings of his first community of young people on his hands and they looked to him for a lead and for guidance and inspiration in their lives. He had to find a way forward, not only for himself but for them also.

CR

Notes for Chapter 3

[1] Interview with Señora Luz

[2] The name Manquehue comes from the district and is taken from the mountain which overlooks it and is called Manquehue (an Indian name meaning Place of the Condors). This school - founded by French Priests and now still thriving under lay management - must be distinguished from the school called San Benito of the Manquehue Movement founded later by José Manuel actually on the lower slopes of the Manquehue mountain.

[3] From an early age José Manuel read avidly about the subjects tht interested him, everything from history, religion, dogs and horses to politics, myths and legends, clocks and watches and family history. He even became something of an expert on airplanes.

[4] Interview with Señora Luz

[5] His name was Hugo Montes. He is now a deacon and Oblate of Las Condes monastery

[6] Interview with José Manuel

[7] The book was 'Buddhist Philosophy' by a Jesuit, Fr Ismail Quiles, SJ.

[8] Interview José Manuel

[9] The Benedictine monastery of the Holy Trinity in a suburb of Santiago called Las Condes. It is a small monastery devoted to prayer and study and hospitality without other external pastoral works. It is the only Benedictine monastery in Santiago and attracts many through its liturgy and the reflective quiet and peace it offers visitors. Set high on the side of one of the foothills of the Andes it overlooks part of Santiago and its white modern buildings are a well-known and attractive landmark. It stands as a silent witness to spirituality and peace. Fr Gabriel Guarda had a career as a distinguished architect before becoming a monk. Some years after this he was elected Abbot of the monastery.

[10] Job. 42,5

[11] Ex. 33,19

[12] Jn. 15,15

[13] Apoc. 3,19

[14] Hb. 11,39

[15] It is recommended to all by the Vatican Council in the words: "Such is the force and power of the Word of God that it can serve the Church as her support and vigor and the children of the Church as strength for their faith, food for the soul and a pure and lasting fount of spiritual life." Vat.II - Dei Verbum n.21

[16] Hb. 2,15

[17] Vat.II - Dei Verbum n.21

[18] The three vows proposed for monks in St Benedict's Rule, which are still the vows taken by monks today, are 'stability, conversion of life and obedience'. There are various theories about the wording of the second vow but all agree that its root meaning is commitment to the monastic way of life described in the Rule. The first vow of stability is uniquely Benedictine. It means in the first place fidelity to a particular community in a particular monastery. In this sense it is the community not the particular place which is primary. Then there are deeper spiritual meanings which involve the idea of constancy of spirit, reliability in faith and practice, endurance in monastic values, perseverance to the end against all odds.

[19] José Manuel remembers that his decision was triggered by an encounter with one of the boys while he was there. It left him with a strong sense that he was called to work there.

[20] Interview with José Manuel

[21] Interviews with José Manuel

[22] Interview with Alejandro Allende

[23] Interview with Jonathan Perry

[24] Jn 13, 34-35

Chapter 4 ~ The Movement conceived

The first meeting of the Movement at Pentecost

After the meeting with the Cardinal in March 1977 José Manuel and his 8 young followers began to discuss the future with a new sense of unity and confidence. It was now clear that José Manuel's vision transcended the confused politics of the time. They had found that vision helpful and relevant to their own experience, offering them a way forward which inspired them in life. Politics in those days tended, whatever side you took, to slide imperceptibly into confrontation, hatred, revenge, violence. The Cardinal's message was different. It was a consistent call for reconciliation. José Manuel himself sought to live the same lesson and to teach it to his followers, but there were still some problems with their families as José Manuel remembers:

> Some of the families did not understand, because they thought the bishop was a little bit red. That was a matter of politics. I had abandoned politics some years before. Through all the Allende government I was not involved. The only help I gave was to someone in a legal way to help him through friends via my father, when he could have problems with the military, and I received a very nice letter of thanks.[1] But there was no more than that. I had discovered Christ and I supported all the action of the Church. On the whole the families understood this, but perhaps some of the young people experienced a bit of persecution at home. They themselves were not political. The Movement was nothing to do with politics, but it was Catholic in the sense that it was in communion with the Church - it was not exclusive Catholicism nor separated from everyone else. We got on well that way, so that the Cardinal sent us a letter urging us to continue.[2]

It had happened, as though by chance, that the Movement started in the framework of a school - the Manquehue School where José Manuel had taught the original confirmation class. He was still a teacher there and the boys who formed the nucleus of the new Movement were now alumni at University, but they came back to visit him at the school and to work with him there. The school itself had gone through a difficult transition. A few years earlier the French Fathers, who had been in charge when José Manuel was a boy, had withdrawn from the school to engage in other pastoral work. At that point a lay Headmaster, who was not a Catholic, was appointed. The school had always up to then had a strong Catholic religious character but with the new lay Headmaster there were many changes. This led to much concern among parents about the Catholic ethos of the school and the Cardinal was persuaded to intervene and appoint a Catholic Headmaster, who was Mgr Alfonso Puelma Claro.

It was Mgr Puelma who had first invited José Manuel, after his first three years with Fr Gabriel were over, to do some part time teaching and take the confirmation class, from which unexpectedly the Movement started. Mgr Puelma had a well-merited reputation for understanding the young and knew what he was doing. He must have been delighted at the development when some of that first class of José Manuel's wanted to stay with their new teacher and find ways of expressing their new Catholic vision in social service. They made a retreat with José Manuel at the Old House in Leyda in early March of 1977 during which they wrote to Mgr Puelma offering to work under him in the school. After some initial hesitation, he decided to accept their offer and, as we have seen, he had something to do with their crucial meeting with the Cardinal. Having accepted their offer he then gave them much help and encouragement.

He wrote an article in the School Paper, the Manquehino, giving them his generous support. At the same time José Manuel was appointed to take responsibility for the Pastoral Department of the school[3]. José Manuel threw himself into this new responsibility. He devised and published a very full program for religious teaching in the school. The Cardinal himself wrote a generous letter in support of this program. It was presented as a program of Catholic Action but was more than that. It sought to promote a real personal acceptance among the students of the Church in its social action, in its spirituality, and in its life of prayer and the sacraments.

The group was now really committed. Their commitment was spiritually oriented and openly based on the word of scripture. The spirit which would later shape José Manuel's Movement was already alive. On the list of the helpers in the school's Pastoral Department, drawn from among senior pupils in the school and former pupils now at university, there were already names of several who would later be among the earliest Oblates[4] of the Movement. Here in the Manquehue School they had under José Manuel's leadership just the challenge they were looking for to pass on to others the word of God in the gospel they had themselves come to value so much.

The new Pastoral Department in the Manquehue School was thus important for José Manuel's Movement, for which it marked a clear new departure. The benefit to the School also was important and widely appreciated. It was José Manuel's personal ambition to encourage positively through his program the development of the boys' spiritual life throughout the school. Already in 1976 he had been thinking in terms of a Movement to act as a sort of inspiration to the boys and now, with the backing of Mgr Puelma and the Cardinal, something like a lay movement was already beginning to emerge in the school, although its scope was still essentially confined to the existing school organisation.

And so it happened that they were already working in the school and had begun to coalesce into an organized group when an important meeting took place which was the real beginning of the Movement as a separate, although not yet fully independent, body. This meeting followed closely on the meeting with the Cardinal and the beginning of the school year in March 1977, which also saw the creation of the new Pastoral Department. There had grown up in those days among the young who were following him a strong sense of a new beginning with very definite aims which were an inspiration in their lay lives.

José Manuel responded to this new spirit by calling a meeting of the founding members for Saturday May 28th 1977 at the Manquehue School. Fr Gabriel from the Monastery accepted his invitation to come to the meeting and to preach to them in the morning. After that José Manuel's brother, Juan Eduardo Eguiguren, who had been a member of the first confirmation group spoke for the whole group. José Manuel's father helped Juan Eduardo in writing the text of what he wanted to say.

He so exactly expressed the spirit not only of that moment but also of the direction of the future Movement that some of his words have been preserved as a prefatory quotation to a later publication of the Movement called 'The Way of the Manquehue Movement'.[5] This is an extract from what he said on that occasion, the memory of which is still cherished:

> This is a historic moment for us because on this Saturday the Manquehue Movement starts its life and begins to reveal its nature. This group came together by their own free choice - a group of young Christian men from the Manquehue College with a strong motivation to achieve something. From small beginnings it has an emerging structure which is now assuming a definite shape. The basic characteristic of this Movement can be summed up in one word - friendship - Christian friendship - Christian love. God is love and, if we find our own nourishment in this love and pass it on to our brothers we shall be satisfied and our desire to give will increase. We are young and will keep the doors open to this development. We shall now make a start in giving to others what we have to give but, however small it may be, it must manifest our friendship because that is essential to all Christian living.[6]

Juan Edouardo Eguiguren's address, from which the above is an extract, was the first formal proposal for the future shape of the Movement and on that first Saturday he formally presented a copy of it to Fr Gabriel Guarda. He was speaking and acting on behalf of José Manuel himself and the whole group. What is surprising about this little meeting in the context of the time is its unwavering commitment to Catholic spirituality and work for others together with the firm and explicit affirmation of the Johannine inspiration, which they all experienced so strongly, of mutual Christian friendship in Christ. This became the scriptural foundation of their spirituality. It clearly inspired Juan Eduardo's reflections on that first evening and led them to choose St John the Apostle from that moment as the patron of their new work together.

From the time of that meeting five quotations from St John gave the young members of the Movement familiar reference points in scripture to inspire their life and work together. They are:

A new commandment I give to you, that you love one another even as I have loved you, that you also love one another. By this all men will know that you are my disciples, if you have love for one another.[7]

If a man loves me, he will keep my word, and my Father will love him, and we will come to him and make our home with him.[8]

This is my commandment, that you love one another as I have loved you. Greater love has no man than this, that a man lay down his life for his friend. You are my friends if you do what I command you.[9]

In this is love, not that we loved God, but that he loved us and sent his son to be the expiation of our sins.[10]

There is no fear in love, but perfect love casts out fear.[11]

It is remarkable that, even at this early stage, they were not thinking only of themselves and the pastoral work they were undertaking in their own school. In a typically Johannine way they began looking outward even as they looked inward. There was more than a hint of this and of the future of the Movement also in Juan Eduardo Eguiguren's positive assertion, which looked beyond the walls of the Manquehue School. He said that:

This group stretches out towards other alumni from other Colleges and to University Students and we all do this with a great desire to serve and to grow in our spiritual development.

Eduardo had sounded the keynote of the future Movement in this very special meeting. The next day was Sunday May 29th 1977. Fr Gabriel gave a homily in which he took up the theme of their mission by reading the passage from Acts where the first deacons were made.

The Hellenists murmured against the Hebrews because their widows were neglected in the daily distribution. And the twelve summoned the body of the disciples and said. It is not right that we should give up preaching the Word of God to serve tables. Therefore, brethren, pick from among you seven men of good repute, full of the Spirit and of wisdom whom we may appoint to this duty.[12]

On that text he spoke to them with encouragement and authority. Juan Eduardo Eguiguren's words had articulated their own vision and generosity. Father Gabriel's quotation from the Acts of the Apostles and his application of it to their new work took their minds back to the earliest days of Christianity when the Church was insignificant and powerless. It was a time, like their own, when the forces of power and authority ignored the word of God. Yet the apostles had chosen some very ordinary young people - the first deacons - to play a part in their mission. Those first deacons had nothing to offer in the way of training or experience - nothing but utter commitment to the word of God and their fellow Christians. By developing this theme Fr Gabriel gave them the confidence to believe that they had also been chosen to do something important. Their developing apostolate was not just a youthful dream of no account. It was fully in accord with the mission of the Church. It was truly ecclesial.

José Manuel himself treasures the memory of that day of their first formal meeting together and its significance for all that followed:

> On that day we held our first shared *lectio*, in which we read the first and second chapter of St Matthew together - the visit of the Magi, the flight into Egypt, the return to Nazareth. We met for that *lectio* in the house of one of the first members, Gonzalo Loesser, at ten o'clock at night. From then on for several years we always met on Sunday evening at that hour. The important thing about it was that we thought that this was the moment at which the Movement actually started, because it was the occasion when we shared the Word of God for the first time as a Movement. There was another vital point about that day, which we did not think of at the time, but it came home to us very strongly later - it was Pentecost Sunday.[13]

That Pentecost meeting was a definitive moment - a moment of change for them all and of 'new creation'.[14] Before that week-end the little group was just a small organization like any other working in a Catholic School, but during their time together on that occasion a special spiritual bond was created by shared *lectio* and all the thinking and praying they did together about their own commitment, about their future together. Their sense of community in their work under their patron St John was strengthened. They came away with a new sense of dedication that would last. For José Manuel himself there was an added touch of grace in the fact that it was the feast day also of his mother's patron - Our Lady of Light. Ever afterwards they saw this day as the real beginning of the Manquehue Movement.

This sense of a new beginning on Pentecost Sunday was, however, clearer in retrospect than at the time. We must remember that at this stage the shape and purpose of the Movement was still only beginning to emerge step by step. Essentially they were at the time no more than a voluntary group of young men dedicated to Catholic Action and working within the Manquehue School. The term Catholic Action was, in the pre-Vatican II tradition, the normal description given to any undertaking by the laity of pastoral and evangelizing work under the direction of the clergy. They were working for the Church under Mgr Puelma, the Headmaster,[15] with the Cardinal's blessing. They certainly had broad visions, but they were not yet an independent corporate entity. There were only eight members and their individual involvement in the Movement was strictly part-time because they were all students in the school or at University. They were, moreover, dependent on the Manquehue School for their base and on the personal backing of Mgr Puelma, who was already sick with heart problems, for the work they did there. No-one could have predicted convincingly, at that stage, the later developments of the Movement. Nevertheless it is also true that from that Pentecost meeting in 1977 they had begun no longer to perceive themselves as individuals attracted to working for the present with José Manuel in his department in the School. A new spiritual cohesion and common purpose had been created on that day and it began to grow. From that time the corporate life of the Manquehue Movement was for them a reality.

The Development of the Movement at the Manquehue School
After that beginning other pupils from the Manquehue School wanted to join the Movement and the numbers involved increased. There was a two storey building on the campus which had been the community house of the French Fathers while they still ran the School. Now José Manuel had his office there and from it he worked as 'Asesor' of the Students' Center. His office became the center for the young community of the emerging Movement. It was the base in which they prayed and worked

in the school under the direction of José Manuel. The Students' Center was an established feature of the school and now through José Manuel's inspiration it began to touch the lives of many of the boys and staff. One student of the time, who later joined the Movement and became one of the first Oblates, remembers his first contact with them at this time.

> For my generation in 1978 the work of the Students' Center was very important. It was organized to cover a number of different areas of school life: Sport, *Tutorías*, Social life, Cultural interests, Communications. Many of the students from senior classes took part in these activities. We held regular meetings and organized many activities. There was also someone there who was really behind all this work whom I did not know much at the time. He was called José Manuel Eguiguren and I got to know him a little.
>
> Then he once took me for a walk in the grounds of the College. We talked a lot and it ended in a barbecue in which he took part. After that he gave me his time and the close understanding he had for us students. Andrew Baraona, a classmate who was much involved in the Movement, invited me to take a more committed part in various activities and persuaded me to join one of the communities for *lectio*. My first meditation was memorable. The subject happened to be the man possessed by devils in Gerasa in St Mark's account. I did not fully understand, but I continued going to the meetings more because of my friendship with Andrew than anything else.[16]

That mention of friendship strikes again a note which was very typical of the growing Movement. It had been strongly mentioned by Eduardo Eguiguren at the Pentecost meeting and after that it remained a characteristic which held them all together. It was a friendship in which José Manuel taught them to see John the Apostle in his friendship with Christ as their patron and ideal. As for their own lay vocation, they should see it in Christ's words to his disciples in St John's gospel calling them to demonstrate their following of Christ through their love for each other.[17] In the early stages it owed a lot to the sort of friendship which commonly arises among groups of young working together and sharing their activities. Under the inspiration of St John and the powerful spirituality of regular shared *lectio* it was transformed into a lasting,

Christ-centered spiritual relationship. This became one of the gifts of the Movement which inspired its evangelizing work and which is always seen not in an individualistic way but as a shared community commitment.

The confirmation classes in the school continued. Some of the newly confirmed stayed on with the group in the Students' Center and were welcomed as co-workers. They met weekly for shared *lectio*. Mgr Puelma continued to give every encouragement to their involvement in the School, in work for social action, in helping with games and social events and in the many retreats they organized. Retreats were very important from the beginning in the evangelizing work of the Movement. José Manuel himself had begun it all with the first confirmation group at the old house in Leyda – so full of memories of his own boyhood. Over the years he taught them how to prepare and organize and run a retreat. He gave them the confidence to speak themselves and lead discussions and *lectio*. Then, once the pastoral work in the school got under way, there were frequent retreats both in the monastery and in the diocesan retreat house at Punta de Tralca[18].

It is a significant fact that at this early stage José Manuel was given by the Cardinal and Mgr Puelma so strong a status of spiritual leadership in the school. It was a vital experience for him and his future work. In the Catholic Church there were many uncertainties and controversies about catechesis at the time and it is remarkable that the Cardinal himself showed his confidence in José Manuel by appointing him as his own delegate in the School to be in charge of catechesis[19]. It was an unusual situation. Mgr Puelma had been appointed as Headmaster by the Cardinal and then, in parallel, José Manuel was appointed, also by the Cardinal, to take charge of the whole Pastoral work of the school both inside and outside the classroom. This made him a strong figure in the life of the School with a position of real authority. He worked, of course, in close harmony with Mgr Puelma as Headmaster, who fully supported him. His position was recognized by the rest of the Staff. His spiritual authority was accepted by the boys themselves who quickly responded to his personal approachability and real understanding of their questions about life and about their faith and the meaning for them of Catholic spirituality. The fact that he was a young layman gave a special strength to his work with them. His own original inspiration had been to fill with his new lay Movement the gap left by the withdrawal of the religious community which had founded the School. His aim now was to make a real community of the whole school - boys and staff - with his group of young pupils and alumni as the driving force.

Director of Christian Formation

It was here in the Manquehue School that Jose Manuel first developed the ideals and approaches to the teaching of religion which were to become formative in all his later educational work in the schools of the Movement. In the 1977 issue of Manquehino, the School Magazine, José Manuel wrote an article setting out his ideals and aims for what within the School context he called a movement for Catholic Action. Today it would probably be called a movement for evangelization. In this article he wrote:

> The Movement for Catholic Action is a community - a community of faith, of worship, of love, of good order, united to the local and universal Church, which carries forward the Church's mission to preach the gospel and serve mankind and realizes its apostolate especially in education and in the field of the Catholic School..........The Movement of the Community is centered on friendship and a consciousness that 'no-one has greater love than to give his life for his friends'. Jn.15,13. The movement of the community has a program for education which is at the same time a spirit, a style, a way of living, a program of life for those who come together from time to time around the Word of God, bringing it to bear on their life, on the culture of their society, celebrating it in the liturgy and recognizing it as the original source of its mission in education.[20]

In the same document José Manuel goes on to write of the need to reconcile our daily life and culture with our faith, of the need for a formation which would inspire all school activities with faith, hope and charity. He emphasizes the role of liturgy and the service of others and introduces his own concept of *tutorías* [21], which would become so important in the educational and pastoral work of the Manquehue Movement in the future. The starting point of *tutorías* is that the young often learn the meaning of faith most effectively from each other. The tutors, therefore, are older pupils working under direction and supervision. He describes a tutor's role as being that of friend, counsellor and servant of the younger pupil, who is to be rescued in this way from the anonymity of the mass. It was an idea of great catechetical potential which was to be developed more fully later in the Movement's own schools. There is little, if anything, of his later educational ideals which is not at least adumbrated in this remarkable document of 1978. It reads like the first outline of all that he was to write and teach in later years.

José Manuel had initially been appointed to take charge of the Pastoral Department of the School. It meant that he was given a position affecting the whole school and it gave him the authority to write in the School magazine in 1977 the words quoted above. With such inspiration the years 1977 & 1978 were golden years of growth and development of the Movement within the Manquehue School under the support and encouragement of Mgr Puelma and the Cardinal. José Manuel recalls this period in which the young lay Movement first really came into its own:

> The Movement took on the Confirmation groups in the school and some of those who were confirmed stayed on to join the Movement. We had meetings every week for *lectio*. Mgr Puelma helped us a lot by leaving us to work very freely in the School so, for example we ran all the social action. There was a shanty town near the school (which is no longer there) and we went there to work with poor families. Also we worked on the sports. We organized many, many retreats at Punta de Tralca and in the monastery. The first retreat before the founding of the Movement was at the Old House in Leyda. Before that the confirmation retreat in 1976, from which it all began, was in the monastery. But now in 1977-78 we held many retreats for the children of the school in both places. We worked at the school developing all the cultural activities and socializing and all that kind of thing. I had been appointed with the Cardinal's approval and that helped me in developing this idea of community within the school.[22]

Roberto Quiroga, who was at that time a senior student in the school, has very good memories of these times:

My memory of our experience at that time was of a great spirit of happiness and friendship. The truth is that we had a lot of work to do in sport, social action, communication, cultural and pastoral work. We stayed on at school every afternoon and we were always laughing and enjoying the work together.   Over it all was the constant presence and availability of José Manuel, who guided us and our work in a friendly way.[23]

Changes under a new Headmaster

Then a great change came for everyone in 1979. Mgr Puelma retired because of ill health. A new Headmaster, Fr Luis Eugenio Silva was appointed. There were many currents of opinion about how the school would develop, some of which differed from the Manquehue Movement's vision. The position of the Movement had been well established in the school under Mgr Puelma, but it was still small and dependent on part-time help of students, both in the school and at University. Within the school it was strong - perhaps in a way too strong – but outside the school among parents and others it was still not very well known nor understood.   As soon as the Cardinal's decision about the new Headmaster was known José Manuel wrote to Fr Silva, with the support of his young Movement members, to offer their continued services in the school and Fr Silva made his decision. He decided not to continue along the same lines but to bring in another priest to be in charge of religious education who would take José Manuel's place with a different title and a different program. The Movement could remain in the school, he said, and any of the pupils (of the school) who wished to join it could do so, but it must be as a purely personal choice. On this basis the Movement remained active within the school among those who were interested for another year under its new name Movimiento Apostolico Manquehue[24]. It was still recognized and valued within the school but it had a more limited scope and could no longer enjoy the independence and responsibility which Mgr Puelma had given it.

The resulting gradual severance of the Movement from the School was all done in a friendly way of mutual understanding and there was a ceremony in the Chapel on 13th June 1979 in which a letter from the

Cardinal was read and new badges of the Movement were presented. Now it became a truly independent group without the official links to the structure of the school which had up to this time given it a firm base and ever-broadening scope. Valuable as it had been and still was to the Manquehue school the Movement increasingly had a life of its own and this life was so strong that it had to find new and wider scope both for its own sake and for the sake of the School and the new Headmaster. After trying for a time to continue his work in these new circumstances José Manuel accepted the inevitable and resigned from the School Staff.

Beginning all over again
This was quite a shock for many concerned with the school. His young followers had grown to love him and many of them felt deprived at his proposed departure. However, for José Manuel himself it was not a time for regrets or recriminations. It brought him gradually to a new conviction, which had already begun to take shape, that he must found his own school. The facts spoke clearly. His Movement had started in the classroom. It had developed and become strong among the young both at school and as students in the University. Now for a time there might be scope for some development elsewhere, but the movement must in the end return to the classroom and to the young whose spiritual deprivation in the context even of a religious school in that age was among his greatest concerns. Schools were the strongest creative influence in the lives of the young. Evangelization must, he believed, take place there or it would not be effective.

Fr Silva was right to recognize that the time had come for a change for the sake both of the existing school and of the new Movement. José Manuel's whole concept and charism and programme for action could not be limited and departmentalized as one among other subject departments in a school – each of them inevitably competing for time and resources. His vision was all embracing, unitive, holistic. It concerned the whole of life, the whole of school life, the life of the young stretching beyond school into the student culture and adult life. It affected both the art of teaching and the discipline of learning. As his disciples moved on into University they still came back to the school and were involved not only with José Manuel but also with the boys in the Movement still at

61

school. This and other aspects of the developing Movement made for difficulties under a new Headmaster who inevitably and rightly had his own agenda. The break had to be made, but what was to become of the Movement without the school? That was the great question which now had to be faced in a radical way. The task for the moment was that the group must somehow be kept together. José Manuel remembers:

> Then began the hardest time, because we left the Manquehue School which we loved very much. All the members of the Movement went to their friends and families and asked them for money to help us continue our work for the young. We drew up a document explaining what we were doing. Many gave us money and with that we rented a house and they paid me, because I was now without work and a salary. I was given alternative opportunities to work in other places (in fact I had two offers of jobs) but I did not want to make that break. I wanted to carry on with this work, so I turned the jobs down. The Movement could pay me only very little but I managed to keep going.[25]

The new situation was difficult for everyone. Alejandro Allende, who was one of the first Confirmation group and was by this time a student at University, remembers the difficulties of this time:

> While we were working in the school, José Manuel used to like very much to receive people and to speak with them quite apart from the *lectio*. Some of us were already University students and still he used to speak to us simply about the things of God. This was very important at that time when nobody spoke about the things of God. God was forgotten. It was sad but understandable that a new phase had to begin. It was then that the hardest time began, because we left the Manquehue school, which we loved very much.[26]

They were now completely on their own and faced with difficulties about continuing to work together which seemed insoluble. Considering that they were only students - university students who had their studies to complete, their examinations to pass and their careers to think of - it was a generous decision to shoulder the burden of seeking financial help to enable them to stay together. However their immediate solution of operating from a temporary unstructured base supported by charity - with no clearly defined field of action or source of consistent funding - could not last. The house they rented with the money they had collected provided a temporary base for José Manuel to continue his work with them. By their meetings there and support of him they showed remarkable generosity and tenacity in their growing commitment.

José Manuel himself had to face radical questions about his own future. There were other possibilities on offer for him. There was plenty of sound and sensible advice available enticing him to abandon this forlorn project and go in a different direction. He did not have to stay with this strange new community of the young, which he had created almost in a fit of absent-mindedness. There were not many obvious reasons why he should stay with them. The Movement was no longer wanted in the school in which it had come to birth and to which it had brought new spiritual life. It looked as though the vision had come to an end and he could easily bow out with honour. He had done his work for them and it was time to move on and think of his own future by taking one of the two quite promising jobs which had been offered him. He considered them but rejected them both. They would be incompatible with what he now saw as a vocation from God. It was a vocation to the evangelization of the young and it must come before everything else.

It was at this time, as we shall see, that he got married. That was another radical beginning in which the security of a regular job would have been the greatest of blessings. But he decided to turn away from that apparently safe course so as to devote himself to the group of young people who were trying to find their way to a better lay Catholic life in the world and who had found in him the inspiration and guidance they needed and wanted to follow - if only he could find a way of leading them.

The rented house, the meagre salary, the quest for work to do were the setting of a heroic new start for both the young people themselves and for José Manuel. Equally this decision to stay together without resources or clear prospects can be seen as a strong statement about the emerging self-perception of the Movement and its solid foundation on prayer, *lectio*, friendship in Christ and dedication to his service as their only ultimate resources. It was in 1980 - a time that was difficult for everyone in Chile. It is not surprising that the temporary arrangement of a rented house and nothing but a trickle of donated money came to an end. The money ran out and they found themselves right back at the starting line again. The marvel, the miracle is that they stayed together and never lost faith. In this way was the new vision and their commitment to it tested as though by fire.

Heaven knows what agonies of spirit José Manuel himself went through at this time but for his young followers, as they look back, the time in the rented house was a time of joy and friendship and spiritual growth inspired by little more than faith and hope. Alejandro Allende remembers how much it contributed to the growth and cohesion of the group. He remembers it as giving them a sense of liberty to meet together in friendship, to have the courage to talk of God and their hopes for the future and to live by faith, because they had little else to rely on. The home was a place of welcome for many age groups. It had a living room which was not very big but was normally full of young people and wonderful for big meetings. He remembers the supreme importance for them of José Manuel's presence and availability in his office.

Roberto Quiroga, another of the group, remembers that the rented house meant a lot for him during a difficult time at University:

> At the time I was studying engineering at the University and life there was difficult and confusing. The Movement house was quite different. It was a place for meeting and being with friends, for holding community meetings of the Movement and of course for laughing and having a good time together. I remember with affection the ancient furniture and the ping-pong table. Above all I remember our meditations on the word of God and how they grew at that time in strength and influence on my life.[27]

The life-line of parish work

So for a time the only base of the Movement was that rented house with its battered furniture where José Manuel, still a ready listener and counsellor, was always available in his office. They met there, meditated on the scriptures, supported each other and laughed together; and they hoped and persevered with faith. As it turned out their faith and tenacity were rewarded. José Manuel recalls a new hope that emerged only just in time:

> By the year 1980 the money came to an end while we were still in the rented house. Then suddenly Fr Henry Cortes, the parish priest of Our Lady of the Angels, asked us to start a youth group there. So we closed the house and moved to the parish and worked there for several years.[28]

Continuity with real work to do was thus assured and they started again, welcomed once more into the active life of the Church in the community of a parish. There was need for youth work in the parish and it went well. They stayed there for about five years, working on confirmation preparation, social work, retreats and helping in the liturgy. They had got a real base again, for Fr Henry Cortes provided them with offices and, what is even more important, with wide scope in all the varied work for the young which can be developed in a busy parish. They put great emphasis on retreats. In fact, during the first year at the parish they organized and themselves led many retreats. They were all busy again and busy in the work they loved - evangelizing among young people. The experience in the school had been good, but this was in some ways better. The school had been all for boys but here in the parish they worked with girls as well and they worked with families. In this and many other ways this pastoral work in the parish was invaluable as part of the preparation for what was to come. It broadened their whole approach to the work of bringing the riches of the word of God into peoples lives. It gave them experience with families, with all age groups, with parish liturgy, with preparation for the sacraments and many other aspects of parish life.

Although when we look at the whole history of the Movement the years of this parish interlude may seem like a mere staging post, yet it was a time of great joy, hard work, growing friendships and new experience of living and spreading the gospel for the young followers of José Manuel. They were joined by others - like Rodrigo Vidal who at this time discovered José Manuel although he had never been in the Manquehue School. They used the parish church and offices for their parish work but in the evening they often met together in a little café called Tip y Tap where they could talk about their work and relax together. Those early members of the Movement look back on it as a time of fruitful happiness.

The parish work was, however, an interim phase in which they learnt a lot, but somehow they knew that here was not their permanent vocation. Their earlier experience in the Manquehue school remained valid as an indication of the way they would have to go. It had revealed José Manuel's unique gifts in leading the young to God in a school environment - his approachability, his firm and inspiring lay spirituality, his ability to lead along a road which was demanding but still challenged the young in ways that they were eager to follow. Truly there was scope for much of the same charism in the context of parish life so that nothing was lost or wasted. It was perhaps during this period that they developed fully the style of José Manuel's unique Manquehue retreats founded on the Word of God which, then and later, became so powerful an instrument in his work for the young.

One of the most important and lasting effects of their years in parish life was that through it they discovered and established the independence within the Church of the Movement itself. It made them and everyone else aware that the Manquehue Apostolic Movement with all its works was completely independent, in spite of the name Manquehue, which in any case is not confined to one institution but belongs to the whole district of Santiago which is overlooked by the massive and inescapable presence of Manquehue mountain. In the parish they came to realize fully that they were not merely a useful subordinate group capable of being used by other Catholic institutions. They had an identity in the Church and a mission which was given them to use for others and above all to rescue the young from the confusion and ambivalence of their surroundings.

The truth was that already José Manuel had himself developed a clear and coherent vision which was specifically educational and which could never be fully realized except in the context of a school. Already he had given expression to this vision in a valedictory message which he wrote, as retiring Head of the Department of Christian Formation in the Manquehue School. He published it in the School Magazine for all to read and ponder. This is what he wrote:

His Holiness Pope Paul VI has pointed out in his Encyclical on Evangelization[29] that the break between the gospel and culture is without any doubt the dramatic problem of our time. What the Holy Father asserts of society applies also to the Catholic School. It is necessary to find ways of teaching and of religious practice which are in harmony with the cultural medium in which the pupils live. It must be a system of evangelization which does not do violence to the young but rather converts them to the call of love, which does not harm them and make them hostile, but which comes to terms with the reality in which they live and, far from provoking hatred, inspires pupils to give all the effort they can and demonstrates to them that in the environment in which God has placed them they have a mission to accomplish. For this purpose it is necessary to develop a project of education which can be at the same time a spirit, a style of life, a way of living, a programme of life..... At present this work is going forward zealously based on the Manquehue educational commitment. It is a community of laity which is dedicated to the overall mission of inspiring the pastoral work among the students of the Sacred Hearts of Manquehue at every level. Today the pastoral office is working both on the solution of immediate problems and also on the task of forming a community for the future. And all this must be in line with the directions of the Archbishop of Santiago, the wishes of the Fr Rector and finally with the living experience of everyone involved.[30]

His words at that time were partly a statement about the importance for everyone of recognizing that the problems of schools and of the young were at the heart of the problems of the Church as a whole and of society. Schools reflected and often perpetuated 'the break between gospel and culture' which is at the heart of the problem of evangelization. He was also expressing a personal vision of what must be achieved for the young in schools of the future. It was the future that was most important to him. It was the question of the future that haunted him in his search for a platform from which to work now that the Manquehue School was no longer available. It was this haunting vision that must have been with him daily in the rented house and in the parish work that followed.

The experience in the parish had been a significant step forward, but now he and his young followers had to move on. Everything had to begin again. From now on everything would be new and, however it turned out, it would be created through the Spirit of God working in the Movement itself. They were ready to begin their first school - except, of course, for the fact that they had absolutely no resources or financial backing to do so. How that could ever come about seemed impossible to imagine, but it was all in the hands of God. In the midst of all this there were other questions and problems pressing on José Manuel in his personal life. We must now turn to consider them and their bearing on his emerging vocation.

సు

Notes for Chapter 4

[1] This was Hugo Cancino, a teacher of modern Church History at the University. Professor Cancino was a senior member of an organization called 'Iglesia Joven', which had a mixed membership ranging from loyal Catholics to some who were alienated from the hierarchy and influenced by Marxism. José Manuel and Hugo Cancino discussed everything together, at University. When Hugo got married, he chose José Manuel as Religious witness for the wedding. After the military mobilization of September 1973 José Manuel sought to help him with legal assistance, but he decided to go into exile. Before going he left a letter for José Manuel which he kept and valued as a tribute to their Christian friendship, which transcended politics and ideologies. As such it was a wonderful affirmation of the friendship which José Manuel valued so much and was passing on to his new young friends and followers.

[2] Interview with José Manuel

[3] This appointment as Head of the Pastoral Department was made by the Vicar for Education of the Archdiocese, Mgr Gambino on the recommendation of the Headmaster Mgr Puelma. At the same time the Cardinal made him one of his two representatives on the Board of Governors of the School. These two appointments were for the academic year of 1978. They followed (and were the result of his success in) the initial appointments to be head of the Confirmation class and then of the Students' Center

[4] As the structure of the Movement developed some members, both single and married, made formal promises and became known as the Oblates.

[5] in Spanish: El Camino Manquehino.

[6] Speech of Eduardo Eguiguren

[7] Jn. 13, 34-35

[8] Jn. 14, 23

[9] Jn. 15, 12-14

[10] 1 Jn 4, 10

[11] 1 Jn 4,18

[12] Acts 6, 1ff

[13] Interview with José Manuel

[14] cf II Cor. 5,17: anyone who is in Christ is a new creation; the old has passed away, behold, the new has come.

[15] When José Manuel asked him what he wanted of them at this stage Mgr Puelma's reply was laconic but positive: 'Be there'. It seems that, given what they stood for, their very presence itself was valued by him.

[16] Interview with José Miguel Navarro

[17] A new commandment I give to you, that you love one another; even as I have loved you, that you also love one another. By this all men will know that you are my disciples, if you have love for one another. *Jn. 13,34*

[18] Punta de Tralca is a large, rambling, capacious Retreat Center overlooking the Pacific Ocean. It is owned by the Archdiocese of Santiago. It was at that time operated by the Religious of the Sacred Heart but is now under lay management. There is space for nearly a thousand residents. It has a large chapel, a number of different dining rooms and lecture halls in the scattered buildings spread on the hillside overlooking the sea. Its atmosphere is welcoming particularly to the young. It combines in an attractive mix some of the elements of a holiday camping site, a youth hostel and a religious house for quiet and reflection. Cardinal Silva had an apartment there in which he lived on his retirement.

[19] The word 'catechesis' was used in the early Church to describe the process by which a new convert was instructed in the faith of Christianity. It is commonly used in the Catholic Church today to refer to the various ways in which the faith can be taught to new converts and equally renewed and strengthened among the faithful of all ages.

[20] Article in Manquehino magazine 1978 p47 - see Appendix 2

[21] an institution of the Movement, which we shall meet again, by which older pupils accept the responsibility of sharing their faith with younger ones and encouraging their spiritual growth. *Tutorías* became and remains a vital and valued instrument for the catechesis of the young at school. It has the exceptional virtue, if well organized, managed and supervized, of being as fruitful for the tutors as it is for the pupils. The original idea came to him through José Antonio Navarro, who was one of the original group. He came to JM one day in 1977 with the idea of doing something with the younger boys. José Antonio told JM of the way he had become so important in the lives of the young boys of the football team he had been invited to train and of the need to bring God to them through this relationship. JM latched on to this and immediately began to encourage José Antonio to develop a deeper relationship with the boys and named José Antonio head of a new area of the Centro de Alumnos called *Tutoría*.

[22] Interview José Manuel

[23] Interview Roberto Quiroga

[24] The Manquehue Apostolic Movement

[25] Interview José Manuel

[26] Interview Roberto Quiroga
[27] Interview Alejandro Allende
[28] Interview José Manuel
[29] Evangelii Nuntiandi 1975
[30] in Manquehino magazine 1978

Chapter 5 ~ The Marriage

Two vocations - conflicting or complementary?

José Manuel Eguiguren is married and has five children. That fact - his marriage, his wife, his five children - are all so closely related to his vocation that neither his life in the Movement nor his family life can be understood in separation. His aspirations, the growing Movement, his educational and other achievements and his family are parts of a single whole bound together by a strong lay Catholic spirituality which he was already living himself and teaching to his young followers before any question of marriage occurred. It was just when his way forward seemed to be getting clear that the question of marriage came unexpectedly into the equation. It did not impede or compromise his vocation with his young followers. It brought suffering and difficult problems, but in time it proved to be an enrichment both of José Manuel's own life and of his apostolate which was just beginning.

He began to think of marriage just at the time when, with the encouragement of both the Cardinal and Fr. Puelma, he had successfully formed a group of young helpers and followers who provided a core group of young lay people at the heart of the school. At this stage José Manuel was committed to developing this group with a view to creating a residential lay community where they had their little office, in the house which the priests had formerly occupied in the Manquehue School. The idea was to give the school again a living community – a lay community this time – of prayer at its center. The house was to be the base for this new lay community and its growing activities throughout the school. It was open to all the students and the nucleus was formed by those who were becoming committed to working with him. It was de facto a celibate community, but with no long term commitment at this stage. As such it would not be too far distant from the community of priests who had preceded them. Thus a strong living religious center was again becoming a feature of the school. The group of helpers lived and prayed together and made the Divine Office the center of prayer in the school.

It was just before he left the school for the next phase of parish work that José Manuel wrote in the School Magazine, the Manquehino[1], about the Movements achievement in the life of the school.

What he wrote at that time is important because it shows how far José Manuel's understanding of school evangelization had progressed. Many of the ideas which became so important and so effective in the Movement's own schools later on are seen in this article to be in place already in the Manquehue School: *Lectio divina*, spiritual friendship and *tutorias* are all there. His article is an impressive summary of the work of the Movement at the time.

Thus José Manuel seemed to have no room for more at that time. However, it was then that a close friend, Jorge Bulnes whom he had known since childhood, spoke to him of marriage. He revealed that he had been doing a little forward planning on his friend's behalf. He said that he was himself going out with a girl and had met her sister. He seemed strangely convinced that this sister would be the perfect girl for marriage with José Manuel. With this in mind he wanted them to meet. José Manuel dismissed this proposal. He was completely absorbed with his new plans and had no time to think about marriage. He wanted to get on with his work, which was for God, and he could do without such distractions.

His friend, however, was strangely insistent and in the end José Manuel gave way and agreed to accompany him for tea with this wonder-girl. That is how he met Luz Cosmelli for the first time. He was unnerved to find that his friend had been right. He fell in love with her at once and in that first meeting his resistance to the idea of marriage collapsed. He found that he could after all make time available and continued to meet her and go out with her.

That was on the way to settling one side of the question about their engagement, but there was another side and another problem. Luz also had lay apostolic work to which she was committed. She had her own absorbing interests and visions and plans and she was sure at that time that, even though she liked him, she did not have anything left over for José Manuel. What she had in her own apostolate was enough for her. It had brought peace and purpose to her life after a terrible experience. The nature of her work and its origins were very important to her. Her commitment to it was unshakeable because for her it was a call from God which had come to her in a way unmistakably authentic at a time of profound religious crisis. She got on well with José Manuel and liked him, but against the competition of her absolute dedication to her apostolic work he could not, she decided, have much of a priority in her life.

Luz Cosmelli's story

Luz's story was utterly different but as unusual as José Manuel's. Her father was a Spaniard named Atilio Cosmelli who had come to Chile from Spain after the Civil War. He married a Chilean wife from Santiago but settled in Chilean Patagonia and was later appointed Governor of that wild and sparsely populated province. He settled there with his family. They lived first of all just across the Argentinean frontier in the little town of Chile Chico and later at Aysen in the same district but a little further north. It was in Patagonia that the family grew up - six sisters and two brothers. It must have been a special experience in such an environment. It is an area of mountains and lakes with the ice and snow of the high Andes on the horizon and very little else. Luz grew to love the grand scale, the space and overwhelming beauty of everything. It taught her how close life is to nature in such a setting. The people who lived there were scattered in farmsteads and small villages. It was a free and easy environment in which the world belonged to everyone and everyone belonged to each other. Her childhood in such a home could never be forgotten.

When Luz grew up, however, they had to leave the beauty of that country behind and the family moved to Santiago. Santiago was very different, but it could never obliterate in her the memory of Patagonia. Wherever she went she brought with her something of the wild freedom, the fearless inspiration from the huge scale of those lakes and mountains. It was a gift which never left her.

The Cosmelli family lived at the time of her meeting José Manuel in the district of Santiago called Las Condes and Luz worked as a nurse in a local health center. She was 22 and already feeling a crisis of identity in this new confined town life when she was involved in a terrible accident. She was riding a motorcycle with a child, who was her cousin, in front of her on the machine. She was turning to go into her aunt's house, but there was a car coming and suddenly she realized that they were going to crash. With a quick instinct she flung the child away from her. He fell by the roadside and was unhurt. But Luz herself was terribly injured in the crash that followed her action of saving the child's life. She was in such a bad way that, as people came and began to help, they were sure that she was dead and covered her with newspapers as she lay on the road.

That was how things were at the site of the accident, when it happened that a girl, who was a friend of Luz, arrived on the scene. She saw the body lying on the road and thought she recognized the shoes. She said they must look closer, because it seemed they were Luz's shoes. They uncovered her body and found that it was indeed Luz, but they noticed also that she was breathing. She was not dead.

Luz was taken to hospital and they found that her injuries were terrible. She had five major injuries, each of which should have been fatal, and many bones were fractured. She was deeply unconscious. As she lay there in the hospital her father overheard some doctors discussing her condition and agreeing that she could not last the night. The family were Catholic and that evening her mother took to prayer and decided that, if Luz recovered, she would offer her to God to become a nun. Her uncle, Rafael Carvallo, invoked the help of the Ursuline nuns whom he knew and from them he brought a relic of Pius XII.

Everyone was thus turning to prayer when unexpectedly Luz opened her eyes and said quite simply; "Bring me a priest; I am going to die." A priest came and anointed her. After receiving the sacrament of the sick she said with finality, as though to close the whole episode, that she was now going to heaven. The prophecy, however, did not come true on that occasion. After that moment of consciousness when she received the sacrament Luz lapsed into a coma which lasted for three weeks. In due course she regained consciousness, but the recovery was long and painful and seemed at first to offer nothing but permanent disability for her future.

When she looks back on that time Luz now thinks that others suffered more than she did from the accident. She was unconscious at the worst time of her injuries and unaware of anything. When she recovered consciousness in the hospital she found it difficult to grasp what had happened - or to grasp anything at all. She just lay there - inert, unresponsive, uninterested. She was completely passive while they did things to her body, as though it were not hers. Her legs were in traction, so she could not have moved, if she had wanted to do so. She, who had been so full of life, began in the process of recovery to live a sort of un-life. It was scarcely like living at all. She was kept in hospital for several months. Her physical recovery took a full two years.

At last she got back home. When she got there a new problem of enormous proportions faced her. She had to learn how to live all over again. She had to learn how to walk and discover again how to do things for herself. At the hospital, when they discharged her, they had said she could go home now but as for learning how to do things again - that would be her problem. They had mended her body. She herself would have to find a way of mending her spirit.

Deep down inside that raised another question for her - why? Why should she bother? Why should she take up this challenge of learning how to live again? She felt that in her mind and spirit she had been completely emptied out from within. She was left with no notion of what life was for or why she should attempt to walk or do anything at all. Her life had been given back to her, but the gift was meaningless. She was locked in a crisis in which interest, motivation or the will to attempt anything at all were utterly lacking. The accident and the physical healing were over. Now the problem was to find a meaning in the life that had been given back to her. It was different from José Manuel's crisis at the University, and yet it was not different, because it led to the same feeling that life was empty and meaningless. It would prove, perhaps, to be a hidden point of bonding between them. But that would be in the future. Now back home from the hospital she looked around a world which seemed to offer no future and no hope. Why should she bother to start all over again and learn how to live - how to be alive? She remembers how that 'why?' about life (so typical of the age) had hovered at the back of her mind before the accident. The accident had forced her to face it.

José Manuel's life when he entered University had been thrown into turmoil, perplexity, confusion by the conflict of ideas about life and the purpose of life with which he was bombarded in a disturbed and rebellious student world. No amount of political involvement, philosophical searching nor even the intense partying and mischief that José Manuel was capable of getting up to, could satisfy him nor answer the question – why? They had all failed him and left him in a state of confusion.

In Luz's case it was something different that brought her life to a similar sense of emptiness. The external trauma of a horrifying accident suddenly brought a radiantly positive young life to a state in which she was shattered in both body and spirit. It left her ready for death because her whole being was so torn to pieces that, looking out on life as she regained consciousness and tried to piece things together again, she could find no sense in anything. Even when medical skill had helped the healing power of a strong young body, the shattered spirit inside was still in helpless disarray. Her life had been given back to her, but now it was quite meaningless. She was left with a question to which she must find an answer before she could do anything at all - why? From the world around her - even from the skilled world of medical healing - there were answers to many other questions but not to that question. The question itself came back at her and echoed again and again in loneliness of the spiritual emptiness in which she found herself - why?

Back at home again Luz yielded in the end to the persuasion of her family to make the very painful and to her pointless effort of going through the wearisome, relentless discipline of rehabilitation and physiotherapy. Her mother was advised to get psychiatric help for her, but her mother did not have much use for psychiatrists and was not at all convinced. She said that Luz could and should find her own way without any psychiatrists, and she proved to be right. Luz somehow found the courage to do that. She did fight her way through, so that gradually she built up her ability to live independently. It was a silent, lonely, inner, heroic battle of perseverance unsustained by vision or hope and without any external help. She won through against the grain.

It was a triumph of spirit. Nevertheless, at in the end of that hard and lonely road, when she had returned to more or less normal health and activity, she had not recovered any real sense of purpose. She was back to life, but it was a life from which, in spite of her newly restored physical health, all sense of purpose, vision, interest, meaning had been leached away into oblivion by the hideous shock and lasting trauma of her injuries. It was strange and alarming that her remarkable perseverance which had won through the hard process of rehabilitation brought no sense of fulfillment. But God had not forgotten her and a new chapter was in sight.

With her return to external normality she returned in her family to the ordinary rhythm of Catholic life, however little it meant to her. She resumed the habit of going to Mass on Sunday. It was at Sunday Mass in one of the parish churches that she heard one day an invitation to a meeting with some lay people who were members of the Neo Catechumenate way[2]. They were planning to begin a group in the parish. When nothing else meant anything at all, this invitation quite unexpectedly roused Luz's interest. She surprised everyone at home by saying that she would go to the meeting. A brother and a sister went along with her to keep her company. Luz herself had scarcely arrived at the meeting when she was seized by a conviction that God had sent this to her - that it was meant for her. She went to all the subsequent meetings for catechesis and enjoyed them so much that at the end of each one (there were two each week) she felt sad and thought that it was terrible to have to wait several days for the next meeting. A new life of faith and commitment had risen up from the ashes. Instead of that state of physical well-being without inner meaning, which seemed likely to blight her life for ever, she had discovered a life of spiritual renewal with God in the center. With God in the center the need to serve him through others became a vivid and inviting reality. She now had meaning, purpose, faith, hope and charity and her whole inner spirit came alive. She had been healed not only in body but in her inner self. There was no more emptiness.

The healing which began that Sunday evening at Mass was not a simple return to her state before the accident. It was the beginning of a transformation through a spiritual renewal and never again would she be without purpose and vision in her Christian life. Prayer became a reality, and a very strong reality, in her life as the expression of her newfound friendship with Christ. She was able and eager to go out from her inner isolation and give to others by sharing the joy and purpose of her new life. She became ever more deeply involved in the Neo Catechumenate

Way and soon Luz was made one of the heads of one of their communities. She had found a fuller life now than she had ever experienced before.

Thus it was that both José Manuel and Luz had found their way back from two different but parallel experiences of negativity and emptiness to a meaning and mission in a new life rooted in Christ. There was indeed, as it turned out in due course, a deep spiritual affinity which brought them together and in the end inspired them to give their lives for others and for the family which God sent them and which he blessed in unexpected ways.

The Wedding

So that was it. When José Manuel met Luz and fell in love with her the obstacle to marriage from her point of view was her Neo Catechumenate mission, her grateful and unwavering commitment to it and its deeply felt meaning in the very center of her life. It was some five years after the accident and two years after her becoming a Neo Catechumenist that she and José Manuel had first met. At the time she had undertaken a commitment to some Neo Catechumenate missions in the South. That work took her away from Santiago but somehow they managed to meet. They found they were attracted to each other but neither wanted to give up their vocation in life, which had been refined in both cases by suffering. They both remember it as a difficult time. Nevertheless the relationship did continue through 1978 and it was a good relationship which both valued. Both, however, were committed to their separate vocations. Luz tried to interest José Manuel in the Neo Catechumenate Way and he went to a meeting, but the prospects of either of them being converted to the way of the other were not promising. Each believed in that particular way along which they had been led by the Lord through personal suffering and their own individual spiritual renewal. It seemed that they would have to come together while retaining their individual vocations or not at all. As time went on their meetings became less frequent, but they continued until a crisis came at Christmas of 1978.

For Luz it was a good time, in which all trace of doubt had gone in her new commitments. Her candor could be engaging or disturbing, depending on how you saw it. It was certainly unequivocal when one day she told José Manuel that she was fulfilled in the life she was leading and wanted only peace and her Catechumenate Way community and their work for God. She really did not need anything else - not even José Manuel.

For him things were not yet quite so settled. It was the time when he was still at the Manquehue School, but Fr Puelma was ill and the future uncertain. His vision for the catechesis of the young was stronger than ever, but he had lost the immediate practical focus of his mission. His young followers were faithful and he felt that the Movement was now spiritually strong in itself, but they lacked a clear structure for their common mission. There was nothing yet solid behind him as a basis for marriage. It seemed that they were together facing the inevitable when at Christmas in 1978 they agreed that they would not meet any more. Christmas is midsummer in Chile so it was with that decision that they both went off on their summer holidays, thinking that all was at an end between them.

From that ending, however, there emerged a new beginning - which in the blessings it brought exceeded all expectation. Their shared resolution to bring the relationship to an end did not last. By the end of March 1979 they met again and decided to marry. After the troubles and trials and testing of their different journeys before their first meeting, and after the self-questioning and doubts of their growing relationship, and after their heroic decision to part and go their own ways, suddenly and without fuss they both accepted the decision to which the Lord in their diverse lives had been guiding them. They accepted the fact, by now rather obvious, that they were meant for each other. There are some things in life which become really clear only when we try to walk away from them. No doubt it needed that false break in their love and commitment to each other for them both to understand the depth of the relationship they now shared. They emerged finally from all doubt and confusion with a strength that would endure in heroic faith and hope and cheerfulness through still more suffering and purification and would lead to deep fulfillment in their life together.

They were now finally committed to each other, but they decided against marriage in 1979. It was partly because Luz's mother died suddenly from mushroom poisoning towards the end of that year. Low Sunday 1980 was fixed as the date for the marriage, which would be celebrated after they had each made a retreat - José Manuel with the Benedictines at the monastery in Las Condes and Luz in her own community of the Catechumenate. Fr Gabriel from the monastery and Fr Puelma and Fr Enrique Cortes of Luz's parish were all concelebrants.

The readings they chose - and one that they did not choose - were important and became also prophetic in the course of the ceremony. The gospel was about Christ's resurrection appearance to the apostles while Thomas was absent himself and later would not believe the report that Christ had truly risen from the dead. Then, when Christ came again to them all, Thomas surrendered making his act of belief with the words 'my Lord and my God'. They had arranged initially that the first reading was to be from Genesis and the second was from Philippians 2 about Christ's kenosis and obedience unto death. The reader of the first lesson made a mistake in the text he read out. Yet it proved to be a mistake with a meaning. In fact much later it did not seem to José Manuel and Luz, when they looked back on their wedding day, that the reader had really made a mistake. What happened was that, instead of the passage they had chosen, a different text from Genesis was read out. It was the story about Abraham's sacrifice of Isaac in obedience to God's prophetic testing of his faith (Gen. 22). The preacher was unperturbed by the change of reading and took it in his stride. He preached to it as though it had been intended. José Manuel remembers his message - that the Lord provides for everything and that we should always use Thomas's words to the risen Lord when we approach him in prayer: 'My Lord and my God'. The unexpected reading and spontaneous homily made a great impression at the time. Afterwards the whole episode came to have a very special meaning which they remembered above all in connection with illnesses of their sons Ignacio and Pedro.

Commitment to St Benedict's Rule

After their marriage Luz, while remaining faithful to her Catechumenate community, came also to be very influential in the Movement. Apparently without effort she united three commitments - to the Catechumenate, to her marriage and family and to the Manquehue

Movement. It proved helpful that she already had an understanding of the Benedictines, who had come to mean so much to José Manuel. In Santiago she had always lived in view of the Benedictine Abbey high up on the mountain. Fr Mauro and others from the Abbey went at times to say Mass in their home, so she was familiar with St Benedict and Benedictines.

José Manuel had by now left the Manquehue School, which meant that he was without paid work when he got married, but Luz accepted this. In fact two good offers of work had come his way. One was in the Ministry of Education. The other was to be Director of a school. At first he accepted this latter job, but then he changed his mind and refused it in favor of his new work with the Movement. That was when his young followers were renting a house for meetings of the group and for *lectio*. It was a fragile arrangement. It meant that Luz entered marriage without knowing what would happen about her husband's career and life-vocation. José Manuel had no other work at the time except for the lectio meetings in the evenings at the rented house.

There followed a period of doubt and confusion about the longterm development of his work with the young. He toyed with the idea of returning to the Manquehue School but rejected it, because he concluded that it would not be compatible with following the lines of lay Benedictine spirituality which they were developing. Luz would stay with the Catechumenate, but it was not the way for him. He was called in a different direction. It was a real dilemma - a real problem for both of them - at the very beginning of their marriage.

It was Luz who cut the Gordian knot. One day she was inspired and spoke strongly, in fact she was quite angry. She told him that he must work with St Benedict's Rule to find a way forward. José Manuel rejected the idea at first and said that he had no intention of doing anything like what she was suggesting. But Luz had perceived something important. In spite of her own commitment to the Catechumenate Way she had seen that his work must be Benedictine in its inspiration and founded on St Benedict's Rule. She stuck to her vision and insisted on it. José Manuel remembers how she perceived before he did and insisted on the vital importance to the growing Movement of the Rule of St Benedict:

One day Luz said to me: "you must stop beating about the bush. You must take the Rule of St Benedict and take it seriously and work with it, because I think perhaps the Lord is calling you to do something new for the Benedictine Order, so stop all this dithering." She was angry and I reacted badly and got angry also and said: "I have nothing like that on my mind." But she said "you are called. Stop dithering. You have the Rule of St Benedict. Stay with it. The Lord may be calling you to that way." She said it more strongly than that. I did not want to believe, but she insisted. She was strongly behind me and understood better perhaps than I did. She also had a big influence on me in putting all our reliance on work for God. I still at that time had some tendency to attach importance to politics and other things.[3]

In spite of his initial reluctance to accept what Luz was saying gradually her words sank into José Manuel and made such an impression that he turned more and more for guidance to St Benedict's Rule. So, although she herself stayed with the Catechumenate, it was Luz who strongly influenced him at that time to pursue the Benedictine direction of all his work both in spirituality and in organization. She saw and accepted that he must go a different way from her and was firmly in support of his work as she encouraged him to go forward and to rely on God's word alone. Her perception and insistence were vital at the time. Luz's strong intervention was remembered ten years later by José Manuel when the same Benedictine orientation for his work, which he had by now embraced wholeheartedly, was confirmed strongly by Cardinal Pironio[4], when he received José Manuel in the Council for the Laity in Rome. He was speaking on that occasion with José Manuel about the future and gave him the blessing of the Church on the Movement. Then he added the official and authoritative message that the Manquehue Movement should be not only lay and ecclesial but also profoundly and joyfully Benedictine. It was Luz, right at the beginning when the Movement had scarcely started, who had first perceived that very thing and expressed it fearlessly.

The beginning of married life for José Manuel was unusual. Neither of them had a career. Such a thing was not expected of Luz in Chilean society of that time. It was more serious that José Manuel himself had no prospects of a secure income to support a family. On the other hand they were both committed to the development of authentic lay spirituality within the Church in the world of post-Vatican II Catholic Movements. Luz's commitment was to the already strong and established New Catechumenate. José Manuel's was to a personal vision which was not yet fully a reality. Both were spiritually strong with the strength that comes from faith and suffering. Luz's understanding and acceptance of the situation was remarkable. Once it was clear that José Manuel could not abandon his vision and join her in the Catechumenate, she herself became a pillar of support to the young of her husband's Movement. She achieved this without changing the fundamental commitment through which spiritual healing had come to her. In fact her own Catechumenate community grew and came to be 60 strong. As time went on she became also the mother figure of the growing Manquehue Movement and gave support with great generosity to José Manuel and his young followers as their work and spirituality developed in the coming years. The married life to which they both gave themselves presented at this stage little evidence of economic strength but enormous evidence of spiritual richness. Together they faced whatever might come in a spirit of profound faith. It was a time which José Manuel recalls with slightly bewildered gratitude:

> When we were married Luz came to be very influential in the Movement, especially in her understanding of the Benedictines. Luz gave great support to a lot of what I was doing and is very responsible for the spirit which developed in the Movement. When I got married I had left the Manquehue school. The reason for that was because I thought the Movement was very strong already in itself, but not strong enough to change a structure like the Manquehue school. That is why I had to leave and face the future without a job. But then I got married, so I got married without work. Luz accepted this situation.
>
> So Luz got married with me without knowing what would happen. We lived together in the house where we still live, but it was smaller at that time. Luz was very influential at that time. I was myself very

desperate about the situation because I didn't know what the Lord was asking of me. Both of us were very much enriched by this dilemma. [5]

Luz's comment was simple but eloquent. She said that there have been problems about herself and José Manuel "each having a special but different call from the Lord, but in many ways it has been wonderful.[6]" And so the marriage, unusual in its beginnings, settled down to a life of faith and self-giving and service in which nothing was predictable - in which everything was received as a sign of grace - in which even suffering turned into something 'wonderful'. There is a deep symbolism in this whole story leading up to the beginning of their life together. It is the story of two lay vocations within the Catholic Church brought together by the word of God which was ever calling, motivating, guiding, leading. There is no other foundation - nothing else to explain what happened. The word of God had brought them through what each of them suffered from the cold, dead hand of contemporary negativity. It had prepared them to fulfill a demanding vocation. It had kept them close to Christ in his church. When they decided to choose the word rather than each other, it enabled them to find the word in each other. It prepared them for the families which were to come - the children - the Oblates - the catechumenate community. It had shown them how it was Christ they were called to serve in those families. It had brought them into Christ's presence in everything. It had freed them from the received wisdom of this world - that wealth is the foundation of happiness in marriage. It had taught them where true happiness is to be found in 'the obedience of faith for the sake of his name'.[7] And so they were ready for all that was to come.

CR

Notes for Chapter 5

[1]   See Appendix 2 – Article from Manquehino 1979 – a remarkable record of thinking about laity and lay spirituality.

[2]   The Neo Catecumenate Way is a world-wide organization within the Catholic Church which was founded in Madrid in 1968 by two Spaniards with the intention of bringing down to Catholics at ordinary parish level some of the inspiration of Vatican II. The two founders were lay but there are priests also in this Movement. They seek to revive in the Church today at parochial level the fervour and commitment of the early Church by centering their catechesis and evangelisation on the Word of God, the Eucharist and the Community. Their mission is to evangelise among Catholics in parochial life and to reach out also to those outside the Church. Their work has been successful both in renewal within the Church and in conversion of those outside.

[3]   Interview with José Manuel

[4]   Cardinal Pironio was an Argentinian who had been Archbishop of Buenos Aires and was brought to Rome by Pope Paul VI in 1976 and then in 1984 he became the first President of the newly formed Council for the Laity.

[5]   Interview with José Manuel

[6]   Interview with Luz

[7]   see Rom. 1, 5

Chapter 6 ~ The Children

The Children

We must now follow the story of the children sent by God to José Manuel and Luz. In the year 1981 their first son was born on the 5th May and named at his baptism José Manuel, but he is also known by the nickname Joselo. That was the year José Manuel first went to Ampleforth and then started San Benito[1] on the temporary site. Pedro, the second son, came the year after that. He was born on 18 June 1982. He had to undergo a big operation and almost died. During the operation he got an infection which seemed mistakenly at the time to be the real cause of a strange illness which followed. This illness turned out to be not a passing infection but a permanent disability. Pedro remained a very sick child and was the center of everyone's concern. José Manuel remembers the anxiety of that time:

> Something had happened when Pedro first became sick. I was very desperate about him and I went to the monastery and by chance I met the Abbot, who was called Pedro also, and he said 'How are you?' I said 'Well I'm all right myself but I have a son who is very ill.' We were walking through the Abbey and there was an image of Christ there and he said: 'Wait, let us pray.' And he said: 'O Lord, help your son by your cross. Pedro is suffering down there at home. Take his suffering and cure him and help him.'
>
> When I went down home, my sister-in-law Carolina Cosmelli arrived and said: 'you must take Pedro immediately to the States.' We said 'you are crazy' and all the doctors also said the same. Two days later Luz left for the States. I think that a lot had to do with that prayer of the Abbot. It was a difficult situation and a difficult decision in times that were very difficult. Everything was very expensive and nothing was yet known about the real nature of Pedro's sickness.[2]

Pedro was taken to Boston in the United States in December 1982 by Luz and her sister Barbara and was for a time between life and death as Christmas approached. It was a time of great anxiety and anguish. Then came a wonderful experience to help them. It was on the 28th December, the Feast of the Holy Innocents - the tiny children who had been mindlessly slaughtered by Herod in his hope of killing the Christ child. José Manuel was almost in despair as he listened on the telephone to Luz in the United States telling him about Pedro's illness. While speaking to him on the telephone she prayed out loud to God for her son, pleading for the cure which she knew God could give. After listening to Luz and sharing her distress, José Manuel was also deeply upset and began praying himself:

> I was in my room and started praying the Office of the Innocents and suddenly I felt the presence of the Lord. It was more real than anything else there at that moment. That presence was like an anchor in my heart keeping me firm. I was completely strengthened and knew that nothing bad could happen. I felt that I was in touch with the Holy Innocents, celebrating with them, they were living persons and I entered into the mystery of God and was filled with peace. I understood that we may be alive or dead, but whatever happens we have been given the gift of eternal life and so we should not worry ourselves.

It was good, he thought, that the Church preserved the feast of the Holy Innocents and celebrated it at Christmas time. During that Christmas season, when Pedro was dangerously ill in Boston, the feast had very special importance for the family. It was a reminder of all the children who suffer and die as innocents and of how it is only Christ who can give any sense or meaning to it all. It was in that conviction and faith that they all prayed.

Luz returned from the Boston hospital with Pedro. She was grateful because he had not died, but still the real nature of his illness had not been diagnosed. The family prayers, however, were answered in the end because eventually, when his strange illness had been really diagnosed and treatment had begun, Pedro did recover partially and was able to live a fairly normal life. Some irreversible damage had been done and he remained always limited by the handicap with which the illness left him.

Then on 2 June 1983 came the birth of Domingo. He was always healthy and strong with boundless energy. A year and a half after Domingo the fourth son Ignacio was born on 14th January 1985. He was perfectly well at first and seemed to be a healthy child until he was nearly one year old. During that first year his temperament came through quite clearly. He was very gentle and kind without making any noise. He was always where the others were, but he remained always very quiet.

Then one day he suddenly had an attack of convulsions which lasted about twenty minutes and changed him forever. For several days he had terrible suffering and looked anxious and disturbed. It was a very difficult time in which he could not eat and everyone could see how tense he was and how much he suffered. The growing community of the Movement were always treated as part of the family and José Miguel Navarro, who was among the first of them, remembers Ignacio's illness vividly:

> It was in that summer that Ignacio Eguiguren got sick. It was an event that had a big effect in binding the family and the whole community together. We all drew closer to each other in our support of José Manuel and his family. This bonding together was especially strong with Manuel José Echenique[3] during those days. Ignacio had been a completely normal baby until suddenly he was transformed by his sickness. I remember going to the house and seeing him with his fists clenched, with his head swollen. He was a baby who was suffering and seemed to be dying.[4]

This sudden illness of Ignacio seemed to be nothing but tragedy and loss. However, as always with Ignacio, in spite of the handicap and suffering there was something that turned to good. Ignacio did not die. He became permanently and profoundly disabled. This had an immediate positive result that everyone, not only in the family but also in the whole young community, became involved in his care. It meant that they conspired to give him not only the physical help he needed but also in many different ways the constant love which alone could really sustain him and inspire him to endure. And so it happened that this terrible illness bound the leading young members of the Movement more closely than ever into the Eguiguren family. They became and remained a closely knit extended family. The gentle, quiet and now completely helpless Ignacio became in a very real sense a central figure and an inspiration which meant more and more to the whole Manquehue Movement.

At the time, however, Ignacio's serious illness caused a great crisis in the family not only because of its gravity but much more at that time because his sickness had not been diagnosed so that no-one knew how to treat him. The doctors in Chile were baffled about the cause of this terrible transformation in an apparently healthy child. There were now two sick and disabled children out of four in the family, which made everyone wonder what would happen to the others.

In fact Luz was still in the maternity Clinic with the fifth child, Maria de la Luz, when Ignacio got ill. The now suffering Ignacio was taken to his mother in the same Clinic. It was on her return home from the Clinic that she made her great decision to take the children again to the United States in the hope of finding a diagnosis. José Manuel remembers the intense anxiety of that time, the arrival of a new baby and Luz's strong decision to act:

> Luz had a new baby, Maria de la Luz born on 22nd June 1986. She appeared to be healthy - as Ignacio had seemed at first - but there were problems yet to develop. Then it happened that one day Luz decided to go to the States again with Pedro and Ignacio and she also took the new baby, Maria de la Luz, with them.[5]

Luz went this time with her sister-in-Law, Zana. She seems to have made the decision to go without really knowing why, but it turned out to be a wonderfully good inspiration which brought many blessings.

The mysterious illness at last understood

At the time of Luz's second departure for the Boston hospital there was no doubt that José Manuel and Luz were faced with a terrible family situation. Two of their little children were ill with an unknown sickness. They had no idea whether the same illness might strike the healthy ones.

For José Manuel it was a time of many anxieties. While all this was happening to his family he had on his shoulders the whole responsibility of the early stages of his first school, San Benito, as we shall see in detail in the next chapter. He was also committed to the guidance and formation of young people who were inspired by him and who needed his care and constant attention in the early stages of the growing, developing community of the Movement. He had started it and it depended on him for spiritual vision and guidance. The sickness of his children could not have come at a more difficult time for him with all these growing responsibilities.

As Luz went off to Boston with the three little ones, José Manuel himself stayed behind to continue carrying the burdens of the growing Movement, to look after the two other boys and to pray. It cannot have been easy in his agony and anxiety to continue in his utter trust in the Lord, but he persevered.

It was summer time in Chile, but winter in the United States. While Luz and the three other children were away, José Manuel went with Joselo and Domingo to his uncle's house to spend the summer vacation in the country. It was there that he received a call from Luz in Boston to say that Pedro was getting better and none of the doctors knew what was wrong with Ignacio, but they were sure that there was no possibility of his recovering. At that stage the doctors had also mistakenly decided that there was no relationship between Pedro's sickness and Ignacio's. When José Manuel told the news from Boston to Joselo he remembers that the boy replied by saying quite simply: 'Well let's pray' and he started praying there and then with his father and Domingo for his mother and the other children in the United States.

Luz returned from the Unites States with no better answers than she had reported on the telephone. Their prayers, however, were answered in the end. Some time after they had returned the doctors in Boston discovered at last what was wrong with the children. They had found that it was a rare metabolic disorder.[6] Pedro had been first affected by it. Joselo, his eldest son, and Domingo were free of it. Ignacio was the worst affected and his condition was irreversible. Maria de la Luz, it appeared, was also affected, but the wonderful news for her was that in

93

her case the doctors said that they were able to contain the illness and keep it under control so that she could lead an entirely normal life.

As soon as this news came Luz and the three children at once went back to the hospital in Boston for further research and José Manuel went with them. He himself recalls that third visit to Boston and what happened there:

> We had a very difficult month during which we were completely tied to the hospital. Only once, while we were in Boston, could Luz and I go out to have supper together. Once they allowed Pedro to go out alone with me, the others they kept in hospital all the time. It was all very difficult.
>
> Then at the end of it all, when we were leaving the hospital, the Director came to see us and said: 'You can come again whenever you want and I must tell you something; we have never had such a good response to treatment from a family.' He wanted to congratulate us because, he said, we had behaved perfectly. But in fact it had not been possible for us to act in any other way, so we thought it was quite funny to be congratulated.
>
> I was very worried at that time about Luz, because in the midst of all this she lost a baby. Just a week before we left together for the States it was found that a new baby she had inside was dead. It was a really terrible shock and strain for her, although her spirit was always strong. In every way it was a very difficult time.[7]

After the long month in Boston they came back home deeply relieved to know at last the medical facts they were dealing with. They had two handicapped children, but at last they knew what they could and could not do for them. They settled down to giving them the support and love they needed. José Manuel reflects on what it now meant for the family and the Movement to care for the completely helpless Ignacio.

> Ignacio has turned out, in spite of or or rather thanks to his disability, to be very, very important to all of us. He is very intense and, although he cannot control any of his movements, he can look and with his face he can make comments very well. Luz has taught him how to pray and it is very strong prayer. His work is prayer and he is conscious of that.

I remember once when he was nine Fr Dominic[8] came to stay. He used to go out and see people, but then quite suddenly he stopped going out. I thought that something was going wrong, but in fact he had discovered Ignacio. He went up to the Abbey and bought for Ignacio a lot of pictures representing the life of Christ. Fr Dominic said that Ignacio had the simplicity of a child but the maturity of one who has suffered. Well, he started with the pictures of Christ's life on earth preparing him for the Eucharist, for his first communion. He prepared him so well that the most important act in Ignacio's life was his first communion, and still the Eucharist is the most important thing for him. It is, without doubt, what he loves more than anything. He loves horses, he likes planes, he loves going traveling - you see we take him everywhere - but what he loves above everything is the Eucharist. This has given him very great strength so that a lot of people come to see him and write to him.

Ignacio has a very strong life in the Movement also. Everyone loves him and they have a very good communication with him - especially some of the Oblates. He is completely dependent on others. If we all trusted the Lord to take care of us as he trusts his mother, we would be completely free and happy. Wherever he goes, people turn to him and love him and, if we ask him to pray for something, he looks at the crucifix and prays. His crucifix belonged to my godfather who gave it to Ignacio. He spends hours looking at it and praying, but he also loves being with and playing with his brothers and sister. He has meant a great deal for Luz and the family and the Oblates and still does. He is like a focus point - a radiation of God's love.

Through our experience with Ignacio I have discovered that happiness is a gift and it does not depend on money, nor on health, nor on whether you are alone or with others. It is simply a gift of the Lord, and he has given it to Ignacio.

When people see him for the first time they often say: 'Oh what a dreadful thing!' It is true that it has been difficult, but in spite of that Ignacio in his grievous handicap has brought among us much more love and happiness than others can imagine.

He and Domingo are close in age and they have a very, very good relationship. When they were small each morning Domingo, when he was already in his school uniform, used to go in his bed to be with him before going out. Domingo spends some time with him every day. When we have gone out in the evening, Domingo goes to him and later we find that Domingo has gone into a deep sleep and Ignacio is awake with Domingo lying over him, and Ignacio is laughing like saying: 'well, what can I do?' So they have a very good relationship.

Domingo has great imagination and entertains Ignacio a lot but with his other brothers also he has very good relationship and Maria de la Luz, as she grows older, has become very close to Ignacio. The boys take him everywhere with them and he has great courage. Once he was hurt and bleeding but he did not mind at all. Joselo is always ready to change his soiled clothes. He really takes on the role of eldest brother. Pedro sleeps next to Ignacio and is always watching ready to tell the others when something is wrong with his younger brother

Ignacio has had a very strong influence in the family and also among the Oblates by entering into whatever we are doing. He has made a great difference to all our lives. From living with him there is something I have discovered - that the life of faith is a life of confidence and that it is God who gives life and love and happiness and trust. I think it is, as someone said, that the scripture wakens us up.[9]

The blessings of handicap understood and accepted

Ignacio on their return from Boston had to settle down and fit into ordinary family life, if anything can be called ordinary in the presence of such a handicap. In plain human terms he is completely disabled. He has no control of his limbs and cannot do anything for himself; he cannot even hold his head up or turn his head or do anything with his hands; he cannot speak.[10] His only set way of responding to questions is by sticking his tongue out for 'yes' and pursing his lips (or rather pulling a face) for 'no'. It is wonderful how rich and swift this method of communication can become with those who are able to second-guess his thoughts – his father and mother, his brothers and sister, some of the

Oblates and the maids who come to the house to assist as domestic helpers. He is carried around the house and goes out in a special wheelchair. He has very sharp ears and swift understanding. He hears everything, knows all that is going on. He is very intelligent. They discovered recently to their astonishment that he understands some English. It seems that he has picked it up through watching films on video with English dialogue, and also through listening to his many English and American friends. He is always interested and he wants to be involved in everything.

His relationship with all the family is very close indeed and it is amazing how they can communicate. He loves it when the boys treat him as though he were normal and, as boys do, pretend to 'rough him up.' He has a sharp sense of humor and is often found chuckling to himself at some absurdity in family life or in a conversation he has overheard. He is very, very important to everyone and at many levels he is the center of life in the house. He is the center because he is completely helpless; he is the center because he must be included in everything and never forgotten; he is the center because he draws everyone to him; he is the center because of his prayer and spiritual stature. Everyone turns to him for prayer. His relationship with his mother is at the center of all his other varied relationships. His trust of her is absolute, but their relationship is free and open and not at all closed or possessive. He is fully conscious that prayer is his own special work in the family and in the Movement.

Ignacio's prayer, his love of Christ in the Eucharist have given a strength and influence which makes a lot of people come to see him and write to him. Among those far away who have developed a special relationship with him are the Benedictine nuns from Campos do Jordao in Brazil. He was taken to Brazil to meet them because the nuns were praying for him and wanted to know him. They held a Chapter where he was present and Domingo was there because he can interpret what Ignacio wants to say.

Like the others he goes to school, a school for severely disabled children in Santiago. When he went there first, there were no prayers, no crucifix, no spirituality. What is more, it was an explicitly secular school, which made a point of distancing itself from particular religious creeds, but Ignacio has changed all that. Ignacio could not live in a place where there was no prayer. Now the children and the teachers and the parents all pray with him and he has brought to the school something of his own spiritual radiance. With some of the other severely disabled children he takes part in weekly meetings of a *lectio* group of the Movement in the School. It is run by two members of the Movement. In their own way these children gain peace and happiness from these meditations on the word of God. Ignacio has brought the blessings of the Movement to the School with him.

The Oblates are for him additional brothers and sisters to give him love and help and support and to share the never failing love of the family. They would not consent to calling their work for him 'bearing a burden' because they do not see it as a burden but as a joy and a privilege. Wherever he goes, people turn to him and love him. No one can tell what the Movement owes to, but certainly it is a debt of deep and lasting significance.

It is important, however, to understand that Ignacio, locked away in his world in which he can see and hear but do nothing else, is not a sweet and insipid little 'saint'. There is a profound underlying normality which appears when he is amused, angry, frustrated, depressed or, in spite of all the help around him, unable to convey his meaning. The very richness of his support may perhaps make him more vulnerable in this way.[11] His mother understands these moods very well and she will never let the doctors suppress or attempt to alter them with drugs. Nor will she allow anyone to envelop him in sentimentality. His handicap does not mean that there is no need to face up to and overcome these ordinary human trials. Fortunately he has love and understanding from those around him and his relationship with them has developed in such a way that they can help him and guide him to a better way than self-pity and resentment. Just as Joselo and Pedro and Domingo, his brothers, can treat him as one of themselves without inhibition, so Maria de la Luz, his sister has a feminine intuition which helps her understanding of his bad moods as well as his good moods. She is very sensitive to them and knows instinctively how to handle them so that their relationship has become especially important to him. Like all human beings he needs understanding as well as spiritual insight to help him surmount the spiritual traps and temptations of our lives. So it has turned out that Ignacio has become an indispensable part of everyone's life. His brothers and sister have agreed in a serious and reflective way that Ignacio through his disability has become a blessing for them all. His relationship with his parents and with each of the children is different, always active, always growing. But, whatever the developments, the love with which he is surrounded is free of jealousy and rivalry. He belongs equally to everyone and everyone belongs to him.

Pedro has surmounted his disability in a different way through his own strong faith and strong character. He has learnt bit by bit how to overcome his limitations, so far as possible. At first he went to the school for the disabled, but at the age of five he wanted to throw himself into a more normal life. He wanted to join his brothers at San Benito school. It was difficult because of the severity of his handicap. His use of one arm is impaired and he has difficulty in co-ordinating movements. He has limited control of his facial muscles so that speaking is not easy. His walking is awkward.

From five to nineteen his time at school was a relentless struggle to control his disability and lead as normal a life as possible. He faced the challenge with astounding success, which was recognized by his peers. In his last year at his graduation ceremony he was awarded the school prize for outstanding contributions of personality and character. When he went up to receive the award all the boys and girls and staff gave him a standing ovation.

Pedro's testimony

When Pedro was already at University in 2002 he went to a General Retreat of the Movement. It is normal in the Movement at such events for some of the young to respond to an invitation to give testimonies about their experiences with the their life of faith and prayer. Pedro on that occasion gave his testimony and this is what he said:

> I begin my testimony at the age of four because it was then that I became fully conscious of both my physical infirmity and of the great restriction it imposed on my diet. I can remember how before that my father took me on his knee to give me every sort of food that I

liked. Then one day my mother told me that I would have to start a very strict regime which excluded cheese, jam, any derivative of milk and meat. It was a really hard blow to know that I had to accept this dietary regime in addition to my physical limitations.

I was growing up bit by bit with many moments of joy but also I met many problems on the way. I remember that on a scout camp I had a serious fall and I had to leave the camp on the second day. It also meant that I had to give up the Scouts. I didn't regret that because I realized that they were not for me. I didn't after that go out much nor take part in extra-curricular activities, which meant that my life was rather confined.

When I was in the eighth grade my mother invited and encouraged me to join a community of the Catechumenate and at the same time I began to take part in a general way in the social action of Colegio San Benito[12]. At the same time I began to develop my personality without hiding or ignoring the cross which I was going to carry always.

Then came my High School education, still at San Benito school, and the third stage of my life as a student. I felt that I was bigger and more mature, but I had no desire to throw myself into life for fear of falling again. But they offered me the opportunity of taking *tutorías* with the youngest children (*prekinder*) and I accepted. These little children were beginning to take hold on life with curiosity and questions about everything. I was faced with questions like – why do you hold your mouth like that? – why do you speak like that? – why do you walk in that way? They imitated me by making faces or mimicking my way of walking. It was then that I realized that this was not the first nor the only time when I would be in such a situation and that usually the best thing was to respond with a good grace.

My brothers Joselo and Domingo had repeatedly taken part in the expeditions among the poor (*trabajos*) and I never felt jealous of them, although I did wonder why I should be excluded. Then it was arranged that they should join the branch for social service and I was invited to join it during the summer. It was there that I learnt to do *lectio* through which I learnt that my physical infirmity did not exclude me from everything. I could gain benefit in the development of my personality, through my good relationship with others and through my cheerfulness. My desire to draw near to God grew stronger. I began to realize that God had given me limitations in many respects but at the same time he had given me gifts of much greater value than my limitations.

I entered the second form with a strong sense of the difficulty of mixing with others but with the ambition to be involved in many activities - in social action among other things.

I took part in a theatre production of 'Twelfth Night' with a very small part of a drunk. I was given that part not because I was a drunk but because often I looked as though I was, although I never had been. To imitate a drunk was easy for me.

I also took part in the activities of Holy Week and in the community works of winter[13]. I must admit that I didn't contribute much to the work materially but I did something for the general atmosphere, for instance, through my cheerfulness. I sometimes gave encouragement to the group and often made them laugh. Just to be there also was good for me.

I continued with many of these activities in the third form. I left the Catechumenate, not because I didn't like it but because I didn't really belong. I joined a community with my companions in the College and in this way I became involved with them. It was the moment at which I felt that I had really become part of my class at last.

As time went on I made great friends in my class, most of whom are still at this moment the community to which I belong. Nevertheless, in spite of this neither they nor the rest of the class ever stopped making typical comments and teasing me in ways which arose from my being the son of the founder and headmaster of the college. I took it with good humour and responded with comments of my own.

I had the idea of getting a driving licence. I took a course in the Automobile Club of Providencia[14]. For twelve days I had to go to Providencia and I did that. I passed the course and they gave me the necessary papers and directed me to municipal offices. There they told me that I could not get a licence because I had not passed the co-ordination tests. I was very annoyed and told the official that I disapproved of discrimination and gave her many reasons to show that I deserved to have a licence. She told me that first I must do the practical exam and that, if I did well in that, I had to pass the vision tests. I passed the practical and also the vision tests and they gave me a licence for six months, then for a year and now for two years.

I was happy and at night time as I lay myself down I said: 'thank you, Lord, because I am as I am, and don't ever leave me'. With these words I opened wide the doors of my disability accepting it as part of myself. I knew that the way before me was full of stones and holes but, if I wanted to reach any goal with the help of God, I must perhaps achieve it at a slower pace than others, but my way would be safe and often better.

I pursued my student life with great determination and joy and with the desire to help others who needed me – both materially and spiritually. During that year I went on the Missions where I perceived that I could make a better contribution than I could in the Works.[15]

Half way through the third form I went to the meeting of youth from all over the world at Rome. It was an unforgettable encounter with God. It gave me the feeling of strength to go forward. This was apparent in the distances that I walked with backpack and other things on my shoulders in a heat that exceeded 35 degrees with no support except tinned food and the few hours sleep we had, so that there could be no doubt that the strength I had was given me by God.

In my final year at school I continued with all these activities until at the same time I took steps to be able get into University. Given my handicap I asked for more time to pass this test but it was not granted me. I began to write letters to different universities explaining to them my situation. My prospects were not very good. My average was low. I did badly in my mock exams. I consoled myself with the thought that I would have a second chance next year. Many universities shut the door in my face without interviewing me, without knowing anything about me. Others said that they would look into it but nothing happened. Others interviewed me. There was only one university that opened its doors wide to me although I did not reach the minimum average. They set me every kind of test and in truth there seemed very little chance that I would be accepted[16]. I was truly aware that without the help of God I was not going to achieve anything.

It was this year also that I was confirmed[17]. One of my friends chose me for his sponsor and in this way convinced me that there are people who value me for what I really am and not by what I seem to be to those who don't look further than appearances. On receiving the sacrament myself I was filled with grace and joy and I learnt to value my life more and more.

During my High School I won some wonderful prizes like the one for Espiritu Benitano of the Colegio San Benito, and my grandfather's prize – the José Manuel Eguiguren Ortuzar prize. I am also the leader of my community of seven members. We meet together every week.

I entered the Catholic University of Santiago to study Law and as a result I have encountered many people of great distinction – not only the ones I have met in person but also in the course of my thinking and developing view of things. It cost me something to adapt – to know how to recognize true friends from those who are merely inquisitive. I am happy with my studies and with the university in which I study and with my new friends who have come to me.

To end with I want to say that none of this would have been possible without God at my side, because in moments of difficulty he took me in his arms and guided me to something better. I also recognize the truth of the saying that the last shall be first, because I, a lower than average scholar, have entered one of the best of universities with the prospect of a highly respected career.

I go to Mass every Sunday and Tuesday to give thanks to the Lord and ask him to continue to guide me. All of us carry crosses – some of us small ones, others big ones, some have crosses known to everyone, some of us hidden ones. My cross is well-known and heavy. The fact that it is well known – is well known. But with the help of God its heaviness is made very light. That is why I never get tired of repeating whenever I think of it: 'Thank you Lord for what I am and for my condition and I beg you not to leave me ever.' Thank you.[18]

That – with only slight editing changes – was what Pedro said to 600 retreatants. He stood up in front of them all and as he spoke his grave handicap was apparent at every moment. His courage, his clarity of thought and expression, his faith and realism were all apparent also. Those who were there thought before he started that they knew him already, but when they heard his testimony they were overwhelmed and torn between laughter and tears and thanksgiving. His spiritual message must have been one of the most powerful witnesses ever offered in a such retreat. But there was something else about it. What Pedro wrote and said was all his own work. However, one can safely say that he was in fact speaking not only for himself but also for his brother Ignacio. The key to the happiness in severe deprivation of both brothers is the same. It is their faith, their trust in God and their close relationship of love with Christ who said: "Come to me all you who labor and are heavy burdened and I will refresh you."[19]

Now that the three eldest children are at University and are looking towards adult life it is possible to say that they have all pulled together and – both the handicapped and the fit and strong – have contributed to unity with their parents and with the Oblates, who have been from the first so important in the children's upbringing. That, however, would be an understatement. It would be true so far as it goes, but in this account we must look deeper. There are levels which go further into the life of the spirit. St Paul drew a picture for the Corinthians[20] about how all who are baptized into the Church exist in Christ. Because of this, he said, even their differences, their weaknesses, their inadequacies contribute to the unity, the cohesion, the importance of what each had to contribute to the others. He begins by saying that all our gifts, great or small, are indeed gifts – not our own doing – not for ourselves but for others; they come from one Spirit. 'To each is given the manifestation of the Spirit for the common good.' Then, taking the analogy of the body, he shows how the members of the body, however different, however weak, can contribute to the unity and strength of the whole body: 'giving the greater honor to the inferior part so that there may be no discord in the body, but that the members may have the same care for one another. If one member suffers, all suffer together; if one member is honored, all rejoice together.'

That is the underlying spiritual reality that became manifest over the years in the Eguiguren Cosmelli family and in the relationship of the extended family of the Manquehue Oblates with them. It is mentioned briefly and inadequately here because it has been so important in the overall development of the Manquehue Apostolic Movement itself.

CR

Notes for Chapter 6

[1] San Benito is the name of the first school founded by José Manuel. Ampleforth is the Benedictine Abbey in England which he first visited in that year. See Chapter 7 below

[2] Interview with José Manuel

[3] One of José Manuel's earliest followers and later an Oblate of the Movement

[4] Interview with José Miguel Navarro

[5] Interview with José Manuel

[6] Glutaric Aciduria Type 1 (GA1), which can inhibit the metabolism of 2 amino acids leading to damage of the part of the brain which governs movement, especially fine movements. The damage is liable to occur during the first 3 years of life. Ignacio was grievously affected, Pedro much less seriously.

[7] Interview with José Manuel

[8] Fr Dominic Milroy from Ampleforth Abbey in England, who had been a friend since José Manuel's first visit to England.

[9] Interview with José Manuel

[10] His father and mother took him back again to Boston in the year 2000. They hoped that something could be done to enable him to use a computer. For this, however, they discovered that he needed to have control over one movement which could then be used to activate the computer. But Ignacio has no such movement under his control and so nothing could be done.

[11] When they took him to the USA in 2000 they visited with him the Amish community in Pennsylvania where a number of children with the same affliction in varying degrees are cared for by a devoted American doctor who has given his life to this work. One of the things they noted was that Ignacio was more involved in and stimulated by the life around him than other children like him. Probably this is partly due to his intelligence and partly to the exceptional 'normality' of the care he has received in the family and the constant stimulus of their loving involvement with him.

[12] The first of the Movement schools founded by José Manuel. All his children went to school there. See Chapters 7 & 8

[13] Yearly projects in which students from the Movement schools spend a week or more in poor districts in the country and work on construction and repair works for the community.

[14] A district in Santiago near the center of the city and some distance from his home.

[15] Missions are expeditions in which students from the Manquehue schools take part for help, support and evangelization in deprived areas of the country. Works are similar expeditions for repairs and construction for those out in the country who cannot afford them. Both types of expedition are regularly organized by the schools.

[16] Pedro worked entirely on his own in his application for University. He wanted it that way. He was given special consideration in his application to the Catholic University for Law. They hoped that they could work with his handicap, and after initial difficulties Pedro proved to be a capable and conscientious pupil.

[17] The final year of high school at the age of 18 is the normal time for the reception of Confirmation in Chile.

[18] Personal testimony of Pedro Eguiguren Cosmelli

[19] Mt. 11, 28

[20] I Corinthians 12, 4-26

Chapter 7 ~ The First School
Colegio San Benito Part 1

Growth of the Movement between two schools

We have seen how a group of young students from the Confirmation class of 1976 stayed with José Manuel and how he founded the Movement with eight of them at Pentecost in 1977. This first community, based at José Manuel's office in the Students' Center, attracted others, who became involved in both their prayer and work. This was the beginning of a new sort of life in which, apart from their university studies, they were learning the meaning of a deeper spiritual commitment. During this time of growth and development their contact with the monastery was important as Alejandro Allende remembers:

> My first contact with the Benedictines was the visits we made to the monastery where Fr Gabriel Guarda gave us various talks. He began them always with some reading from scripture and added others during the course of his talks. Then there were the retreats at Holy Week which gave me a profound sense of meeting with Christ. Perhaps it was due to being together in silence, living a new experience and seeking to understand more. During these visits and retreats we always meditated with José Manuel on the word of God. There were times when we took part in the prayer of the monastic office in the monastery. Thus we got to know the Office and the Rule of St Benedict, although we never suspected that the Lord was showing us the way to our future charism as lay Benedictines.[1]

At the center of this group was José Manuel inspiring, teaching and guiding them in the school and later in the rented house and in their work in the parish. They were learning to live a lay life which was truly for them 'a new creation' with its commitment to *lectio*, the prayer of the Office and apostolic work for others. The demands this made on their time as University students was not without its problems. There were some who drifted away or simply could not find the time for this extra commitment. There were others who, like Rodrigo Vidal, had not been at the Manquehue school but discovered José Manuel and his incipient Movement at this time and never looked back.

There were developments also in their work for others. Besides their work in the parish of Our Lady of the Angels, which was their base, some of them began working also in the parish of St Peter in the district of Las Condes under the pastor Fr Sergio Venegas where they started some communities for *lectio* and meditation. Another group, to whom we shall return in Chapter 9, began work among the poor in local settlements known as *campamentos*, where they looked after the children and prepared them for the sacraments.

Little groups or communities of the Movement were growing up around this time which met weekly for shared lectio and mutual support. They included women - especially after the core group had left the boys' school. These women, some of whom were married and some single, sought primarily renewal of lay life based on the word of God in scripture. So their spiritual renewal also began with *lectio* in small communities.

In 1982 José Manuel brought to an end the mixed groups and invited Ana Maria Salazar to start separate communities for women. The custom began at this time of naming the communities after a patron saint. The first women's community was named after St Benedict's sister Saint Scholastica. Several other communities for women were also formed during these years.

It was later on that one of these women's communities adopted as patron Saint Frances of Rome who in the fifteenth century led a remarkable life as both mystic and evangelizer in Rome.[2] In due course one of the women's communities was named after her and became the first community of women Manquehue Oblates[3], who made the promises for life. The shape of the Movement as consisting of small communities for *lectio* and meditation and mutual support all of whom co-operated on an equal basis in various works of evangelization was established at this time. The Benedictine connection was in place already but it had not yet become fully formative in their lives. That would come after the founding of the first school.

The work of the Movement with the parishes and in the campamentos for the poor brought a vigorous and expanding life to the Movement. Those who were young at the time and working with José Manuel remember it as a time of happiness and fulfillment. It was a wonderful contrast to the formal demands of university study. They really were enjoying life, even though it was a demanding life.

Nevertheless these scatttered communities were not in themselves satisfactory as a permanent arrangement. They did not provide a firm base for the future because the Movement's position in the parishes depended entirely on the current pastor. Moreover what the young people did for the Movement was done in their spare time. More important still was the lack of formal educational work. The article which José Manuel had written in the Manquehue School magazine[4] makes it clear that in his own perception there was an urgent need to bring the gospel itself into the lives of children at school. That was his means of saving them from anonymity. It was for him an imperative mission. He needed a school so as to be able to teach the young about the riches of their Christian heritage based on the power of the word of God in scripture and the sacraments of the Church. He had a vision which could be realized fully only in a school.

A new foundation
It was Fr Gabriel and Rafael Valdivieso[5], José Manuel's brother in law, who now pressed on him the idea of founding an entirely new school of his own. Rafael Valdivieso was a banker and had a good grasp on the problems of finance and organization. Although he was never himself a member of the Movement his business and financial experience were vital to the next stage of the Movement's development. As early as 1980 he was able to put on the table a serious proposal for financing the project. Substantial help for this was offered by another group which actually produced from one of the Banks an attractive proposal for financing the initial building and development. This scheme, however, was linked to a different Catholic religious organization which had its own aims and vision for the pastoral education of the young and their program did not quite coincide with the ideas of the Manquehue Movement. They made conditions for the loan which were not acceptable, because they would

have deprived the new young community of its liberty to pursue the new-found vision that inspired it. After considering the proposal carefully the Manquehue Movement decided against it. It was a disappointment but the decision was wise. They needed liberty and scope to find their own way and develop their own spiritual path and educational vision.

Fr Gabriel and Rafael continued their discussions of ways and means in their support of José Manuel. During 1981 two lines of advance emerged. Rafael inspired the first through which in that year the first financial stepping stone, which made everything that followed possible, was put in place. José Manuel's father at this time and until his death in 1986 was strong in his support and encouragement of his son's growing Movement. He together with José Manuel himself combined with Rafael Valdivieso and a fourth partner Jorge Cerveró in a commitment that they would find the necessary capital to make a start. They were ready to put forward their own money to get the school going. This was an initiative of tremendous importance, inspired by generosity and faith, which at last made possible the independent base which the Movement needed and from which it in fact developed and grew in strength.

The plan made action possible but with very little margin. Faith and hope were stronger than the actual finance behind the project. A site was found on the lowest slopes of the Manquehue mountain in an area which at that time was undeveloped but which now is full of residential buildings. At once a search was started for a house in which the school could begin its life while the building started. A suitable house was found in the district of Santiago called Providencia. It was a substantial house with plenty of grounds for the little boys of 4 years old to play in. It was called San Benito and another house was rented near by to enable the girls to start. All seemed ready to go, if the pupils could be found.

As for Fr Gabriel - he was concerned about José Manuel's desire that the school should be truly Benedictine. The monastery at Las Condes had no educational experience, but he had recently met Fr Dominic Milroy - at that time Headmaster of Ampleforth College, a Benedictine school in northern England. Fr Dominic's mother was Chilean and he had recently visited his relations in Santiago. José Manuel, Fr Gabriel suggested, should write to Fr Dominic and ask how a Benedictine school should be run. He remembers what happened:

112

During these years Fr Gabriel told me to write to a Benedictine monastery that has a school and he suggested that I should write to Fr Dominic Milroy at Ampleforth in England. So I wrote asking him to send me something about the school. He sent me an article he had written for the 1500th anniversary of St Benedict and he said that it was not possible to understand about a school without visiting it - and that is true. [6]

José Manuel might well have considered himself already well prepared for starting a new school in Chile. The Manquehue School had given him invaluable experience in the education of the young and their pastoral needs. He had learned a lot about the administration of a school from his closeness to Fr Puelma. He had gone far in the development of his own vision of how to meet needs of the young in religious education. His standing at this time is shown by the fact that he had actually been offered the job of Head of another school after leaving the Manquehue school. It was a compliment to his abilities but it would have crippled his visionary work with the young. So he had turned from that prospect of a safe career and instead carried forward his vision in difficult circumstances through evangelizing work in the parishes and the *campamentos*.

There was only one way forward that appealed to him. To fulfill the mission he had undertaken he must create a new school. Nevertheless there was something more he wanted to infuse into the whole project - the Benedictine dimension of education. For this, as Fr Gabriel urged him, he must visit an actual monastery with a long tradition of Benedictine education. What Fr Dominic said was true. He must make the long, long journey to Ampleforth.

The visits to Ampleforth

The seeds of his attractions to the Benedictines had been planted during the years he had spent with Fr Gabriel in the monastery. After he had moved to the Manquehue school he had tried to adapt to the devotion of the French Fathers' Order, which was to the Sacred Hearts of Jesus and Mary. He makes this clear in the article he wrote in his last year there.[7] However, he was also delighted to find that the French Fathers were themselves committed to the Rule of St Benedict for spiritual guidance, although this had not been very strongly applied in the Manquehue School itself. Luz had strongly confirmed him in following the Benedictine way and now that he was on the point of starting the great enterprise he showed typical thoroughness and humility in wanting to be sure that he really did understand the Benedictine ideals as they applied to education. Up to now, after all, he had never yet had any contact with a Benedictine School.

The visit was accordingly arranged to Ampleforth Abbey and College in England through the Headmaster Fr Dominic Milroy. To nearly everyone else in Chile this journey to Yorkshire seemed quixotic and difficult to understand. It was in the fall of 1981 when they were preparing for the opening of the new school in its temporary quarters in March 1982 - the beginning of the school year in Chile. Why ever should he leave them to struggle through the preparations and go off to the other side of the world alone. It seems that at the time it was only José Manuel's mother who welcomed the idea and supported it. She had been anxious about her son's apparently wild plans since he had left the University and not settled down to a regular job, but she thought that his desire to model his school on the Benedictines was rather sane. In spite of the distance and physical difficulty of travel and the many other arguments against this bizarre plan, she welcomed it:

> I loved to see him off to Ampleforth on this and subsequent visits. The first time was terrible for him. But I didn't think he had gone mad. I thought it was salvation. Rafael Valdivieso[8] said 'he is mad to go off to England like this at such a time'. But in spite of thinking that, Rafael still supported him. I did not agree that it was mad to go. I thought it was great, because I knew he would be given a way to follow (by the Benedictines) and so he would not have to invent one......With Benedictine support behind him I knew that José Manuel was not just founding a sect.[9]

It was a long journey to Yorkshire and a trying one especially for him with his disability. Quite apart from that it was not immediately obvious how a remote Benedictine Abbey in England could help much with his new lay foundation in Chile. For some reason José Manuel was adamant;

he must go and find out what he could about how to give his new school a truly Benedictine spirit. Arguments against the plan had little effect on him. The journey was long and difficult. By the time he arrived in London much of his enthusiasm had drained away. He began to wonder if he should turn round and go home, but in the end he decided to persevere.

A strange episode when he got to London encouraged him. It seemed like a heavenly confirmation of the path he was treading. There in London he was offered and accepted his very first pupil for San Benito school.

> While I was in London a Chilean[10], who was working in England for the Chilean copper company, and his wife said that they knew I was starting a school and wanted to register their son with me. So he was registered in St James hotel in London.[11]

That was his own laconic account. He was always able to accept the extraordinary as though it was quite ordinary. That meeting in a London hotel was treated by José Manuel as though it might be expected that, coming from the other side of the world, he should be asked there to accept his first pupil for a school which was still not much more than an idea in his head.

After that start in London he set out on the long train journey to the north. There was nothing further to encourage him until he arrived at the Abbey and then he felt strongly that everything changed for the better. He experienced a definite affinity with the spirit of the community.

That first visit of José Manuel to Ampleforth in 1981 proved important not only for him and the Movement but for Ampleforth as well. It was the beginning of an association which, as time went on, brought many blessings both to the monastery and to the school. Many things began slowly to grow as a result of that visit. Many lives were deeply affected and drawn closer to Christ as a result of José Manuel's courageous and visionary decision to go himself to see a Benedictine school against all the sensible arguments put forward to deter him at that time of political tension and chauvinistic confrontation on both sides of the Falklands war.[12] José Manuel's solitary and painful journey of

Catholic faith and Benedictine solidarity was itself a symbol of new life and reconciliation. It was a moment of grace whose effects would prove to be far-reaching both in England and in Chile. José Manuel remembers the impact that first Ampleforth visit made on him:

> On my arrival at Ampleforth I first met Fr Benet, the Second Master. I was shown everything in the School because I spent four days there. There was a boy, named Nicholas Duffield, who looked after me and showed me round and Fr Dominic took me to different events in the School. But what was much more interesting than the academic work of the School was the monastery and the whole Ampleforth world which had a big spiritual impact on me. It was much more than I expected and like a new meeting with the Lord. The Benedictine spiritual way of seeing things was a big shock and very impressive. On subsequent visits for several years my impressions were confirmed but the impact was very strong in the beginning when I arrived, and it soon made me feel very much at home.
>
> When originally I had gone to Fr Gabriel at the Benedictine monastery in Santiago what attracted me was that he was very open minded and here in Chile that spirit was difficult to follow without getting into trouble with the Catholic Church. The same open-minded spirit was much broader at Ampleforth. Not only the spirit but also the mind of Ampleforth was made for me and that was why I felt very much at home in a way that gave me a deep spiritual experience. I felt also that this was the way I should go, but without knowing how to do it. I saw Ampleforth as the Church in miniature and the experience of seeing it in that way was an experience of great significance for me.[13]

The visit to Ampleforth was extraordinary in its consequences and it proved important as much for the general development of the Movement as for any explicit reasons connected with the educational work of San Benito school. Father Dominic Milroy remembers that first visit to Ampleforth and reflects on its significance:

> When he first visited Ampleforth in October 1981, two things immediately became clear. He had a thorough knowledge of the text and spirit of St Benedict's Rule, and he knew exactly what he was

looking for. Within two days he had identified and absorbed not only the general ethos of our school, but also the hidden attitudes and mechanisms that made it work. Many of these we ourselves were inclined to take for granted. It was 'second nature' for us, but he needed to 'unpack' them if he was going to be able to translate them into his own culture as well as into the methodology, the spirit, even the architecture of a school that did not yet exist.

The whole point of what was happening is that here was a venture that was entirely lay, entirely from scratch, entirely unsupported and unfunded by existing clerical institutions and at the same time entirely rooted in the Rule of St Benedict and the concrete traditions of Benedictine education. There was even a poetic and providential wisdom in the fact that the monastic school against which the vision had been tested was thousands of miles away and therefore unable and unlikely to interfere.[14]

The first visit was only a beginning. In the following year José Manuel again took time out from the young of the Movement and the crucial early stages of the San Benito school to make that long journey once more. He decided to go again in spite of his disability which, as he now knew, made travel so difficult.

This second visit happened at the worst of all possible times because the Falklands conflict between Argentina and England had disrupted communications and made any such journey longer and more tiring. However this second visit in 1982 was no mere repetition.

He had only a short stay at Ampleforth from Tuesday to Saturday, but it was important above all because he met Fr Columba Cary Elwes who gave José Manuel vital help towards the understanding of English Benedictine monasticism and its relevance to the spiritual mission of the laity in the modern world. His conversations with Fr Columba on that and subsequent occasions did much to establish a strong relationship with Ampleforth Abbey.

It was on this trip that I met Fr Columba.[15] I think Fr Dominic, on that occasion, did not know quite what to do with me and he said he would find Fr Columba to meet me, which turned out to be a very good idea. Fr Columba took me to St Wilfrid's House in the School for our discussion. It was a strange and amusing experience, because there was a cat there which went for Fr Columba's head. We spent some time trying to settle the cat but we couldn't, so Fr Columba suggested we should behave as though the cat were not there. We did that and went through the whole meeting with the cat jumping up and down. In spite of this, I developed a very good relationship with Fr Columba and he had a very good influence on all that we were doing in Chile. That was good and I think the Lord sent me that opportunity. He remained very interested always and knew about all my problems and told me many things that were helpful.[16]

The English Benedictine Tradition

José Manuel's conversations in depth with Fr Columba Cary-Elwes were about the Benedictine tradition[17] in its pastoral, educational and apostolic outreach as well as its contemplative, prayer-centered heart and how the two could and should be inseparable. It was just what he needed at a time when his lay Benedictine community was taking shape. It began to throw a new light on this strange connection which had so quickly sprung up across the world forming a bridge which could help the development of the Movement in a way which was authentically Benedictine. Ampleforth was particularly helpful at that time to José Manuel in his search for a lay and apostolic expression of the Benedictine spirit.[18]

What he found at Ampleforth was in many ways a new world to him because the Spaniards had never in the early days brought the Benedictines to their colonies in South America, although the Portuguese had brought them to Brazil. When they did come to the American Spanish lands in the 20th century it was from the enclosed, contemplative tradition of the nineteenth century Benedictine revival in Europe. Both traditions are right to claim authentic descent from St Benedict, who had fled from the world to seek God alone but later himself began Benedictine education by taking young boys into the monastery and teaching them. He also took the first steps in Benedictine pastoral apostolate on his arrival at Monte Cassino by preaching the gospel to convert the local inhabitants. The two traditions are complementary to each other.

As José Manuel met with this tradition at Ampleforth he found that the monks cherished the monastic life of the monastery and the search for God in prayer and community living, not only as their own way of seeking God, but as their way also of bringing others to him. He also came across monks who listened to him and 'wasted time' hearing him out. He experienced at Ampleforth a sincere and powerful Benedictine hospitality.

It was this tradition, combining monastic spirituality and the apostolate, that attracted José Manuel. The same spirit was what he wanted for his own lay Benedictine Movement in Chile. It helped to inspire him to forge for the laity of the 21st century his new and unique concept of an extended lay Benedictine community[19] living a lay life in the world. The details of how this came about will emerge later in this story.

The important point at the moment is that he found at Ampleforth just the concepts in a genuine Benedictine tradition, devoted both to monastic prayer and evangelization, which he needed for his new vision of lay Benedictine life. This would not be an imitation of what he found at Ampleforth. In many essentials it would be entirely different but his experience there helped him and gave him added confidence in developing his new concept of lay Benedictine education and evangelization in Chile. It was thus that his second visit to Yorkshire helped. It was especially in his meetings with Fr Columba Cary Elwes, who understood his aspirations about lay Benedictine evangelization, that he found what he was looking for. They struck up a relationship which grew stronger for both of them as time went on. Fr Columba's influence and his understanding of José Manuel's aspirations are still remembered with gratitude in Chile. For José Manuel at the time they came as a flood of light and strong encouragement for his developing vision.

The first Gringos

During the first visit to Ampleforth one of the senior boys in his last year at school, Nicholas Duffield, approached José Manuel with a new idea. He was thinking seriously about a vocation to the priesthood and had been impressed by meeting José Manuel and hearing him talk about his new venture in education in Chile. It was a time when it had become quite normal for boys in England on leaving school at the age of 18 to spend a year abroad to gain experience before starting at University. Some of them went to take part in various forms of voluntary service or to work with missionaries in Africa. Nicholas, with this on his mind, said he would like to go to work for a year in Chile. José Manuel remembers the occasion:

> I was in the Upper Building[20] Guest Room at Ampleforth one day when the door opened and there was Nicholas Duffield who had showed me round the school on my previous visit; and he said 'I want to come to Chile'. So we spoke about it for some time and I said OK but come with a friend, not alone, because you will probably feel lonely. He said he would come with Tim Jelley.
>
> They were the first two that came. They came in March 1983. They stayed at my home, because we had no gringo's house or anything like that. At that time Pedro was very sick and I was very worried about it and anxious also about Luz and Domingo who was born on June 2 1983.[21]

It is important to note that it was the spiritual vision which José Manuel had communicated in his talks that attracted Nicholas Duffield and led him to make the request. For him, as for so many others later, it was the personal impact of meeting José Manuel that inspired him. As time went on it was just this aspect that emerged as incomparably the most important in the visits of other English boys who followed the example of Nicholas Duffield and Tim Jelley. Some of the gringos over the years may have been looking for practice in Spanish, or adventure in South America or a way of filling in the gap year. But there were many who saw and responded to a spiritual vision of how lay Catholic life could and should be lived and they came back enriched beyond their wildest imagining.

The spiritual growth of these young men as a result of their time in Chile was at first beyond any expectations at Ampleforth, although in time it came to be expected as almost normal. There was never any doubt that the gringos received more than they gave.

When José Manuel agreed to the visit of the first two gringos and welcomed them into his own house he showed great generosity. It was a difficult time for him and his whole family because of Pedro's illness. The richness of the outcome, especially for the gringos, was beyond anything they could have dreamt of at the time. These first gringos learnt rapidly by living with José Manuel, by being involved in the Movement and by sharing in prayer and work. This pattern continued and developed year by year, although later gringos lived, not in José Manuel's house, but in a house of the Oblates. Through the great generosity of José Manuel and the Oblates other young leavers or university students from Ampleforth went each year to serve in the Movement for a few months or a year. With few exceptions they came back with deeper faith through which they were spiritually better prepared for life. Many of them went back again to Chile and there were some who, as we shall see, committed themselves for life to the Movement.

The experience of the gringos in Chile was so strong that it led some of them on their return to England to establish at various universities a new English Movement for *lectio* and mutual support in small communities just as they had learnt it in Chile. This English development was the work of some gringos from Ampleforth who had learnt so much in Chile that they wanted to persevere with *lectio* and the lay spirituality they had learnt there. Some of them persevered in this practice together after University. The survivors of these groups now work in England independently of but in spiritual harmony with the Movement in Chile.

The First Pupils

As we have seen the first pupil for the new school, called San Benito, was registered in London by a Chilean couple who were there for business reasons. It was strange that when José Manuel left for England shortly before the opening of that first school year he had plans and dreams and a rented building but still no pupils. Then his trust in God was rewarded on his crazy visit to England by finding his first pupil there in London. That was not the end of the wonders. On his return to Santiago the first enrollment filled up quickly and was complete just in time for the opening. There were 130 children to start the school. It was as though

God were making it clear that the future was in his hands and not subject to any ordinary process devised by public relations experts.

All the pupils in the first years as the school was building up came like that - without advertising, without enticement, without effort; they just arrived promptly on time. The time was ripe. New schools were needed. José Manuel attracted parents and they trusted him, but that was not enough to explain everything. The Holy Spirit seemed to have things in hand and needed no assistance. The parents turned up with their children and the places in the first year were filled without effort. In many ways it was a tense and anxious year when everything was new and untried and no-one could see the shape of the future. Nevertheless it went well. San Benito had been launched and the Movement at last had a course, a direction and an ideal to live for, no longer in the abstract but incarnated in the lives of these children to whom they were now committed.

Gradually the young members of the Movement transferred from the parish to this new work, but they did not all move at once. Some of them went on working in the parish for several more years while those who had gone to work in the *campamentos* were preparing the way for San Lorenzo school. Gradually the majority left parish work and were concentrated in the growing school of San Benito.

The house the Movement had rented in the district called Providencia was adequate for very small boys in the early years. There were girls also and a second house nearby was rented for them and called after St Benedict's sister, Saint Scholastica. It was under separate management but, when they moved to the new site, boys and girls came together under one Headmaster but in separate classrooms. The boys are on the west side of the range of buildings, the girls on the east. They normally work separately but can easily mix for certain activities.

All went well on this basis in the two houses in Providencia for the first years. There were professional teachers of course but also there were the young men and women who had been working under José Manuel in the parish and other work. They were called tutors and they taught the children through the way of the word of God in scripture. They were always with them in recreation time. The impression from the photographs and accounts of the time is that the whole experience for the children was one of great happiness. It was the beginning of the real Manquehue enterprise and it went well. The site was quite a distance from where most of the children lived and parents took turns to deliver and collect them, which brought many of the parents close to the enterprise. They used to arrive with cars packed with tiny children who had been taught to sing a merry song on the way about their wonderful new school with detailed instructions about where to find it. They only had to sing it to instruct any new driver where to go.

By the beginning of the school year in March 1985 San Benito had outgrown the rented accommodation and everyone was more than ready for the move to the new site. The new buildings were in the district of Vitacura. From behind the school they looked straight up to the huge Manquehue mountain and there was at that time very little else to be seen except the mountain and open ground. Life for both teachers and pupils, when they moved into the first buildings, was quite unlike that in a well-established school. Alongside the teaching and all other activities substantial construction operations were going on all around. It brought a sense of creativity to the environment of learning because the building that was going on was for the future – for their future - and for a whole new series of ideas and ideals.

Building had started in 1984. The plan was to move along the line of buildings, creating a sector at a time to satisfy the needs of the coming year and provide for one year's intake at a time. It gave the pupils and the staff quite an interesting experience. Daily they shared the site with the builders who were moving ahead of them and completing a new section just in time for each school year as it came. The builders kept just ahead of the growth of the school and were scarcely out of each new phase when it was occupied by the encroaching hoards of children.

Provision for the girls moved as fast as that for the boys. They mingled with the boys in break and play time, but had their own accommodation and their own classrooms. At the end of the line came buildings which were smaller and more like home for the infants - until the huge family was complete and reached 1600 pupils ranging in age from 4 to 18. Rafael Valdivieso managed the finances and helped them along by persuading the parents to invest in the growth of the school by downpayments when a child entered the school which were returnable when the child's education was completed. He and the architects and contractors coped with insistent demands and it must have been easier to do this because the whole project was vibrantly alive in a process of creation which was not merely physical but human and spiritual as well. Youth was really on the move in those years.

Everyone had to understand priorities and no-one was allowed to alter the spiritual priorities which José Manuel kept strongly in the forefront of everyone's mind. The Chapel was small, but it must be there in the building schedule. The parents' association gave money for a bell so that the children and teachers would know when it was time for Lauds and Midday Prayer and Vespers. It was the right thing for a Benedictine institution where *Nothing must come before the Work of God.*[22]   It was a witness to the spiritual priorities and the Benedictine character of the new school right from the beginning.

The Movement & a new educational vision

The focus of this account must now concentrate on the educational developments of the Movement starting with the first school San Benito. We must remember, however, that at the time San Benito was founded as a school the Movement itself was still at quite an early stage of its growth and there was a long way to go in the development of its spirituality and organization under the inspiration of St Benedict's Rule. That spiritual growth, through a typically Benedictine process of self-discovery, provided the underlying motivation for the overt educational development. The two - the Movement itself and the school it had created - were and still are woven together and they may seem at times to be almost identified. This is especially true because the Catholic & Benedictine vision of the Movement is consciously and deliberately expressed and realized through the educational policy and practice of San Benito school and the others which followed.

In spite of this it is important to make a distinction between the Movement and the School and to keep that distinction always in mind. The Movement itself has now developed to a point where it has a corporate existence of its own which is not essentially dependent on the schools it has founded. The fundamental mission of the Movement is to to teach its member to live out their baptism, in a spirit of what is today called re-evangelization. It applies to all ages although it is currently realized principally, but not exclusively, through the schools. If the educational undertakings of the schools were by any mischance to come to an end, the Movement could and would continue to serve the Church in its lay life through the lay spirituality it has developed and to carry its mission of evangelization into other aspects of lay life.

It has already begun to do this in some of the other works of the Movement which have developed since the early days. However dominant and important the schools are, the Movement is always impacting other aspects of lay life through its members and followers of every age and occupation in the Church and society. It will become more clear in the course of this account that the Movement is not simply concerned with formal education of the young. It is dedicated above all to evangelization and re-evangelization not only in schools but also in every aspect of lay life. Their educational vision is holistic and as a lay Movement its mission stretches out to the whole of lay life at every age. Nevertheless at this stage our concern must be with the Movement's educational developments and with the importance of these developments in the shaping of the Movement itself.

☙

Notes for Chapter 7

[1] Alejandro Allende - quoted from El Quaderno No 15

[2] St Frances of Rome was married at a young age and, while she was still married, founded a group of Benedictine Oblates. When her husband died, she became a Benedictine Oblate herself. She won over many of her contemporaries to a life of fidelity to the gospel. So many gathered round her that she founded a congregation of Benedictine Oblates. By her life and work as a committed laywoman she provided a perfect model for the Manquehue women's communities. As the prayer for her feast day expresses it: 'she was a model both for married life and for monastic life.

[3] Later, when the Movement was fully established, those who after a period of formation formally committed themselves to the Movement in accordance with the Little Rule were called Manquehue Oblates.

[4] See Appendix 2

[5] Rafael Valdivieso was a banker with experience in development plans. Although not a member of the Movement himself he was a close friend of José Manuel and made a vital contribution by his financial planning and business expertise to the building developments for San Benito and San Lorenzo & San Anselmo schools.

[6] from interview with José Manuel

[7] see Appendix 2

[8] See endnote 5

[9] Interview with Señora Luz - José Manuel's mother

[10] Patrick Cussen McKenna. His wife was Loreto Vial and their son (the first registered pupil of San Benito) was Andres.

[11] Interview with José Manuel

[12] The Argentinians occupied the Falkland Islands off the coast of South America. They officially belonged to Britain and the British Prime Minister sent a force to dislodge them.

[13] Interview with José Manuel

[14] from 'Benedictine presence' paper by Fr Dominic Milroy

[15] Fr Columba Cary Elwes, who was by now in retirement at Ampleforth, was fluent in Spanish and eager to help. His experience was broad. After a period as Housemaster in the School at Ampleforth and then as Prior in the monastery he

had been sent out to St Louis in Misouri USA as founding Prior of Ampleforth's foundation there in 1955.   Later he had experience also in Africa where he worked for a time with Glenstal monks on their foundation in Nigeria.

[16] Interview with José Manuel

[17] The Benedictines were strong in England from the earliest Anglo Saxon period of the 7th century right through until the destruction of the monasteries by Henry VIII.   However, once Elizabeth had imposed and consolidated the Protestant settlement in England, many young Catholics were anxious to carry on the Benedictine tradition and eventually succeeded in founding two English houses on the continent.   These new English Benedictine monks claimed continuity with the Benedictines of the Middle Ages through the re-foundation of Westminster Abbey during the brief Catholic reign of Mary (1553-1558). The new English Benedictines in exile re-founded the English Benedictine Congregation which at that time consisted of the monasteries of St Gregory's at Douai and St Laurence at Dieulouard in Lorraine.   These were followed by St Edmund's in Paris.   At the French Revolution these monks were expelled from France and refounded their monasteries in England at Downside (St Gregory's from Douai) and at Ampleforth (St Laurence's from Dieulouard).   St Edmund's in Paris eventually became Douai in Woolhampton in Berkshire.   For a fuller treatment see Chapter 14.

[18] This was a point made to me by Abbot Gabriel Guarda on a visit to him in the monastery in Las Condes in Santiago.   I said to him that I felt almost like an intruder because he in his contemplative Benedictine monastery had been the initial inspiration of the Movement through his three years of *lectio divina* with José Manuel.   He replied that, if you look through the history of the Benedictines it is so diverse that it was important for him to go to just the Benedictine tradition that was relevant to him.   That, he thought, was the tradition of Ampleforth, which was why he sent José Manuel there.

[19] This is a new concept developing the idea of a Benedictine community and applying it to those leading a lay life of Benedictine commitment.   It is explained as follows in *The Way of the Manquehue Movement*:   'The name 'Extended Benedictine Community' is designed to signify that, just as a monastery is established as a community which serves under a Rule and an Abbot, so also the Community of the Manquehue Oblates is formed of a group of people who serve under the Rule of St Benedict and a Responsible who governs them. Just like a monastery the Extended Benedictine Community represents the organization of an alternative society which seeks to establish an intimate union between faith and life, in order to achieve in this way a full development of the

fruits of baptism by making the gospel the basis of their lives and invoking the help of the Holy Rule. In contrast to a monastery the Extended Benedictine Community consists of laity and not of monks. Although it has its own physical space it is not confined to a particular place but reaches out to all the areas of life work and recreation in which the Oblates move.'

[20] The name of one of the school buildings which at that time contained, among other things, accommodation for guests to the School

[21] Interview José Manuel

[22] St Benedict's Rule ch 43

Chapter 8 ~ San Benito Part 2

New creation - new structures

In the Chilean world outside, during those first years of San Benito School, it was a time of anxiety and uncertainty. The military government was strongly in power and the people of Chile with their long tradition of democracy were restlessly yearning for change and new elections. Noone quite knew how things would develop or where they would end. It was a difficult time for everyone and the pain was felt in San Benito. Among the supporters and parents of the school there were some who longed for the return of true democracy. Others in those unstable times looked to the military as the one source of stability. They supported the regime, not because they liked it, but because they saw good reasons to fear that nothing else could defend the country from the specter of instability and the alien grip of irreversible international communism.

José Manuel tried to keep in line with the Archbishop, Cardinal Silva Henriquez, who was outspoken in defense of human rights. He did what he could to support those who suffered from the denial of these rights and at the same time he always sought to promote reconciliation through his readiness to enter into dialogue with both sides of the political divide. Inevitably the tensions and conflicts of interest in public life were reflected among the supporters of San Benito. None of the political problems of the day deflected José Manuel from his vision of lay spirituality and his pursuit of fidelity to the gospel and the Church and to the Cardinal's wise and sensitive leadership. At San Benito there was a calm spiritual vision under the inspiration of St Benedict's Rule which was appreciated by all who worked in San Benito at that time. It was becoming an oasis of spiritual calm and was recognized as such by many who came into contact with the Movement and its work.[1]

For the small group of young people, who were being led into an unknown future by José Manuel in spite of the dark clouds that surrounded them, this was a time of building and vision for the future in which everything was positive and everything was creative. With limited educational experience so far they were learning how to start a school from nothing and then how to run it successfully. Many things were tentative and experimental, but one thing was not tentative - the Christ-centered vision, the values, the standards which they were communicating to the young. These were founded on the word of God in Scripture and inspired by St Benedict's Rule with its emphasis on community, on prayer as the foundation of all, on *lectio*, on the fraternal charity of chapter 72 of the Rule, on the constant personal affirmation of *acogida*.[2] That was what they wanted to give the young. This vision was there explicitly from the beginning. Before the school began on the temporary site the Director of Studies, had called a meeting of the young men and women of the Movement, and given them unequivocal guidance about the standards they must meet:

> You are going to be the first tutors of San Benito and I want to make sure that you all have the right attitude of complete commitment to the good of the young for whom you will be responsible. If you are not so committed, you had better go and I shall get someone else to take your place.

That moment was important for the self-image and motivation of the tutors. It made them realize that they were not just filling in part of the timetable as a formal obligation. They were there to give something which was now part of themselves - how to live their lives in Christ through their baptism and *lectio*. At the time one of them, conscious of this unique gift, made the comment that, if they with their vision and commitment failed to achieve this, nobody could succeed.

That meeting with the Director took place right at the beginning in the first temporary site before even the first day of classes. It had a lasting impact on the tutors which carried over into the new site. They were to give themselves without stint and share the vision for Christian life based firmly on the Word of God which they had already learnt in the Movement. They were university undergraduates in various disciplines from agriculture to economics and law. They were not professionally trained as teachers in the ordinary sense. What they did have, however, would become a richer resource. The Director of Studies had established absolute priorities, right at the beginning before the enterprise had really started.

It was a defining moment for their future mission and it brought explicitly into play in the new school what these young teachers had been learning while the Movement worked in the Manquehue school and the parish. It was richer in its spiritual and moral content than the traditional vision of school life and school relationships. And it was precisely in relationships that it was different.

Among pupils in school the normal relationship with their teachers is a 'we-they' mentality. It may work quite well for some formal teaching and learning purposes but it leads too often in practice to a largely passive receptiveness on the one hand and an actively dominating management on the other. This may be hardened by authoritarian discipline or weakened by the well-meant attempt to soften everything through abandoning authority in the interests of the idea that all are really on a level together. The idea of such equality is a fiction without the theology of baptism and the diversity within unity of the gospel. Through baptism we are all made one in Christ but within that fundamental unity we have different functions and distinct duties.[3] Without the foundation of such a spiritual vision attempts at leveling in schools usually end in lack of discipline, lack of order, lack of learning, lack of achievement, lack of spiritual growth. The new relationship of San Benito grew on a foundation deeper than either authoritarianism or disorderly liberal egalitarianism. It was built on the spiritual truth of Christian relationships which were consciously and clearly seen to arise from shared baptism into Christ with strong Christ-centered mutual obligations and spiritual debts.

The problem that faced the Movement at this stage was to convert this vision into structures which would work while still maintaining the other essential aims of teaching and learning in schools. That was not easy. They had to achieve it in association with many professionally trained teachers who were not members of the Movement. Those teachers brought with them invaluable professional expertise, knowledge and experience. They had to be won over to the new vision and their gifts integrated with the Manquehue vision.

131

Manuel José Echenique at this time became General Secretary of the Movement under José Manuel and later their principal authority on education. He remembers the structures that were developed at San Benito in its early stages:

> The organization of the school was in three main areas.
>
> The first was the academic area, which was under the direction of Luz Maria Eguiguren (known as Lute), who at that stage was not yet a member of the Movement. The academic work was basically very good but it did not bear any special seal characteristic of the Movement. It was an educative vision of how to get the school going academically but it did not yet have a specifically Benedictine character.
>
> Secondly the planning and administration of the property was under the direction of Rafael Valdivieso. Again there was nothing about it to reflect specifically the spirit of the Movement. Its originality was in the fact that San Benito was perhaps uniquely organized and administered in its finances according to the management structures and principles of a modern business. That was achieved through Rafael's expertise and personal business experience.
>
> Thirdly the area in which José Manuel had direct influence was essentially to do with relationship with the pupils - the boys and girls - through *tutoría* and friendships in general. This happened really through the way in which the tutors and members of the Movement, who had a permanent presence in the school, were inter-acting with the students, but the way in which this relationship was fostered was not at that time formally inserted into any official structure of the school.[4]

It was the third area under José Manuel himself which in fact provided the vital and unique inspiration of the school. It was concerned with the day to day interaction between tutors and pupils - with personal and religious growth - with the interface between family and school - with mutual understanding and empathy between the pupils and teachers on which so much depends. There was a sense in which it affected everything on the timetable, because it aimed to inspire a fundamental spiritual vision which facilitated all activities and was at the deepest level the source of all motivation. That is how it came to be recognized by all, not as a separate department, but as the defining context for everything and everyone in the school. It was the unique contribution of José Manuel himself to the school. His own personal contribution was great but he worked also increasingly through his disciples - the young tutors.

The Young Tutors

The young tutors were the young men and women of the Movement - not yet Oblates, because that status within the Movement had not yet been formalized. We must remember that the Movement itself was still, like the school, in the process of creation and formation and the young tutors were vital to both.

The young tutors were constantly with the children. They had been taught the importance of rescuing students from anonymity in institutionalized education. They got to know them personally and took an interest in their ordinary needs and problems. They were intent on communicating to the children the word of God, the meaning of their baptism and the lay Benedictine vision which was renewing their own lives. They were in their early twenties and they carried into their work with the pupils the concept of *acogida* or warm, self-giving welcome, seeing Christ in everyone. It was in fact what they had learnt from the gospel and the Rule of St Benedict. These tutors initially did not hold formal positions of responsibility in the school structure, but as time went on they became more and more involved in everything. It was Jorge Baraona who insisted on the tutors being gradually brought into the formal school structure. Jorge brought an energy and organization to the early life of the San Benito that was invaluable and, like others at the time and also to come in the future, he provided José Manuel with the creativity and practical administrative skills that enabled his vision to take form and life.

That was how things started with the professional teachers in charge of the regular educational structures and the young tutors providing inspiration and pastoral and personal support. Then the time came when one of the Form Masters (who was one of the professional teachers in charge of a class) fell ill. Then one of the young tutors, José Miguel

Navarro, took the leap and stood in for him. It was a big step forward for the Movement and all the more important because it worked well. Soon he was followed by his brother, José Antonio Navarro, and then finally others were brought in.

The meaning of this development was that José Manuel, as Headmaster, was no longer alone in pursuing his vision among those in positions of responsibility in the school. It was in this way that the young tutors, who were members of the Movement, although young and without formal training as teachers in the traditional sense, blossomed into Form Masters working alongside professionals and learning fast as they worked. In spite of lack of teaching qualifications they had a university background and were, of course, well trained in a unique way by José Manuel himself. The training was infectious and spread rapidly through teachers and students. It was above all a training in what might well be called 'the art of communicating Christ to the young.' The change through which some of the young tutors started working as professional schoolmasters was an important step in the development of San Benito itself and in its relationship with the Movement. There were some of the young tutors, like José Miguel Navarro and Manuel José Echenique who decided to abandon university studies so as to devote themselves wholly to the Movement. San Benito as a school became rapidly more integrated into the structures of the Movement and more attuned to its vision and ideals.

Naturally, it was a change that had its problems. Manual José Echenique remembering those days, when he was himself one of the young tutors, recalls how inexperienced they were and what difficulties they faced. He comments that they were in fact amateurs and that anyone looking for professional educational expertise would not at once have recognized it in them.

That led to tension and debate among the teachers. There were differences of opinion about how to define the right relationships of authority and friendship between teachers and pupils. It is a debate which often happens in schools but seldom with the open-ness with which it was faced in San Benito during that crucial stage of early growth. There it was soon recognized that the young tutors, with José Manuel as their guide, had discovered the importance of basing their relationship with the pupils on a friendship which was centered in Christ. What they brought to the staff and pupils of the school was no empty theory but a living and effective reality. They had shown that they knew, on the firm basis of the gospel itself how to meet children on their own grounds, how to play with them and be with them and enter to some extent into the hurly-burly of their lives. The skill with which they did this put them exactly in the right position to help when help was needed and to bring positive and quite strong influence to bear on their spiritual, human, educational development.

There were some professional teachers on the staff who at first disagreed with the young tutors and thought that authority should come first and prevail over all other relationships. Only after that was established could there be room for a friendship, which must be secondary to authority and restricted by it. That was a well-established traditional view, but it was different from the new vision of José Manuel himself and the young tutors. It relied too much on the affirmation of authority as paramount to allow the development of that mutual understanding which was so important to the Movement's vision. The disagreements were real but fortunately at San Benito they were not allowed to generate confrontation.

From the point of view of schools in general there was nothing remarkable about the fact that this sort of debate was taking place. What was remarkable was that the young tutors' vision was coherent, well argued and based on their living experience of teaching the gospel outside the world of education as well as within it. It was also well founded on scripture and St Benedict's Rule. Its aim was not vague companionship but it was a deliberate attempt to bring the teaching of the word in scripture and the wisdom of the Rule to bear on the actual problems and confusions of the young. This gave the tutors' relationship with the young an unusually objective strength quite apart from the increasingly impressive pragmatic fact of its manifest success in the school. Moreover, with José Manuel behind them the young tutors had a growing confidence which commanded respect and they received a remarkably open hearing among the other teachers.

Of course it was also important that the young tutors were eager to learn from the teaching experience of the professional teachers. Thus it was that the tutors, instead of being stamped on and then driven to working, as it were, under-cover in a way unrelated to official structures, they were able to have real influence on the official development among the teaching staff and students of San Benito. Their relationship with other teachers, who had been contracted to teach as professionals, was not as difficult as it might have been. Although there were complaints about the perceived inefficiency and unpredictable ways in which the tutors often operated, everyone began to recognize and value the special relationship which these young tutors and form masters were developing with the pupils. The great value of this relationship in their growth and learning became daily more apparent. The ethos of the school was being established and it proved to be an ethos which was attractive not only to the pupils but to the teachers and parents as well. It was the beginning of a new understanding between teachers and pupils, based on the meaning of baptism into Christ. It would grow stronger over the years and become the mark of education within the Manquehue Schools.

An exceptional and important aspect of tutoring was the daily use by the tutors of the word of God in the Bible through the daily habit of *lectio divina*. The tutors were all Members of the Movement and their own lives had been not only influenced but they had been radically changed by *lectio divina*. They themselves had experienced in their lives all the confusions and temptations both of the country they lived in and of the world at large. They saw them, however, with a difference because they had learnt how to look for guidance and inspiration in scripture. They did not hesitate to teach the pupils how to look in scripture for the solution of their personal problems. They could do this convincingly because that same source of the word of God had given birth to the Movement and given not only José Manuel but the tutors themselves their positive spiritual perspective in life. The young tutors were single minded in their care for their pupils and could often be seen taking a pupil with a certain problem out of class in order to listen to him and offer the *acogida* they had been taught by José Manuel. During the conversation at some stage they would invariably read some relevant passage of Scripture as a way of letting the Lord shed His light on what was happening. It showed great tolerance on the part of the professional teachers that they were able to take this sort of interruption in their stride. It also revealed an astute appreciation of the true value of the interplay between spiritual development and learning.

The impact on the pupils was profound. Many of them had come to San Benito from other schools and were able to appreciate the difference and understand what was very exceptional in San Benito and that it was all for their benefit. One of them remembers that she had been settled in her previous school. She did not like it much but she was settled and she had friends, when suddenly her parents moved her to this new school San Benito. She resented this and reacted against the new environment, but she was soon won over completely by the atmosphere - the ethos - of this new school. Like many others she found that the secret worries and doubts of childhood were no longer swept aside by institutional needs and the inexorable march of the curriculum. There was a warmth and personal affirmation which overcame fear.

The children who came into it from other schools discovered through *lectio* with the tutors that God is not remote and inaccessible but that he is as close as the word of scripture and that he loves them. This truth came alive to them also through the *acogida* of the tutors who were near enough to them in age to understand, to share and to give the support and guidance they most needed. Thus they discovered in their vulnerable years of growth an attractive vision of values and purpose in life to which they could relate through the encouragement of the tutors who were young enough for them to identify with the example they gave.

The Formation of the Oblates in relation to the Schools
In the laying of these foundations what was achieved was at a cost to the young tutors themselves. Although they were members of the Movement the young men and women who became the first tutors were not yet committed as Oblates. They were still searching and were not yet finally established in this unusual vocation. They could not yet see where exactly they were going or what would happen to their lives. They might, for all one could tell at that time, end up as priests or monks or nuns. They might become farmers, engineers or anything. For the moment it was enough to learn how to live their baptism to the full in lay life - in any lay life. It was in part their own need, not only that of their pupils, that they were concerned with in their teaching. There was an

137

immediacy, therefore, about their attempts to meet the spiritual needs of their pupils. The pupils were receiving *acompañamiento*[5] from those who were, indeed, strong in their faith and trust in God but still in need of some answers themselves, still finding their way. The pupils often joined forces with tutors in a common search, which made it all the more real.

Some of these young people had joined the Movement for reasons unconnected with caring for the young and no one had asked them if they wanted to be teachers or tutors. However they found that working in the Movement had come to mean working with children and families in San Benito and San Lorenzo. They accepted this in the spirit of Benedictine obedience, as an inner call to the imitation of Christ in seeking God and bringing others to him. Their obedience was strengthened by the inner Christ-centered imperative of giving to others what they had received themselves. The educational character of the Movement within the Benedictine spirit was forged in this way.

It was in this pragmatic way also that they learnt to use the text of the Rule of St Benedict and found in it powerful guidelines for the development of their own lives within the Movement and for their guidance of the pupils for whom they were responsible. One of those who later became an Oblate remembers:

> What really made us turn to the Rule itself to find the principles on which we could organize the various aspects of the life of the school was that there was no monastic community behind us to give us a claim to be called 'Benedictine'. And so we had to discover in the Rule and make explicit the characteristics of a Benedictine education. As we did that, we began to discover that the school became not only the work of a community but rather as a community in itself. As such it was a community which sought to serve God and for that reason the Rule could be applied to the various departments and activities of the school in a way that respected the particular character of each. That is how we set about reading the Rule and comparing with it as honestly as we could the whole of our scholastic life. And so we discovered gradually how the Rule responds to each one of the questions that cropped up day by day. [6]

It was thus that the actual text of the Rule gradually assumed a primary role in the formation of the Oblates and also in the moral and religious education of their pupils. It was all done, of course, with the knowledge and strong encouragement of José Manuel himself. It all led to the production some year's later of the Movement's own pocket edition of the Rule with index and cross-reference. The first edition came out in 1995. The Rule itself really began to assume a primary role in the schools and among the Oblates towards the end of the eighties and in the early nineties.

Manuel José Echenique as General Secretary of the Movement worked closely with José Manuel. He reflects on the personal influence of José Manuel during these early years in San Benito:

It is important to reflect on the role of José Manuel at this stage. He was building the school on the foundations of the Movement and the Movement was basically comprised of young people, who were not old enough to take on much formal directorial responsibility. One can see, therefore, that on the one hand there was a huge pressure on him at the administrative level. In spite of that what is most impressive is that he was able always to put personal contact first, talking with people in a spirit of *acompañamiento* and *acogida*. He devoted hours and hours of time to talking with people some of whom are now not even members of the Movement any more. It is also surprising and impressive that he was able to inspire great confidence in the parents who committed their children to his care.[7] He was able to transmit to them that this was an educational project which really was getting somewhere. His role at this stage was interesting in that respect. On the one hand you can see that he must have experienced loneliness at this time but also he had very great personal faith. He was building a school on friendships and searching for God but he did not have a clearly defined professional project for achieving this. He was creating it as he went along.

For example one can look at the emerging relationship with Ampleforth at this stage. It was a relationship which was only beginning. José Manuel was going there every year himself but without really knowing quite why he was going. The young followers he was working with were even less clear about it. Gringos were coming from England and people were asking why they were coming and what they were here for. It is arguable that on one level having English people working directly in the school could be perceived as lending a certain prestige to San Benito - more so then than now - but what else besides that did it mean? It is easy to look back now and see that all these initiatives of José Manuel have in the end led to positive achievements, but at that time the people he was working with him had no understanding of some of his schemes and priorities. He himself was intuitive. He was largely living by faith and intuition, which is an unusual starting point for such a large and complicated project.[8]

San Benito was growing year by year. The buildings are well designed with variations of shape and angles so that they avoid the threatening effect of a massive facade. The main entrance leads into a spacious open area or courtyard - useful for activities and meetings - and behind that further up the hill is another range of buildings containing the refectory and kitchen. This is raised on pillars so as to leave a covered open space to be used for activities during rainy weather. Other buildings continue the line east and west and within each section there are other open courtyards of varying sizes and on changing levels. At the far end on the east side are buildings on a smaller scale for the kindergarten. Although they are all in one style each section has its own individuality. Variations in the angles and settings help to avoid some of the worst aspects of institutional design. Although the building is for a large school of 1600 pupils the design helps to preserve the Movement's belief in the significance of the individual.

As the building progressed there was each year a new form of boys and a new form of girls and the oldest pupils, who were the foundation members, moved into the new accommodation they had seen taking shape the year before. One of the Oblates was a foundation member of the school and remembers that time:

There was building going on there all the time. There were new houses going up around and we were playing with the building site materials and the builders' helmets; it was part of life. We felt that the school was ours - like our house. It was very much a sense of beginning something new and the school was being founded and built around us so that we were part of a new project.[9]

Their needs were changing also and new pastoral initiatives were called for. For instance, when these first pupils reached the ages of about 13/14 it became apparent that *tutorías* taken by the young tutors were not as effective as when they were younger. Changes were then made to meet the needs of greater independence and responsibility in these teenagers. Instead of the *tutorías* they began to form the first groups or communities for *lectio* drawn from the pupils of San Benito themselves. At a later stage from 2001 onwards there was a yearly combined retreat for all of this age from the three Manquehue schools. The retreat focused on this big new step of forming their own shared *lectio* groups. At the end they were invited to volunteer to form the new communities. They were for teenagers but on exactly the same pattern as the already established communities for adult members of the Movement. It took courage and insight to start this adult treatment of young people within the ambience of school.

The vital point about this change was that, after several years of *tutorías* led by someone older, they were now themselves forming their own communities for shared *lectio* with their own contemporaries. They were being invited to respond to the challenge of facing their own faith in a more mature way through *lectio* together in their new communities. They were helped both by friendship and loyalty to each other with the security of following in the now established way of their elders. It was a positive step towards spiritual adulthood in which they began to see as their own responsibility the growth of their deepest convictions about their lives and where they were going. They learnt also in their communities how to join with others in finding their way in the confusion of life through reading and listening and prayer together. The retreat in which all this was made clear to them offered them a new beginning in which they began to recognize their own responsibility for spiritual progress.

At the same time as the decision for communities came another critical step. Once they were settled in their communities for *lectio* they were invited to learn how to give a helping hand in faith development to their juniors in the school by taking them for *tutorías*. That was how the older pupils began to recognize their responsibility for the younger in San Benito. They were taught that it was a spiritual relationship rather than a school-based duty. Of course they were helped and guided by the tutors and as time went on quite specific guidelines were developed to direct and co-ordinate the work and to provide sympathetic adult supervision.

Once the students had opted for this service they never looked back because they had made the transition to Christ-centered responsibility towards their younger brothers and sisters. Helping others who were younger in their religious perception and commitment became one of the characteristics of the young in San Benito. They found their own way better by helping those younger to find theirs. The whole process became a lesson about how to receive in giving and how to give in receiving. It was based on Christ's own words "it is a more blessed thing to give rather than to receive."[10]

The pattern for these older pupils is the same today in all the schools. Their communities meet outside the normal curriculum and timetable. There is no obligation to join, but the opportunity and invitation are given with careful explanation and preparation. A high percentage of a class normally opts to join a community; in 2004 an overall average of 72% in the three schools opted to join a community of the Movement for shared *lectio*. When the scheme was launched José Manuel was himself involved in the new venture, especially with the *lectio* of the first group, although he was not himself in charge. From now on this pattern of *tutorías* for the youngest pupils and *lectio* communities for the older students with responsibility for *tutorías* lower down the school was firmly established.

Working with Colegio San Lorenzo

At this time also, when the first communities were growing in San Benito another big step of great importance for the Movement was taken. The older pupils of San Benito began to work at *tutorías* in San Lorenzo.[11] This called for both courage and generosity. When the San Benito pupils first went down to San Lorenzo in Conchali they were entering a world which was new to them. In the early days of San Benito and San Lorenzo the well-to-do and poor areas of the city were more sharply divided than they are now with little contact between them. The children of San Benito in their family life would have been kept strictly apart from the poor in such areas as Conchali. Now in entering this world they were invited by the Manquehue Oblates, and under their guidance, to take a real interest in the lives and hopes and fears of the young of San Lorenzo and to accept a degree of spiritual/catechetical responsibility which was unusual at that age. It was another big step in which they learnt that in the world of spirituality and evangelization there is no difference between the rich and the poor.

One of the first pupils from San Benito to start *tutorías* in what was to her a new world of San Lorenzo loved it and derived so much from it herself that, when she left school for university four years later, the loss of these visits was one of her greatest regrets.

For the pupils at San Benito this new development naturally led to new ways of thinking about the social divide between rich and poor. Those who went to San Lorenzo to give *tutorías* acquired a high profile and were seen to be doing something which was extra and important. A new relationship began to develop between the two schools. Two worlds began to come together and find ways of relating to each other. A new understanding grew up. In due course other things came from this, like sharing retreats, missions and work projects[12] in the holidays, which was to the enormous benefit of both schools. These community projects were well established as a vital part of the education of the young in both schools. When taking part in such projects students all live together for a period, work together and pray together. That was an essential part of the experience from the first and through such experiences deeper understanding and friendships were formed.

Of course, what was happening was quickly noticed by the parents and there were understandable anxieties both at San Lorenzo and at San Benito. The poorer parents were as anxious that their children would not be corrupted by contact with the rich as the rich ones were about their children being exposed to the world of the *campamentos*. Ways through these difficulties were possible and were actually found because the overall inspiration of both schools was the Manquehue Movement itself

143

with its lay Benedictine vision. In the light of this vision the wealth or poverty of pupils and parents was irrelevant to the main concern of the Movement, which was the evangelization of all who came within their influence. If the word of Christ in the gospel could be brought to the center and kept there, then economic and cultural problems would become more manageable.

Suddenly it became clear that both schools were unique, and that made them able to tackle and face up to many problems experienced by families and children who were growing up in a divided world. They were problems which were too often ignored in South America. Many parents of San Benito took notice and asked questions. For instance some of the parents began to assume that San Benito was contributing from its fee revenue to the running of San Lorenzo. They protested about this. It had not been their intention, in sending their children to San Benito, to pay fees which, they suspected, were geared to the support of San Lorenzo also. They were immediately reassured and told that there was no such financial link. The two schools were on the same foundation but operated independently with separate funding. San Lorenzo did not benefit from the fees the parents paid for their children at San Benito. Whereupon other parents complained that this was wrong and strongly asserted that San Benito ought to support San Lorenzo, which was a wonderful testimony to this lay Movement's evangelization of the parents. This led to a reconsideration of the whole question of the relationship between the two schools. The financial independence of each school was reaffirmed. Nevertheless in response to the parents who wanted to help San Lorenzo a new foundation was set up in Chile which was called the Friends of San Lorenzo dedicated to raising the funds that were needed to run San Lorenzo.[13] This foundation gave everyone the opportunity to give help where it was needed, but to give it freely.

During this period José Manuel was the driving force and inspiration behind the building up of the Movement and the two schools, San Benito and San Lorenzo. His main support was the group of young people who had followed him into this work for Christ and his Church. They gave him support, but they also depended on him for spiritual formation and guidance. He was carrying a formidable responsibility in finding ways of realizing his lay Benedictine vision. He shouldered this responsibility at a time when in his personal life he had great anxieties about the future and health of his own family. He might have been forgiven for taking time off from worries about the schools and the future of the Movement.

In some ways the key to his achievement was that, in spite of the administrative burden, he succeeded in putting personal contact with the young for whom he was responsible before everything else. Day after day he made himself available to others, as though they alone mattered to him. He lived to the full the ideals he preached to his young followers through *acompañamiento* and *acogida*. He devoted hours of his time to listening and talking to people - not just to the key figures in the Movement but to many who were not even members of the Movement, but were to him children of God and brothers of Christ. He inspired confidence in this way not least among parents, who may have come to him expecting formal educational expertise. What they found instead was a layman who was building a school for their children in which friendship, mutual affirmation in Christ and the sincere and open search for God through his word established a genuine spiritual dimension in their education for lay life. He was able to inspire them with the conviction that here was an educational project that was meeting those inner spiritual needs of the young in their ordinary lay life which are denied or neglected in secular education with disastrous results. It was a vision for their children which they learnt to value by the results.

Administration of San Benito

In the early days José Manuel worked in San Benito as Founder and Headmaster. He was ably assisted by Manuel José Echenique as his deputy in many respects, who also became Secretary General of the Movement and accompanied him on his yearly visits to Ampleforth Abbey in Yorkshire. Manuel José remembers that he did not really at the time understand the purpose of these visits to a monastic Abbey in a country so remote from Chile both physically and in its culture. In those years he did not even speak English but accompanied José Manuel in a spirit of obedience and to give him support. In spite of this, when he actually found himself at Ampleforth his perception changed. This happened through a strong spiritual experience he had in the Abbey Church. After that he was able to share and support José Manuel's perception of the importance of this relationship with the Abbey and community. This was important in the development of the mutual understanding with Ampleforth which was the background of the gringos' experience in Santiago.

There was no lack of requests from among the English boys at Ampleforth. They stayed usually for about six months, although some asked to be allowed to stay longer. The happy consequence of this generous investment of time and effort was the great spiritual benefit it brought to the gringos. Ampleforth at that time was a school for boys only, but there were also some girls from England who joined the gringos between 1986 and 1996. Manuel José and the Oblates carried the burden of arrangements for their stay in Chile. In due course Manuel José Echenique became vice-rector, or Assistant Headmaster of San Benito, until in 1999 he became Chairman of a new body called Dirección Educational Manquehue, the purpose of which is to coordinate the educational practice of all the Manquehue schools and make sure that the Benedictine vision of the Movement is kept alive in them. DEM, as it came to be known, held regular meetings of the Heads of the three schools so as to unify their educational work. Above all it carried forward and encouraged ways of bringing the reality of Saint Benedict's Rule into all the Movement's work for the young. This work of DEM not only strengthened the bonds between the three schools. Its work was influential in the following year in establishing the yearly Cunaco meetings.[14] There were further changes later in the administration of San Benito with the introduction of Deans in the various works of the Movement. Manuel José Echenique later became Dean of San Benito and Mario Canales Headmaster.

This account has concentrated so far on the aspects of education which were special to the Movement and were seen by many to be the chief attraction of the school. There were other aspects worthy of note like the retreats and expeditions for service of those in need and the work of the scouts. These are very important and will be dealt with more fully in chapter 13. There was also a full range of sports. In the early years space for games was limited and the boys and girls had to be taken by bus to other playing fields. There was a wonderful development, however, in the year 2000 through the purchase of land opposite the school which provided space for a fine running track and football field and gymnasium. This really completed the basic facilities for the school.

Parents & academic standards

It was to be expected in a lay Movement that from the first there was great concern about the parents and a desire to involve them in the lives of their children at school and especially in their catechesis. The Movement looked upon the parents as being involved intimately in the mission of the school to their children. The idea that parents should stand aside and leave education to the professionals was not accepted. The Oblates began by experimenting tentatively with *lectio* groups for husbands and wives together. Experience led them later to re-organize in separate groups for men and women. This was not wholly welcome and so the project was put on ice for a time to give space for reflection and discussion.

The second phase started in the most natural way because it was inspired initially by some of the young children themselves. Parents - especially mothers - tend to hear of everything from the child's perspective that goes on in school. Some parents were struck by the strong religious conviction and solid formation their children were receiving. They wanted to know more. One mother, for instance, was fascinated to see her eldest son getting more and more involved in the spiritual side of the school. She decided that she ought to find out from the inside what was the secret of this good influence the school was having on her son. So she got involved and joined one of the communities for *lectio*. After that she never turned back from her own commitment to the Movement and in due course became one of the married Oblates and a very committed supporter of the Movement. This sort of development, which led many parents into the adult communities of the Movement, involved mothers to start with rather than fathers, but fathers also were drawn into this new world.

There is no doubt that this introduction of regular, stable community prayer founded on the Word of God and the Divine Office became increasingly effective among adults - parents and grandparents. It may be seen as the second major phase of the educational outreach of the Manquehue Movement. This time it was into the world of adult

147

religious education. One of the Oblates is in charge of the organization of these adult communities. The life of these communities has a momentum of its own within the apostolate of the Manquehue Movement. They are no longer dependent on the schools. They are well established among University students and in the world of work. This outreach of the Movement is always growing. In 2004 there were 135 groups with 1199 members.

San Benito was founded and developed on strong spiritual lines. That did not mean that academic standards were neglected. In Chile, as in the United States or England, a school which cannot compete academically will not survive. The parents who are sensitive to spiritual and moral standards will not pay the price of accepting inferior academic achievement. Fortunately San Benito has been consistently successful in holding its own academically. However strong the Christian vision of the school it would not survive if its academic standards collapsed. There have been examples in Santiago of the effect of rising and falling academic standards. Catholic schools have traditionally been among the best academically. San Benito, therefore, had a strong tradition to follow while it brought its own special charism of strongly committed lay Catholic spirituality which is rooted in the Movement. Evidence of its success can be found in former pupils who are now successful in Law and Medicine and Commerce in Santiago. This has been achieved without accepting some of the more stringent practices of selective schools in rejecting pupils on purely academic grounds. The family dimension is always important. This has not prevented the school from maintaining the good academic standards which parents looks for.

They are reluctant to part company with a child who falls behind in work for whatever reason and they make special efforts for disabled children who are capable of facing the ordinary curriculum. They tend to go further than other schools in trying to find a way through when faced by individual learning difficulties, whether of character or ability. This is done in the belief that it is best to keep working with the child to encourage the motivation that can overcome many such problems. They believe that the pursuit of high academic standards does not contradict the Benedictine inspiration of San Benito and should be pursued but not at the expense of other considerations which touch on the human, spiritual and family development of a child. The high standards themselves should be pursued for the right, generous reasons and not for the wrong selfish ones. In this way everything can be brought into the balanced Benedictine ambience of the whole enterprise.

Those with experience in the education of teenagers know well that motivation or lack of it is often the most critical factor in the progress of a boy or girl at school and university. To some it comes easily at first and then unaccountably falls off. Some are slow to start with or simply uninterested. Then something happens and they change almost overnight and become achievers beyond all expectation. There are a thousand different patterns in the growth and death of motivation among the young, but one thing is certain: its importance cannot be exaggerated. The point to be made here is that the holistic approach of the Movement in which the inner spiritual life of the pupil is of great importance is a wonderful way of bringing the young through the inevitable crises of motivation. At the center of what the Movement does for them is the word of God in *lectio divina*. This together with the personal affirmation of *acogida,* of friendship, of spiritual companionship which find expression at every stage through *tutorías* and the Movement communities, retreats, missions, work and its very special version of scouting - all taken together form the unique contribution of the Movement's educational work to this very fundamental problem in the education of the young.

Although many cases could be quoted in which individuals have been rescued by the Movement from the terrible damage of inner emptiness, it is more difficult to show how an even greater number have been saved from it by prevention. The sheer happiness and sense of purpose and confidence which is induced by the gospel-based relationships with God and each other is the protection from negativity which the Movement education offers to all its pupils. It is often the means of saving them even from the threat of negativity and despair. It is the secret and source of their motivation in facing life. It is the greatest gift of the Manquehue Movement not only to the young in their schools but to all the adults also in their small communities for *lectio*, meditation, companionship and mutual support in the spiritual crises of life. It has brought the light of new life to many fathers and mothers and a new escape also from the isolation and depression of old age to many grandparents of the children in their schools.

However, it is also important to recognize the failures and the mistakes. They occur in San Benito as much as any other school. . In fact, José Manuel is well known for admitting in public the mistakes that might have been made. In graduation ceremonies for instance in front of the whole school and all the parents, he was often seen asking forgiveness for errors and any harm the top year feel has been caused during their time as students. There are many people who love their time at San Benito. And there are others who are indifferent. Of course this must be true because what the Movement offers them is the gospel invitation; and the gospel invitation must be free at every stage. Evangelizing at this age cannot ever be concerned with reaping harvests but only with sowing seeds.[15] The reaping - the conversions - may come much later or not at all. All that is in the hands of God for each one of us. The role of Christian education is to do the sowing well and nurture whatever growth appears. That is what the Movement is committed to.

The Documents of the Movement

As we have seen the three key areas of administration, academic structure and pastoral development in the school were in the early stages run in parallel and treated as being distinct in themselves. All three were developed successfully during the creative stages of a growing school, and those concerned worked in with each other satisfactorily. Then in 1991-2 Manuel José Echenique took over the actual running of the school as Associate Headmaster. In 2001 he became Headmaster. His aim was to integrate the whole enterprise so that the way things were done in all three areas would flow from the Benedictine character of the school. This was the deliberate aim - to make the gospel-based Rule of St Benedict determine the whole ethos of the school. It was not good enough to leave that simply to the *tutorías* and let the other two areas go ahead on their own. Unity and cohesion would be lost in that way and there would be danger of disorderly experimentation in different ways and areas. As usual José Manuel saw it in spiritual terms with the eyes of St Benedict, who insisted on the physical unity of his monastery at Monte Cassino for spiritual reasons:

The monastery itself should be constructed so as to include within its bounds all the facilities which will be needed, that is, water, a mill, a garden and workshops for various crafts. Then there will be no need for monks and nuns to wander outside, which is far from good for their monastic development.[16]

This meant for him that a Benedictine education must be holistic. The whole of school life must be inspired by the Rule. So Manuel José took in hand the task of drawing together all the threads which had gradually developed during the growth of the schools and of the Movement itself. His aim was to make sure that the whole undertaking of San Benito in all its aspects was so thoroughly Benedictine in inspiration that no one could change it and it would be impossible to go back. This integrating process was the inspiration of his period in charge. He confesses that at the time when he started he had little idea of what such a challenge would mean. It involved taking the Rule along with other Oblates and reading and re-reading it in order to discover what St. Benedict was trying to say and how his wisdom could be applied to every aspect of school life. It was a community effort.

However during this period of consolidation he had an essential tool which was not available in the first years of the school. This was the codification of what the Movement stood for in its lay, Benedictine, ecclesial mission.

José Manuel had been working ceaselessly to articulate in writing the developing vision by which they were living and working. The result was a substantial booklet named *Minima Regla*[17]. It went through many stages of development but at last even José Manuel was satisfied and it was printed principally for the Oblates of the Movement to guide their lives and for members who are aspiring to become Oblates. Following in the guidelines of St Benedict's Rule it expresses for today how lay men and women, both single and married, can live their lives under promises of fidelity and perseverance in charity with each other as they pursue the call of their baptism to evangelization and the growth of the alternative way of life within Christ's Kingdom to which he called all mankind in the gospel.[18]

Now this Little Rule for Oblates of the Movement is in place and always available with its clear and uncompromising expression of the Benedictine genius for laity living and working in the world and with its truly innovative expression of what is meant by an 'extended Benedictine lay community'. It was followed by the publication of *El Camino Manquehino* - The Manquehue Path - a less formal and partly historical exposition of the Movement's visionary application of the gospel to modern lay Catholic life. All the early years were a preparation for these two documents of codification which have done so much, built as they are on the Scriptures and on St Benedict's Rule, to bring the Movement and its various works to maturity. The *Camino* is an invaluable help for parents, teachers, students in University life and for adults engaged in the world of work or eager to develop spiritually in retirement. These two documents have been successful in opening up doors in many directions.

These publications and the work of integration under Manuel José were invaluable aids in the period of development, but in San Benito itself, as Manuel José pointed out, there is one thing which has been the same throughout. It has had great influence on the establishment of the spirit of San Benito and has been vital to its continuing success among the young. It is, the presence of committed and enthusiastic young people working at ground level with the students and always closely in touch with them. The young who started the school are now of a more mature age and hold more responsible positions or have left and found their vocations elsewhere, but there are new ones always coming on who are down on the patio at break times and after school talking with the pupils and bringing to them in terms they can understand the wisdom of the gospel and of St Benedict. This is the work of grass-roots evangelization. These young teachers work still today in the same spirit that went to shape the beginnings of San Benito so many years ago. It will be important for the future never to lose sight of that welcoming and understanding contact with the young adults, which José Manuel perceived and encouraged from the beginning. It has much to do with the special identity of San Benito and will continue to be vital for its future.

CR

Notes for Chapter 8

[1] Mgr Cristian Precht was Vicar General to the Cardinal at that time and a few years later he wrote to Fr Dominic Milroy at Ampleforth: 'In the Movement there is a quality of spiritual life which is surprising and gratifying. This is so above all because this spirituality has been built up by laity. One would have to be blind not to be able to see the action of the Holy Spirit in these adults and young people - both in the way they live and in the works of service which they are undertaking.'

[2] acogida is a Spanish word which means 'welcome', but it is stronger than the English word and in the Movement from an early stage it became a key word to express not only welcome but also the generous affirmation of and commitment to another person in charity.

[3] See St Paul: Gal. 3,28 - There is neither Jew nor Greek, there is neither slave nor free, there is neither male nor female, for you are all one in Christ Jesus. & Rom. 12,4 ff

[4] Manuel José Echenique interview

[5] The word means 'companionship'. In the Movement 'spiritual companionship' was preferred to spiritual 'guidance' or 'direction' to express the way of learning gospel truth.

[6] Interview with Cecilia Bernales

[7] Looking back on the early days he once commented that could never understand why parents had been prepared to entrust their children to him in his youth and inexperience.

[8] Interview with Manuel José Echenique

[9] Interview with Nicolas Meneguello

[10] Acts 20, 35

[11] for San Lorenzo school see chapters 9 & 10

[12] 'Missiones y trabajo' are explained later in this chapter.

[13] In England also a fund-raising group was set up later by Mrs Anna Mayer, the mother of one of the gringos who had spent nine months in Santiago working in the Movement. The English foundation is also called 'The Friends of San Lorenzo' but it is separate and independent.

[14] The Cunaco meetings (named after the House in Chile where the first meeting took place) are held yearly by José Manuel and some of the Oblates, to which representatives from some other Benedictine schools are invited. Its meetings are always concerned with the development of education in conformity with the gospel and Saint Benedict's Rule.

[15] see Luke 8, 4-15

[16] St Benedict's Rule Chapter 66

[17] see Appendix 3

[18] see Mt. 5 & Lk 6. 17-49 & other texts

Chapter 9 ~ The Second School
Colegio San Lorenzo Part 1

The Movement & deprivation material & spiritual

The Movement had first taken shape among the children of the affluent who were able to pay the fees of an independent school. However, since the Movement was firmly based on the gospel it was to be expected, especially among South America Catholics, that even at the earliest stages José Manuel's young followers would look outwards to the evangelization also of the poor and deprived. Real deprivation in Santiago at that time, when the country was still poor and the economy fragile, was close at hand. It was close at hand in the same city, but in separate enclaves. That meant that, although they did not have far to go to reach the poor, that short journey brought them to a world that was utterly different from their own. It was a different world but the work they did there was in its essence the same.

In San Benito the Movement's commitment and work had followed the lines laid down by José Manuel while he was still in charge of the Pastoral Department in the Manquehue school. He described the three aspects of the work in this way:

First, "there are the communities for the celebration of the Word, which rely on a way of meditation taught by a Benedictine monk of Las Condes." That he described as the primary source of all the Movement, giving it a true Christian character derived from the Gospels.

Secondly, came the organization of groups for education and service. He gave a rich definition of the purpose of these groups. They were "to develop the many spiritual, intellectual, artistic and physical gifts of the members and to dedicate them to the service of others." The close relationship between the development of personal gifts and the service of others was vital.

155

Thirdly, came the actual services these groups undertook for the benefit of the community. To this he added a comment of great importance for the development of the Movement's work. The actual service or work undertaken by the groups "is always understood to be the fruit of the first two."[1]

That is to say that without *lectio* and the constant development of their spiritual and human gifts the work they undertook would be at best impoverished.

When we say that the most important part of the work of the Movement was evangelization, we must be careful to avoid the narrow interpretation of that word which is common today. It is normal to think and speak of evangelization as primarily a form of church recruitment. It is especially important to correct that misconception now when we come to the Movement's service of poor communities. For the members of the Movement, when they went to the poor it was just the same as when they went to the children of the rich. It was to bring them the gospel of Christ in all its richness with the full meaning of baptism and community life and common prayer and reliance on the word of God in scripture. It was all that, but it was also explicitly to welcome them into the shared friendship in Christ which had meant so much to the first young members of the Movement. That welcome was offered to them as equals. Every hint of patronising, every suggestion of superiority was excluded. The inspiration came from Christ's words in St John:

> I give you an new commandment: you must love one another just as I have loved you. It is by your love of one another that everyone will recognize you as my disciples.[2]

In his gospel Christ's call to love was universal, knowing no barriers of status or rank or race or condition. There is no change in that call today. For the young of the Manquehue Movement this truth has been the inspiration of all the work they have undertaken. It was the inspiration also of their earliest efforts to serve the poor. The needs of the poor seemed at first to be different, but beneath the surface there was an identity of spiritual need.

In the world of money and property and status from which these young people came it was easy to recognize how profound was the need among the rich and successful for the deeper spiritual vision which can be found only in the liberating love of Christ. It was not a problem unique to Chile. All over the affluent West the dangers of godless secularity were apparent in the alienation of many young people, the confusion of values, the escapism of addictions, the false gods of greed and ambition, the lack for so many of any ultimate purpose in life or meaning or vision or hope. Inevitably the dangers were there also in Catholic Chile. The young of the Movement were seeking to meet such negative influences by bringing the love of Christ to the children and families among whom they worked at San Benito. They were dealing there with a world they knew and understood, because they had experienced it.

When they faced the world of real poverty, into which so many were locked in South America, these young people were moving into a world which was for them still largely unknown. In South America the rich and poor lived close enough to each other, but they were still separated by an impenetrable divide of incomprehension, fear, hostility which easily breaks out into violence. The most obvious needs of the poor on the surface are different and apparently more immediate. They suffer from the need for the essentials of life – food and clothing, shelter and security, warmth and work, the care and education of their children, and the means to look after the sick and the elderly. That was the area of social work. It was urgent and obvious, but underneath it there were other needs which were not so different from the needs of the affluent.

At an early stage the Movement learnt that, if these spiritual needs of the poor were not met, the good effects of social work would remain superficial and could be undermined. There was urgent need among the poor for realistic personal affirmation and self-respect, for love and purpose and hope and vision and the deep stability which cannot come from anything but the fundamental spirituality of knowing and loving Jesus Christ. It is easy to say that the affluent and the poor are all one in Christ, but it was necessary for the poor to experience it if the words were to become real.

These were among the needs of the poor in Santiago on which the young work groups of the Movement began to focus in their early experience. They had something special to bring, because they based all their work explicitly and deliberately on the Word of God in scripture

157

and on communities for meditation and on welcome and friendship in Christ. They never neglected material needs, but they did not confine their attention to material needs. They set out to share with the poor, as brothers and sisters, the source from which their own lives had been changed by the word - *lectio divina,* the incomparable gift of *acogida* and the recognition that Christ lives in those who are in need, as he taught in the gospel.[3] These were the means they used to establish, if they could, the reality of a community through which they sought to cross the social boundaries and prejudices and assumptions that tend to make a supposedly Christian society radically un-Christian.

These warm relationships, which they had learnt from José Manuel through reliance on the word of scripture, accompanied and enriched their work for the material needs of the poor among whom they moved. They had very little financial resources. They were to a large extent weak and powerless and inexperienced themselves. The task was enormous. They were working part-time while studying at university. In their vulnerability they faced a frightening task, but they did so relying on their faith and hope. In this they were like David as he faced Goliath trusting in God alone.

Beginnings of work among the poor

There was a *campamento* of squalid shanties for the very poor near the Manquehue school and there they started working in a kindergarten which had been established for the children. The groups of young people spent time with them in play. There was nothing that lasted of this work, apart from the invaluable experience they gained, because the *campamento* was moved by the government and the land used for housing.

The group that had started in this way stayed together when they left the Manquehue school in 1979 to begin their university careers. They looked for other work to do - something to bring some sort of help for these poor families in their immediate needs and with that help the light and warmth and vision of the gospel. They went further afield and found work in a poor district of Las Condes which was not so deprived as the first *campamento*. This went on for two years. They worked there in preparing children for confirmation in association with the local parish. By the time the children were confirmed the group had decided to move more directly into the center of the problem. They wanted to face up to the most radical needs of the poor who were still trapped in their own environment of destitution - to move right into the areas where the corrosive effects of inescapable poverty were greatest. From their experience so far they realized now how much they had to learn and how absolute must be their dedication and clear their priorities, if they were to succeed. Their generosity was great but their involvement was only partial because they were students still and could do this work only at weekends and in other periods of spare time from their studies at University. It was not enough but it was a start.

After those first two attempts had come to nothing, they moved to a different area where some other women, unconnected with the Movement had been trying to work with the families. The young university members of the Movement took over from these women and started work on the new site called *Campamento Guanaco* in the district known as Conchali. This was the beginning of the venture which developed so well that in the end it led to the founding of the Movement's second school for the poor which they called Colegio San Lorenzo.

The groups began by helping in the parish with some of the children. They must have been developing a real expertise, because the size of the group of children grew steadily. Soon there were some of the mothers whose confidence they won through the children. They began to work with them also and then there were some young people whom they attracted.

Mario Canales was working with this group of young and José Antonio Navarro was helping the group of women to find ways by which they could earn for themselves. They started knitting and making things to sell in Santiago so as to bring in a bit of money for their families. With them also was Francisco Loeser, son of the bursar of the Manquehue School. He had a gift for dealing with young people and in giving *tutorías* to children. There were others taking part and they all went to Conchali faithfully early every Sunday morning by bus. That was how they found their feet in this work of service to poor families. They began to make headway and were gradually gaining the confidence of the families so as to build up a real relationship with them.

Learning in Conchali

Conchali is in an area north of the city center of Santiago but at that time quite separate from it. A range of the Andes foothills (which in England would be called mountains) stretch out to the West dividing the plain in that region. They include the Manquehue mountain with San Benito at its feet. The city center lies inside that range and to the south of it, while Conchali, and far beyond it the airport, are to the north. Today there is a road not far from San Benito which crosses the range through a pass in the hills and goes on past Conchali to the airport. It has brought the whole area more closely into contact with Santiago. In those early days the road did not yet exist and Concahali was isolated - an impoverished world apart. The young members of the Movement had to go down to the city center and get a bus round the mountain to approach Conchali. It really was a journey into another world.

When the Movement started working there in the early eighties it was all very poor and desolate in stark contrast to the modern city on the other side of the hills. There was very little communication between the two worlds at that time. Conchali and the people who lived there were in a forgotten land. They were conveniently shut out by a mountain over which there was as yet no road. The *campamento* itself was served by dirt roads straggling between the shanty houses. The dirt reverted to mud when it rained.

When they first arrived there were no public services of any kind. Some time after they had started work there, an effort had been made with minimal street lighting and there was main water to a small brick structure, constructed by the government on the site of some of the houses. This was the peak of housing development for the poor at the time. Apart from that the houses consisted of one low storey cobbled into a wretched living space from random boarding and battered sheets of corrugated iron. They were ugly and squalid to look at. They were crowded sadly together in a disorderly pattern. But the people that lived there were not downtrodden. They had a quiet dignity and a pride which made the most of the little they had. Deep humanity struggled heroically to survive the deprivation of resources, of basic human needs and status.

The women had family instincts and generous care for their children, however little power they had to do much for them in material terms. It was the women's genuine concern for their children that originally inspired those who had started working among them to dream of San Lorenzo as a school and not only a school but also a center for the social and spiritual needs of the families they worked with. But that idea and any possibility of its realisation was a long way off when they first arrived in Conchali.

Conchali and the whole area around it have changed a lot since those early days. The growth of Chilean economy has had an effect on the lives of these poor people in some ways that are good and in some ways that are bad. There is more employment in a substantial industrial development which has grown along the new road over the hills from Santiago on the way to the airport. There are more cars about and more pretentious shops, symbols of a culture that is alien but tempting. There are fewer shanties. Some three or four storey blocks of apartments have appeared together with proper roads and better facilities all round. In some vital ways these apartment blocks improve the lot of the poor, but they bring with them inevitably the negative tendencies which are so familiar in 'high rise' living developments all over the world. Marketing and advertising have invaded the area. The dark clouds of the drug culture and the negative sides of teenage culture are there, threatening the integrity and destroying the values of the young and sometimes their lives also. The seductions of the consumer society find a foothold even among the poor. But besides these changes, thanks to the selfless work of the Movement, there is also Colegio San Lorenzo, which is dedicated to the spiritual service of the church and the people of this whole area. It stands out still, but in a different way and against different odds, as the symbol of an alternative lifestyle - alternative to hedonistic secularism because it is founded on the rock that is Christ.

But to see how this came about we must go back to the beginning. In the early days of weekend work - it was in 1983 - the young men and women of the Movement who worked in Conchali organized a Christmas party for the children. Christmas comes at midsummer in Chile, which made the *campamento* more tolerable. The party was a great success.

Everyone was having a good time, but Mario Canales remembers a moment of truth in the midst of all the jollity:

> There was an old man there. I can remember well his face and eyes. He said to me that this is a beautiful party. I said yes it is. Then he said: 'but it will end as it always does' and I asked him what he meant. He replied that many people come to the *campamento* in their cars to play with poor children. They give them candies and they have a fantastic day. But then the winter will come and there will be rain and the streets will turn into mud so that you will get mud on your shoes. And then you will disappear for evermore.

That was the moment in the party that Mario remembered. He thought again and again of what that old man had said to him in the midst of the party:

> He was a man, but for me he was an angel of God as well, and he brought a message for us all. He left a very deep impression. He made us understand that we had no right to come there to satisfy our need to help. We must come to serve people in reality - to serve *their* needs, not *ours*. When we first went there we did not know what we were going to face in that shanty-town. We were like children, and that man taught us that what we were faced with was a really serious challenge which could not be satisfied with a few children's parties.

The lesson they took home from that Christmas party was that if they were to work in Conchali it must be with a real commitment of the whole Movement to the people there. They must be ready to face any difficulties that might arise without knowing beforehand how the whole venture would develop. In fact, when they reflected and talked about it, they began to see the new dimension of their call in terms of Benedictine stability. They must go there and stay there with the people and stay with them in every aspect of their lives. They had begun this work of service and evangelization while still at school, but now they were facing all the harshness of the adult world and had to find a way that would go far beyond the passing glitter of Christmas parties. Their efforts had been unequal either to their original vision or to the needs of the people in Conchali. In the face of such profound need the best they had been

162

able to give appeared to be no better than dabbling in the problems. They must find some way to commit their lives, to share the hardships of these people and accompany them in their search for a new way in life.

The groups started more serious work. The focus turned from what they could do for the people to what they could enable the people to do for themselves. It was an important step to the evangelization of service, following the Christ who said 'I am among you as one who serves'.[4] They worked with children to help in their upbringing. They organized more effectively the groups of women to work at knitting and sewing and provided them regularly with materials. Then they found ways by which the products of their work could be sold. This was a small but vital step for these poor people towards independence, self-respect and self-reliance.

That was the first work-project and it prospered. It strengthened their perception that it was not enough to give paternalistically like Father Christmas. They should seek to establish among the poor families themselves the means of affirming their own sense of achievement and the self-respect that went with it. They started a small health center with a young woman medical student who was still studying at university. She gave her weekends to teach the mothers how to care for their own health and their children's. The Movement tried hard to belong - to find a role for themselves within the community they had come to love. Gradually they made headway - at first with the women and children and the young. It was not quite so easy with the fathers of the children. They were often absent and had their own agenda outside the family. They were more difficult to win over. Nevertheless, some of the men also slowly began to appreciate what was happening and to take an interest.

From the first this group of the Movement brought with them to Conchali the special weapon of *lectio divina* of the word of God in scripture, which they had made their own. They began, not by distributing largesse, but by sharing the word of scripture with them in meditation groups. It struck at a deeper level than any social work they could do. They were learning how to pass on the light of the word of God, which had transformed their own lives, to those for whom they now worked. Among the families they had come to know they formed

163

small communities for *lectio* of the word of God in scripture. Thus they introduced them to the Bible and to prayer. It was a powerful instrument which gave strength and stability to the other work they were doing. It also brought - as only the word of scripture can - a perspective which came from beyond the harsh, immediate limitations of the life in the *campamento* but which was deeply relevant to it. It gave their new work its unique and lasting character. It was unique and lasting because in giving themselves they gave also Christ himself through his word.

For the poor, as for the rich, the Manquehue vision was the gospel vision. One of its greatest gifts, which now formed a strong bond between the young members of the Movement and the poor of Conchali, was the truth that the word of scripture which they brought was the word of life equally for themselves and for the poor they served. There are not two gospels, one for the affluent and one for the poor. There is only one. The gospel began to bind these young student members of the Movement to the people and the people to them with the unique power that comes from Christ himself. They had made at last a true beginning, but it was only a beginning.

Their work was still only weekend work. That degree of commitment was too tenuous for the needs to which they were called to respond. How tenuous and inadequate it was came starkly home to them one Sunday when they learnt that a baby had been killed by a truck in the shanty town during that same week. It had happened on the previous Monday, but they had not known anything about it and had gone on with their own lives in bland ignorance for a whole week. The families they were coming to know and love in Conchali had grieved and mourned all week for the child. The child had been buried and life had gone on leaving behind an aching gap in the life of one family, but the young members of the Movement knew nothing about it.

Then at the weekend they learnt about the week-old tragedy. It had taken all that time during which they, who thought they were showing their love and support, had been unaware and uninvolved and unable to help in the actual shock of the cruel loss of a child and in the grief of the family. For them it had been just as though it had not happened! They began to see that this free-time link was all very well, but it was too weak and too limited in its scope. They were accepted by now and they understood better what was needed, but they were still only on the edge of these peoples' lives. Stability was at issue again – the commitment of real stability in their relationships with the families. It was another turning point which brought into focus many questions hanging in the air about the future - questions which were waiting for an answer. Was the Movement's involvement in Conchali to be a passing episode of no lasting importance, or was it to go further than that? If it was to go further, how could that be achieved?

The idea of a School & how it came to life
It was at this time that the idea of a school entered seriously into the talking and thinking of the Movement. However the idea did not originally come from the Movement. The new fire was kindled by two girls who were university students studying for degrees as teachers. They were Magdalena Salazar and Mary Ann Kramer. They had conceived an ambition to start a school for poor people somewhere in Santiago. They had no idea how to do it, but at the time Magdalena was Roberto Quiroga's girlfriend, whom she subsequently married. She talked to him about their wonderful idea and he suggested she might approach the Movement for support.

That is how the idea of a school for the poor first entered the thinking of the Movement. But it was no more than an idea conceived by two young students who were full of dreams and plans and talk about the project but had no resources to bring it about. It looked as though it would remain forever a beautiful idea which could be talked about endlessly but could not be realized in practical terms. That was not good enough for Magdalena Salazar and Mary Ann Kramer. They must do something practical, so they turned to José Manuel himself with their idea of a school for poor families and they asked him directly if he himself would sponsor it and make it a work of the Movement – just like the growing San Benito. He could do wonders there, so why not for their great new idea of a school for the poor? This was at the end of August 1985.

José Manuel, however, at that time was not looking for any additional major responsibilities. He had more on his hands than he could manage. This was the situation that faced him at that moment:

San Benito had moved from temporary accommodation to the new site and new buildings involving huge financial liabilities. He was carrying the commitment for the evangelization and spiritual care of the children of San Benito and the corresponding responsibilities for staff and buildings. Each year there were demands for new resources, new organization, new personnel. He had on his shoulders the responsibility for the young who had committed themselves to his new Movement. He had not only to attend to their spiritual formation but also to devise the unique parameters of that lay formation from the Rule of St Benedict. Moreover, it was just at that same time that his worries about the mysterious illness of his little son Pedro and its threat to his other children reached their peak. One might have thought that he and the Movement were fully committed for some time to come but Magdalena and Mary Ann wanted a new school for the poor and awaited an answer. Only José Manuel's own words are adequate to tell what happened next:

> In addition to my other worries at this time there were two girls who came to me with a project of making a school for poor people. One was Magdalena Salazar, who is now the wife of Roberto Quiroga and the other one was Mary Ann Kramer. I was very doubtful about it all because of the worries we had over dealing with the Movement and San Benito and I thought we were not ready. But, thanks be to God (and unfortunately for me at that moment) my father was there when the girls came to see me. Afterwards he asked me what these girls wanted. I said they wanted me to make a school for poor people, but it is impossible. My father wouldn't accept that. He said 'you cannot destroy the hope of these girls; something must be done.' That was what he had to say about it, and it made so powerful an impression on me that I decided in spite of everything that we had to make a start. So I said we could do it if Mario Canales, who was deeply involved in the work in Conchali, gave up his chosen career in architecture to take responsibility for this school. So I went to Mario and said to him: 'Are you ready to be in charge of a school?' He said yes he would but he did not really know much about it. Then he asked what financial guarantees I could give him. So I said 'None. We have nothing.' He came back every week with the same question

and I always said: 'Nothing, and the only thing I can say to encourage you is that the gospel says that, if you give one for the Lord he will give you a hundred,[5] and that is much more security than I can give.' So we had a lot of discussion with those who were keen to do something.

My father was very involved in this and he said to me that he was President of a Foundation and, if we had a definite proposal, he could get money from the Foundation, but only enough to make a start. The girls then came to me to talk about it all. When they said that they had a name they wanted to give the school. I said that, in that case, the name for the school was the one problem left now. I told them that I could not accept their name. We wanted to call it San Lorenzo because of our close friendship with Ampleforth and St Laurence is the patron saint of Ampleforth Abbey and College. They replied there would be no problem about that and agreed. That is how Colegio San Lorenzo started.

Mario's call

Behind this laconic account something of vital importance for the whole future of the Movement lies hidden. At first José Manuel could not face the idea of a new foundation backed by no resources which the two girls were innocently demanding. What made the difference and changed his decision was the faith of his father who stood beside him quietly listening and who then also helped him with some money. But there was something else at stake without which nothing could have happened and which was of great importance to the future of the Movement. What he was now asking of Mario Canales and his future wife was a total commitment to the Movement involving the abandonment of his career prospects. Undoubtedly the idea was not entirely new. While still in the pastoral department of the original Manquehue School he had written that what was needed among the young was a commitment which was "at the same time a spirit, a style of life, a way of living, a program of life". Now came a moment of decision about the acceptance of a new program of life for the young people who were asked to take on this new school in Conchali. They had been finding time from their University studies or their careers to work there. Now they were explicitly asked to move from part time involvement to a total life commitment. That was the new invitation which Mario Canales and the others were now facing. It was a huge step forward in the concept of the Movement.

Mario was engaged to be married. He was studying architecture with a view to a career as architect. He had no teaching qualification, and yet he was being asked to give up his chosen profession to become the founding Headmaster of a new sort of school in the *campamento,* where his voluntary work up to now had been fitted into his University study. He was now faced with a harsh choice of accepting the unknown in this new school in Conchali or leaving the Movement. He discussed the whole situation with his fiancée Magdalena Errazuriz (who is always known by her nickname Manena). She also was already involved with the Movement's work in Conchali and was in fact at the time running the sewing group.

At that point there was another unexpected and encouraging move. Their only *pied à terre* in Conchali so far had been the abandoned hut with no attractions or facilities. Now the Mayor of Conchali made an offer that is a testimony to the impact already achieved among the families by the young members of the Movement working there. The Mayor offered them a site which was well placed and quite big enough to start a school. It had been a community center but - like all community centers in that run down area - it had petered out. That offer of the Mayor was a challenge. Mario and Manena discussed it all and agreed to accept all the demands on them that were involved whether known or unknown - and most of them were at the time still unknown.

Mario went to José Manuel and said that unexpectedly a site had been given him. That was enough, he said, and now he was prepared to make the attempt. He would try to make a beginning of the Movement's school for the poor. It meant a profound change in every aspect of his life and that led him, as he entered the married state, to ask what security he would have in this new venture. Mario could not forget José Manuel's reply in Spanish. It was *Nada* - the favourite word of St John of the Cross[6] - nothing at all. Together Mario and Manena began their marriage looking squarely at the material implications of that word for them and their family.   With a wonderful courage born of faith they accepted.

Besides being an act of faith and courage for them and for the others who would join them in full time commitment at San Lorenzo, what happened to them was part of a strange stirring in the whole Movement at the time. Among the young tutors in San Benito also during these years a desire was growing for real Benedictine commitment. It all led in a few years to the formal establishment of the core group of the Movement, called Oblates who take promises for life - some of them in the celibate state and some as married. The joint commitment of Mario and Manena was an important step on the way that led to the ultimate shape of the Movement.

The assets available to the Movement at the time were easily counted. In Conchali they had the support of the Mayor and several families. Soon they had about fifty tiny little children of four years old waiting eagerly to go to the school. They had the promise of a site and no money at all except for what José Manuel's father had given them to make a start. Yet they had something else which was the strongest factor of all. It was something which no amount of money could have given them. They had the conviction of profound faith in the work they were undertaking strengthened by the invitation of the families and the support of José Manuel and his father and they had the support of the other young men and women of the Movement who were ready to go with them. Their faith was shared by all who were concerned and especially by the families and the children who would fill the new school. It was enough and the signal was given to go ahead.

As we have seen, José Manuel's father had played a vital role at this critical stage of the story. He had changed everything and made the next step possible. From the first he had taken the keenest interest in all that his eldest son was doing for the Movement, but his greatest interest moved to the San Lorenzo project, as soon as he heard of it. With unerring clarity of perception he saw its importance and made it his own special concern. Although he was gravely ill he went to all the meetings about it. It may be that he saw the need for a balance between rich and poor in the Movement's work, or he may simply have seen San Lorenzo as the area of greatest deprivation in the growing apostolate of the

Movement, which would therefore always need support. Or it may have been just an intuition that led him to his great decision. Whatever the reason it was he who made the first step possible, as Mario remembers:

> From the first mention of a school in Conchali there was one person who was very important for the beginning of San Lorenzo. That was José Manuel's father. He was very sick and almost dying but for some reason he was very, very interested in San Lorenzo and was always at the meetings about it. Somehow he himself arranged the money we needed for starting. I went to his office and he gave me money in cash for the start of San Lorenzo. I put the money in the bank and that made the beginning possible.

When the beginning of the school year arrived - March 1986 - they had the money and they had 50 children to start two kindergarten's, one for girls and one for boys. There was a teacher for each, and there was a social worker also. Magdalena Salazar was Director of Studies, Mario Canales was Headmaster, Francisco Loeser was tutor. Cristian Baraona had been working with the Movement from the start of the work in Conchali. Now he began to come from his business in the city to San Lorenzo once a week to deal with the accounts, which were thus professionally handled from the start. Everything came together just at the right time.

The opening ceremony took place in March 1986 and José Manuel's father was there at the opening ceremony. Without him San Lorenzo would never have been more than a dream, so his presence that day was of profound importance to him and to everyone involved. It was later that year, in November, that he died and, as he lay on his deathbed, it was San Lorenzo that seemed to be his great concern. He begged his son not to forget San Lorenzo and to look after it as best he could. That deathbed request of his father put a sacred seal on his son's determination to see the San Lorenzo project through to completion, whatever the difficulties might be, and there were many obstacles yet to be overcome.

There was some provision for running costs from public funding at the time. Even in the poor areas of Santiago the Government invested in schools for the children. The Government did not contribute to capital costs but any Institution which was willing to found, build and staff a school could qualify for a grant towards the running costs. A *per capita* grant was made for each individual pupil attending the school.

It was understandably normal for Institutions which took up this offer to aim at attracting the largest possible grant by making the classes as large as possible. Classes of up to 45 pupils were acceptable in the area. It was common practice, moreover, to maximize the grants by holding two sessions every day, one in the morning and one in the afternoon - each for a different set of children. There were even schools in which 3 sessions were held. In this way they could double or treble the grant and so make a profit as a return on their investment. Thus the interests of the pupils were inevitably sacrificed in the pursuit of profit. Under this system in the deprived areas the children who attended school in the morning were let loose on the streets in the afternoon and vice versa. This arrangement together with the huge classes made any real spiritual and moral guidance at best highly problematic. The teachers in these schools worked hard to do their best for the children and to establish good standards, but it was not easy. The system was economically sound but morally and educationally questionable. As to the spiritual needs of the children and more general family support and welfare, such schools had nothing to offer.

The Movement did not want to start another school like that, nor did the families who were already involved in the planning of the Movement's project. They knew all about those schools and did not want another for their children. The understanding already established and the consultation in progress led to a quite original scheme for the school's operation and the goals it would aim at.

It was quite a new plan for Conchali. Everything was to be for the good of the children and their families including explicitly the spiritual welfare of both. If this was the primary aim, then God would provide what money was needed, if they stuck to that solid principle. This was how the fundamental idea of San Lorenzo emerged and was defended, as time went on, against all attempts to scale down the commitment in a way that would fail to meet the real educational and spiritual welfare of the children and of the families. From the start Colegio San Lorenzo was to be a second home and center – a strong spiritual and moral support - not only for the children but also for the families. There would be only one daily session of classes, but the school and its facilities would be open all day for the children while they were at a school. Then, when schooling was over, they would be welcome at San Lorenzo for all their lives also if they chose to come back. There would be no clearing them out at the end of the morning to make room for the next session in the afternoon, in spite of the sacrifice of the extra grant money.

Colegio San Lorenzo, moreover, would be open not only to the children but to their families also during and after school. San Lorenzo would help them with other essential support - in a medical center, run by volunteers – in a social center – and, as time went on, with other support and educational services also. It would provide them with a unique center of centers in the chapel where the Blessed Sacrament was present and where daily the Divine Office was to be sung. The Divine Office was an integral part of the work of the Oblates and Movement members, but it was not their private affair. As in San Benito everyone - the children, the teachers, the families were welcomed to join in the prayer, which was the spiritual dynamo that kept everything alive. That was how the idea of San Lorenzo developed and all the Benedictine spiritual vision of the Movement was to be poured into it: in the daily prayer of the Church, in *lectio divina*, in *acogida*, in *spiritual companionship*, the spiritual bonding of a praying community, in the welcome extended to all as though to Christ himself. San Lorenzo was to be, not just an ordinary school, but truly "a school for the Lord's service"[7] inspired and sustained by the extended[8], lay Benedictine community of the Movement.

The first step

The full development of what has been described took time. To start with the Movement had this abandoned site which had been intended as a community center. It was protected by a wire fence. It had a dirt floor for the children to play on. There were wooden huts for classrooms, offices and storage. Between the huts there was an open space for the children to play in - luckily they were small four year olds for whom a little space went a long way. That made it less crowded and they could play football there and run about.

This site gave a wonderful start, but everything went so well that it soon became too small. By the second year it was bursting at the seams and everyone knew that something larger and better must be found if the project was to survive. The Mayor of Conchali was again very helpful and through him they got to know of another possibility a large open space which was controlled by the Government. They went to the Ministry to talk about it. It was a large area, which had been used as a garbage dump and it was in very bad condition and now derelict. Negotiations had to begin with the military government during which it became apparent that the authorities did not in fact have any immediate alternative plans for its use. Nevertheless they just did not want to give it up.

When the talks proved inconclusive, the authorities said that the final decision would rest with President Pinochet so a meeting with him was suggested as the only possible way forward. It was arranged that José Manuel with Rafael Valdivieso and Mario Canales were to see him. It happened that Fr Dominic Milroy and Fr Timothy Wright from Ampleforth Abbey were in Santiago at that time on a visit to the Movement specifically to help with the problems of San Lornezo. Their presence would be helpful and they were invited also to come along to the meeting in the hope that their standing and the interest of Ampleforth might strengthen the case and they at least could not be suspected by Pinochet of being communists. It was not an easy meeting but in the end Pinochet gave them the site.

It was a great achievement in difficult times and their anxieties seemed to be at an end. By this time the old site was desperately over-crowded. The wooden huts were almost on top of each other and only a small courtyard was left in the middle. On this central area the boys played football on two pitches forming a cross with the square in the middle common to both pitches. The hope that both games would not want that central patch at the same time was often disappointed by a united dash of four teams of small children invading the central reserve at the same moment. The melee that resulted probably added to the boys' enjoyment, but it was not satisfactory.

Planning on the new site had already started when the election[9] was held and the new Government of President Aylwin came into power. Instead of smoothing the way for the development of San Lorenzo further this change gave rise to an entirely new problem. The man in the new Government who would have to give the permission turned out to be an architect who had an idea for making a park in that area. He was determined to stop the building of San Lorenzo so that he could have his park. Meanwhile the football games - not to mention the teaching - on the old site became more and more problematic.

Negotiations proved to be difficult because the idea for a park held great attractions for the Minister in charge of this department, who was Alberto Etchegary, the man who organized the wonderfully successful visit of Pope John Paul II in 1987. As to the site in Conchali, there would have to be another major decision before anything could be done. An official process was needed to change the use of the land – and the Minister was against this on principle. He was strongly attached to the idea of providing the park and nothing else in this derelict area. It was a worthy cause but in direct collision with what seemed to the Movement a much worthier cause of San Lorenzo. They were dismayed to hear that the Minister was reported to have said that he would never consent to change the designation or alter his plans. It was a moment of real crisis and brought back all the acute agonies that attended the birth of San Lorenzo.

It was at this point of apparent impasse that Mgr Cristian Precht, the Pastoral Vicar General of the Archdiocese, intervened. From the early days he had been a great friend of the Movement and was well aware of their problems. Now he interceded with the Minister and explained the whole nature of the San Lorenzo project. He made it abundantly clear that San Lorenzo was not political but truly ecclesial and had the full support of the Church in Santiago. This was one of the many signs of friendship and support for the Movement which Mgr Precht gave José Manuel in those early years. His intervention now was invaluable. It saved San Lorenzo and cleared the way for the government's approval for the new use of the site in Conchali as a school and pastoral center. When Mario went to see the Minister again he gave the final permission for San Lorenzo to move to the new site. After all the acute tension and drawn-out anxiety which had haunted them there was great rejoicing in the Movement and among the families and children of Conchali. It really looked as though they could at last move to a permanent site which would be their own.

That, however, was not after all the end of the problems. At the beginning of all the negotiations a survey of the ground had been done by experts who found that it was good for building. It was on this advice that planning had gone forward. However, when workmen actually moved onto the site, they discovered that somehow the survey had missed one important area where a big excavation had at some earlier date been filled up with garbage and it had then been covered over. Work for the school had already started on the site when the foundation specialists intervened and said that it must stop because this part of the ground was unstable and to continue would be to throw money away on buildings that would not survive. The experts were gloomily sure that there was no solution. The site could not be built on, and it seemed once again like the tragic end of a beautiful dream. Of course there was much prayer in San Lorenzo and in the Movement generally.

The prayer was answered and something must have touched the experts' hearts, because they thought again and produced a solution which opened up a way forward – at a price. They proposed sinking piles in the area of instability to carry the foundations. Of course, it made the whole project more expensive, but the Movement did not hesitate to go ahead trusting in God to find a way for them to see it all through. They had in mind the spiritual and human interests of the little children, now crammed into the old site, and their families also, to whom they were committed irrevocably. So they trusted that God would provide. Their faith and their prayer were answered. After all the agony Colegio San Lorenzo would be able to continue and it had a future on a site which allowed for all the development they foresaw.

CR

Notes for Chapter 9
[1] see Appendix 2
[2] Jn. 13, 34
[3] Mt 25, 40 ' Truly I say to you, as you did it to one of the least of these my brethren, you did it to me.
[4] Lk. 22, 27
[5] cp Mt. 19, 29
[6] Spanish Carmelite writer on mystical prayer.
[7] Prologue of St Benedict's Rule, last para.
[8] see Chapters 15 and 16
[9] In 1988 the military government held a plebiscite in the hope that their tenure of power would be confirmed by the people, but the people, in accordance with the long democratic tradition of Chile, voted for free elections.

Chapter 10 ~ San Lorenzo Part 2

The New Site

The permanent buildings for Colegio San Lorenzo at last began to appear above ground on a site now owned by the Manquehue Movement. After so many agonies of uncertainty about the future, work started in September 1990 and the first essential buildings for the smallest children were ready for occupation by the beginning of the new School year in March 1991. The old site was gratefully returned to the mayor of Conchali. Established now in their own permanent buildings Mario Canales and the other teachers and assistants began to learn quickly. There was much to learn since they were beginning to create something entirely new.

Their first aim was to integrate into one what had been attempted elsewhere by two separate facilities among the people of Conchali. There were the schools, which were valued by the community in spite of the fact that they had very large classes with double sessions and minimal social activity. Then there were the various community centers, which had been less than successful when run by temporary week-end workers. This had been learnt from the Movement's first failure on that pattern in the *campamento*. Now on the new site the Movement brought the two together so that the school became the backbone of the community center with a permanent on-going community life. That was what made possible the new concept of working for the benefit of the families and their children.

In order to achieve this integration four centers were established on the school site. They were: the Social Center, the Sports Center, the Pastoral Center and the Cultural Center. Through the school and these centers San Lorenzo became quite quickly a permanent on-going source of realistic service through education, social support, spiritual inspiration and evangelization. It meant that San Lorenzo was run and managed in a way quite different from other schools.

More important still than the integration of services to serve both children and families was the Manquehue spirit, which is the gospel spirit, in which all this was done. Mario remembers those early days and his discovery by experience what a difference there was in the role he had undertaken from that of a traditional Headmaster of a school:

> The school site was open all day, even after the children had gone home. The families as well as the children were in fact invited to participate in the school. At first it was difficult to persuade them, but now more and more come and get involved. Even if they don't have children in the school they are welcome anyway. The aim of the School is not merely to give education in the sense of teaching the children various skills. The aim is to teach them to know Christ and to have experience of the community. As time went on and they became more and more accustomed to this welcome, some of them joined a *lectio* group of the Movement. So it happened that, even in the early years, two of the women became fully involved in the work of the school and in the Movement.

It did not all happen at once. At first the parents' shyness was difficult to overcome, but as time went on more and more began to participate and, of course, it was the mothers who were the first to adapt to this wholly new situation. It was they who had at the beginning asked the Movement for a school which would really care for their children. It was they who were the first to overcome their shyness and find the courage to contribute where they had never before dared to think that they could contribute. They worked with the lunches for the children. They took part in the Divine Office in the chapel, they were welcomed to and learnt to take an active part in retreats. They learnt to take part in *lectio* groups. It was the mothers who looked after the kitchen area and prepared the lunches for the children. From this early stage they became, not only a part, but an essential and valued part of the whole enterprise.

Development in this direction was not easy at first but gradually the families began to understand that this school was different. It was not a place to leave their children for their studies without venturing themselves to follow them past the gate. They were made so welcome

178

that for some - both mothers and children - it began to seem like a wonderful extension of home. There were some very exceptional features which were so new that it took courage to appreciate them. There was the chapel and Divine Office and welcoming *lectio* groups. Some of the mothers at an early stage took part in the Divine Office, in retreats, in *lectio divina*. They were helped by the welcome of the Movement. As with San Benito the deepest aim of the San Lorenzo project was evangelization through a community bound together by the commitment to seek God together as lay men and women and so work among others for the kingdom of God in the world of today. This was the aim which gave its identity and its mission to the extended[1] Benedictine community and which gave its special character to the work of San Lorenzo among the poor.

Tutorías taken by San Benito pupils

Tutorías had been established at San Benito by the young Oblates and were now working wonderfully, but here at San Lorenzo in the early stages the Oblates had other responsibilities and there were no older children to help the younger. That is how it happened that boys and girls from San Benito came to San Lorenzo to take *tutorías*. They came not only to supply a need but to establish also a priceless link between the two schools - a link which was founded on the gospel perception of spiritual equality that transcended all other divisions. About 20 of them came down to San Lorenzo once a week for an hour of *tutoría* working under the guidance and supervision of one of the experienced adult members of the Movement.

It was of course difficult in many ways at the beginning. The tutors themselves needed help and encouragement. They were only 15 when they started this work, but they rose to the challenges and their weekly presence soon became well accepted and welcomed at San Lorenzo. Many of the San Benito pupils valued that experience as a real spiritual benefit for themselves. One of them, who was among the very first to start *tutorías* in San Lorenzo remembers the experience with real gratitude. She was only 15 when she went with the first group from San Benito to tutor the little children in what was to her the unknown world of Conchali, but it was one of the things she remembered with gratitude as much later she looked back on her experience in the Movement. Weekly *tutorías* at San Lorenzo became for her one of the things she looked forward to at the time partly because she herself learnt so much from the experience.

It was an exceptional situation. The two schools were at opposite ends of the social spectrum in Chile but the Movement, through this practice of *tutorías,* had succeeded in cutting through the divisions to create understanding based on the spiritual bond which alone had the power to unite them. Naturally it went further than *tutorías.* Some San Benito pupils became involved also in retreat work and in the scouts for San Lorenzo. The whole of this brave initiative, which started even in the early stages of San Lorenzo, is perhaps the essential spiritual and human foundation of the good relationship and co-operation which currently exists between the two schools. It was a natural outcome that the pupils of San Lorenzo, as they grew older, started to take *tutorías* themselves and to be involved in retreats and other activities.

The whole idea of *tutorías* had, as we have seen, been worked out originally by José Manuel while he was still on the staff of the Manquehue School of the Sacred Hearts. He perfected it, before ever he started a school of his own, as a way of communicating the faith to children. He saw how children have the open-ness of heart to respond generously to the word of God in scripture. He saw also that they are naturally eager and ready to be taught about it. However the gap of experience and understanding between the young child and the adult is such that it is not easy for them to share the deep inner responses through which faith grows. This is where another young person, who is only a few years older, can establish a mutual understanding which goes beyond what is possible for an adult. A break-through occurs because the younger can really identify with the older in sharing fears, anxieties, joys and hopes. Above all they can discover together through the word of scripture the wonder of true faith in Christ. That faith grows more strongly where the older boy or girl takes an interest and helps the growth in confidence of the younger through a brotherly or sisterly interest in all the activities of the younger one. So the tutor learns to take a real interest in what interests the younger child. Faith is thus situated in the reality of life as actually experienced by a given age-group in all its ordinary events. This can be seen in the celebration of a birthday where the real meaning of a birthday has not been drowned in the desire for self-indulgence and expensive presents.

I learnt about this one dark evening at San Lorenzo when I met a small boy who could hardly speak for the joy of telling me that it would be his birthday the next day. He had talked it through with his young tutor and that had made real both his understanding and his delight. There would be no rich presents for him as he returned to the poverty of his home, but the joy he was experiencing already was better than any satisfaction the most expensive presents could have given him. For him his birthday and whatever little presents he might receive had been set in the context of God's word and Christ's care and love for us.

I was reminded on that occasion of a conversation in England with a woman who had grown up as a Catholic in the poverty of the great depression of the late twenties. She told me of the deprivation of their lives but then added: "but we stuck together and we were happy. Nowadays", she added, "people have more than we had, but they are not really happy any more."

The unifying force of *tutorías* and the general involvement of San Benito pupils in San Lorenzo was part of a broader development. It was not long before some of the parents of the pupils of San Lorenzo found their own lives being gradually transformed. They found that they were actually invited to become involved with their children's spiritual development. They found, when they accepted, that in this school the primary aim was not to enable the young to make their mark on life through the transmission of secular knowledge and money making skills. They are taught in the classroom the knowledge and skills which they need. The pupils God-given gifts - both intellectual and practical - are developed well. The primary aim, however, is to teach them to know Christ in the milieu in which they live and to have experience of a community founded on him and living in his name.

It is at this level that a real break-through began to happen when some of the parents joined the Movement. Many of the pupils also found their lives radically changed. The change was usually not dramatic conversion but a gradual growth like the utterly surprising growth of a little seed. Christ himself took the germination and growth of a seed as the theme of his parable of the sower about grace acting and developing within us. The work of San Lorenzo was always very close to that parable. It was the work of Christ's grace that became apparent in the lives of the young who responded to the challenge of the school.

Some of the earliest pupils, who began as little boys in the first days of San Lorenzo on the old site, have now completed their education and left school. Of these students some are now voluntarily coming back to the school to work there and give *tutorías* and also to teach sports and help in other activities. Their motivation for doing so is an essential part of the story of San Lorenzo – the story of the young to whom it brought a new vision of a new world with new challenges for themselves in the way they were to live their lives. Some of them are ready to speak openly of their experience. It is quite normal for the young in Movement retreats to give carefully considered testimonies of their own spiritual experiences in various circumstances. Two of the early pupils of Colegio San Lorenzo spoke to me about what the school had meant to them and what it had done for them.

Testimony of Roberto Avila

Roberto Avila said that through being a pupil at San Lorenzo his whole life has changed. Everything would have been different without the school and the Movement. His family was Catholic but coming to a Catholic school like this was a new experience of Catholicism. The teachers, he said, were not just professionals doing a job. Speaking very personally about them and about the school, he said:

> They were real people and their teaching was different. The first thing I started to understand was the word 'love'. I learnt very much about love during my time in the school.

Roberto's way through school was not all smooth. He had many problems but there were always people there and ready to help with the love he had discovered on his first arrival. He found that the *tutorías* were very important and they helped him to discover the meaning of love. However it was not only the weekly hour of *tutoria* that counted so much as the presence all the time of 'real' people who helped him and he mentioned in particular: Anthony Dore, Rodrigo Vidal, José Miguel

Navarro and Christian Destuet (all of whom are now Oblates). He says that they brought into his life what he now recognizes as 'spiritual companionship'.[2] Describing how they were always beside him in good times, joking with him, talking with him and giving him strength, he recalled that:

> In the bad times they were there also always helping me, always giving me affirmation, always with the Word of God and with the Rule of St Benedict, with prayer, with friendship, and also with games at good times. That is really what has struck me and moved me more than anything else.

All that Roberto experienced in this way, he said, was 'the work of God'. His circumstances were all against it. Both his parents were working all day and he was too old to be left in his grandmother's care. He had nothing to do except go out on the street. It was boredom in the end that led him to drop in on San Lorenzo, which was always open for students in the afternoons and evenings. About these occasions he said: "There I discovered Rodrigo Vidal who gave me a lot of *acogida* and a lot of company." Roberto enjoyed going to Rodrigo's office, eating chocolates and playing and enjoying the companionship. But he added that at the same time Rodrigo didn't just pat him on the back. He made him do things.

> For instance, he asked me 'why don't you do *tutorías*? - why don't you go and take part in the scout group of the school? - why don't you do this or that?

Rodrigo gave him companionship but he also said:

> Well, you have to *do* things, because if you don't do things you will be doing wrong and not making progress' - and that is why I started to improve.

Roberto said that things were never simple; they were often changing for him. Things were up and down. Sometimes he had very high moments and sometimes very low ones. He remembers a time once when things were very low.

The only things I thought and talked about were going out with friends, having parties and drugs.

Somehow Anthony Dore, who was an Oblate and tutor in the school, knew what was happening and came up to him and spoke to him – sometimes every day.

He didn't tell me to stop doing what I was doing wrong. No, he just advised me to pray, read the bible and never leave *tutorías*.

Roberto said that the influence of these people in the Movement was so important for his growth and development that he came back, when he was no longer a pupil, and he is now working in the school at San Lorenzo and involved with the Movement also. But looking back on his school days he speaks of his last four years as bringing a sense of 'vocation' and relaxed dedication to working at *tutorías* with small children in the school. There were new experiences at this time also. There were the technical projects they were introducing at the school. The work experience in outside firms to which they introduced him helped him to become more confident and to get to know the world of others.

Then there was Confirmation[3] which was for him a very important event:

I felt that Jesus was really present there and that he was going to be present in the new way. It meant that I was starting really to live my life.

He then began to work with a real sense of his own responsibility for his life and with less dependence on others. It was at the time when he came to the end of school life that Roberto was invited to think of joining the Movement and to stay on to work at Colegio San Lorenzo. He did not know how to reply, but he remembers a firm conviction that he was now not dependent on San Lorenzo. God would provide whatever he needed and he could be found anywhere. In fact he left school and went to work with a firm where he would get professional training and a qualification.[4] About this work experience he says:

184

I discovered what the world had to offer me. I discovered a world that is empty and devoid of love.

He said that it made him face some radical questions about what he was really looking for in life. He had a strong sense that the world he met outside was a contradiction of the ideals he had learnt at San Lorenzo.

I felt that I needed all the school had given me. And by that I mean not just love but also working with people, creating things and making a new world.

Shortly before his work-practice with that printing firm came to an end he had a conversation with the Headmaster of San Lorenzo, José Miguel Navarro, who offered him the chance of working in the school. But then there was another offer. The company in which he was working offered him a job to stay on there and continue to study and earn money doing what he had been prepared for at school. It was an offer that contained not just the security of a job. It opened the prospect of a whole new life with the glitter, the promises and the dangers of the market place. Roberto made his decision; "I turned that offer down and chose instead to work in the school." His father and mother were at first not very happy at the decision and asked him;

Why are you doing this? You always said that you wanted to work in printing. Why don't you carry on and do it?

Roberto's reply was that he felt happy – deeply happy - working with the Movement in San Lorenzo. His parents seemed to understand at once and replied that he should do what he really wanted to do.

Roberto at this time felt that he was truly giving himself completely to this decision he had made. He had just before that spent a period in the Movement's Formation House[5] and it had clarified his appreciation of what life has to offer – the true and the false, the real and the artificial. He sees that his decision owes much to his experience in the Formation House

It was very, very important experience and instead of the empty world I have seen I prefer my alternative society in the Movement.

Testimony of Rodrigo Vasquez

Another of the earliest pupils of San Lorenzo is Rodrigo Vasquez. Looking back on his experience in the School and in the Movement he sees it as a great influence for good in his life. He says that it was only by chance, as it seemed, that he went to school at San Lorenzo. He moved there from another school at the age of twelve. He did so rather reluctantly, but a friend of his was changing to San Lorenzo so he went also.

> They showed me a lot of love and I started discovering real friendship in the classes there.

He was a Catholic and used to Mass on Sundays at his parish church,

> but it was when I got to San Lorenzo that I really discovered the Mass and the Office of the Hours.

He liked also the school religious teaching in the top class, that is the original founding class, which he joined. In the first year he found *tutorías* something very new and very difficult. But in the second year, when with help he had to learn how to do *tutorías* himself it was different.

> Then through *tutorías* I actually met people, like Rodrigo Vidal and Julio Bahr, who showed me what the school was for, what they wanted of me, what it meant to be Benedictine, and I discovered the Office and I discovered Christ. It was then that I heard what seemed like a call of Christ. I really liked very much praying and singing the Office. I started getting to school earlier so as to take part in the Office of Lauds and sometimes I stayed on in school in the afternoon to take part in Vespers. I really started liking and looking forward to this prayer.

At the end of the year he had to decide whether to stay for the technical course, which was just starting at San Lorenzo, or leave and accept his mother's offer to move to another school.

> I decided to say 'no' because the friendships I had made with some of my classmates were very strong.

Also he had found great strength and support in his new community for *lectio divina*.

> One of us always had to prepare the themes and readings, and once I had to do the preparation. That was with the help of Francisco Loeser and Julio Bahr. That was a turning point because when I did the preparation and we had our meditation, I felt the call to stay in San Lorenzo. That is what I had in mind when I started the last four years in the school.

Incidentally in these years Rodrigo got to know better "all the people who had talked to me about Christ". He mentions especially Anthony Dore and Cristian Destuet, who talked to him a lot "about service and working for others and loving others and spending time for them." Cristian introduced him and the whole form to a group called 'Auxilio'[6]. Rodrigo started working there although at the beginning he didn't want to and went to the first meeting feeling 'ill and absolutely horrible'.

> In spite of that I liked a lot what was said there. We were taught to build up a service team with people of the class. We started going to an old people's house and I really liked showing love to people and helping. I discovered that there is so much to do in the world, although there were so many people saying that there is no way and nothing we can do to change the world. I discovered with that group that I was going to help to make the world different by very simple things like going once a week to see these old people.

In the school itself Rodrigo had the experience of giving *tutorías* to two different classes of smaller boys.

> It was then that I discovered how much I liked this work with children – to meet them in the corridor and say 'hallo' and know their names. This gave me a great sense of fulfillment in giving a real meaning to my life.

Then Francisco Loeser became head of Rodrigo's *lectio* group. It became stronger. They started having *convivencias* and they learnt to be more ambitious in their *lectio* and "got to know each other much better. It was a time of growth in the community life of the group." During that year also Rodrigo had to take some older groups for *tutorías*. It was more difficult than with the smaller children but he said to himself:

> Well, I like this work and I will stay here, and I don't care if it is difficult, I shall see it through. I continued also going to summer and winter works (*trabajo*) outside Santiago, as I had the year before.

Rodrigo still had doubts about whether he should continue working in Colegio San Lorenzo, because he didn't think it very attractive as a career. He didn't know what to do "but we worked together and met and talked a lot and prayed together." The result was that for Rodrigo things gradually changed and began to take shape more clearly and he began to realize what Christ was asking from him.

> Also the Movement was beginning to have a new meaning for me. It was a very important year. The following year continued happily along the same lines I was going deeper into everything. In my last year, when I was in the top year of the school, it was quite a difficult time. Many important things started to happen and there were many important changes. I wondered what was going to happen to me and what would happen to all the others around me.

He was now doing work experience in a company and there would be a test at the end of the year with the chance to go to University "but I did not know whether I really wanted that." In some ways things were not going well but

> there were some good things that happened at that time. First of all there was Confirmation, and it was good to continue doing what I was doing then and what I am still doing now in the school. Then there were my friends. They meant a lot to me and I felt them like brothers. Many of them were the same people as the *lectio* group and they were very close to me, helping, listening, giving me strength in difficult times.

Rodrigo made one move in the middle of this year. He went with another young Catholic to see José Miguel Navarro, the Headmaster of Colegio San Lorenzo, to ask about the possibility of a job in the School. The problems he had been experiencing faded into the background and he felt a real call to give to the children in the school "all that I had received." So he made the request with the idea that during that coming year he would have to decide finally about his future.

At the end of the year he did his final exams for university entrance and did professional practice. It all made him think and

it seemed to me that the world outside the Movement was empty and nobody seemed to care about anyone else.

It was the world he would have to work in on leaving San Lorenzo behind and he didn't like it. But the pressures mounted and he was offered huge opportunities. He was offered a place at University

and it was not offered to many of my classmates at San Lorenzo. I began to wonder what would happen if I did go to University and then got good results which would give me a qualification and a career in the world of work, but I decided to continue working in the School and not to go to University.

That was not all. After finishing his work experience in a printing firm he was offered a job to continue working there.

But I did not hesitate and immediately said no, although it was a difficult time to get a job working in a company like that.

I was losing a very big opportunity and many people were asking me why I was turning down a chance like that. The answer came in the very same week when I was helping on a retreat with the eighth form in San Lorenzo. That was the work, I discovered, that attracted me more than anything else. From then on I continued doing the same things - I went to the winter works during the holiday time and especially I was still doing *tutorías*.

Rodrigo saw the whole of that year as a time of growth and new understanding during which he really felt part of the Movement. The next thing for him, to which he looked forward very much was a period in the Formation House. He was thoroughly settled at San Lorenzo in his new role there and had developed very good understanding with the children, so that he could really communicate with them in a way to help them in their lives.

I definitely want to stay here and continue working in the school especially in the *tutorías*, because I feel that the biggest call of God is to be there with the children.

The evidence of these testimonies of young men who have come through the school and become members of the Movement reflects the spirit of San Lorenzo. The pupils and the parents from Conchali who have joined the Movement through becoming members of *lectio* groups are creating at San Lorenzo a community which draws its inspiration directly from the gospel and the Rule of St Benedict. It is sensitive to the children and to the local people themselves. It is not an alien imposition from outside but a new creation from within belonging to the people of Conchali themselves.

The community has grown spiritually from and through the formative ways in which the Movement expresses its true nature in all its activities. They are: shared *lectio* of the word of God, the divine office, *tutorías, spiritual companionship*, the daily use of the Rule of St Benedict as a guide to life and the retreats that are organized regularly for the pupils and members of all ages and the parents of the Movement schools.

These retreats are not a private exercise of personal spirituality. They are community events of continuing spiritual formation shared by all who want to be involved. Holding these retreats every year has been very important for parents and pupils alike. It has helped them to understand and identify very deeply with the apostolic and evangelizing spirit of the Movement. The Movement's presence in Conchali has become a powerful spiritual resource and a significant support in the many human needs of such a community.

The New Buildings for the Millennium

San Lorenzo started life on the new site with the bare essentials. By 1998 the Communications and Technology Center had been added with excellent computer and printing equipment for the older children, which would prepare them to go on to further studies or get employment on leaving school. There was a little chapel for the Office of the Hours, which St Benedict calls The Work of God, and there were some small offices for administration - which provided only a tiny room for the

Headmaster, who did not ask for something grand and impressive but who certainly needed more room than he had in that first office for his daily pastoral work for children and adults alike. That was all there was. Provision had been made in terms of space for future building but the necessary funds were not there.

During all the first 15 years the provision of a midday meal for all the pupils and staff was a real problem. When the time for lunch came round some of the mothers of the children came together in the kitchen area and helped to prepare the food. It was always a cold meal set out on specially made individual plastic trays and then carried round the campus to children in all the individual classrooms. When the meal was over the children carried the trays and mugs back to the kitchen area and then returned to their study while the mothers washed up. The generous, tolerant and co-operative spirit in which all this was done was truly wonderful. It was very much in line with the ideal of San Lorenzo as a community and family school, but it was far from ideal as a practical arrangement for a working school.

As funding came in for development the whole picture was gradually improved and it was in the millennium year of 2000 that new buildings at last transformed San Lorenzo by providing the facilities which were really essential to the fulfilment of its mission. The builders had scarcely left the site when everyone came together for the blessing on September 27th 2000. It was a fine day and the liturgy in the open air was beautiful and moving. It fully involved the children, the parents, the Oblates and the Mayor and people of Conchali. It was an occasion of great joy and hope for the future together with profound thanksgiving to God for all that had been achieved and for the gifts of donors and for the faith and perseverance and self sacrifice that had made it all possible.

By the year 2000 the school roll of San Lorenzo reached exactly 722 boys and girls and they certainly needed and valued the new developments which were blessed in that September. In the new building is included a simple, strong, holy and impressive new Chapel which stands at the corner of the site near the entrance. It had been built a few years before the millennium development but it is really part of the new San Lorenzo. It stands at the intersection of two streets, like a sentinel to the whole project, holding the cross up and proclaiming its meaning.

Then there is a Gatehouse and Porter's Lodge with a way into the School and a separate way to the community rooms, the medical and social centers. Here the parents and families are welcome and there is provision for catechesis and *Lectio* etc. This development of 2000 at last makes it possible to activate fully what had been there in embryo from the beginning - the dual nature of San Lorenzo as a school and a community center with a catechetical mission or outreach to all who want to come.

There is much that is new also for the school itself. There is a Library, offices for the Headmaster and staff, which are fitting for their purpose but not lavish. There is a room for *tutorías*. There is a big dining room (the first they have ever had) which can also be used for assemblies and drama etc. And there is a fully appointed kitchen. At last the real essentials are in place.

The Medical Center is part of the social center. It is staffed on a voluntary basis by mothers of San Lorenzo. It did not wait for the new buildings but started from the very beginning in a hut on the site. The staff work as a group to look after the children in what ways they can. They teach them hygiene and health-care and give help and support and advice to the mothers. There are doctors and a dentist and nurses who give their services free on regular visits. These doctors and nurses are normally parents of children at San Benito and members of the Movement. Under their direction the staff of the medical center do a lot for the health of the children and also for the families, chiefly through preventive work and through teaching the children basic hygiene. The dentist was a member of the Movement and also for a number of years head of a group for *lectio* among fathers of the San Lorenzo children. He comes once a week to work with the children at the school and also for some families. This work is part of the Social Center which looks after other general family needs for instance in employment, in diet, in counselling. It is there that parents of the children can get basic help and advice in dealing with the bureaucratic demands and threats of modern society.

Technical Education

In the early stages of San Lorenzo it was intended that the school would take the children to the 8th grade up to the age of about 14 and after that they would leave and go to other schools to prepare for employment. As the time approached, however, it became clear that, if they followed that plan, the first children would have to leave San Lorenzo and all it stood for at too early an age. They would have to leave just when they most needed the strength of this community in learning to face the problems of life and when they themselves could contribute more to the school as senior pupils. A better plan was needed. Fourteen is a sensitive age for children when the confusing world of teenage development is beginning for them. It is a time when a secure background and clear guidance and continuity are more than ever needed. It was certainly not a time to turn them out from such a community school as San Lorenzo and so cut them off from the source and stay of their spiritual and human formation at the time when they need it most. Above all it was just not the time for the young of Conchali to make a break in their catechesis and to separate them from the living community source of that catechesis in the Movement. There would be a real danger of destroying all the good that had been achieved in their lives so far. What was really at stake was the children's Christian formation.

All that became very clear but, if they were going to continue their studies at San Lorenzo, then the extra years of school study must have purpose and content of real value to the children. It must help them to get employment and have a stake in society. That is how discussions focussed at an early stage on some form of technical education. Some years before the development of 2000 this question had to be faced. The trouble was that to extend in this way the education offered in Conchali by San Lorenzo further funding would be needed. The need for well-informed planning was accepted and also for dedicated teachers who were trained in the technical subjects to be studied.

Funding has always been, and still is, a perennial problem for San Lorenzo. The policy which had prevailed so far and had never disappointed was to get on with the work within the limits of the resources available and trust that God would supply what was needed. That prayer of hope was always answered. But now something more than funding was needed. People also were needed who had the skills and knowledge both for planning and teaching courses that would be of immediate practical benefit. Such expertise was not available on the existing staff at San Lorenzo. It was just as this need became apparent that new friends came on the scene in Conchali. They had just the knowledge and expertise that was needed and they proved able and anxious to help. It made possible the development of plans to meet these new needs.

The Technical courses to be offered

A full range of technical courses was for many reasons out of the question. After a careful study with the help of experts the Movement decided to concentrate on teaching communication skills, which would include printing, computer work and graphics. These were seen to be the best courses to offer a wide range of opportunities in the world of work both for boys and girls. It was a popular and promising decision. Immediately there was a lot of interest from printing companies who gave generous help in the formulation of the curriculum and the provision of equipment and also by sending trained personnel as instructors.

This was a good start, and this new initiative was supported by other developments outside San Lorenzo. There was a new road through the district which went out to the airport and made possible the growth of a local industrial center. Thus a local need for young trainees in a wide variety of enterprises had suddenly grown up. Then again these communication skills were not an end in themselves but were needed in a very wide range of employment. Once they had basic training in computer skills, printing and graphics the young boys and girls from San Lorenzo might hope for interest in what they had to offer in most forms of commercial enterprise. These courses could lead equally well to further training in highly technical work and to the development of the best secretarial and administrative skills. This initial training provided in the technical area of San Lorenzo would, in fact, be capable of leading in very different directions and it was equally suitable for girls and boys. What they learnt in their final years at school would be a foundation for further training in a variety of firms and would, as some firms quickly recognized, give these young people a very useful 'head start'.

Last years of prepation for the world of work

These last years of technical education at San Lorenzo brought other benefits besides initial training for work. As in San Benito, so here in Conchali the pupils who stayed on for these courses were invited and encouraged to join one of the small *lectio* communities of the Movement and these (with their *acogida, spiritual companionship, convivencias, and periodic retreats* etc) were much more than traditional prayer groups. They brought a wealth of warmth, friendship and community into the young lives of those who without this support would face loneliness and isolation in the early stages of the world of work. There were, of course, some who did not opt to join a community or who decided not to stay on for the technical courses. All of them, even after leaving the school, are always welcome to visit at San Lorenzo. In fact I remember, when I was with the Headmaster one day, how one of the young boys came up to speak to him. It had been decided that he was not going to stay on at school for the technical courses. He seemed to accept that but there was one thing about he wanted to be assured. Could he come back for *lectio* and for the retreats. There was no problem about that and he was made very welcome. At San Lorenzo they are always welcome to come back.

That was how the last element of the curriculum of San Lorenzo fell into place and made it possible to give many of the boys and girls a realistic start in life. It was made possible by the generosity of many who were ready to help in the realisation of the Manquehue mission. All the technical expertise was available to make it work. Before the decision the whole problem seemed completely impossible, but once the decision was made everything fell into place. In true community spirit the parents and the children of San Lorenzo were all kept fully informed and involved in the process of putting this development in place. This strengthened the decision of the Movement and maintained in this new venture the precious sense of common purpose and co-operation which from the first had inspired the Movement's work in Conchali.

Training courses for adults

Already about five years before the building developments of 2000 a beginning had been made in San Lorenzo in offering training courses for adults. With the new buildings this has come really into its own. The enterprise is organized and maintained, like the school of San Lorenzo itself, by the Institute of Saint John the Apostle. This is the legal structure which provides support for San Lorenzo. In part of the new buildings flanking the gateway there are now offices devoted to this work for adults. The organisation for Adult Training and Employment created there is recognized by the National Service for Training and Employment. Its outreach goes beyond the district of Conchali itself and is open to adults especially in five districts in the north of Santiago of which Conchali is one. This means that for adults the outreach of the Movement through San Lorenzo has stretched far beyond the district from which pupils come to the school.

Two types of course are on offer to these adults. There are simple courses designed to help in the home, such as dressmaking, hairdressing and cooking. Then there are more advanced courses giving training in practical work which is capable of generating income through the offering of services to a neighbourhood. A new type of course began in 2001 for the achievement of basic and middle-grade standards in academic study which are recognized and approved by the Ministry of Education. These are offered for adults who have been deprived of a full education and look for some opportunity for learning more at times which fit into the actual conditions of their lives at home and at work. In full accordance with the nature and purpose of the Movement these courses for Adult Education are inspired by the desire to welcome those who need them into the community of the Movement and the sharing of the word of God in the scriptures. This is in accord with the primary mission of the Movement to evangelize. There is nothing strained about this. It is based on *acogida* and is simply the natural way in which the Movement works.

A New Headmaster

Mario Canales had been chosen as Headmaster of San Lorenzo at the beginning. The whole Movement had supported him in bringing the community in Conchali through the birth pangs and growth problems arising from difficulties and obstacles which had seemed at the time beyond the strength of anyone to surmount. The enterprise had been blessed by God and had grown year by year. Now in the millennium year the new buildings were in place. The curriculum developments for technical training were working. The community work and support for all the families was developing. The local involvement in the Movement itself was growing. The millennium buildings were completed. Mario Canales was now needed for another major growth area of the Movement which was the coordination and development of all its social work. It was time for a new Headmaster to be appointed and he was another of the Oblates, José Miguel Navarro.

Like Mario Canales, his predecessor, he was one of the earliest followers of José Manuel and he had also been one of the original tutors in San Benito and one of the first celibate Oblates. In the March (the beginning of the school year) in 1999 he took up the challenge of guiding the Movement's work in San Lorenzo for the next stage of its mission. It was a moment to assess the achievement so far and look to the future.

The new Headmaster, José Miguel Navarro brings to his work for San Lorenzo experience from the earliest years in the Movement's Catechetical work and strong commitment to its development among the children, the staff and the parents of Conchali. He expresses his understanding of the vision of the Movement which is being realized in San Lorenzo by pointing out that:

> There is always a danger – especially in South America – of looking at San Lorenzo as simply a social project depending on financial and social expertise. There is a constant need to recall everyone to the principal objective which is to evangelize all those who are involved in it, following the spirituality of the Manquehue Apostolic Movement which flows from the Rule of St Benedict in communion with the Bishop of the diocese.

San Lorenzo is based on an approach to the problems of Conchali in which "someone in a relationship of loving welcome (*acogida*) has taught them to use the Bible, to encounter Jesus Christ, and to accept him as personal Saviour and Lord and King of their lives."[7]

There is now a good infrastructure of buildings and facilities. The relationships between older and younger pupils has been well established and in this the help of pupils of San Benito has been invaluable. A vital source of success so far has also been the *acogida* and *tutorías* which are the key to the whole work. It has been an outstanding work of the staff who have always been ready to listen and to make an effort to respond to the needs of so many people who are involved with the College.

Inevitably, given the circumstances of Conchali, there are urgent, immediate problems like drug addiction, alcoholism, adolescent pregnancies and so many other things that belong to the realities of our time. San Lorenzo's principal concern is to be welcoming and to preserve the capacity to listen, the ability to love, to maintain confidentiality, to preserve a relationship of true friendship. In this the key is in the work of the tutors, the role fulfilled by teachers in charge of departments, the responsibilities which everyone who works in the College must accept. What they all need to do is to cooperate closely with each other about the role which each one must play and to make sure that everyone delivers the only possible response to what in reality emerges from a meaningless situation – and that is to respond to the message of Christ. To this end every effort is made to work at the formation of teachers, the tutors and all the staff of the College.

In addition all must work with the auxiliary systems which are maintained to help in this work, namely psychology, psychopedagogy, workshops for sport and cultural pursuits, conferences with teachers in charge and the tutors and several other external resources. Every effort is made to avoid short-term solutions and evasions and to make San Lorenzo ever more explicitly a project coming from the very heart of the Manquehue Apostolic Movement with real fidelity to its principles.

There are some fundamental pillars on which this purpose rests like praying the Divine Office in as worthy a way as possible, listening daily to the word of God, which has found a concrete form in the reading of the gospel before every meeting, having *lectio* in all the retreats, in the teachers' courses and days for study. Also there has been work on the concept of Community by basing it on the attentive reading of the Rule of St Benedict. Other fundamental pillars both among the pupils, the officials and the teachers is the formation of groups for *lectio divina* to meditate on the word of God week by week. In this respect some very good work has been done by the former alumni and officials who are involved.

In addition to this a welcoming *acogida*, which already exists is being strengthened and together with it a strong development of the sense and practice of community among the pupils and staff. Experience and the recollections of former pupils show clearly that what has most affected them and helped them, especially in times of difficulty, has been the time, sympathy and understanding and support shown them by individual members of the staff and assistants, who have always been available and ready in school and out of school to give time and attention to those who are lonely, in difficulties and in need.[8]

These words reflect a world which is already significantly different from the world of the students' meetings in the abandoned hut of the early days in Conchali. Nevertheless the spiritual vision which inspired the Movement in the early days is essentially the same, although it is richer and more developed through much experience. It is the gospel vision of how to make the poor and deprived truly our brothers and sisters through sharing with them the truth of the gospel.

The coming years will see further changes and new problems for the Movement's mission to the children and adults of Conchali in Colegio San Lorenzo. The Movement's fidelity so far to the initial vision of evangelization and service inspires confidence that the same fidelity in the future will bring God's blessing on whatever lies in the future for the Oblates and Members of the Movement in their work with and among the people who come to share in their search for God.

Notes for Chapter 10

[1] See chapter 7 – endnote 19

[2] Spiritual companionship is a vital element in the mutual help and support of life in the Movement – particularly among the Oblates. It takes the place of what used to be called spiritual direction and goes much further than that ever could because it is based on Jn. 14 – a form of friendship and mutual help based on friendship with Christ as a present living reality.

[3] The sacrament of Confirmation is in Chile normally received at the age of 17/18.

[4] This was a printing firm in line with the technical project at San Lorenzo.

[5] A House - in Santiago at this time - presided over by two of the Oblates. Young members of *lectio* groups in the Movement went to stay there for some months to have the experience of community living, prayer and study. It prepared them for deeper commitment to the Movement and its works. It was later replaced by the foundation of the Movement Houses of San José and Santa Hilda in Patagonia.

[6] This was *Auxilio Maltes* a service project which for a time the Movement ran in conjunction with the Knights of Malta.

[7] Little Rule for the Oblates 1, 10b - 14

[8] From reflections by José Miguel Navarro

Chapter 11 ~ The Third School
Colegio San Anselmo

A new creation

When you leave the main urban area of Santiago to cross over the shoulder of the Manquehue mountain going northwards towards the airport, the road enters an extensive plain which not long ago was open country. To the west on the left of the road is Conchali where Colegio San Lorenzo is now well established and flourishing in an environment which is still poor and deprived but has better facilities than it had when the school was founded. As you proceed along the road you drive through a new growth of industrial and business development reflecting a lot of foreign investment in the Chilian economy. More industrial and residential building is also creeping along the hillside to the right of the road stretching in some places out into the plain. After a mile or two, as you continue northwards, there is a road to the right which crosses the plain and finally climbs up the foothills into the High Andes mountains. It passes the shrine of Santa Teresa de Los Andes[1], goes on into the little town of Los Andes itself and then climbs up a pass through the mountains into Argentina.

Long before this road reaches the mountains there is a branch road to the right which leads into an open plain. On three sides this area is flanked by mountains and at the far end it is separated from the urban complex of Santiago by the Manquehue mountain, on the other side of which is San Benito school. As the economy of Chile grew in the 80's and 90's and the working population increased in Santiago, this whole area, which is called Chicureo, was designated for residential development. Its disadvantage initially was its distance from the center of Santiago, but a tunnel is planned which will make the area almost part of the urban complex. Its great attraction for homes is that the air is free from the pollution which in the center of Santiago becomes a problem whenever the wind drops and the polluted air becomes trapped in the bowl of the mountains. Another advantage for families is the sense of space and freedom in the whole of that area, which means so much to growing children and to their young parents as well. That is what led to the choice of this area for residential development.

After a number of other sites had been considered Chicureo was chosen also by the Movement as the right site for its third school, Colegio San Anselmo. The increasing demand for places at San Benito had led José Manuel and his Council to consider the foundation of a new school. During the early nineties the reputation of San Benito school had grown but the demand for admission to the school had grown faster. It was a demand which could not be controlled by academic selection. That was unthinkable, because it would have conflicted with the Movement's aim to serve whole families. There were so many applications for admission to the school that the Movement would soon be forced to refuse some of the families to whom they were already committed because the elder brothers and sisters were at school in San Benito.

Another reason for the decision was to enable the Movement itself to grow and find increased scope for its educational work and evangelization. The matter was carefully considered in the Council of the Movement with the prayer inspired by St Benedict's words in the Prologues of his Rule:.

> This, then, is the beginning of my advice: make prayer the first step in anything worthwhile that you attempt. Persevere and do not weaken in that prayer. Pray with confidence, because God in his love and forgiveness has counted us as his own sons and daughters.[2]

The decision was made and San Anselmo School was opened in Chicureo in 1995. At that time the basic services for residential development had been brought to the area and installed. The roads and even the street lighting were in place. Only the predicted mass of houses was missing, although there were already a few dotted about in twos and threes, while more houses were under construction in scattered parts of this extensive area. They looked rather lonely in the empty township grid, which was waiting in expectant solitude for the sound of voices and the liveliness of the families who would come to begin their lives there. In the early days San Anselmo was on its own in all that emptiness.

There was a sense of pioneering as the first buildings took shape, but it was combined with a sense of purpose and confidence inspired by the Movement's now well established principles about how to teach and evangelize the young. The sense of a new beginning on the now familiar Catholic Benedictine lines of the Movement was strengthened by the newness of this housing development and the youth and energy and the faith of all who came to be involved in it.

The Oblate who was chosen as Headmaster to get the school started was Roberto Quiroga. He had been working at San Benito as Director of Studies. He and his wife Magdalena (who as a young student had been so strongly influential in the earliest beginnings of San Lorenzo) moved with their children to a new house near the chosen site for the new Manquehue school in Chicureo. There were 55 pupils in the first entry, all tiny children of 4 years old. In fact, the new buildings were not ready and this first class of San Anselmo began its life in the Kindergarten buildings of San Benito, while the construction of the new school in Chicureo got under way. Here San Anselmo followed the early pattern of both San Benito and San Lorenzo. The first children and teachers began life in temporary accommodation. The San Benito kindergarten children completed their classes in the morning and the little ones for San Anselmo had theirs in the afternoon.

When this first class moved out to Chicureo there was plenty of space on the new site for San Anselmo - much more than had been available for San Benito. The layout of the buildings is more generous and there are ample playing fields available, so from the first there were wonderful assets for the children on the new site.

In working out the plans the architects benefited from all that the Oblates had learnt from the planning and building of San Benito and San Lorenzo. They made the most of the sense of space and light and air which belongs to the whole area and the mountains that flank it. As the building progressed the children and staff moved in from their temporary quarters in San Benito and the school began to take on a distinctive character. However, as Roberto Quiroga remembers, there was no intention of starting a different sort of school:

There was no specific aim or project which marked it apart as a Movement school. The idea was to repeat the experience of San Benito with a few minor adjustments and modifications, but they were only details about how to realize exactly the same thing that was already a reality in San Benito namely, evangelization through encounter with the Word in scripture in line with the wisdom of the Rule of St Benedict.[3]

In spite of this San Anselmo from the first had a character of its own. The staff and children are faithful to the principles and methods that were worked out for the Movement in San Benito. They work always in close co-operation with Manual José Echenique, who was at that time the co-coordinator of the educational thinking and practice within the Movement[4]. Nevertheless this new school was not simply a clone of San Benito. San Anselmo in its own environment developed its own character and unmistakable individuality.

At the beginning the vision of the ghost town of Chicureo, with no houses in sight but plenty of streets and street lighting, made one wonder if this empty school in an empty place would ever manage to fill up. But the children came all right. They began in 1995 with 55 pupils. By 1999 there were 580 pupils and 80 staff, including teachers, cleaners and kitchen staff. The Chicureo housing development is now thriving and other schools have moved into the area to supply the growing needs for the education of children. But San Anselmo, through the foresight which went into its conception and planning, had the advantage of being in place and working from the first before there was any competition. It quickly became part of the scene - a well-established and well-loved center, where a short time before there was only a desert in which the earliest buildings looked rather desolate without shape or context in the windswept empty bowl of land lying between the mountains. For those with a historical sense these lay Benedictines of the Movement were creating an echo of the early Celtic and Benedictines monks in Europe bringing the gospel, literacy, creativity, light to a different sort of emptiness among the relics of the Roman Europe which had been shattered by the barbarian invasions. But that early physical emptiness of Chicureo is a rapidly receding memory. Now San Anselmo is all seething with life and, because of the spacious design of the buildings and the whole ambience, the children look as though they belong and the school belongs to them.

Building a new community

Thus the initial emptiness of Chicureo changed and became full of promise for the future, especially in the daytime when the little children were brought on site by their parents. In the evenings and at weekends, however, in those early days the life went out of it again. For Roberto, the Headmaster, himself the first two years were difficult and lonely. He had the support of his wife - an Oblate like himself - and his young family, but in the school itself he was at first the only member of the Movement working on the staff. Having been used to working in community he found it hard - especially in the second year. He was separated from the rest of his own Manquehue community and he felt it in his work. Nevertheless he was there for a new beginning not for himself but for the whole Manquehue community. He had left his old community specifically to build a new one. Now without the support of their immediate presence he had to remain absolutely faithful to *lectio* and prayer while thinking carefully about administration and everything that had to be done each day. Part of the way in which he faced this problem in his meetings with San Anselmo's new teaching staff was by witnessing openly from the first to the Catholic and Benedictine principles which would inspire the teaching and the pastoral care of the new school. He recalls how he tried from the first to share with them the vision which inspired him:

> It was important from the first to bring the teaching staff into the prayer life of the schools and also into the Benedictine style we follow in our staff lunches with silence and reading. The prayer together was vital but so was the community lunch. For St Benedict sharing prayer in the oratory and meals in the refectory are the two strong moments of community life. It was important in building up a new school community that everyone, and not just members of the Movement, should be together at lunch. The fundamental ideals of

the Rule were for everyone who was part of the new school community.[5]

This sharing in community life was a good start. After the initial shock of meeting the monastic principle, still so alive among the laity, these professional teachers settled down remarkably well to a vision about their teaching vocation which was quite new to them. It invited them to accept an integrated approach which was foreign to the tendency towards compartmentalization of teaching, and of every subject within the curriculum, to which they were accustomed. Now they were being invited to combine their teaching of the received curriculum with sensitivity to the spiritual needs of the young. They became aware of the call to take part in the formation and evangelization of a new generation of young Christians. They learnt that prayer was seen by the Movement as the essential inspiration of their professional work. That was very new and quite a problem. Making the God-centered prayer of the Liturgy of the Hours an integral part of the school day was not easy for them at first. There had not been anything like that in their training as teachers, but they were being invited to learn about it from example and discussion. Roberto himself remembers how:

> In the first years I often went to the chapel to pray the Office by myself - or I might invite a couple of members of the staff to come to the chapel to pray with me, and they might well wonder 'what is all this?' It led to conversations with them in which they learnt about St Benedict's vision which recognizes our spiritual weakness and our need of God's grace.[6]

The first two years were the difficult time. In the third year other members of the Movement came to strengthen the core community and this made things easier. There was Anthony Dore and Macarena Garcia and later they were joined by Ignacio Canales. The spirit of the Movement had been there at the beginning, but it gained strength with the arrival of the other Oblates and members of established Manquehue communities. Fortunately they were helped enormously as time went on by the generous response of the professional teachers to the vision to which they were being introduced by the Movement.

The wisdom of St Benedict

Already in the schools of San Benito and San Lorenzo this lay Benedictine Movement had found in practice a real correspondence between the spiritual needs of growing children and deep scriptural wisdom of St Benedict. The Oblates themselves were learning to live the Rule in a new way in their own lay lives and that helped in their teaching and pastoral care.

Things inevitably looked different at first for the trained professional teachers with whom they were now working. Teachers who had no knowledge of the scriptural basis of the Rule or its place in the Movement needed to be convinced about its relevance in their work. It was necessary to inspire in them an appreciation and love of the values that had come to mean so much to the members of the Movement. It was not easy to achieve this, especially when it came to themes that are out of fashion in the secular world.

The theme of obedience[7], which is so important in the Rule was difficult because of the secular assumption that it is outdated. It seems at first to be opposed to cherished ideas of personal freedom and independence. Parents, however, (and most of the young teachers were parents) come quickly to see its value for children. But what about adults? Well, even for adults, they had the example of this strange lay Benedictine community. The lay Oblates were committed to the gospel reality of the obedience of Christ and our call to imitate him. Perhaps, after all, it was a key to inner spiritual freedom not the end of it. The Manquehue proclamation of the importance of obedience in spiritual formation of the young had a solid foundation. It could not be discarded out of hand by any who would follow the gospel seriously.

The centrality of *lectio divina* was easier to deal with. The teachers quickly became accustomed to it. Every week at San Anselmo there were faculty meetings which began with a gospel reading. Every month the whole staff met for an hour and a half. Again they started with a gospel reading and it was always clear that the agenda was about their God-given responsibility to the children and the families. Through these meetings and through the daily Office and the *lectio* (with its daily inspiration of the word of God from scripture), and the *tutorías* and the spiritual companionship in the spirit of the Rule, which had become the

207

great instruments of the Manquehue educational vision, the staff began to develop a true community spirit in the Manquehue style. This bound them together as in a single body with a single purpose for the good of the children. The chapel was no longer for the Oblates only, as more of the teachers and children began to join them at Lauds, Midday Office and Vespers.

Thus at San Anselmo, as in San Benito and San Lorenzo, the great themes of St Benedict's Rule were from the first used to enable the children, the staff and the parents to understand and make their own the riches of Catholic living. It is not easy to get a hearing for scripture and St Benedict in a world which so often looks for inspiration to competition in everything from sport to the market economy and which offers little to the development of personality except the desire to lead and to dominate over others.

Can humility[8], for instance, which is so dear to St Benedict, be linked to the encouragement of self-esteem in the young, which is so often the aim of modern educators? Roberto, in promoting the Manquehue vision for San Anselmo, argued with the new teachers for the positive value of humility because it teaches us to see ourselves as we really are. That involves recognizing the potential for good with which we have been gifted and then in gratitude working to develop it for the good it enables us to do for others. It is a better basis for self-esteem than fantasies of self assertion. It is strengthened - not weakened - by St Benedict's insistence that the good in us comes from God and is there to be developed with gratitude.

The theme of correction is also important for St Benedict in education but it is often neglected today and rejected by extreme libertarians. They would like to abolish it altogether from education, but it is integral to any process of really caring for and guiding the young. It is important in the Movement schools as an expression of love. To deprive children of the guidance they need through correction in finding their way between good and evil is to deprive them of an essential element of love.

There were other Benedictine themes that proved helpful to the education of the young. St Benedict speaks strongly about the evil of murmuring in a community. The word he uses is often translated unsatisfactorily as 'grumbling'. What he means by murmuring is a hidden and almost conspiratorial criticism of leadership in a community, which destroys peace and mutual support, which in the end makes it almost impossible to respond to good.

Care of the equipment and goods[9] of the school and of all that they use and handle is another lesson from St Benedict which is important in the educational vision of the Movement. It is not instinctively appreciated by the young. It needs to be taught from an early stage. If it is not taught, if it does not come into their growing understanding of themselves and the world they are born into, then they will be ill-prepared for the lessons about the conservation of our environment which have been so disastrously ignored in the world of today.

In the early stages of San Anselmo school it was a primary aim of the Headmaster, Roberto Quiroga to lay the foundations in terms of these Benedictine principles, which were the inspiration of the Manquehue vision. It gave a real sense of purpose to the new staff and it was gradually shared by the parents to the great benefit of the growing school. A really united community grew up from the first so that now all those who are directors of the school are glad to meet and pray together as one Manquehue community. It has become the normal practice at San Anselmo. Progress among the teaching staff can be shown by the fact that two *lectio* communities of teachers were soon created.

It is important to make these points about the spirit which inspired the early stages of San Anselmo. That spirit was of vital importance because of the school was founded and grew up in the midst of growing affluence of the country. It was an important strength in the spiritual witness of the school that many of the teachers enter into the prayer life and the liturgical round, and they are all able to contribute to the varied spiritual input in a way that earlier developed at San Benito and is now a reality also at San Anselmo as it develops its own characteristic style within the genius of the Movement.

Two new developments
At the beginning of the academic year in 2002 José Manuel, as Responsible for the whole Movement, urged all the Oblates and members to make a 'preferential option for the young' in their work for

evangelization. The idea appealed strongly to Roberto Quiroga as Headmaster of the new young school of San Anselmo. He invited a group of young men and women, who had been at school at San Benito and were now at university or beginning their careers, to commit themselves as tutors at San Anselmo. They had remained faithful to the Movement and were members of university *lectio* groups. What Roberto asked of them was to visit San Anselmo at least once a week to take tutorías with the pupils. There were also occasionally convivencias for the whole group in Roberto's garden. These young tutors brought an element of inspirational disorder into the well-organized round of school life. The teachers found these student teachers difficult to assess but welcomed them with some anxiety and began to refer to them half in irony as 'the fantastic young people'. However they were accepted and settled down and became part of the scene at San Anselmo. They had a high profile which was appreciated by the children and parents, so that in time there was general agreement about the importance of their contribution. In a way typical of the Movement they had brought new life into the school.

There was a precedent for this development. During San Benito's early days the presence and support of young people (many of whom later became Oblates) had been invaluable. Now in San Anselmo 'the fantastic young people' were filling a similar role and keeping the Movement young and so more closely in touch with the children. They brought with them a conviction about the Catholic vision of the Movement which the pupils could understand. They came from different universities and different faculties but, through their shared work at San Anselmo, a great friendship grew up between them which added to the strength of their influence.

Then a second new development came a year later in 2003 in response to changes in the Movement since the early days. The whole Movement had by now become strong and diverse with outreach in the three schools, in the formation house of San José in Patagonia and through all its other growing commitments. José Manuel, as Responsible, saw the danger that under the educational and social pressures of running schools the original vision might lose its power.

There was great need to strengthen the spiritual vision of the Movement which was the essential core from which everything else must come.

With this in mind José Manuel, supported by the Council of the Oblates, decided to reorganize the work of the Movement on a pattern of 'deaneries', which is an idea taken, with some adaptation, from St Benedict's Rule.[10] During the early days of San Benito and San Lorenzo José Manuel himself had been able to keep in close personal touch with everyone involved. He had not been so concerned to monitor organization as to inspire personally the spiritual vision of those who gave life to the organization. This he achieved through the spiritual companionship which was his special genius. Those who saw what he was doing never ceased to wonder how he managed it on top of so many other responsibilities, but there came a time when even his exceptional gifts were over-extended. That was the time for the creation of deaneries. At San Anselmo Cristobal Valdes was appointed Dean at the beginning of the school year in March 2003.

As Dean his principal task was concerned with the Oblates who by this time were working with Roberto in the school. Whereas in San Benito the Oblates had from the first been a dominant factor in every aspect of the development of the school and community, in San Anselmo they had come rather later on the scene to assist Roberto in his initially lone witness to the Manquehue Benedictine vision. It was necessary that the Oblates should be seen in fact as a community, not in the loose sense of a group united in common work but in the very specific sense of a lay community united by their commitment to St Benedict's Rule. This was the center of everything and must be established in the deanery as such.

There is always a tendency in education for the curriculum, the day-to-day demands of pupils and the ambitions of parents to define the nature of the community. In a Manquehue school this would have been an impoverishment. There must be room for the vision of St Benedict, which would in fact enrich all those other elements. It was the community of Oblates who must embody that vision in San Anselmo. To achieve this with greater clarity was the task of the Dean and to relate all the work of the other groups and the activities of the pupils to this center. They had found that a lay Benedictine community is a reality which is profound though difficult to define. It was essential that it should be manifested and perceived by everyone in the concrete realities of everyday life. The Dean, representing but not supplanting the Responsible, and the Headmaster could now work together to achieve this for San Anselmo.

The gap between faith and living

It was really the achievements of the Movement in San Benito and San Lorenzo that made possible the creation of San Anselmo. This school, however, was founded and began to grow in a different and more affluent time. It was a time of economic growth and prosperity. The parents who moved out to Chicureo and sent their children to San Anselmo were on the whole young and making their way in a rapidly developing economy. There were new personal and cultural perspectives opening out in the country at large. The growth of the Chilean economy had brought with it a degree of affluence and confidence which was already a long way from the experience of Chile in the sixties and seventies.

The developing economy brought great and necessary benefits, but it also brought a shadow side which came from the secularization of society in the west. The new technological industrialization from North America was often linked with an alien assumption that economic growth and affluence are the essential and only keys to human happiness and progress. The result wherever this assumption became dominant was that the idea itself of human happiness was insidiously debased to fit the limited and often dehumanized categories of the market economy and rampant consumerism. Such an attitude to life was gaining ground in Chile during the early years of San Anselmo.

In this climate of opinion education itself was in danger of being reduced to a method of passing on the skills that open the way to making more money. To many this seemed to be justified by the false assumption that material prosperity itself leads to true happiness as a natural consequence. It was leading in the West to a climate of material affluence and increasing spiritual poverty. This shadow side of economic growth had its effect also on Catholics - even on Catholics in Chile, where Catholicism is still the country's official religion and was historically the tap-root of its culture.

An 'official' religion can at any time become formal and unreal and the danger is greatest when a gap begins to yawn insensibly between faith and 'real' life - between the Christian vision in which 'man does not live on bread alone'[11] and the anti-vision of what is called the 'real world' of technology, consumerism, the profit motive and relentless competition for the markets. This gap does not necessarily involve a sudden repudiation of the faith. Faith can easily be relegated to the background of life and kept in reserve for its expected long-term effect - a refuge for bad times or a consolation for the end of life. In that case faith is preserved in a sort of half-life or 'sleep-mode', which is not very operative, not very alive, not very real. In this sleep-mode it does not impinge on practical decisions and so it leaves one free to concentrate on material work and pleasure to the increasing neglect of what in truth matters most to human beings.

The real meaning of faith is then gradually forgotten and is considered to have nothing important to say about the education of the young. It is simply an 'extra' for those who happen to want it with nothing to say about 'real life'. In this way the gap between faith and life comes almost imperceptibly to be established as an assumption easily accepted because never truly examined. Catholics can learn to live with the gap because it threatens nobody and inspires nobody.

The Movement had arisen in response to the dangers of such spiritual impoverishment and sought to ward off the various specters that arise from the gap and threaten human life. At San Anselmo Roberto from the beginning and the other Oblates, when they joined him later, sought to enable the young to avoid the dull and obvious road of falling victims to the gap and losing themselves the spiritual emptiness it engenders. To achieve this it was necessary to witness openly to the truth of the gospel in all aspects of life - in the classroom, in play, in leisure occupations, in moments for the God-given ability of children to have fun, above all in the moments of seriousness and reflection. The task was to help them face the truth about themselves and the meaning of life which the gospel offers to all. This truth is often evaded or suppressed in the lives of the young today, because it is neither understood nor encouraged nor affirmed by the example of parents, of teachers, of society at large. And yet, if they are given the chance, the young often show a spiritual awareness beyond their years.

In the early days both the new teachers and the new parents had much to learn at San Anselmo about the gap and its effect on the education of the young. They are able to testify to some profound experiences which arose from their encounter with the faith that is at the root of the Manquehue educational work.

Thus it is that in the days when Roberto was building up his teaching staff there were some strange chances and improbable coincidences that brought teachers and parents to the school. The growing reputation of San Benito influenced one, while another was attracted by the surrounding hills and unspoiled countryside of Chicureo as a place to bring up a family. Whatever the original interest they came without preconceptions of what they would face when they were interviewed by Roberto. That meeting was an unusual and unexpected experience for the first teachers and the first parents as they approached this apparently solitary man who spoke to them of a vision the Movement cherished for these first tiny children in his charge. It was the vision of a large community empowered to help and guide them by the word of God in scripture and the Rule of St Benedict. He may have seemed solitary to them at first but he spoke from the strength of the whole Manquehue community. Perhaps there were some who turned away from anything so challenging but those who responded had a tale of gratitude for the world that opened up for themselves and for their children.

The bridge of the word of God

For one teacher parent the first spark of her interest began with a visit to San Benito as a possible school for her children. She was amused to find that they took St Benedict's Rule seriously and patronizingly thought how 'out of date' these people seemed to be. She stayed for the Office of Lauds and sensed a strange spiritual awakening, but she quickly got over that. San Benito was not the place. It was to Roberto at San Anselmo that she went from there. Now her quest had changed. She was looking for a teaching job while at the same time thinking of the education of her children. She knew that the schools of the Movement stood for the practice of Catholicism, but, as for herself, the gap between faith and life was yawning wide and she did not think her Catholicism very relevant to the things that mattered in life.

Faith for her was a fragile thing. She had many doubts and no answers to them. Nor did she feel any appetite for further seeking nor expectation of progress in or revival of faith. Like many others in this state of mind she had already looked elsewhere for spiritual nourishment and followed others into the western penumbra of Buddhism and Hinduism - all without much profit.

Her first encounter with Roberto struck her with unexpected force. "How is your life of faith getting on?" he asked with irrepressible candor. The question was unexpected and abrupt. It was so unexpected and so on target that it brought her to tears as she was driven to review the gap that had grown in her life between the Catholicism of her upbringing and the present chaotic state of her religious life.

She began as a result of that interview with Roberto to build the bridge through the word of God in scripture which had also brought José Manuel and many after him across the gap to the discovery of the wonder of living faith. It was the bridge of the word of God which is best built through *lectio* to which Roberto introduced her. The experience of *lectio* then and afterwards brought her great peace. It brought her happiness also and it was a happiness which did not desert her later when it was tested by adversity. She encountered sickness, suffering, and in due course she had to face death and bereavement. Looking back she said that, after crossing that bridge, the shape of her life had not changed much. It was still that of a professional teacher and mother of a family, but she had changed completely in her hidden inner self through the bridging of the gap in the reconciliation and integration of her life in Christ.

A journey from emptiness to fulfilment

Another, although baptized as a Catholic had been brought up in a secularized school in Santiago in which religion was ignored. There was no hint of it in the curriculum, no mention of God. It was blandly assumed that religion and the Church were meaningless survivals from the past, and the past was dead and best forgotten. Atheism was the thing now in which everyone could be comfortable.

As a pupil in that school she did not really accept atheism herself but formed a secret independent idea that God probably does exist but is so remote from human life that he is quite irrelevant to it. As a belief it remained in the background and did not disturb her nor influence her life in any way.

A break, however, occurred to disturb this immunity from faith. She did not complete her schooling with the atheists. Instead a change of school was considered for her. Her mother began to think of a Catholic school but not her father. He was against so radical a change of direction. He thought that such a change for the child would mean the loss of her personality through the domination of nuns. Religion must be excluded. That was essential. She ended up at a College which was secular, mixed and lay - to satisfy her father - but it was liberal enough to permit each week one hour of religion - to satisfy her mother.

One day at school in some sort of wild experiment of liberalism they all attended a Mass. That was too much for her to comprehend. She was lost. She had been baptized as an infant but had learnt nothing about the Mass. She knew nothing whatever about what was going on at the altar. Her curiosity was roused and she turned to her companions for some explanation. Here was another way of beginning to cross the gap which we find built into the modern experience in so many ways. In response to her inquiries, her companions and one of her teachers led her steps along the way she had begun by her inquiry into the meaning of the Mass. She did not hold back. She even made her first Communion and later was confirmed. Her confirmation especially made a strong impression on her at the time and seemed to bring God near to her. But he came near in a distorted image. He was not quite such a remote inaccessible figure but still retained the old intimidating aura. That had not been changed by his nearness. In fact she thought he had got too near, and now appeared as a terrifying, inflexible figure intent on punishing anything she did wrong. In this way, while still at school, she went to Mass and read the gospels. After school it did not last. During five years of further study she did not bother any more about God nor risk getting near to him, nor did the Church have any significance for her. That religious episode of her schooldays was a thing of the past. The gap had taken over again.

216

When she married it was to a husband who came from a Catholic family. For him also the gap was operative, but in a different way. It was the way the gap can operate with Catholics at any time but especially today. Religion for him was there, but it took second place to everything else, and everything else occupied the whole of the screen of life. She and her husband had an amicable agreement. They were content with their life together, their work, their children, and that was enough. There wasn't any room for God. Neither of them felt any need for him. They were both comfortably settled at the other side of the gap, contentedly facing the other way.

They moved to Chicureo to get away from the confining stress and pollution of the city. At the time they had two sons, the elder just ready for school. They had heard of San Benito and that made them wonder about San Anselmo, but it certainly seemed too religious for them. Like many parents confronting the gap she felt how much she would have loved many aspects of the Catholic formation she observed at San Anselmo, but she knew now that all that dream was over for her. Anyway it was clear that she and her husband did not qualify by their lifestyle for San Anselmo. Theirs was not the sort of attitude to religion that San Anselmo seemed to stand for. It was consoling in a way. They knew they would be rejected and their sons with them. However, just to see what happened, they sought acceptance by these ardent Catholics. After the interview, in which they avoided pretence and told everything about their lack of religious belief, their boy was accepted for the school. They were profoundly surprised at this deal across the gap, which was offered beyond all expectation. What did it mean?

They went cautiously to the first meeting with the staff and there in that first meeting at the school her husband astounded her by suddenly volunteering to be a delegate on pastoral matters. She was furious. How could she and her husband pretend to deal with pastoral matters when they did not go to Mass - even as a mere formality. But it was too late. The die had been cast and the Holy Spirit was on the move. They found themselves in a *lectio* group and it was led by Roberto himself, the Headmaster. What was really surprising was that the group prospered and grew in numbers so that it had to split into other groups. After two years of this new experience of growing familiarity with the word of God they were asked to direct a new group. They accepted and in the end took on three groups. At every stage of this strange transition of their lives, as they edged their way – propelled by the unseen breath of the Spirit - across the gap, they found themselves enriched, ever more fulfilled, ever more committed, ever more at peace.

It followed that this mother newly awakening to faith was in due course invited to join a Manquehue community of women. She agreed to this partly from curiosity, but it proved to be a dangerous curiosity. Things were getting more and more out of hand. The day came when Roberto invited her to take charge of a Manquehue community of women which was being formed in the area of Chicureo. The steps followed each other inexorably and each was positive, constructive, renewing, encouraging and unexpectedly welcome. There was no dramatic upheaval in her life. She was still the same wife and mother, but now God was no longer remote and threatening. He was a loving father. Jesus was her friend. Mary was no longer a plaster figure in the sky but a mother close to her in understanding and love and quiet support. Cynical rejection of everything had evaporated from her life. *Lectio* had become part of her life, and every word of the Bible had a positive message for her - a message of love, guidance, healing, support. Her life had been enriched by what she had learnt through gentle stages about praying the Office, about mercy, about compassion, about obedience, about the service of others, about tolerance, about listening, about taking part in the Mass every Sunday - not in order to fulfill a religious duty but because of her love and need of the Mass. She had found her way finally across the gap.

The key to the jigsaw puzzle

There was another who on looking back saw the course of events which brought her to San Anselmo as a series of chance meetings, chance decisions, chance events which made no sense in themselves but somehow in the end formed a new and unexpected pattern in her life, like the pieces of a jig-saw puzzle coming together to form an improbably fascinating picture. She had been living a happy well-organized life as an infant teacher. She was completely happy and content with her husband, her job, her three children. They were Catholics. They went to Mass each Sunday. Yet there were times when they felt there was something missing.

Then came the question of a school for their eldest son. There was a nearby Catholic school, which they knew well and liked the people, but they thought they should look further. At the same time they were thinking of moving to Chicureo and a leaflet about San Anselmo came into their hands. Gradually they felt themselves drawn into its orbit. Without any real effort on their part their son was accepted for San Anselmo, but when his mother visited the school she thought, as an established Catholic, she knew better than they did. Frankly she thought these people were slightly mad, because they prayed too much and took everything too seriously. As she listened to them she decided that she did not understand anything they were saying. Her son, however, did not share her own negative reaction. He took to everything that happened in the school immediately and with joy and he was really happy to be there. She was surprised but gave in for his sake - hopefully.

They were not left alone. They were invited to form a pastoral group for families and then came the fatal blow. They discovered *lectio*. It was something new the like of which, in spite of their Catholic background, they had never heard of or experienced. It brought a cost with it in time demanding effort and perseverance, but it opened up a new world for them, which, in spite of their tame, secure, traditional Catholicism, they had never suspected and in the end it became a real necessity to get to know more about it all.

From that first pastoral group the members were separated to form other groups. A deep need grew up in the mother to go further in her commitment and to learn more. She joined a Manquehue community for *lectio* and then was called on to become its leader. The prospect of that responsibility caused her a lot of agony. She had discovered the Rule of St Benedict and knew what he says in his chapters on the Abbot about the demands made on one who takes on spiritual responsibility for others. She had never seen herself in this light and it was difficult to face its implications, but somehow she knew that God was directly 'calling her to cross a river'. She had been trying to live with one foot on either side but it would not do.

She considered herself a coward and wanted to hold back and stay with the familiar. But at that very moment she remembered the first time she had done *lectio*. It had been Christ's words to the disciples 'Do not be afraid'[12] that stuck with her and came back with great power again at this moment of fear. That was the end of her cowardice and she went forward across the gap into the full reality of the new life in Christ.

Looking back she saw the pattern of the puzzle that had been her life. She saw in her life God's fatherly love, his tenderness and concern in guidance, his correction through sorrow and suffering. Now at last, even when she is faced with grave problems, she has the certainty that God is guiding her life and those of the ones she loves. On what had been the other side of the gap, which is now her side, she came to understand that the key to everything is to love and to give unstintingly.

Allowing God to become the center

Looking for the right school for the first child in a family is always an anxiety and perhaps it is not often that parents on that search have the wonderful experience of finding a school which involves a lifelong gift for themselves as well as for their children. It happened to one such parent who approached San Benito about his eldest little son the year before San Anselmo was opened by the Movement. There was no room at San Benito, 'but what about trying this new Movement school in Chicureo?' It seemed like a gift from heaven because they had just bought a plot in Chicureo, simply as an investment. The matter was decided for them and their first son joined San Anselmo even before they had built a house nearby.

Very early on in the school year (which starts in March) they found themselves with many others being led round the Via Crucis[13] on Holy Saturday - an experience which impressed them deeply. They were impressed by the meditation on the Passion. They were especially impressed because it was led by a layman, who was their son's new Headmaster.

Everything was new to them - the whole district, the people, the style of this lay community who seemed to have so much to give. There were meetings with the teachers and other parents in which they began to get to know people and to feel more at home and to be comfortable with those who influenced the direction of the school, 'of whom the most important, it seemed, was God'.

These years when the school was beginning were not without problems, but they were reassured by the example of how the Movement had succeeded at San Benito. In their first year came an invitation to form a 'pastoral group'. They were happy to respond. They had no idea what a 'pastoral group' might be, but they felt personally affirmed by the invitation and said 'yes'. It turned out to be the first pastoral group of the College and it was led by the Headmaster. What they did was completely new to them. They were plunged into *lectio divina*. They found themselves reading the Bible seriously, making comments on what the readings had meant personally to them. It was quite a new experience for them to express their intimate personal response to the word of scripture. They found the courage to overcome their embarrassment and then they experienced a sense of happiness and liberation as they left the meetings after such exposure to profound and timeless issues of life. Moreover they found a deep and growing bond of friendship with the others in the group - a friendship which has lasted.

After the first group they were called to form others, and then came the time when the husband was invited to join a community of the Movement, while his wife was invited into a woman's community. It was a big step forward. The pastoral groups had been partly social in their orientation. This new community of the Movement took them into a deeper experience of personal dialogue with God through his word in scripture. And at home they began reciting Compline together each evening. Their spiritual life advanced day by day towards a deeper commitment, happiness and fulfillment.

They took part in the General Retreat[14] in September and it was a new and powerful experience for both of them. They came away enormously enriched and began living quite naturally in a way they could never previously have envisaged - with Compline in the evening and Lauds at San Anselmo before going to work. There were other things of great importance also. For instance before writing about his experience the husband prepared himself by reading a passage from the Bible and praying the Our Father so that whatever he wrote might be in the light of God.

To summarize his experience of San Anselmo he wrote:

I have not mentioned the academic education offered by San Anselmo to my children. I have five sons and four of them are at the College and I know this about them: that they are happy at school and they have made good progress in learning to read and write and to study and they get good reports on their progress. Above all the vital experience of the whole family is that by allowing God to become the center of our lives together we have experienced the reality of his love.

The spirit of Saint Anselm

San Anselmo as a school and community is growing still. It will not reach its full measure of over 1600 pupils until 2007. It is close in spirit to San Benito and San Lorenzo, but the process of its growth has been a new experience for the Movement. For the growing Movement itself the founding of each of the three Manquehue schools was an adventure with great issues at stake. Although the main issue was the same in each case, namely the evangelization of the young in an age of secularism, the actual experience in each case was different. At San Anselmo the sense of pioneering on an empty development site marked the beginning. Then life grew stronger with the hordes of tiny children and the community of teachers, many of whom were also parents, and the young parents who found new inspiration not only for their children but for themselves also in this unusual school.

Then came the 'fantastic young people', the strengthening of the community of Oblates and the creation of San Anselmo as a deanery. While all the necessary academic learning and the games and other activities were developing all the time there was also another sort of learning which flourished at San Anselmo. It was valued above everything else by the Movement. It came from the word of God in scripture and the wisdom of St Benedict. This combination of learning and evangelization was not essentially different from what went on in San Benito and San Lorenzo, but it had its own characteristics in Chicureo.

The patron chosen for this new school was the Benedictine Saint Anselm. He had the misfortune of being forced into the position of

Archbishop of Canterbury, but his real life came before that. It was the life of a monk in Bec Abbey in Normandy. There he was known and especially loved as a teacher of the young. It was in response to them and with their co-operation that he composed two of his great works.[15] In fact, in the way he wrote and the purpose for which he wrote he took the advice of his students in preference to opposite advice of his great predecessor, scholar and archbishop, Lanfranc. His relationship with the young whom he taught was one of strong friendship centered in Christ. His method of teaching was not the imposition of learning but the encouragement of interest through mutual understanding. While teaching he revealed his inner self. While offering guidance he invited them to share a journey. They were saddened to lose him to what was taken to be a higher calling. He had known how to give them not only knowledge but friendship. His correspondence reveals how the friendships of these days lasted when he was moved from the monastery to be archbishop.

It may be that these details were not in mind when Saint Anselm was chosen as patron of the Manquehue school in Chicureo, yet somehow it proved to be the right choice at each stage of the school's development. In a context far removed from the monastery of Bec in the early middle ages the unique spirit of Saint Anselm seems to have found new life today in this lay Benedictine community and in Colegio San Anselmo of the Manquehue Movement.

≈

Notes for Chapter 11

1 Santa Teresa was a young Chilean who was born in 1900 and died as a Carmelite in the Carmelite convent of Los Andes at the age of 19, making her profession on her death bed. Her published diaries and letters reveal a young life of self-sacrifice and prayer reaching the heights of mystical experience. There were many miracles and a very strong popular cult and she was canonized by Pope John Paul II in 1993. Her shrine just outside Los Andes is now a great center of pilgrimage.

[2] The Rule - Prologue para 2

[3] Interview with Roberto Quiroga

[4] It was about this time that the Directorio Educational Manquehue (DEM) was founded under the chairmanship of Manuel José Echenique. It monitors, supervises and unifies all the educational and evangelizing work of the three schools.

[5] Interview with Roberto Quiroga

[6] Interview with Roberto Quiroga.

[7] See St Benedict's Rule - Prologue and Chapter 5

[8] See St Benedict's Rule - Chapter 7

[9] See St Benedict's Rule - Chapter 32

[10] Rule chap 21: "Deans should be chosen from among the community, if that is justified by its size. They should be chosen for their good reputation and high monastic standards of life. Their office will be to take care of all the needs of the groups of ten placed under them and to do so in all respects in accordance with God's commandments and the instructions of their superior."

[11] Luke 4, 4

[12] Jn. 6. 20

[13] The Way of the Cross – a Catholic devotion following in prayer and meditation Christ's steps in his passion.

[14] Besides the many smaller retreats for groups in the schools or among the adults or the students of the Movement, General Retreats are held every two years. They take place from Friday to Sunday in a Retreat house and are usually attended by about 600 from all age groups.

[15] *The Monologion* and *The Proslogion*

Chapter 12 ~ Deaneries and Foundations

Introduction

We have seen how the beginnings of the Movement were interlocked with the beginnings of the first school of San Benito. Both were the result of José Manuel's search with his young followers for the guidance of God in their desire to serve him and his Church. While their work in practice focused on the schools of San Benito, San Lorenzo and San Anselmo there were other works of great importance for the mission of the Manquehue Movement apart from the demands of formal education. The influence of the Rule of St Benedict was growing during this period and putting down deeper roots. Both the Rule and the schools were influential in the development of a concept of the apostolate of the laity which was as new as Vatican II and as old as the gospel. It led them to work beyond the classroom also among adults of all ages to bring the gospel to life in the lay world today. It led to the gradual assimilation of spiritual principles of the Rule of St Benedict into a new vision of lay life in the Church. It led to the development of a new kind of lay Catholic life in the Movement which was important for their educational work but also went beyond that and affected every aspect of their lives, whether they were married or celibate. It led to new undertakings and initiatives, some of them related to the schools, some of them quite separate.

In this chapter we review some of these foundations and initiatives. But first of all we must explain the way in which the Movement in the 25th year of its existence was reorganized into deaneries. This was done in 2003 and involved changes and developments of great importance in the Movement's work both in the schools and elsewhere.

1   THE DEANERIES OF THE MOVEMENT

At the beginning of the academic year in March 2003 José Manuel made a radical change in the structure of the Movement and its mode of operation. Until then the organization had been largely dictated by the work to be done whether in the schools or elsewhere. It was based on a pattern which is familiar in the secular world, which distributes and delegates the responsibilities for work to be done and indicates the chain of command through which those with delegated responsibility 'report' to their superior or 'boss'. It was, therefore, the work of the Movement and the way in which the responsibility was shared out that determined the whole structure.

It became apparent, however, as the Movement grew and became more complex that the original vision of personal *acogida* and the interior reliance on the word of God in community might be lost in the impersonal demands of organization. The Movement was not immune from the danger, which is so commonly felt in all organizations today, that the structures themselves can take over and dominate the personal lives of individuals. Such developments would be quite contrary to the spirit of the Movement.

There are well-recognized types of malaise from which all complex organizations are liable to suffer. What often happens is that those with delegated responsibility are made to feel that they have to fight their battles alone without proper support and understanding from above. But then again it may go the other way. The one with delegated responsibility may feel that he is not sufficiently trusted, that constant interference from above prevents him from achieving what he is there to achieve. It is common knowledge that such problems – and many others like them – bedevil the work at the human level of institutes and organizations. The larger the organization the greater the threat to human peace and fulfillment. Organizations with a religious perspective, dependent on faith and charity, are not exempt from such problems. They come with human nature and they belong to all times.

In writing his Rule St Benedict was clearly reflecting his own experience when he foresaw possible difficulties about the delegation of authority to the Prior and to Deans[1]. He would have written at greater length if he could have foreseen what would happen in medieval monasteries as they became large and powerful. The great officials of those monasteries were known as 'Obedientaries'. It could happen that they exercised a power and authority within their own area of administration in a way which seemed almost independent of the community and the Abbot. It is a tendency which haunts every human organization with unfortunate consequences.

There was no danger of this sort of rigidity developing in the early stages of the Movement, when it was small enough for José Manuel to be close to everyone with his spiritual influence and support. As it grew larger, however, the task of being in touch with everyone on the basis of spiritual companionship was too demanding for one man. He foresaw that others would have to help him and that is why he re-organized the Movement into deaneries.

He was guided by St Benedict who, even in his own comparatively small world had foreseen dangers in the delegation of the Abbot's spiritual authority. In foreseeing them and dealing with them he sought to bring everyone involved back to the spirit of the Rule in which all are seeking to serve God together and in doing so to support each other. In fact that is the only way to deal with such problems, but it is a way not accessible to the materialist secular world. It has, however, been precisely the message of José Manuel from the beginning of the Movement and he achieved it in the early stages through his personal influence and support. He had managed to keep closely in touch with everyone and he saw this as a primary obligation and a way of affirming and supporting the priority of the personal spiritual growth of individuals over the demands of a work ethic and its distortions of life. In the *Minima Regla* he had written about the Responsible:

> The most important office of the Responsible is the exercise of spiritual companionship; that means being available to the brethren with encouragement, directing their attention to the word of God and guiding them lovingly towards Christ and towards becoming more truly the Church in the way of the Movement.[2]

Now that the Movement had grown in size José Manuel had to teach others to assist him in this task. He turned for inspiration about how to deal with this to Chapter 21 of the Rule of St Benedict:

> Deans should be chosen from among the community, if that is justified by its size. They should be chosen for their good reputation and high monastic standards of life. Their office will be to take care of all the needs of the groups of ten placed under them and to do so in

all respects in accordance with God's commandments and the instructions of their superior. They must be selected for their suitability in character and gifts so that the abbot may, without anxiety, share some responsibilities with them.[3]

That was the key to the decision and the last point was the most important. The deans were appointed to maintain the personal inspiration flowing from the top and to motivate the spiritual commitment from which the Movement had started and on which its true life depended. The organization was to be centered on the spiritual needs of the *people* involved rather than on the *work* to be done by them. So in 2003 José Manuel appointed Oblates, whom he called Deans, to give support and affirmation to those engaged in each of the areas of work of the Movement. They would share his authority in personal guidance without being absorbed in administration. They would thus be able to share with him the task of spiritual companionship and support of the those who were doing the work. He wrote briefly about the introduction of this change to all who were involved:

> The most important consequence of this change of focus is that the structures which were formerly there to govern the Movement will now be there to give support principally through the Deans and also through the Secretary General.

It is important to note that, as a result of this change in the scheme of organisation, those with delegated responsibility for the organization of work – like, for instance, the Rectors of the three Schools – are not deprived of the fullness of their responsibility. Nor is there any change in their authority. The difference is that they are supported now by the Dean who offers them spiritual companionship, understanding and the inspiration of the word of God and of the *Minima Regla* in the fulfilment of their responsibilities.

The Dean does the same for all those who are working with and under them and so brings a new inspirational dimension into the work life of all who are concerned in this particular work of the whole Movement. The Dean is able to do this because he or she is there as the representative of the Responsible in order to fulfil precisely that task of 'spiritual companionship' which is so strongly affirmed in the *Minima Regla* to be the chief duty of the Responsible.

It may help to see how this new arrangement works if we take one deanery – that of San Lorenzo – as an illustration. The Dean is responsible for the spiritual, personal guidance in the first place of the whole working community which consists of all who are members, at whatever level, of the Movement and then in a special way of the Oblates, the aspirants (who are seeking to become Oblates) and of the *lectio* groups which will include some of the older pupils and members of teaching or administrative staff and even some of the parents. The Oblates and aspirants meet together for Lauds & Holy Communion in the morning before work starts. Then again they come together in the same way at midday for the midday Office and for lunch which the Oblates and aspirants have together in a separate dining room. They have lunch in silence while listening to reading in true monastic fashion. This prayer, this silence, this reading and the conversation which follows it are a profoundly important spiritual experience in the course of a busy working day, and it is presided over by the Dean. The same is the case with the evening prayer of Vespers, when the day is over. Pupils and staff who are not members of the Movement are, of course, welcome to join the Oblates for Lauds, Midday Prayer and Vespers, if they wish. Many of them do so from time to time – especially at times of need or deprivation. The Dean will take part in the work of the day and will also be available throughout the day to give support and spiritual companionship to all who may need or desire it.

It will be obvious that, although José Manuel took the idea of his deaneries from the Rule of St Benedict, he did not follow St Benedict's concept exactly but adapted it to the very different needs of his lay Movement. St Benedict's deans were responsible for a group of ten members of the larger community. The Manquehue Deans have a wider but in some ways a more limited responsibility. Their mission is not to take over the responsibility of the Rector (Headmaster) and other officials but to give them spiritual help and support in fulfilling their responsibility and to share with them through spiritual companionship the burdens and challenges of their office.

229

The Secretary General works closely with his assistants under the Responsible in overseeing the whole organization, helping to establish guidelines, providing administrative support and encouraging the different areas of the Movement to work together.

2 THE HOUSES IN PATAGONIA OF SAN JOSÉ AND SANTA HILDA
The meaning of Formation

The members of the Manquehue Apostolic Movement stretch out in concentric circles which embrace those who are fully committed and many others whose association is more tentative. All of them are learning and seeking in the spirit of the Scriptures and the Rule of St Benedict. That means that a process of formation is going on all the time. The word 'formation' is used to indicate that it is different from the process of 'training' which in various contexts is common in the secular world. Formation is a process of learning a way of life in which everything depends on the voluntary acceptance and inner assent of the learner. It often begins in the Manquehue Movement through communities for *lectio divina* and Movement retreats, and then through consciously following in community the guidance of the two key documents: the 'Way of the Movement' which guides all the members and the 'Little Rule' which is especially for the Oblates but may be used also by others.

In the early days at the Manquehue School, in the parish and during the emergence of San Benito school José Manuel personally guided in formation the young followers who came to him. As their own formation came to maturity they were themselves learning how to form others. Although José Manuel himself was always available to the Oblates and more committed members of the Movement, especially the young, he could not do everything and others had to co-operate with him in teaching those who wanted to know more and to become more fully involved. To achieve this it was not enough to arrange meetings about the word of God, the Rule of St Benedict, the spirituality of the Movement and the discipline of this way of life. More time, more concentration and more space for prayer and reflection had to be made available for the process of learning.

So it came about that a Formation House was established in which aspirants could for a year or more live a life, which except for work outside in the university or to earn their living, was separate and structured. In this environment they were able to learn more, to give more time and space to prayer with the reading of the scriptures and in this way to discern their vocation. Various temporary Formation Houses were established at different times as the need arose, including one for the Formation of women when some of the women members wanted to deepen their commitment and discern the validity of their desire to become Oblates. These Formation Houses, however, were not themselves permanent but lasted only until they had fulfilled a specific need.

The work of these early Formation Houses was fitted into a busy and demanding daily life in Santiago. Their effect was impressive but at an early stage a need was felt for more time and space to devote to intensive spiritual reflection, reading and practice in prayer and community life. A quieter environment also away from the city and its distractions was desirable. And so it happened that in the year 2001 a new community of San José was set up in Chilean Patagonia as the Formation House of the Movement.

The Foundation of San José de Mallín Grande in Patagonia

This new House was far away from the Movement's center in Santiago. Already in the days when San Benito and San Lorenzo were in the early stages of their development José Manuel used to go with his family and the Oblates, and often some of the other young members who were not yet Oblates, down to a remote farmstead in Chilean Patagonia. There in the summer months of January and February they could share in greater quiet and intimacy the life founded on the word of scripture, the Rule of St Benedict and the Divine Office and at the same time relax and read and meditate. The circumstances were ideal and beautiful beyond the imagination of city dwellers.

The farmstead itself belonged to the family of Luz Cosmelli de Eguiguren, José Manuel's wife. When her family was living in the small township of Chile Chico, she and her brothers and sisters had all been brought up in that wild and wonderful country. When their father,

231

Atilio Cosmelli, was made Governor of the whole district and had to move his home to Aysen, he had built the farmstead of San José on the lakeside in a lonely area of great natural beauty and had bequeathed it to the family. After his death they agreed to keep it and to share its use at different times. It was here that José Manuel and the Oblates used to gather for their summer holiday.

That was the first use by the Movement of this distant retreat. Then there was an entirely new development in the year 2000. The whole ambience of this farmstead, of San José, was so perfect for retreat, for reflection and personal discernment and for spiritual formation that they decided to set up a community of the Movement there as the nucleus of a permanent House of Formation. In that summer they began to build a new house in the area not far from the farmhouse by the lake. It looks down on an enormous lake which is some 80 miles in length and varies from two or three to some twenty miles in width. It is surrounded by mountains of searing beauty with ice and snow of the High Andes closing in the western horizon, because in this region the Andes mountains run down the Pacific coast and shed their glaciers into the ocean. The population of the whole region is small. Their livelihood traditionally comes from subsistence cattle and sheep farming, though these days the timber, mining and the tourist trade offer more hope for employment. They are a sparse and hardy race because, although the summers are warm, the winters are bitterly cold and the snow can be deep.

The Manquehue community for this Formation House follows the charism of the Movement and makes the fruits of their following of the Word and the Rule and of their prayer available to others who come to learn with them and from them. The process of formation, founded on St Benedict's Rule and the Minima Regla of the Movement, had been developed in the earlier Formation Houses in Santiago and was perfected in this austere and beautiful environment.

They do manual work on the farm and in the household. They have ample time for prayer, meditation, reading under the guidance of one of the Manquehue Oblates. Pastorally the community serves the neighboring farmsteads and small villages of the area in whatever way they can. It was very important for them that on their arrival there they were immediately welcomed by the Bishop of the whole vast region, who in his four page news sheet, which goes to everyone in his diocese, greeted them warmly. It was in the issue for the feast of Pentecost 2001 that he wrote:

> We also extend a warm welcome to the brothers of the Community of St Joseph of Mallín Grande[4], five young laymen, inspired by Benedictine Spirituality (prayer and work) are bringing strength to our Church of Aysen through the dimension of contemplation. This is a presence which little by little we shall get to know better so as to recognize its value and incorporate it into our pastoral work. May the Blessed Virgin Mary protect us in her compassion and may we feel the warmth of her heart making our work fruitful. I greet these brothers and give them my blessing with affection.
>
> Luis Infanti de la Mora,
> Bishop & Vicar Apostolic of Aysen

There is a local itinerant priest who goes round the widely scattered farmsteads and townships in the area and, whenever he can be in that area, he visits the Movement at San José. They work in harmony with him for the care and support of the local community. He has even commissioned them, on occasions when he has to be absent, to hold celebrations of the word and communion services in the local chapel in the village of Puerto Guadal.

The resident Manquehue community of three is intended to be the stable center of this new foundation and they welcome other groups from the Movement to stay for from four months to a year in that demanding paradise. San José has isolation and many of the attractions of the eremitical life. It has the quiet, the complete separation from the pressures, the confusions, the contradictions of contemporary city life. The four pillars of Manquehue spirituality provide the basis for the formation of the young: the search for God through *lectio divina* of the Scriptures - community life together - the celebration of the liturgy of the Hours - the sharing of common work.

Cristian Destuet gives an outline of the life these young people live at San José:

Our aim is to help people coming here to have a personal encounter with Jesus Christ, who is alive and risen, and is present in each person's life. The way in which they can do this is by living the spirituality of the Movement, something which most (although not necessarily all) of them have had some experience in before coming to San José.

This is the reason why *Lectio Divina* is our principal activity of the day together and is done twice, in different forms and at different times. God really speaks to our young people and they become strongly aware of His presence in their lives.

Community life according to the Rule of St. Benedict is also central. The young people often find themselves making significant changes in their way of thinking, moving from self-centered thinking to having an open heart and mind. They find themselves asking more and more, "What does the community need?" This change is almost impossible if it is not supported by faith. This community life is very intense and can often include lots of problems and sometimes frequent arguments that force fraternal correction and reconciliation, so we can live out what St. Benedict says, "Rid your heart of all deceit. Never give a hollow greeting of peace or turn away when someone needs your love."[5]

The Liturgy of the Hours builds up the community. By striving to become one voice together, we unite with the whole church and we live the Paschal Mystery, offering with Christ a sacrifice of praise.

Manual labour brings the young to discover that they are co-creators with God. What becomes important is not so much what sort of work they do, but the dignity of what they are doing as human beings. They collaborate towards supporting the community by working on the farm.

Acogida is vital to each person. It requires taking a lot of time to listen to each person, to get to know each one's personal history, helping them to listen and respond to God who is speaking to them.

It is not necessary to be a member of the Movement to take part in this experience.[6]

All members of the Movement were kept well informed about this new venture and they have been quick to understand the reason for it.

The whole idea soon became popular especially among the younger followers like the university students of the Movement in Santiago. Almost at once there were many of the young who volunteered to spend time there.

The House of Santa Hilda of Whitby
The first House of San José was followed in 2002-3 by the foundation of a Guest House nearby which was originally managed for a year by a doctor and his wife from the Movement. Then it was taken over in 2003 and run for visiting guests by a community of women of the Movement. This community of women is named after Saint Hilda of Whitby. Young women university students are accommodated there for four to six months of formation and there will be other members of the Movement who will visit from time to time to help in the work and studies. In order to achieve this there will be need of further buildings - in the same simple but strong wooden style - to complete the project. It is a growing project but the interest of the young already brings hope of a great future for this work.

3 THE INSTITUTO SAN JUAN APOSTOL &
THE CORPORACION BENEDICTINA DE MANQUEHUE (CBM)
Every religious organization which handles funds must hold and administer those funds through a corporate organization which is recognized in Canon Law and conforms to the requirements of the civil law of the country in which it operates. It is desirable that this organization should be 'non profit making'. In the early 80's the Movement set up such an organization which was called after the Movement's principal patron *Instituto San Juan Apostol* - The Institute of Saint John the Apostle. Initially this Institute was responsible for all the works of the Movement, but one of its concerns (perhaps its most urgent concern from the start) was the governance and handling of funds for Colegio San Lorenzo. Before long San Lorenzo became its sole concern and other responsibilities were transferred to the *Corporacion Benedictina Manquehue*. This was necessary so as to reassure the donors, on whom San Lorenzo depended, that all funds received would be devoted to the cause of San Lorenzo and to none others.

Then there were the Houses where the celibate Oblates live, who were earning by their work for the Movement but did not have possessions and capital themselves as individuals.[7] A separate Association was set up for these houses which is a legal entity conforming to civil law. There were separate legal Associations also for each of the schools and for the other official works of the Movement, which included the Bookshop and other later undertakings. All these other corporate associations are managed by *the Corporacion Benedictina de Manquehue*. Thus the *Instituto San Juan* is the corporate body which manages and is responsible exclusively for San Lorenzo School and Social Center and the *Corporacion Benedictina de Manquehue* is ultimately responsible for the management of all the other associations, funds and activities of the Movement, although there are some variations in the statutory provisions of each of them.

4 DIRECCIÓN EDUCACIONAL MANQUEHUE - DEM

With the foundation of San Anselmo the Manquehue Movement had 3 schools to run. Each school was at a different stage of growth, in a different area of Santiago and was required to attend different sectors of Santiago society. There was obviously a clear need to foster co-operation and mutual support among the 3 schools and above all develop and apply in each one a common Manquehue vision of education. The job was given to Manuel José Echenique in 1999, who set up what was to be called the "Dirección Educacional de Manquehue".

José Manuel had written the first article about a Manquehue approach to education in 1978 and since then he and those who had gathered with him in the running of the schools had developed this initial vision, but Manuel José and the newly founded DEM recognized at once the burning need to move on and give convincing answers to the fundamental questions about what the Movement was doing in its schools: what does it mean to educate according to the Rule of St. Benedict? What does a Manquehue school expect of its students, teachers, parents, tutors? What role, for instance, does academic study play in a Manquehue school? What is the Tutoría? There were many questions to be answered and the DEM has, since its beginnings, worked hard, researching into Benedictine education past and present and what the

Hierarchy of the Church is asking of schools. They have set up inter-school working groups who were asked to help in formulating a common educational policy applicable to all the different aspects of school life. The DEM has worked continuously with the headmasters of the 3 schools, bringing them together for regular meetings and providing them with the support and guidance they require as headmasters. It has also developed a formation program for teachers, tutors, and parents. The work with the teachers has been an important step in involving them in the Movement's Benedictine vision of education. The majority of the teaching staff are not members of the Movement and it is essential for their support and understanding, if the schools are really to achieve their deepest aims. It has also played a critical role in the Cunaco Group, set up in 1999 as a small group of Benedictine educators from Ampleforth Abbey, Worth Abbey, St. Louis, Sao Geraldo of Brasil and of course the Manquehue Movement who are all committed to developing thought on Benedictine education and initiatives in their respective schools. It has been and continues to be an important Area of the Movement's work.

5 CASA DE SANTA MARIA EN SABADO - THE SEDE

The organization and basic services of the Movement emerged and grew as they were needed like a living thing. In the early stages everything was done in San Benito, because that was the only building available. However, it was apparent that something more was needed and a search began for another house, which would serve as a center for organization and also for a number of other Movement activities which were growing rapidly. The money was raised and a house began to be rented in 1996.

This house rapidly became a nerve-center of the whole organization. It was known as the "Sede", which is roughly equivalent to Headquarters. It was named after Our Blessed lady on Saturday. In the Roman Liturgy Saturday is dedicated to Our Lady whenever another feast or seasonal liturgy does not occur. This liturgy of Our Lady on Saturday is observed by the Movement as a special expression of their devotion to Our Lady.

The opening of this house was like a gift of God to the Movement, so that quite suddenly things began to fall into place and the move of various activities to the new house became both possible and more

237

necessary than ever. The Corporación Benedictina de Manquehue was the first to move in to the Sede and soon it was from here that the Movement's own bookshop, the Librería San Juan, was run. Then came the Center for Benedictine Studies which also began to base itself in the Sede. The Center had the aim of inspiring studies in Benedictine spirituality and articulating the lay Benedictine character of the Movement. Under the direction of Lute Eguiguren, José Manuel's sister, the Center developed a full and varied program of lecture courses, and revived the Movement´s twice yearly review "El Quaderno" which obtained a wide circulation within the Diocese of Santiago, as well as providing valuable expertise in the preparation of training courses for teachers and parents in the Movement's schools. The Movement's weekly newsletter, El Boletín was run from the Sede too. The Boletín gives all the basic information for the week about Liturgical events, Feasts, Retreats, special meetings and activities as well as the times of Divine Office at the Movement's main centers. It gives a list of the Gospel readings for the week to help Lectio meetings. In addition to all this vital information, which is so important for the ordinary members, the Boletín always includes an editorial piece relating to the Liturgical time of year or some special event affecting the Movement.

The Sede also provided a base from which all the Lectio Groups could be run. For many years the Ramas, as they are called, (Branches in English) were headed up by Carolina Dominguez before she became Dean of San Lorenzo. The fundamental aim of the Ramas is, in all the aspects of organization, simple and profound – namely to facilitate through these branches the living encounter through the word of Scripture between each of the members of a lectio group and Christ, the risen Lord and to keep them in touch with the center and with all the life of the Movement. General retreats, the monthly General Vespers, to which all are invited, and other occasions and convivencias were all organized in the Sede. Material helpful to the various groups was also prepared there.

The Liturgy Area, set up in 1997, under the direction of Isabel Gross was also based in the Sede. From the beginning the greatest care has been taken to celebrate the liturgy of the hours with reverence and faith, following St. Benedict's guidance. In the Area Liturgia music and direction are provided for the daily celebration of the liturgy in all the Houses of the Movement. Also special liturgies are prepared and rehearsed for Holy Week ceremonies, for Pentecost, for the Liturgy in which Oblates make their own personal oblation by which they are committed to the Movement, for the First Communion and Confirmation liturgies at the Movement's schools, and for any other great celebration of the Movement.

The Sede quickly became the administrative anchor of the Movement. It provided a chapel, a spacious meeting room and plenty of space for secretary and offices. At first it was essentially an office building but in due course, with the establishment of the deaneries, it became also the community center of one of the Manquehue deaneries. In this way the Sede developed from being an office building to becoming a part of the "extended monastery" of the Manquehue Movement in which the celebration of the Liturgy of Hours, shared *lectio divina*, a shared meal in silence and a common timetable ruled by the bell are the key Benedictine elements which define its character. All other deaneries follow a similar pattern of life. As such it became a focus for members of the Movement of all ages, with many members of the Movement turning up to pray at different hours and *lectio* groups and other activities taking place in the evenings, especially among the young, often late into the night.

6 ESCUELA DE SERVICIO MANQUEHUE
MANQUEHUE SCHOOL FOR SERVICE

The Escuela de Servicio Manquehue was set up under the direction of Mario Canales in 1999. Its purpose was to find ways in which the schools and other members of the Movement could extend the Manquehue vision of love and service in areas of need outside the schools themselves. In this way Mario and his team organized opportunities for social action for the schools and for the communities of the Ramas. They had no doubt that wherever there is human need it is in the last analysis both spiritual and material. Seeking to supply material needs while ignoring the spiritual is as misguided as ignoring material need while seeking to supply spiritual want. Their ideal was reinforced by St Benedict's Rule who wanted his disciples to welcome all guests who came to the monastery and to see in them Christ himself.[8] The powerful guidance from St John and St Benedict has always been taken seriously by the Movement. It lay at the roots of the foundation of San Lorenzo and of the commitment of all their schools to the work of *Missiones* and *Trabajo* for the help of those in need in the countryside.

As time went on and the organization grew it was important for them that their work for others should not be dominated by the demands of administration and economics and so rendered impersonal, as can so easily happen. They strove always to keep alive in all their work for others the personal dimension of a one-to-one encounter with the Lord himself. In the broader perspectives of contemporary society there was always in the heart of the Movement a concern to help the deprived through social action but to do so through lively faith in the presence of Christ in them.

The Escuela de Servicio sought out and made available to the schools projects in the area of work and missions for the young of the Movement. At the heart of all these projects was the meeting with Christ through faith in the lives both of those who come to work in areas of need and in the lives of those for whom they work. This radical equality before Christ of those who give and those who receive was an essential part of their aim in all their work for the needy.

Particular times and occasions were chosen to foster this work. In the Branches or Lectio Groups during Lent everyone is encouraged to undertake a particular work of community service. In the schools they hold each year a week of Service during which each of the young are encouraged to undertake at least one task for those in need which will make them aware and open their hearts to the needs of our less fortunate brothers and sisters. Such experience leads on to further commitments and to the development of real friendships and mutual understanding. Groups of the young go back to the same areas again and are welcomed not just for what they bring but much more for what they are and whom they bring, namely Jesus Christ. This is the real heart of lay evangelization.

Opportunities for particular acts of service were also created and at any time the young of the Movement volunteered for them. These might be for visiting the elderly, the sick the neglected and performing simple but vital acts of kindness for them. Special days or 'workshops' are also organized for *lectio* groups and families to heighten the awareness of members of the Movement of what the needs are and what they can do and above all to inspire them in all this work with a lively faith in the presence of Christ and the need for prayer and *lectio* as the radical inspiration of all this work. The Manquehue School for Service worked to enable all these varied activities for the help of those in need. When the Deaneries were established this work was divided up between the Deaneries, so that each Deanery carries on the work of Mario's group in finding and organizing service projects for the school or Ramas which it oversees.

7 HOSPEDERÍA SANTA FRANCISCA ROMANA

This very special Manquehue foundation owes its origins to a group of parents of San Lorenzo. In 1997 they met in San Lorenzo chapel to ask God's blessing on a new work they were undertaking. It was to bring food and comforts to homeless men and women who slept under the bridges in central Santiago. Of course that was not enough for the Manquehue ideal. They brought not only food and comfort but Christ and faith in him to these destitute groups. They found them, including children, trying to shelter and sleep in cardboard boxes and plastic rubbish bags. Their first efforts were well received and this encouraged them to visit these homeless people regularly.

They were especially struck by the number of women - some of them with children - who had no home to go to. It was this that gave them the wild idea of founding a house of refuge to give these women some sort of temporary shelter and help. It was a wild idea because they were poor themselves and had no resources of any sort to make it a reality. However, just as had happened so often with San Lorenzo itself, a generous donor appeared when she was most needed. She provided the funds for this new venture and in August 1999 the house, which was called Hospedería Santa Francisca Romana, was opened in central Santiago. The patron, Saint Frances of Rome, was a laywoman and Benedictine Oblate whose life story, as a lay Benedictine in the fifteenth century had attracted the interest of José Manuel from an early stage. She was a married woman who lost her husband in a Roman brawl and then, as a Benedictine Oblate, gathered other women about her to

241

evangelize and care for the poor. Her work, though highly unusual for a woman in those days, was approved by the Pope. She was a mystic and visionary with great influence at that time and was canonized fifty years after her death in 1440. The Manquehue Oblates count her as one of their patrons.

The house down in the city center of Santiago was opened and the first resident welcomed on 16 August 1999. Quickly it became a place of refuge for homeless women - often with children who are welcomed and cared for also. There is a trained and qualified manager and as many as a hundred volunteers work there at one time or another to look after those who come there for shelter at night. To visit it is to experience a strong sense of joy and peace which is in sharp contrast with the harsh outside from which these women have come. It is one of the most valued works of the Movement outside the schools.

8 TUTORS AT THE SEMINARY

At the beginning of the academic year in March 2003 the Rector of the Major Seminary in Santiago asked José Manuel Eguiguren to send Oblates of the Movement to teach the new seminarians who were just beginning their studies about the Manquehue practice of *lectio divina*. This invitation came with the approval of the Cardinal Archbishop of Santiago and was both a great compliment and a formidable challenge for the Oblates who were sent to the seminary each week to fulfill this task. In the twenty five years of its existence the Manquehue Movement has become known in Santiago as a lay Movement working within and for the Church and the importance they attach to the daily practice of *lectio divina* is well known through their small communities of lay people of all ages who meet weekly for *lectio divina*. The recognition of this led to the invitation from the Rector of the Seminary.

In the Church since Vatican II the old monastic term *lectio divina* has become known among the ordinary faithful as never before. Many books have been written about it which have put forward various explanations and theories and recommendations. For many it has become simply the Latin term for any form of spiritual reading, but for the monks of St Benedict originally and for Fr Gabriel who taught José Manuel it has a special and precise meaning in connection with scripture.   The

Manquehue Movement itself has never wavered from the initial perception which meant so much to José Manuel Eguiguren during his three years with Father Gabriel Guarda in the monastery of Las Condes. At that time from a condition of doubt and confusion he came to a profound and living conviction that Christ himself is present for us in the Word of Scripture and that *lectio divina* is the way of responding to that presence and the guidance it brings in the day to day realities of our individual lives. The Oblates and other followers of the Movement have learnt to base their whole life and work on this perception and to depend on daily *lectio divina* and the prayer it inspires as an essential spiritual support for their way of life. In this they are simply following the guidance of Vatican II in *Dei Verbum*:

> For the word of God is living and active and it has power to build you up and give you your heritage among all those who are sanctified. Prayer should accompany the reading of Sacred Scripture, so that God and man may talk together; for we speak to Him when we pray; we hear Him when we read the divine saying.[9]

The message of the Oblates who now began working with the seminarians was simple and direct. It was to recognize the presence of Christ in the scripture readings and to concentrate on the simple but demanding question: 'what is Christ saying to me, and demanding of me, here and now in my life through this word of scripture? Six of the Oblates were assigned for this task at the Seminary. They began with a retreat for the Seminarians from Thursday evening to Saturday midday. After that introduction they led workshops with the seminarians once every week during which they worked together on chosen texts. The response of the seminarians was very strong and positive and some of the older seminarians began to ask why they were not given the same course. As a result of this response at the end of the first semester the Rector called in the Oblates and told them that, whereas his first invitation had been tentative and experimental, he now wanted to make the arrangement permanent and to extend it by starting a parallel course for the older seminarians.

At the beginning of the academic year in March 2004 the Rector extended this work further asking the Oblates to take lectio workshops for the Theologians as well. This they have now started so that the whole undertaking at the Seminary has now become a major commitment for the Oblates. It is not only a major commitment for them. It is also a quite remarkable opening up of their apostolic work in a way which will certainly have many unforeseen consequences. For José Manuel and the Movement it is a wonderful confirmation of their mission within the Church of Santiago which, beyond all their dreams, brings them right into the work for the formation of young priests. Not only the commission by the Rector but also the wonderful reception by the seminarians gives them added courage and affirmation in their own lay vocation. It is a very remarkable thing and perhaps a sign for the future of the Church that a completely lay Movement should be entrusted with such work by the Rector and Archbishop. Such sharing, understanding and co-operation brings into being new hopes and perspectives for the future. This, the latest of the commitments of the Movement within the Church of Santiago may well prove to be one of the most far-reaching and fruitful of all their works for Christ and his Church.

80

Notes for Chapter 12

[1] The Rule - chapter 65 & chapter 21
[2] Minima Regla de los Oblatos n. 6
[3] St Benedict's Rule Chap 21
[4] Mallín Grande is the name of one of the small townships on the shores of the lake, which gives its name to the whole district in which San José is built.
[5] St Benedict's Rule Chapter 4
[6] For further details of the life at San José see Appendix 4
[7] They follow St Benedict's precept that there should be no private property. Thus the property held by Benedictines should be held in common. "Everything in the monastery should be held in common and no-one should think of claiming personal ownership of anything." RB ch 33. The married Oblates are different and they contribute at an agreed rate to the common funds.
[8] "Any guest who happens to arrive at the monastery should be received just as we would receive Christ himself, because he promised that on the last day he will say: I was a stranger and you welcomed me." Rule chap 53
[9] From Vatican II Document on Revelation (Dei Verbum) nn21 & 25

Chapter 13 ~ The Movement's Educational Vision

The Chilean framework of schooling

Throughout the twentieth century the system of education in Chile from grade schools to Universities was probably the most advanced in South America. By the 1980's from each age group as many as 96% of children were attending the 8 years of grade school (basico) education and 75% were attending the four years of high school (medio) education. In tertiary education the number of Universities had increased to 41 and there were also strong professional institutes and centers for technical education as alternatives to University. Up to the time of the military government the limited number of Universities were funded by the government. They charged different levels of matriculation fees but tuition was free. From that time onwards the number of private Universities charging tuition fees increased rapidly.

Of the grade schools (from 5 years old to 13) and high schools (from 14 to 18) those which did not charge tuition fees were subsidized by the State on a per capita basis. Some of these were state run and some private. The private ones were mostly run by the Catholic or Protestant Churches, although some schools were owned and run by other financial interests. From the 1960's onwards the state provided limited funding for the schools where tuition fees were not charged and added funding for the provision of breakfast and lunch daily during school sessions. This had the desired effect of leading to a strong increase in attendance.

In order to establish consistent standards and monitor performance the government set up an authority to lay down a basic curriculum and approve textbooks to be used by all schools at both grade school and high school levels. It also established control of the final examination which qualified students for admission to University. This is a basic qualifying examination and it is left to the Universities to deal with further assessment of applications and determine the level beyond the basic they require for different faculties.

From this summary it is clear that from grade schools right through to Universities both state owned and privately owned schools are both accepted and must conform to the minimum standards officially laid down.   It was this system that made it possible for the Manquehue Movement to establish its schools.   San Benito and San Anselmo are in the privately funded sector for those who can afford tuition fees while San Lorenzo, because it does not charge fees, receives per capita grants for tuition and also funding for school meals.   Much further funding is needed for San Lorenzo to cover all that it offers and the exceptional care it provides for the families and their children.   To cover this sum year by year the Movement is dependent on charitable giving.   It is this charitable giving which makes all the difference for the families and children by bringing into the realm of possibility all that the Manquehue Movement seeks to do for them.   It also makes it possible to treat the young from both types of school as equal and so bring about the integration in the life of the Movement of the young people who come both from deprived and from affluent backgrounds.

The educational mission of the Movement

The first point to be made about the task of the Movement when it entered into this Chilean educational scene is that it accepted the overall educational standards which were demanded and proceeded to work within the parameters set down for all schools in Chile.   Only by fulfilling these standards right up to university entrance requirements could they attract and keep pupils in their fee paying schools and justify the grants - both those from government and the gifts from charities - which they received for San Lorenzo.   This meant that from the first good teaching and academic rigor were essential.   Beyond those standards, however, there was much more that the Movement sought to give through their schools.   These further aims were not based on a private theory about the aims of education.   They were based upon the word of God in scripture and the teaching of the Catholic Church.

In the early days when José Manuel already had a following of young people he asked Cardinal Silva Henriquez whether there was anything he could usefully undertake with his young followers as work for the Church. It was in the seventies and at a time of difficulty in the Church worldwide. It was the time when Catholics at every level were trying to come to terms with the decrees of Vatican II, especially the changes in liturgy, when there was evidence everywhere of revolutionary talk and angry, often destructive, idealism among the young. The Cardinal's reply was probably not quite what José Manuel expected at the time, but it was clear and positive. It was a call to found Catholic schools which were truly Catholic and would teach the gospel to the young with the new ways he was discovering through his own experience.

In Santiago something had been happening, which was happening elsewhere also at the time. There were many in the Religious Orders, both of men and women, who were interpreting the Council as a call away from educational work in schools to more direct social action among the poor. This interpretation was questionable in the light of the text of the Council documents, but it had powerful support and led many to conclude that they should devote themselves to direct social work among the very poor rather than to continuing and renewing their traditional role as educators not only of the poor but also of the middle and upper classes. Catholic education of the young at all levels of society had for four centuries been a valued vocation among religious men and women. Now it was suddenly being widely devalued and abandoned by the Orders which had over many years built schools everywhere. Hence many Catholic schools were suddenly handed over to laity who were ill-prepared for the challenge of passing on the faith to a generation which was particularly restless and resistant to their efforts. In many cases the result was either the closure or the disastrous secularization of these schools at a time when a renewal of their mission within the Church and of their methods of passing on the faith were needed as never before.

Faced, as he was, with this situation in Santiago it was understandable that the Cardinal, seeing the evidence of José Manuel's exceptional influence on the young, had explicitly pointed him towards the foundation of Catholic schools. They were to be different from the old Catholic schools which had been run by nuns and priests. They would be renewed in the pattern of Vatican II both in the fact of their being run by laity for the laity and in the spirit of renewal which would inspire them. Following José Manuel's own discovery of the word of God during his three years at the monastery, they would return to the origins of Catholic faith by taking the word of God in scripture as their primary inspiration. They began working on these lines while still serving as assistants in the Manquehue School. After that and after their experience in parish work, the great decision to found their own schools was inspired and encouraged by the Cardinal's initial call to them to take on the challenge of Catholic education as committed lay people.

At this stage José Manuel and his young followers were already learning new spiritual dimensions in their lay lives of service through lectio divina and the Rule of St Benedict. It was these models that they brought with them into education and from which an educational philosophy has grown up with the Movement itself and has been given coherent expression by the spiritual vision which inspired it.[1]

From the beginning the Movement has stood for something much deeper and much more realistic than the mere acquisition of personal skills. Of course, it does not accept the secularist dogma which either excludes religion from school life or tolerates it only in so far as it is no more than an optional extra, which may be added to the rest of the curriculum but may equally be omitted without damage to the whole of education.

The aim, then, is to enable the pupils, while growing in their personal lives, to develop their native gifts and the different potentialities of the character and disposition which God has given them. To this end high standards in everything that is taught, from academic subjects to art and music and sport are an integral part of the aim. But the development itself of gifts and skills is subordinate to the greater aim of understanding the meaning of our lives and our vocations before the God who gave them to us.

This view is not forced on any pupils. It is offered to them to accept or reject as they grow through it to maturity. The difference is that in a Movement school they are never deprived of the means to learn about and understand this Christian view of who and what they are as children of God. Naturally, like all other adolescents today, pupils do not take everything with meek co-operation. There are storms and crises in Manquehue schools, as in others. However the personal relationships, which have been built up from an early age through all that is implied in *acogida* help greatly in the resolution of problems. Some go through times of withdrawal from what is being offered them. They may come back at school or after - or they may not. Such problems at this age are also opportunities, because adolescence is a time of life for sowing seeds rather than reaping harvests; and there are many stages in the growth of a seed. The problems which arise are wide-ranging and include also times of rejection of God and religion. All the rich meaning of the parable of the prodigal son[2] is alive and active in the Manquehue approach to such problems.[3]

The Word of scripture & tutorías in the schools

Besides academic excellence, then, there is a deeper aim to be achieved in and through all the activities and all the growth that the academic and other goals of a school imply. It is an aim that can be summarized, but not adequately described, by the word 'evangelization', that is the bringing of the 'good news' of Christ to our fellow human beings in ways that they can understand and assimilate. José Manuel himself expressed in simple and compelling terms his own experience and his desire to share it with others:

> At a time when nothing seemed to make sense to me, a Benedictine monk handed me the Sacred Scriptures and taught me to read them in such a way that it seemed as though Jesus Christ himself was revealing himself to me, risen and alive, shedding light on my life and filling it with meaning.[4]

Having received that gift he wanted to share it and, when he was faced with a class of largely unwilling and uninterested eighteen year-olds, he saw at once that what they needed was what he had himself received:

> All I did with them was to take the Bible and set about discovering how the Word of God speaks to each one individually. Their response was remarkable. We soon became filled with ideals. We wanted to do things, change the world. We became very good friends. We decided to organize ourselves and we called ourselves the Manquehue Apostolic Movement.

251

It was thus that, when a potentially hostile confrontation was converted into a shared experience, it began to take shape as an educational program. It developed rapidly. This rapid growth was due partly to José Manuel's genius for friendship. It was also partly due to the fact that among the young with whom he was dealing he was faced by those same crying needs from which he had himself suffered so recently. They are, in fact, the crying needs of the young at all times. Sometimes these needs are suppressed. Sometimes they break out in violent ways. Sometimes they are diverted into the pursuit of false ideals. Always they are there.

It was to lead the young to the Christian response to these needs that the Movement started their schools. As they sought in this way to pass on what they had received they gradually discovered something new. When the original group gathered round their teacher, they were drawn together and led onwards in their work by a strong experience that led to the creation of a special instrument of the Movement, which they called *tutorías*. One of them remembers the early days:

> We felt that we simply had to be with the children and tell them about our experience of Jesus Christ. A very special relationship began to grow up between a number of the older students and the younger ones. They helped train the younger sports teams, helped them with their studies or simply played with them in their free time. We began to discover how this special relationship, which we began to call *tutoría*, was in fact a precious vehicle for talking to children about this living God that had so much to do with their lives and all that was happening to them, who spoke to them through his Word and who heard their prayers.

It was in this way that at a very early stage, the whole concept of *tutoría* had taken shape. It is the second vital element, after sharing through *lectio* the Word of God in scripture, in the educational theory and practice of the Movement. *Tutoría* is, in fact, so important to the Manquehue educational vision that José Manuel has described it as 'the soul' of his schools so that without it their "whole educational project would fall apart". It is a unique feature since most of the tutors are still students (at school or university). They are not qualified educators in the ordinary secular sense of having a degree or other official academic certificate, although some of them have that sort of qualification. Their qualification for this work comes from their complete commitment to Christ through baptism, the sacraments and the daily practice of *lectio* in the Movement and the Movement is responsible for and guides their performance. This concept and how it worked out is so important that we must spend a little more time on it.

The word of scripture is the primary source book for *tutorías*. It is always available. Everyone in a Manquehue school has his or her own Bible. In *tutorías* they learn how to use it and listen to it. José Manuel explains:

> Simply reading the Word is not good enough. What is needed is for the Word to be brought home to each person. We must remember what the Ethiopean eunuch in the Acts said to Philip: 'How can I understand, if I have no one to guide me?'[5] This is where the tutors come in. They must play Philip to the children. A tutor might be a senior student, an alumnus (former pupil of the school) or one of the younger members of the Manquehue Movement who is assigned to a specific group of children with whom he or she over the course of time builds up a strong personal relationship. This enables him or her to take a real interest in the children's well-being and how they are getting on at school and at home with a love that ensures that no child gets lost in a crowd.

Elsewhere José Manuel describes this as 'rescuing a young person from anonymity'. Right from the beginning each child in the Manquehue schools is affirmed and saved by his tutor from feeling 'out of it'. This can achieve something of great and lasting significance. It is a way of evangelization enabling the child to identify with the mission of the School and of the laity within the school and in the Church – precisely as laity. This encourages the development of self-confidence, because self-confidence cannot grow in the vacuum of isolated self but only in the context of acceptance by others through love. The tutors themselves have experience of that context of love, just as the older children of a family do if it is founded on love. As younger members of the Movement every tutor has already been on the receiving end of *tutoría*. Thus, when they volunteer to be tutors, they know well the needs they have themselves at an earlier stage experienced. Now it is their job to care personally for the younger children, to 'rescue them from anonymity' and 'reveal a living God' to them through the word of scripture, a God who speaks to them in the word of scripture and is at work in their everyday lives.

The young tutors, of course, work under the guidance and supervision of one of the Oblates, but that is in the background. It is important that a tutor is seen to be a real young person and not just an agent of adults. That makes the tutor one with whom small children can identify as an individual, so as to rescue the young not only from the spiritual neglect of anonymity but also from the domination of 'peer groups' or 'gangs'. A tutor can come to have an enormous influence in the life and faith of a younger boy or girl. Few adults are as credible in the eyes of an eight or ten your old as is an older student of sixteen or eighteen. Once the relationship is established it is not only in the weekly period that the tutors work with the pupils. They join and help them in many other activities, such as sport, outdoor activities etc. They help them to celebrate important events like birthdays. They become a constant support and inspiration to the younger pupil.

It may seem dangerous to let the young lead the young in this way, but it is important not to be unrealistic. The ordinary fact of life in western schools, as every parent discovers, is that the young are anyway led by the young through peer-group pressures and the teenage culture. The way of *tutorías* within the Movement is realistic in accepting this fact and providing an 'escape route' of real spiritual depth. It is effective in rescuing many from the worst effects of a spiritually empty common culture of peer-group domination.

The time comes, however, when the young children must move on.

The weekly *tutoría* periods end when the children reach the age of fifteen. At this point the students can opt to join a shared *lectio* group run by the Manquehue Movement. These groups of between six and twelve people meet once a week, out of school hours, and currently just over half of the fifteen to eighteen year olds in our schools belong to a *lectio* group. It is important to mention that these *lectio* groups are not just something for the students. There are *lectio* groups made up of parents, teachers and maintenance staff as well. In their weekly meetings the students proclaim the Word and share with each other or pray out loud what God is saying to them. Each group is headed by a slightly older member of the Manquehue Movement. In school the whole tone of *tutoría* changes from about this age on. The relationship between the tutors and children gradually gives way to the provision of spiritual companionship for as many of the senior students who want it. [6]

Spiritual companionship arises naturally from shared *lectio divina* and from the weekly welcome of each other by the members of the community. It is closely related to the personal affirmation of each other, which in the Movement is called *acogida* and is quite simply an expression of the call to see Christ in each other which comes from the gospel[7] and is strongly repeated in St Benedict's Rule[8]. Since all are following the same way they share their experience with the word and this is the foundation of their community. This sharing brings encouragement and confidence through which in Christ they rescue each other from the spiritual isolation and the loneliness that can be so profoundly threatening at this age. They are now growing into the way of life of the Movement under the guidance of the gospel and the Rule. The Movement through *lectio, acogida, tutorías,* spiritual companionship and the mutual support of the meditation communities has been doing nothing more than passing on to the young the teaching of Peter to the first generation of Christians:

> Love one another deeply from the heart. You have been born anew, not of perishable but of imperishable seed, through the living and enduring word of God.[9]

Religious Education classes
Not everything, however, in their religious formation is left to the students encounter with the word of scripture in the rather informal groups for *tutoría* and the Manquehue communities. There is a strong religious education department in each school with qualified teachers

who operate alongside the *tutorías* but independently of them. In these classes they are taught about the history of Christianity and the Church, about Vatican II and about the doctrinal and sacramental life of Catholicism. To cover this there is at least one double teaching period a week for everyone. This more formal teaching is able to relate to the context of the living Church the whole religious development which the students have experienced through *tutorías*, and in their communities, and through the sacraments, and the Mass and the daily Divine Office.

Manquehue retreats

Integral to all this work of the *tutorías* and the communities and religious education is the retreat program.

> One vital aspect of *tutoría* is the retreat programme whereby we send every form, between the ages of ten and eighteen, to a retreat house in the country for a whole weekend once a year. There they are given talks on different subjects by senior students, old boys and old girls or members of the Manquehue Movement and they work in groups developing certain key concepts such as fraternal correction and friendship. We insist that the resurrection of the Lord be proclaimed in every retreat and we make sure that this is complemented by an experience of *lectio divina*. The retreats are an important part of the process of creating space where the students can learn to listen to God.[10]

Retreats have always been part of the Manquehue program. It was during a retreat that the first proposals for the formation and mission of the Movement came from the young followers of José Manuel. Every stage since then and every moment of decision - whether for individuals or for the whole community - has been marked by a retreat. The retreats last from Friday afternoon until after a midday Mass on Sunday. It is important to go away from the school and its classroom associations, so the Movement retreats are always held in one of the local retreat houses which are right away from home and school. A very popular place is the big diocesan retreat house on the coast overlooking the Pacific called Punta de Tralca. Retreats are not only an educational exercise. They are a vital part of the spiritual life of the Oblates, aspirants and ordinary members of the Movement. All the Manquehue retreats are run by the Movement itself with talks by laity who are members of the Movement. They may be Oblates or they may be alumni (former pupils of one of the schools) who are now at University or in the world of work. There are work groups on various topics and throughout there is a strong sense of spiritual friendship in which fraternal correction and guidance are easily accepted. The community experience and the individual experience are united in one Christ-centered experience. When there is a priest available for the sacrament of reconciliation and for Mass, he is there not to lead the retreat but for the Mass and the sacramants. The directors of the retreat are laymen and women and they lead the prayer (apart from Mass), the group meetings and the main sessions. In this the Movement is - as in so many other ways - authentically lay and exercises to the full the gifts of their baptism.

Preparation for the Sacraments
There is one characteristic of the Church in Chile which is not to be found everywhere. It is that all Catholic schools, once they are approved by the Archbishop, are also recognized as 'Pastoral Units' and as such they are integrated into the diocesan structure. They come under both the Youth and Educational Services of the diocese and relate directly to the pastoral outreach of the Bishop through his Vicars for Youth and Education. This opens them up to many inter-parochial activities under the aegis of the diocese. The pupils and the staff of a Manquehue school will, when they are at home, be involved in the life and activities of their own individual parishes, but at school they will also be involved directly with broader activities, which are school based and occasionally come under Vicars for Youth and Education of the diocese.[11] At school preparation for the sacraments is vital:

> The Sacraments do of course have a central place in our schools. The students make their First Holy Communion and Confession at ten and are Confirmed at eighteen. Preparation is done by intensifying tutoría, Lectio Groups, service projects and religion classes in the months prior to these key moments. When it comes to preparation for First Communion and Confession we put the parents through a

parallel preparation process lasting a total of six months and many end up by opting to join a *lectio* group once this process is completed. Students and parents are encouraged to attend Sunday Mass together in their own parishes as a way of strengthening their life in the local church. At the schools, Mass is celebrated on the year's main feast days and solemnities and on a more frequent basis in smaller, form groups. Daily communion is available for all in Lauds. Regular confession is also available, thanks to priests who come to work with us on certain days of the week. All sorts of priests work with us, diocesan, Benedictines and others, but it is worth mentioning that while they provide a ministerial service they are not involved in the school's organization nor in its academic side. Their job might best be compared to being chaplain to a convent.

Service Projects, Mission & Scouts

Service projects form a vital part of Manquehue religious education:

> Another important part of this process are the different service projects we run with our students. St Benedict invites us to recognize Christ Himself in the guests who arrive at a monastery, in the poor, the old, the disabled, and indeed in all those who are in need. By bringing students into contact with this Christ present in the needy we are able to create a further space for listening to the Lord. However, for the service projects to become an authentic and explicit contact with Christ we have come to realize the importance of incorporating *lectio divina* and the Divine Office into such activities and for the service activities to be done with others, in community.

Out of these projects any of the older boys and girls who wish to participate choose between work camps and missions. The work camps involve carrying out some form of community service in places like old people's homes or poorly funded rural schools and chapels. The students work in simple building and repair projects or help out with painting or cleaning jobs.

Missions are a well established in the tradition of the Chilean church. What is normally meant by *misiones* is that priests, supported by laity, go to villages or areas without a resident priest to teach the people and bring them the sacraments. In the Movement it is the laity who go to places where there is no resident priest and their aim is to bring them inspiration and encouragement especially through *lectio divina*.

For the young of the Movement in the schools the missions are organized by the students themselves under the guidance of the Oblates. They are thus taught to take the initiative and learn how to do it. These projects involve going away to a rural area where the students spend long hours going from house to house in pairs, inviting people to take part in a moment of prayer and reflection on the word of God. They also organize evening meetings in the local chapels or other suitable meeting places setting up prayer groups and teaching the people about shared *lectio divina*. They visit families and individuals (especially the elderly) to give them the welcome and affirmation which is so typical of the Movement, to encourage them and give them confidence in their faith and prayer and practice.

Another very popular form of community expeditions outside the school curriculum is Scouts for the boys and Golondrinas[12] for the girls. The troops of San Benito, San Lorenzo and San Anselmo Colleges follow worldwide international scouting practice but have their own special character of strong spiritual dimension. They are popular active and well-organized but, as so often with the Movement, there is much more than that to say about them.

Within the well-known framework of scouting St Benedict's Rule is explicitly used to give a spiritual dimension to the experience. This is in harmony with the whole aim of the Movement and it gives a deeper meaning and challenge to scouting which adds to its attractions. The ordinary activities of living together in community, of camping, of caring for each other, of facing the challenge of demanding tasks, of providing for the needs of each, of support, of forbearance, of generosity, of self-sacrifice, of acquiring community skills like cooking, hygiene, first-aid and of exercising responsibility for the sake of others – all these are given a spiritual meaning which is easily understood by the young through the direct use of St Benedict's precepts.

Scout camps last for a week to ten days in the summer and for two or three days in the winter. They are planned and staffed by University students of the Movement and senior pupils under the direction of the

Oblates and are so well organized by the young themselves that they can take as many as 200 in a camp ranging in age from 10/11 to 18.

These Missions and work camps and scouts often involve real conversion experiences in the young who are generous in accepting real hardship and hard work to do this work together. When away on these projects they live a highly disciplined life centered on *lectio* and the Divine Office. They live in harsh conditions in which there is little comfort for them, but they are happy in the work they do for those in need.

> The boys and girls find the rhythm hard, especially when it is their first camp or mission. However, by the end of the week they are invariably talking about a sense of fun and fulfilment that is difficult to find in their normal lives. And what is really remarkable is that over a period of a week or more our students voluntarily live out so much of what I have been talking about. They have the opportunity to work with the Rule and value many of its aspects. For instance they see sense in defining a "cloister" to keep the community together over the time that they are in mission or on camp. This cloister is a cloister without walls and is different for different people: a key concept in the life of our Extended Benedictine Community. The students work in community, celebrate the Divine Office and practise *lectio divina*: Ora et Labora. *Tutoría* and spiritual companionship flow naturally. The strength of the friendships that spring up is extraordinary. Indeed, there is no better recipe for building and creating friendships than working hard together to repair a roof, or walking for hours with someone else just to get to a remote house in order to share a kind word and the Word of God. They discover that, with both friendship and a sense that is beyond themselves -like helping someone in need-, they can happily put up with the cold showers, weariness, poor food, extreme temperatures, hard floors and general discomfort. The boys and girls learn many other things too, like the fundamental need for putting someone in charge, as experience quickly shows them that without authority community life falls apart and nothing gets done.

I would like to make a comment apart here. It is remarkable to see how the involvement and initiative of our older students in activities like *tutoría*, missions and scouts means that they learn to speak openly about Jesus Christ. We have seen how this produces something wonderful in our boys and girls: a deeper and more mature faith, a faith that is opted for, a faith of assent, a faith, I believe, that is more likely to survive and shine in today's society than a faith that simply comes to us via tradition and culture.

Experiencing God - and facing reality in the world

The emptiness of severely secular education cannot be filled by religious instruction which is cold and impersonal. To avoid this, José Manuel believes the love of Christ and the love of each other which he came to teach us must be alive and active. Without them there is no real Christianity, whatever the external trappings may be:

> Christian education will end up by becoming sterile unless at the same time we insist on both proclaiming a risen Jesus Christ and creating space for that all-important encounter with him. I am often asked what sort of school leavers we are looking to produce. My only reply is to say what we want is men and women who are able to listen to and respond to God's vocation for them. This vocation is often neither what a young person is expecting, nor is it credible in the eyes of their family or 'society', nor even in the eyes of the people at the school. Our vocation is the word with which God addresses each one of us. It comes from God, not from us or other people. As a result, to educate is not only a matter of teaching a person to be attentive, to listen, but also of accompanying that person in their response to the word. Such companionship must be a question of helping, correcting and encouraging a person rather than directing them with ready-made ideas and advice. Our schools, like monasteries, are places where we learn and practice love. Moreover if a school is conceived to be an extension of the family, it is like a family, a place where we can understand from our experience of human love what God's love is like. We should not lose sight of love when we are talking about Christian education.

Here the position of prayer in education becomes a vital issue. In the secularist's world it has not only been crowded out by the explosion of knowledge and technology and all the interesting things they can do for us. The secularists are also terrified of it and want to exclude it from schools, because it introduces a world which is out of their control. In this way they distort not only the lives of individuals but they also impoverish the very meaning of community. In the Movement a very different idea prevails, as José Manuel explains:

> Prayer plays a significant part in all that I have been talking about. The *lectio divina* taught in *tutoría* reveals a God who not only speaks, but who also responds. The children first come to know about this thanks to the testimony of their tutors (who are so near them in age that they can easily identify with them) and in time they discover this for themselves through their own experience. Knowing that God responds to our prayers, knowing that God is available, is without doubt one of the main incentives for prayer. Indeed, this seems to be what St Benedict is telling us in chapters 19 and 20 of the Rule on The Discipline of Psalmody and Reverence in Prayer, and it is the spirit of these chapters that we wish to convey to the different age-groups in our schools. We have made sure that each school has a regular choir for the Divine Office open to everyone. Lauds, Midday Office and Vespers are celebrated there Monday to Friday and the children know that they can join in whenever they want.

Of course the students do not all respond by attending these Offices daily but they know that the bell is an invitation and a witness to something of great importance in the life of the school. It is there for them at moments of crisis or need. When they respond they learn prayer through joining an active, living community of prayer in which they and their seniors are one before God. They are thus rescued from total ignorance about the centrality of prayer and worship in a well-balanced human life.

Thus they learn to deepen their belonging to Christ and to his Church as a community of prayer. Everyone is involved and they can recognize their involvement. The school becomes through this prayer a community of communities involving, in Colegio San Benito for instance, 1500 children, 700 families and 250 staff for the whole site. Their primary involvement in this community should be through prayer.

By this practice of common prayer they learn to value the truth that through baptism and confirmation the laity have a share in the priesthood of Christ, as the Catechism teaches:

> The whole community of believers is, as such, priestly. The faithful exercise their baptismal priesthood through their participation, each according to their own vocation, in Christ's mission as priest, prophet and king. Through the sacraments of Baptism and Confirmation the faithful are 'consecrated to be...a holy priesthood'.[13] The ministerial or hierarchical priesthood of bishops and priests and the common priesthood of all the faithful participate, 'each in its own proper way', in the priesthood of Christ[14]

Community is a much used word today and it is so often misused that it needs to be explained. José Manuel has plenty to say about it as part of his educational vision:

> We need community. We are all weak. We cannot make it alone. We need to belong to 'the ranks of brothers'[15], who can correct us, teach us and be available for us. We need the support of others. This is true for our students as it is for us. Moreover, our schools must be communities built up in love. Our being united to Christ through his Paschal Mystery in baptism will never reach its full development and true fullness unless we live in love. Jesus told his disciples: 'a man can have no greater love than to lay down his life for his friends'.[16] In order to live this love we need community. Chapter 72 of the Rule is clear about this and it is our constant point of reference. This love cannot be theoretical love. It must be real and personal. I am convinced that our parents commend their sons and daughters to us because they love them. Our schools must be a place where we can prolong that family love. In carrying out this task *tutoría* is irreplaceable. It is the guarantee of that personalized love. In this light I have no doubt that *tutoría* is the soul of each of the Manquehue schools.

The creation and preservation of true community in the schools, as elsewhere, in the Movement is closely linked to *acogida*, which is a relationship treasured in the Movement. José Manuel describes it and asserts its importance:

> St Benedict saw Christ in his guests and, when in our schools we insist on *acogida*, we are calling for an attitude that recognizes and adores Christ himself in another person. It is a way of opening one's heart to the love of that other person, of making space in one's thinking and of listening to another among all the preoccupations and tasks that absorb the mind, of making every effort to meet others' needs from one's own resources, whatever their requirements may be – whether material or spiritual. Then, just as St Benedict insists that the word of God is an essential part of being hospitable[17], so too is this *acogida* incomplete if we are not prepared to make room for the word of God in our relationship with others. We insist above all that the more experienced tutors practice *acogida* with the students, especially the older ones. They must be prepared to 'waste' time in order to be available to any students who approach them. It is difficult to provide enough of these experienced tutors to meet the needs, but this *acogida* is so important that we spend a lot of time looking for the right ones.

Friendship in Christ
These principles and practices of the Movement in their schools which have been outlined all tend to encourage friendship but it is a very specific sort of friendship, namely friendship rooted in Christ and in his call in baptism. Such friendship is, and was intended by God to be, a strong influence for good but, if it is left rudderless in the tide race of teenage life, it can easily be changed into a powerful influence for evil. Friendship among the young does not have to be invented by their elders. Wherever young people live and play and work together it is natural that friendships rapidly develop. It is sadly inevitable, however, that distortions will disfigure these friendship wherever strong ideals and clear guidance is lacking to the young as they grow up.

For instance, friendship may become exclusive and disrupt community. It may lead to gangs and gang warfare. It may lead to the exploitation of one group by another - the exploitation of the weak by the strong. It may cause isolation, misery, despair among those not accepted in the group. It may lead the innocent into a self-destructive way of life through sexual license and deviation. It may lead to violence, alcohol and drug abuse. Thus friendship among the young at school and after can become a gift of incomparable beauty or a dangerous snare for the unwary.

José Manuel understood this so well that he strongly encouraged friendship among the young and gave some guidelines for his followers[18]. He says that friendship in Christ in the Manquehue Apostolic Movement rests on five central principles:

> The first is that Christ himself must be present in a true friendship. The second is that it must be open, mutual and expressed by each one to the other; it cannot be on one side only. Thirdly, there must be room for fraternal correction in every friendship in Christ; he quotes St Benedict on the need to speak the truth to each other with integrity of heart and tongue.[19] Fourthly, it should be open to the community because healthy friendship enriches the community and radiates love to others. Fifthly, Christian friendship leads to and encourages a shared mission so that friends wish to live Christ's kingdom, evangelize and serve others.

Order, discipline and freedom in the schools

The children who attend the Manquehue schools have all the goodness and strength but also the weakness and waywardness of ordinary children with very human potential for good and for evil.

> Our schools are made up of weak people like any other community. We are fragile, sinners, often incapable of doing what we really want. We know it is love we desire, but it eludes us. We fall short of this true love of God and neighbour. We need help.

The balance needed in dealing with this human situation they learnt from St Benedict:

> What we mean to establish is a school of the Lord's service. In the guidance we lay down to achieve this we hope to impose nothing harsh or burdensome. If, however, you find in it anything which

seems rather strict, but which is demanded reasonably for the correction of vice or the preservation of love, do not let that frighten you into fleeing from the way of salvation.[20]

This passage has helped the Movement create schools which are not places for those who already know but for those who want to learn, not for those for whom achievement comes without effort but for those who need help. Again the inspiration comes from the gospel: 'it is not the healthy who need a doctor but those who are sick.'[21] José Manuel writes:

> Within this 'school of the Lord's service' order and discipline are essential. A brief glimpse at the Rule is enough to tell us this. It is full of detailed instructions on how to run a monastery; times, place, responsibilities, punishments. However, St Benedict leaves us perfectly clear that order and discipline are means not ends in themselves. He warns us at the end of the Prologue of the need for 'a little strictness', but he also explains that this leads to 'our hearts overflowing with inexpressible delight of love'. Chapter 7 takes us through a journey of *ascesis* and negation which at the end of the day brings us to 'that perfect love of God which casts out all fear'. Finally the Rule culminates with that wonderful description of the fullness of fraternal love and eternal life which we find in chapter 72.

This concept has led to the sort of rules and disciplinary measures that are needed for the good of all. Their purpose is not to limit or restrict students but to enable them to achieve greater freedom within themselves and in their relationships with others. They exist not only to 'amend faults' but also to 'safeguard love' - a framework for correction, guidance, encouragement. About this José Manuel himself comments:

> We have come to see correction and *acogida* as two different manifestations of a single charity. Love without correction is nothing but a vice. Correction without love only ends in rebelliousness. The aim and purpose of punishment must be to produce an inner change. Disciplinary measures are not there to administer justice but to heal the person who has committed a fault. This means that those who are responsible for discipline must be aware that they 'have undertaken the care of the sick.'[22] They should develop their 'skill for

winning souls'[23], which is a task that demands creativity and tact because 'every age and level of understanding should receive appropriate treatment'[24]. This does not mean that we should be simply less demanding of some, rather we should look to treat each student with a view to what we can expect of him or her and what is the best way of achieving this 'so that the strong may have something to yearn for and the weak nothing to run away from'[25]. With younger children it is important 'to cut vices out as soon as they begin to sprout[26], because when children get older it is more difficult, and in this way they learn 'good habits and the delight of virtue.[27]

The ideal of human wholeness

It will be clear from all this that the educational aim of the Movement is holistic - aiming to develop the best potential of the whole human being rather than specializing and concentrating on a few limited skills. In developing this educational vision José Manuel was influenced by St Benedict's holistic understanding of human life:

> St Benedict sees every moment of the day, every place, every activity, every person as part of a whole pointing towards a single goal – God. The traditional Benedictine motto *Ora et labora* poignantly expresses this vision of prayer and work as twofold aspects of a single path. God is to be found everywhere by the person who searches for him. The pagan splitting of the world into material and spiritual is entirely alien to the Rule. Nor is there any hint in the Rule of that division of the Christian life into the active and the contemplative. We have discovered how the Rule seems to offer a convincing way of living out the Vatican Council's call for a stronger union between faith and everyday life.

The search for wholeness in education is not easy today. It is not easy even when the ideal is clearly expressed and pursued in schools – as it is in the Manquehue Schools. In this age of the explosion of knowledge and the overkill of communication technology the competitive pressure on the young and their parents is relentless. It drives them against their will to sacrifice everything to immediate achievement that can be turned into cash. It inevitably leads to imbalance in the individual. In Chile, as elsewhere, schools are judged largely by their success in getting their pupils to the best universities. The intensity of this drive for success threatens the pursuit of wholeness not only in spiritual development of the young but even in their human growth and fulfillment. Everywhere in the world it is difficult to maintain a balance in education even in the realm of ordinary human endeavor. To go further and find room for growth in the spirit as an essential part of the education of the young is even more difficult. The prospect for the future from the encroachment of an obsessive dedication to personal achievement threatens the health and peace of all future generations. The brilliant and largely successful work in this area of the Manquehue Apostolic Movement deserves to be understood and its example followed. There is a phrase in St Benedict's Rule which has been treasured through the ages: 'so that God may be glorified in everything'[28]. 'Everything' is the key word. Every aspect of our lives should reflect the glory of our creator - not as a grim obligation but as the key to radiant happiness in the fulfillment of our being. St Benedict's phrase fits very well the Movement's holistic approach to all that goes on in their schools.

 හ

Notes for Chapter 13

[1] The Movement's close links from the start with the Archdiocese of Santiago meant that they received much help from Mgr Gambino, a Salesian priest, who was Vicar for Education for Santiago at the time. As a Salesian he was himself inspired by St John Bosco's evangelization of the impoverished and neglected young in Turin in the late 19th century. Mgr Gambino introduced the Movement to the post Vatican II documents on Catholic Schools and evangelization published by the Congregation for Education in Rome. These and other diocesan documents inspired by Vatican II kept the Movement in close touch with Catholic developments in educational thinking.

[2] see Luke 15. 11 - 31

[3] Of course in the Manquehue schools not everyone is conformist nor happily content with the religious ethos. In an interview with some university students who had been at San Benito I was given an enthusiastic report of their own experience but they added that not everyone among their contemporaries liked the school and its ethos as they had. "Those who have a negative experience" they said "well, they just don't like studies; they find academic work difficult and so just don't like the school and studying. Those who found the religious aspect too strong for them with going on retreat every year - that was something they just didn't want to do. Some people end up by hating the Movement, usually as a result of having a bad experience in a set-to and coming out the worse. They complain that if you think in a different way about life, there is not much space for you."

However, it was very good to be taught religion by lay people: "Having lay people in charge of religion - the tutors and Oblates - was good because it meant that they were much closer. It would have been very different having them dressed as priests or monks because there is a distance produced by clerical dress."

[4] Quotations in this chapter, unless otherwise stated, are from José Manuel's 'Creating a New Benedictine School' (1999). Although many of the items in this chapter have been dealt with in the narrative of the founding of the schools, it is important that they should be gathered together in the words of the founder himself.

[5] Acts 8.31

[6] José Manuel: Creating a new Benedictine School

[7] Mt 25.40

[8] Rule chapter 72

⁹ 1 Peter 1, 23
¹⁰ from Creating a new Benedictine School
¹¹ The schools in practice come under the aegis of two Vicariates: La Vicaría de Educación y La Vicaría de Joven Esperanza. The Vicaría de Educación looks after interschool activities and matters relating to education in general. La Vicaría de Joven Esperanza looks after general youth activities in the diocese which means that they have to come into direct contact with the schools in coordination with the Vicaría de Educación.
¹² Golondrina means swallow. It is the name in Chile for female scouts or Girl Guides.
¹³ Vatican II. LG n10.1
¹⁴ see Catechism of the Catholic Church 1546 & 1547
¹⁵ Benedict's Rule 1. 5
¹⁶ Jn 15.13
¹⁷ cf. Benedict's Rule 53.9: Then some sacred scripture should be read for the spiritual encouragement it brings us, and after that every mark of kindness should be shown the guests.
¹⁸ These guidelines will be more fully examined in Chapter 15 on the Spirituality of the Manquehue Movement.
¹⁹ Benedict's Rule Chap 4.28
²⁰ Benedict's Rule Prologue 55ff
²¹ Mk. 2, 17
²² Rule 27, 6
²³ Rule 58,6
²⁴ Rule 30,1
²⁵ Rule 64 19
²⁶ Rule 2, 26
²⁷ Rule 7, 68
²⁸ A phrase from chapter 57 of the Rule which is often taken as a Benedictine motto, since it summarises the over-riding purpose of everything that happens in a Benedictine monastery.

Chapter 14 ~ Lay Movements
in the Church Today

The Council, Newman & the Laity

Pope John XXIII after his election in 1958 called together in Rome the second Vatican Council[1] to consider the state of the Church. He invited ecumenical observers to attend and sought to make the Council as open as possible. What he asked for from the Council was inspiration and encouragement which would renew the Church and open it to the world within which it lived and thus lay foundations for better understanding between the two. It was an ambitious and inspiring program, but it led to some problems. Before long within the Council itself two rather different models of the Church became apparent. Each model had its strong defenders within the Council and this made Vatican II in the controversies which followed typical of all the Councils of the Church since the Council of Jerusalem in apostolic times.[2] Both models of the Church were reflected in various shades of theology at the time of the Council and afterwards in Catholic communities throughout the world.

There was a model which proclaimed the Church to be essentially solid, changeless, hierarchical, handing down from the Popes, Councils and Bishops deductive guidance covering every moral and spiritual problem that could assault mankind. Many cherished that sort of description as a faithful reflection of their understanding of the sacred tradition of the past. For those who were captivated by it there was no way forward except by retaining the same perceived tradition and relying on it alone in the face of every challenge, every new experience, every new change and development in human life.

The other model which began to emerge during the Council, to the joy of some and dismay of others, was confessedly new yet claimed also to be deeply rooted in the most ancient sources of Christianity. It was a model of a living, growing, developing, Church which, while being faithful to its roots and sources in the gospel would nevertheless be able, through new growth and development, to respond constructively to the rapidly changing future which was opening up with increasing speed before mankind. Pope John XXIII appeared to be the prophet of this model of the Church with his well-known appeal for *aggiornamento*[3] and his reported plea for an opening of the windows of the Church to let in some air.

This model of what the Church is like was not a claim that there was or could be a new revelation, nor did it suggest that the ultimate spiritual truths of Christian doctrine were altered or made redundant by social and political changes, or by scientific research and technology, or by the changes these brought about in human life. It did, however, claim that *our ways of understanding* the mystery of divine truth inevitably develops as our knowledge grows so that the *meaning* of scripture was capable of development to sustain and guide that developing understanding. There are times in the Church's life, it was claimed, when certain developments are vitally necessary for the continuing mission of the Church. As in the past, so in the present there was, they asserted, need for the Church first of all to discern and understand and then to welcome and assimilate such developments.

This model of the church was strongly influential in some of the Council's most important documents. Among other changes it led to a new model of the role of the laity within the Church. That did not imply that the laity had been neglected in the years before the Council. There never was any doubt that the laity were valued members of the Church with an important role to fulfill in its life. However this role was often seen before the Council as being in practice absolutely subordinate to the Pope and bishops and clergy. That meant that the laity were called to support the initiatives of the Pope and bishops but had little scope for initiatives in the Church themselves and in their own right. They were always valued and constantly encouraged to take part in what was called Catholic Action in support of the Pope and Bishops and under their immediate direction. When they did so that was the peak of their special vocation in the Church. It was seen as a vocation which came from and was subordinate to the hierarchy. It meant that in the ultimate analysis the Church - even the Church of the laity - was a radically clericalized structure. It was an understanding of the Church which depended heavily upon the authority structure of the hierarchy consisting in Pope, Bishops and Priests.

The new model of the Council, which claimed also to be the original position of the New Testament, approached the question of lay status from a different point of view. The status and rights and initiatives of the laity within the Church were not derived from hierarchical decisions. Baptism was now seen as the source from which lay pastoral initiatives and responsibility were derived. That in itself recalled St Paul's proclamation of 'one Lord, one Faith, one Baptism'[4], which points to a radical unity founded on common faith and common baptism. In that vision, of course, lay life in the Church must be in communion with the Pope and the local bishop of the Catholic Church. All are baptized into communion with the mystical body of Christ, which is the Church. That means that they owe obedience to the legitimate authority of Pope and bishops. However, within that communion the laity have their own status and responsibilities as laity, which are not derived from decisions of clerical authority but from their baptism. Thus the radical mission to evangelize for both clerics and laity alike arises from their common baptism through which they are incorporated into Christ and given a part in his mission. That is what is meant by calling the laity's mission truly 'ecclesial'. It means that their evangelizing activities are - in their own right - truly part of the mission of the Church

It has often been said that the life and writings of the great English Cardinal Newman had a striking influence on the Second Vatican Council. The spirit of Newman, it was said, brooded over the Council. The Council sought to renew the Church by going back to the sources in Scripture and in the Fathers of the Church. Newman, before becoming a Catholic, had led in the Anglican Church a movement, called the Oxford Movement, which sought to renew Anglican doctrine and practice. The source of his own teaching and practice was the Fathers of the Church, both Greek and Latin, in which he was better read than any Englishman of his age or subsequent times. It was that patristic vision which - for Newman and Pusey and Keble - was to renew the Anglican Church. Relying on their teaching Newman discovered that doctrine and practice had developed over the ages in the living church. He used this discovery to explain and justify first of all the developments he recommended to the

Anglican Church and finally his own perception that the Catholic Church, with all its developments which he had previously thought unjustified, is the true Church of Christ. And, he argued, it is so precisely because of these developments, which enable it to be faithful to the teaching of Christ through the ages. He came to see that the Catholic Church of his day was the true descendant of the Church of the Fathers and the true home of the belief he had learnt from them. "The Fathers", he once said, "made me a Catholic"[5].

Newman saw this development as a manifestation of spiritual life which began in New Testament times. Thus in a sermon in Oxford in 1843 while he was still an Anglican, commenting on the text from St Luke's gospel: 'Mary kept all these things, pondering them in her heart.'[6] he had said:

> St Mary is our pattern of faith both in the reception and in the study of divine truth. She does not think it enough to accept, she dwells upon it; not enough to possess, she uses it; not enough to assent, she develops it.

Of scripture he went on to say:

> Its half sentences, its overflowings of language, admit of development; they have a life in them which shows itself in progress; a truth which has the token of consistency; a reality which is fruitful in resources; a depth which extends into mystery.

He saw that in the profession of faith there is an inward reality which goes deeper than the words in which it is expressed. He insisted on

> The reality and permanence of inward knowledge, as distinct from explicit confession, [so that] even centuries might pass without the formal expression of a truth, which had been all along the secret life of millions of faithful souls.

Later Newman wrote of how there are times when it is necessary "to change in order to remain the same." That was the sort of change that happened in Vatican II as the Council itself recognized explicitly in the Document on Revelation in a passage of great importance for the interpretation of the Council:

There is a growth in insight into the realities and words that are being passed on. This comes about in various ways. It comes through the contemplation and study of believers who ponder these things in their hearts. It comes from the intimate sense of spiritual realities which they experience. And it comes from the preaching of those who have received, along with their right of succession in the episcopate, the sure charism of truth. Thus, as the centuries go by, the Church is always advancing towards the plenitude of divine truth, until eventually the words of God are fulfilled in her.[7]

Thus the Vatican Council took up a theme which Newman had made his own. It was a theme which had guided him into the Church - the theme that there are aspects of Catholic teaching and practice which are capable of and in need of development in response both to the development of the Church's understanding of scripture and to changes in human life and knowledge. Such development had never meant for Newman a distortion of fundamental teaching, but it had meant that the word of God was indeed *alive and active*[8] in a living church and that new meanings, nuances and applications arise from the word through prayer and devout reflection especially in times of development and human change. It is to be noted that such development occurs from within the Church and from the center of prayer among the faithful including the laity. Genuine development can never be achieved by impositions from outside by secular agencies whether they are political, academic or social.

The development with which we are concerned, namely the status and vocation of the laity within the Church was one which Newman himself addressed and wrote about particularly after he had become a Catholic. In this he was well ahead of his time, and occasionally wrote things which caused alarm among traditional Catholics who were wedded to a rigidly static view of Catholic doctrine and practice. On one occasion after a learned exposition of evidence from the Fathers of lay involvement in the early doctrinal controversies of the Church he quotes from another author a description of the Council of Ephesus in 431 and the lay support and involvement in it. Then he adds this comment:

My own drift is somewhat different from that which has dictated this glowing description; but the substance of the argument of each of us is one and the same. I think certainly that the teaching Church is more happy when she has such enthusiastic (lay) partisans about her as are here represented, than when she cuts off the faithful from the study of her divine doctrines and the sympathy of her divine contemplations, and requires from them an implicit faith in her word, which in the educated classes will terminate in indifference, and in the poorer in superstition.[9]

Newman's teaching and writing on the status and vocation of the laity within the Church was greeted with suspicion in his day, but it took root and flowered in the Vatican II. It was there, as we shall see, that the autonomous status and vocation of the laity was made abundantly clear. This does not diminish their 'obedience of faith'[10] in Christ – an obedience which extends to the pastoral authority which Christ himself had given his Apostles and their Successors and calls for the preservation at all levels of genuine 'communion' with the Pope and the local bishop. The Council re-asserted that within that obedience to Christ in his Church the laity have both the right and the obligation to exercise an ecclesial role which is truly their own and not created by hierarchical authority. This conciliar 'development' was destined to have an ever deeper and richer effect in the life of the Church. It is in this sense that the developments in the vocation of the laity in the Church and its source in the sacrament of baptism, which are part of the theme of this book, are all to be understood as proceeding from the teaching of Vatican II.

To the younger generations of today Vatican II is a remote event of long ago. For them it seems far from their immediate world. However, its effect is not over, any more than the effect of a seed is over during the growth of a mature tree. The vitality of growth and development of the Church is always evident in the ongoing experience of the faithful. And so in a contemporary form the work of the Council years is still alive today among the young as well as the not so young, whether they truly appreciate it or not. The positive teaching of the Council is still being assimilated and put into practice but there are also persisting echoes of the two models of the Church which struggled for recognition in the Council – the model of a static unchanging Church and of a living developing Church. The memory of those models lives on and they still influence in differing ways the growth of the Church, sometimes in ways that are positive, sometimes negative. The adherents of these models are often referred to by loose and inaccurate descriptions such as conservative, traditional, even reactionary on the one hand and as liberal, open, contemporary in their thinking on the other. They still tend to view each other with suspicion. The controversies which arise from this suspicion keep the tensions alive without necessarily clarifying the real issues very much.

There is nothing surprising about this. The work of the greatest Councils takes a long time to come to full fruition in a worldwide Church of great diversity and richly contrasting perspectives. Bishop Butler who, as Abbot of Downside and President of the English Benedictine Congregation, took an active part in the Vatican Council as a member of the Theological Commission, devoted himself by his writing and speaking to explaining the Council's work after it was over. In the early stages he thought that it would take a long time - perhaps 30 years – for the ordinary faithful to understand the Council and fully absorb the wonder of its teaching. Towards the end of his life he changed that estimate. By that time he thought it would take more than 100 years. That was a truly Benedictine estimate in its patient readiness to think in centuries and to wait upon the Spirit to teach the Church (both clergy and laity) how to absorb the teaching of the Council and make it real and vital in their everyday lives.

There lay behind this patient attitude also a deep appreciation of the potential extent of the work of the Spirit which the strange and unprecedented event of the Council had unleashed in the Church and on the world. Bishop Butler was right about how long it takes for the work of such a Council to come to full fruition. There are conciliar developments still which are enthusiastically welcomed by some Catholics but treated with suspicious caution by others. Among them is the growth of Movements in the Church and particularly of lay Movements.

The Lay Apostolate
What the Council in fact did was to change the concept of what it means to be an ordinary lay person in the Church. It did so by recognizing explicitly what scripture teaches, namely that baptized members of the

laity have received from the Lord their own vocation and their own mission as lay people within the unity of the whole Church. It is a vocation which is complementary to and different from the vocation of the ordained clergy and the vocation of those living a consecrated life as Religious. It is a vocation and mission which are essential to the Church and reach fulfillment in their own lay milieu and in the ever changing world of lay life. Their vocation to holiness is real and urgent and their way to holiness is to be found in their lay life and not in some sort of partial imitation of the way to holiness which belongs to the different vocations of Clergy or Religious. In the Council's model the laity were to be no longer auxiliary troops at the disposal of the clergy for special needs. Their apostolate derived not from any particular commission from Pope or Bishops, however important these might me, but directly from their baptism and from the nature of their integral belonging to Christ through their membership in his Mystical Body. It is from and within that membership that their special vocation comes to life.

One of the most important documents issued by the Council was specifically concerned with the apostolate which belongs to the laity as such. Speaking of the ordinary baptized laity it says:

> The Christian vocation is of its nature a vocation to the apostolate as well. In the organism of a living body no member plays a purely passive part; sharing in the life of the body it shares at the same time in its activity. The same is true of the Body of Christ, the Church: 'the whole body achieves full growth in dependence on the full functioning of each part' (Eph.4,16). Between the members of this body there exists, further, such a unity and solidarity that a member who does not work at the growth of the body to the extent of his possibilities must be considered useless to the Church and to himself.[11]

This is a strong statement making the apostolate a right and obligation of the laity which they acquire simply because they have been baptized into Christ. After that it is not surprising that the Council went on to assert unequivocally that the laity in their lay status share in the priestly, prophetical and kingly office of Christ himself and so have their own special share in the sacred mission of Christ to his apostles:

In the Church there is a diversity of ministry but unity of mission. To the apostles and their successors Christ has entrusted their office of teaching, sanctifying and governing in his name and by his power. But the laity are made to share the priestly, prophetical and kingly office of Christ; they have therefore, in the Church and in the world, their own assignment in the mission of the whole people of God. In the concrete their apostolate is exercised when they work at the evangelization and sanctification of men; it is exercised too when they endeavor to have the gospel spirit permeate and improve the temporal order, going about it in a way that bears clear witness to Christ and helps forward the salvation of men. The characteristic of the lay state being a life led in the midst of the world and of secular affairs, laymen are called by God to make of their apostolate, through the vigor of their Christian spirit, a leaven in the world.[12]

In trying to adapt our minds fully to the real meaning of the Council in this passage we need surely to pay special attention to the phrase in which it says: 'the laity are made to share the priestly, prophetical and kingly office of Christ.' For those who, with understandable nostalgia and veneration, look back to the triumphs and sufferings of the highly clericalized medieval and post Reformation Church this passage may seem difficult. We must reflect, however, that it does not imply any disparagement or diminution of the sacred status within the Church of bishops and priests. Rather it strengthens that status and enriches it and the whole church by revealing the precise meaning of the lay vocation. The laity by their intimate union with Christ through Baptism and the Eucharist are, in their ordinary lay lives, associated with his mediation[13] as priest between God and mankind. This is true even though they have not as laity the power through the sacramental reception of ministerial priesthood to represent him by celebrating the Eucharist. To confuse the laity's sharing in the priesthood of Christ through their baptism with the priesthood of ordained ministry is only to distort and so diminish the reality of the priesthood of the laity. Theirs is a special and different vocation. Through their baptismal sharing in Christ's priesthood they take the reality of Christ's mediation for all mankind right into the heart of the lay world in which they live as witnesses and living signs of its reality and as exemplars of what that reality can mean in lay life.

Then after priesthood comes their sharing in Christ's mission as prophet. This means that they are empowered and called to witness to the truth of his word in their own milieu through their word and example - and it must be through their lay words and lay example that they do it. Neither in this nor in any other aspect of their mission must they be seen as a pale imitation of the ministerial priesthood. That would be to fail in their vocation to be lay icons of Christ.

Finally in their kingly sharing they also are invited to the ultimate witness whereby they can stand with him (or rather he can be manifested in them) just as he stood before Pilate deprived of every civil honor, every human authority, everything the world can give and yet supreme in the spiritual power by which through his death and resurrection he manifested the truth of the Spirit. That is supremely kingly because it is the only aspect of the office of King which survives the death to which all else that is human comes.

These three aspects of lay spirituality are particularly clear in the martyrdom of St Thomas More perhaps the greatest of the canonized lay saints. In laying down his life for his friends and praying for the king and his persecutors he shared in the priestly redemptive sacrifice of Christ. In witnessing to the truth at the cost of his life as a layman in his lay state he shared in the prophetical office of Christ. In accepting the loss of office, property, family, freedom and life he shared in the kingly witness of Christ before Pilate, on calvary and in his resurrection.

The Council underlines how lay life can be and should be based on the imitation of Christ when it insists on the importance of their preserving *their living union with Christ* in a way that accepts and affirms their lay lives:

Neither family concerns nor other secular affairs should be irrelevant to their spiritual life, in keeping with the words of the Apostle: 'Whatever you do in word or work do all in the name of the Lord Jesus Christ, giving thanks to God the Father through him.'*(Col 3. 17)*.[14]

With these words the Council takes a further step towards a new vision of Catholic lay life. It does so by insisting that for laypeople who are baptized into Christ their holiness does not consist in stepping aside from their lay occupations and obligations so as to seek holiness through a partial imitation of Religious life. It is within the framework of their lay occupations and obligations that they must seek holiness and will through grace attain it. Rather than stepping aside and devising some pale imitation of the life of dedicated religious, they must bring out for all to see the signs of the kingdom in their ordinary lay lives, by prayer, by the integrity of the lives they live, by the self-sacrifice of Christ-like love and by finding space for God right in the lay context of the lives they lead.

Baptism - the essential starting point

Among the fundamental truths which were new in expression and application but in their essential teaching as old as the gospel itself was the Council's re-affirmation of the true meaning for the laity of their baptism. This was so important and so central to the new expression of this ancient and scriptural vision of Catholic life that the Council dealt with it in a document about the essential teaching on the Church itself:

> Christ the Lord, high priest taken from among men, made the new people 'a kingdom of priests to God, his Father'. The baptized, by regeneration and the anointing of the Holy Spirit, are consecrated to be a spiritual house and a holy priesthood, that through all the works of Christian men (and women) they may offer spiritual sacrifices proclaiming the perfection of him who has called them out of darkness into marvelous light. Therefore all the disciples of Christ, persevering in prayer and praising God, should present themselves as a sacrifice, living, holy and pleasing to God. They should everywhere on earth bear witness to Christ and give an answer to everyone who asks a reason for the hope of an eternal life which is theirs.[15]

This passage is theologically explicit in its proclamation of the reality of lay vocation within the Church. It places the source and origin of that vocation in the sacrament of baptism including its call to holiness within the lay state. From the very beginning of the Manquehue Movement this same perception of their vocation through baptism to the apostolate and to holiness in the lay life ranked close to *lectio divina* of the word of God as the formative inspiration of their life. This meant that becoming a member of the Movement – at whatever level – involved a conscious rediscovery of the sacraments of Baptism and Confirmation and a realization (a making real) of their lay mission and a shaping of their lives in Christ. It meant for very ordinary men and women coming to terms with St Paul's words that they are through baptism 'a new creation'[16].

In the light of this and other texts in St Paul the baptism of adults calls for the conscious acceptance of a profound conversion and re-orientation of life. Where Christianity is well established and baptism is received in infancy the spiritual reality of the sacrament must be realized through gradual development of understanding and free acceptance in adult life. If that free acceptance is to be realistic and spiritually fruitful it must involve the perception of what St Paul means by 'new creation'. This perception about themselves and their lay lives grew strong among the lay people of the Movement through their reading and reflection on scripture. The vital instrument was *lectio divina* through which they learnt from the word of scripture. This spiritual growth of the Movement coincided with developments resulting from Vatican II elsewhere in the Catholic world. It corresponded also with developments in the administrative structures in Rome, where the teaching of the Council about the role of the laity in the Church was reflected in the reorganization of the Curia in Rome.

Developments in the Church and the Curia

In the Roman Curia there are ministerial bodies or 'dicasteries' which are usually called Congregations. They are presided over normally by Cardinals, who have immediate access to the Pope. Each of them is commissioned to deal with some particular area of the Church's work and apostolate. Before the Council there was a Congregation for Religious which cared for men and women who were known collectively as 'Religious' (monks, nuns, friars, sisters and all members of Religious Orders). They were the ones who took religious vows committing themselves to live a life which was in varying degrees apart from the life of the laity and specially consecrated to God. Whether ordained or not, they had a special status in the Church.

Pope Paul VI reorganized the Roman Curia in the light of the Council and he changed the Congregation for Religious. He gave it a new name so as to recognize that laity also might dedicate their lives to God while remaining in the lay state. Its new name is the Congregation for Institutes of Consecrated Life and Societies of Apostolic Life. This rather cumbersome title has been adopted to include not only the traditional Religious Orders but also the rapidly growing organizations of laity who take vows while remaining authentically lay.

That reorganization brought together the old Religious Orders and some more modern lay religious bodies, which are sometimes partly lay and partly clerical and sometimes completely lay. However, this change proved to be insufficient to deal with the way the Spirit was moving in the Church and another 'dicastery' has been added to the Curia in the years since Vatican II which has had various names and today is known as 'The Pontifical Council for the Laity'. This Council cares for the needs of the many lay Movements which have grown up in the Church and which have a corporate life but without the formal dedication of 'vows'.

The nature of such Movements is that they are formed by groups of laity who come spontaneously together to work for Christ and the Church. They may take 'promises' and commit themselves in various ways, but they do not take formal religious vows which would assimilate them with those who live a 'Consecrated Life'. In this way the Curia recognizes and encourages a critical development in the life of the Church while blessing and offering help and guidance to the laity involved.

There is further an important difference about the Council for the Laity. The Congregation for Religious and Consecrated Life exercises jurisdiction over those who live in vows as members of Orders. The Council for the Laity does not exercise any special jurisdiction over the Movements and lay groups with which is it involved. They come under the ordinary diocesan discipline of the Church and the Council for the Laity exists to support and facilitate their lay vocation. This is an important affirmation and encouragement of a measure of lay autonomy under the supervision and guidance which is necessary for communion with the Church.

These contemporary lay Movements are different from the earlier 19th and 20th century Catholic Action. The organized laity of Catholic Action were for the most part controlled and governed by the hierarchy and they were always governed by the local Bishop. The new Movements are different. They are usually inspired, organized and recruited independently by lay people and then seek the general approval of the Bishop. They claim to have an identity, vocation and mission within the Church which is their own and authentically lay yet fully ecclesial. Of course, in order to operate within the Church and be understood and accepted by the faithful they must be in full communion with and recognized by the local Bishops. They can also seek a more universal recognition from Rome and it is for this that they come into the oversight of the Pontifical Council for the Laity through which they are integrated into the pastoral and apostolic outreach of the Church.

The Manquehue Movement was first recognized officially by the Hierarchy in a letter from Cardinal Silva Henriquez in 1979. Then on 29th October 1993, when José Manuel visited the Council for the Laity in Rome Cardinal Pironio gave the Movement his *Laudatio* which signified the general approval of Rome. During the same visit he was encouraged to seek fuller recognition at the diocesan level. With the assistance of Mgr Cristian Precht in Santiago this process was hurried forward and finally on 8th September 1994 the Statutes of the Movement were recognized under Canon and Civil Law by Cardinal Oviedo, who was at that time Archbishop of Santiago. In such matters both the Archbishop of Santiago and the Pontifical Council in Rome are guided by the teaching on the laity in Vatican II and also, after 1988, by another important post-conciliar document on the laity issued by Pope John Paul II. This is his Apostolic Exhortation on the laity, which followed the Synod on the Laity in 1988 and is entitled *Christifideles Laici*, that is 'The Laity who are faithful to Christ'.

Christifideles Laici

The Synod of Bishops has been called together in Rome at intervals since the Council to assist the Pope by considering key issues about developments arising from the Council. In 1987 their subject was concerned with the role of the laity in the Church. In the following year,

1988, Pope John Paul II issued an Apostolic Exhortation to the whole Church called *Christifideles Laici* that is *The Laity who are faithful to Christ*. This document reaffirms and develops the teaching of the Council. It is an essential document for the understanding of the role of the laity in the Church of the present and future. A few quotations from it will help us to set the Manquehue Movement in its true context within the growing and developing Church. It is a rich document, which reaffirms and develops the teaching of the Council and it should be read in its entirety. It has become a primary resource in the development of the life and mission of the laity in the Church. It begins by considering seriously the true nature of the laity and the sources of their dignity and standing in Christ's Church.

> In giving a response to the question 'Who are the lay faithful?' the Council went beyond previous interpretations which were predominantly negative. Instead it opened itself to a decidedly positive vision and displayed a basic intention of asserting the full belonging of the lay faithful to the Church and to its mystery. At the same time it insisted on the unique character of their vocation which is, in a special way, to 'seek the Kingdom of God by engaging in temporal affairs and ordering them according to the plan of God.' 'The term lay faithful' we read in the Constitution of the Church of the Council 'is here understood to mean all the faithful except those in the Holy Orders and those who belong to the religious state sanctioned by the Church. Through Baptism the faithful are made one body with Christ and are established among the People of God. They are in their own way made sharers in the priestly, prophetic and kingly office of Christ. They carry out their own part in the mission of the whole Christian people with respect to the church and the world'.[17]

Again and again during the course of this document the Pope comes back to, emphasizes and explains the participation of all the laity in the life of the Church within the 'priestly, prophetic and kingly office of Christ'.

> The Church's mission of salvation in the world is realized not only by the ministers in virtue of the sacrament of Orders but also by the lay

faithful; indeed because of their baptismal state and their specific vocation, in the measure proper to each person, the lay faithful participate in the priestly, prophetic and kingly mission of Christ.[18]

Pope John Paul emphasizes that baptism into Christ is the sacramental means through which men and women are incorporated into Christ himself, made members of his body which is the Church. Thus baptism is source and inspiration of lay life in the Church.

Incorporation into Christ through faith and baptism is the source of being a Christian in the mystery of the church......it is no exaggeration to say that the entire existence of the lay faithful has as its purpose to lead a person to a knowledge of the radical newness of the Christian life that comes from baptism, the sacrament of faith.......baptism regenerates us to the life of the Son of God; unites us to Christ and to his Body, the Church; anoints us in the Holy Spirit making us spiritual temples.[19]

As he surveys the life of the laity in the Church the Pope also notes with gratitude and approval the rapid growth of lay Movements in the Church since the Council:

In modern times such lay groups have received a special stimulus, resulting in the birth and spread of a multiplicity of group forms, associations, groups, communities, movements. We can speak of a new area of group endeavors of the faithful.......in a secularized world the various group forms of the apostolate can represent for many a precious help for the Christian life in remaining faithful to the demands of the gospel and to the commitment to the church's mission and apostolate.[20]

Then, after recognition of what is actually happening in various parts of the Church, comes an affirmation of the freedom enjoyed by lay people in the Church to act in this way as a matter of baptismal right. Although they have this right it can be truly fruitful only within the communion and mission of the Church itself:

The freedom for lay people in the Church to form such groups is to be acknowledged. Such liberty is the true and proper right that is not derived from any kind of "concession" by authority, but from the sacrament of baptism which calls the lay faithful to participate actively in the Church's communion and mission.[21]

The Manquehue Apostolic Movement had already gone a long way in its internal development and external achievement in Santiago before the Synod on the laity and before the Pope's exhortation in *Christifideles Laici*. It is remarkable how close their spontaneous course had been to that which the Synod now proclaimed for the laity. Their spiritual foundations were firmly rooted in the scriptural word of God and in the real meaning of their baptism, in their working from within the communion of the Church, in their desire to serve the Church and its mission, in their confident reliance on authentically lay spirituality, in their returning to old perspectives for lay life which were derived from traditional Benedictine spirituality, in the way they made the prayer of the Church in the Divine Office the center of their prayer – in all these aspects of the Movement which they created they showed themselves to be very close to the post–Vatican II development of the Church. Every item in their early growth was vindicated by the Pope in *Christifideles Laici*. Above all in their absolute fidelity to the uncompromising lay character of their Movement they reflected the Council's perception of a new, powerful and truly lay apostolate. In *Christifideles Laici* Pope John Paul II quoted a particularly trenchant comment about the laity of Pope Pius XII:

> They in particular ought to have an ever clearer consciousness not only of belonging to the Church but of being the Church.[22]

In the Manquehue Movement that consciousness was already well established before the Synod of 1987, and they were certainly helped by the development of other Movements in the Church in Chile. Chileans were already familiar with Movements and other institutes of lay consecrated life like the *Schoenstatt Movement,* the *Neo Catechumenate*, *The Legionaries of Christ, Opus Dei* and many others. Some Movements and institutes are lay throughout, some part lay, part clerical. The Manquehue Movement is entirely lay; but it is also profoundly ecclesial through its full communion with and obedience to the local Church of

Santiago and the Holy See. Its aim is to live baptismal life to the full within the Church and to inspire others to the same course.

Movements usually arise from a group of lay people coming together for prayer, for study, for social, apostolic and pastoral action to deepen and realize more fully their own baptismal commitment. In full accord with Vatican II and *Christifideles Laici* they do not depend on clerical leadership to organize them, lead them or direct them. However, as others join and their 'movement' grows they recognize the need of communion with the local bishop and full recognition through his approval of their statutes and mission. In this they are simply following the supernatural instinct which arises from their incorporation into Christ by the sacrament of baptism. The Church is the Body of Christ and

> by one Spirit we are all baptized into one body - Jews or Greeks, slave or free - and we are all made to drink of one Spirit.[23]

So a truly Catholic Movement seeks the formal external expression of that inner unity through the approval of the bishop of the local Church.

Although Movements arise frequently from lay initiative in the contemporary Church they are not peripheral to the mission of the Church. Once approved and in communion with the Holy See they have a vital role to play, as Pope John Paul has made clear and repeated emphatically at Pentecost in 2004:

> I energetically repeat: 'The ecclesial Movements and new communities are a providential answer, inspired by the Holy Spirit given the present need of new evangelization....This evangelization needs mature Christian personalities and strong Christian communities[24]

The Church's approval for the Manquehue Apostolic Movement was confirmed when it was made a 'Private Association of lay Faithful'. This status was granted it in 1994 by Cardinal Carlos Oviedo, the Archbishop of Santiago. The approval and blessing of the local Church has been further confirmed by the Holy See through the Pontifical Council for the Laity, whose President in 1993, Cardinal Pironio, gave his *laudatio* or approval of the principles and works of the Movement. At that time Cardinal Pironio, who was himself a South American from Argentina and had a great understanding of the laity in South America and their needs, showed his personal appreciation by identifying explicitly the three marks of the Manquehue Movement when he urged them to continue on the way they were following as 'authentically lay, profoundly ecclesial and deeply ('joyfully' he said on one occasion) Benedictine. '

CR

Notes for Chapter 14

[1] The Council met at St Peter's in the Vatican from 1962 to 1965. The sixteen documents which it published, together with many post-conciliar documents published by the Pope after the Council in order to implement the expressed wishes of the Council, had a far-reaching impact on Catholics throughout the world.

[2] See Acts of the Apostles ch. 15

[3] a 'bringing up to date' of the Church

[4] Eph. 4, 5 'One Lord, one faith, one baptism, one God and Father of us all, who is above all, and through all and in all.'

[5] See Letter to Pusey

[6] Luke 2, 19

[7] Vatican II - Document on Divine Revelation *Dei Verbum* n.8 Transl. Flannery

[8] Hb. 4. 12

[9] Newnan: *On consulting the faithful on matters of doctrine*

[10] see Rom. 1, 5

[11] Vatican II - Decree on the Apostolate of the Laity *Apostolicam actuositatem n.2*

[12] Vatican II - Decree on Lay Apostolate n.2

[13] see Hebrews 12, 24 'Jesus, the mediator of the new covenant'

[14] Vatican II - Decree on Lay Apostolate n.4

[15] Vatican II - Constitution on the Church n.10 *translated Flannery*

[16] 2Cor. 5, 17 'if anyone is in Christ, he is a new creation'

[17] Christifideles Laici n. 9

[18] Christifideles Laici n. 23

[19] Christifideles Laici n.9

[20] Christifideles Laici n.29

[21] Christifideles Laici n. 29

[22] Christifideles Laici n 9

[23] 1 Cor. 12. 11

[24] Pope John Paul II address at Vespers on Pentecost 2004

Chapter 15 ~ The Movement's Benedictine Connection

The Benedictine idea and its diversity

It is not possible to understand the connection between the Benedictines and the Manquehue lay Movement without first getting to know something about the Benedictine Confederation. The first point to be made is that the Benedictines are not an Order in the sense in which that word is used to describe Franciscans, Dominicans and Jesuits and other Orders of men and women in the Catholic Church. Such an Order is usually understood to mean a unified body of men or women under the authority of a single elected individual, usually known as 'General'. The members are professed for the Order and can be moved to different houses and a variety of different works by the local Provincial or by the General. In the case of the Benedictines there is no such unified organization nor a central authority governing all. Each individual Abbey is essentially independent, ruled in accordance with the Rule and its Constitutions[1], although it is associated also with a confederation of all the Abbeys in the World. The Abbots of the world meet at intervals of usually four years at the Benedictine Abbey of Sant' Anselmo in Rome when they elect an Abbot Primate. The Abbot Primate has no direct jurisdiction (as the Generals of other Orders do) over the individual Abbeys. He may, however, do much to help them and bear witness to the spirituality of St Benedict's Rule, which is the bond that inspires them all and has proclaimed through the centuries the principles to which all Benedictines are committed.

In spite of the unique spirit and basic lifestyle derived from the Rule, which inspire Benedictine life and make it quickly recognizable, there is a wide diversity in the works undertaken by Benedictines and in the degree both of withdrawal from the world and of engagement in the work of the local Church, which is found in the Abbies of different Congregations and different countries. The Congregations are associations of Abbeys, either on a regional basis or stretching through many countries. Each Congregation has a specific set of agreed parameters, called Constitutions, to establish in greater detail the ways in which the Rule is to be applied in the local context. The Constitutions will also specify the sort of work to be undertaken by those particular Abbeys. Besides these groups of Abbeys organized in Congregations there are a limited number of Abbeys or independent Priories which have been founded for some particular, and usually local, reason and are not assimilated into any of the Congregations. Some of them may come under the local bishop and others under the Abbot Primate who has an oversight of them and arranges periodic visitations.

The broadest division between different Congregations and different individual Abbeys or Priories is between those who do some external work for the Church (for instance in teaching or the pastoral apostolate) and those who devote themselves exclusively to prayer, study and manual work. It often happens that these two groups of Benedictines are distinguished by being called 'active' and 'contemplative'. These names are not quite accurate, however, because common prayer is always paramount and there is a strong contemplative element in all Benedictine life. It is difficult to find accurate descriptions which would fit every case. In fact we are here entering into a characteristic diversity which makes the Benedictine way of life resistant to sharp, legalistic categorization. The diversity goes further still. There are even different Benedictine 'Orders' like the Cistercians and the Camaldolese and Olivetans, which have their own structures and vocations but still follow St Benedict's Rule.

When we turn to the organization of the women Benedictines the picture becomes more complex still. In the medieval tradition Benedictine nuns were enclosed and did not engage in external work. Many such Benedictine communities continue today living in enclosure and they are normally referred to as 'nuns'. Some of these are devoted to perpetual adoration of the Blessed Sacrament as a special continuing prayer for the whole Church. Other enclosed nuns, apart from their life of prayer, are engaged in literary and historical work and research or in the provision of a retreat house or in farming. Then besides the enclosed nuns there are many communities of Benedictine sisters who are not strictly enclosed but engage in various forms of active work in teaching and general pastoral work. These Benedictine Sisters form the largest group of Benedictine women. It is worth noting that in the last published statistics for the whole world in the year 2,000 there were 8,694 Benedictine monks in the world and 18,213 Benedictine nuns and sisters.

This brief summary does not do justice to the wide diversity of ways in which the Benedictines are engaged in the life and work of the Church throughout the world. Nor can it do justice to the strength and spiritual power of the unifying influence of St Benedict's Rule itself. This spiritual influence is stronger than anything mere organizational structure could of itself achieve. It is a strength which comes from the simple but profound teaching of the Rule itself. Enough, however, has been said to make it clear that the Manquehue Movement's relationship to the Benedictines cannot be described in simple terms, as though the Benedictines were a single body under tight and unified control. It is rather a relationship which reflects something of the diversity of a monasticism which has grown in ways that are deep and subtle through the centuries.

There is one special aspect of Benedictine life which was important in attracting the young Manquehue Movement to the Benedictine tradition. This is its age-long association with the laity. Throughout the 15 centuries in which the Rule has been actively followed in the Church there have always been lay men and women associated with the monasteries in different ways in different times and countries. These lay people, both men and women, came to be known as 'Oblates', which is a Latin word meaning 'one who is offered'. It has always been used of those men and women who offer themselves formally in their lay state to serve God in accordance with the teaching of the Rule and are accepted by a particular Benedictine community. While continuing their ordinary lay lives they undertake a modified observance of St Benedict's Rule with certain obligations of prayer, good life and good works which gives them a share in the prayer and often the apostolate of the particular Benedictine community which accepts them as Oblates. They are normally local and are thought of as something like an extension into lay life of the Benedictine family to which they belong.

There is one outstanding saint from among the Benedictine Oblates of the Middle Ages who especially drew the attention and devotion of the Manquehue Movement from an early stage. This is St Frances of Rome. She was married in her early teens, as was normal in those days, and brought up a family. Later she devoted herself as a Benedictine Oblate to prayer and good works. She converted many other women in Rome to follow her example and, so strong were her followers that she took the unusual step with the Pope's approval of founding a separate congregation of Benedictine Oblates in Rome. Prayer was at the center of her vocation and in the midst of all her active work and charity she became well known as a mystic through her visions and prophecies. The inspiration of her life meant much especially to the women of the Manquehue Movement and she was adopted as one of the patrons of the Movement. This remarkable Benedictine example from the fifteenth century is a confirmation of the validity of the extended Manquehue Benedictine community living as laity in the world and bringing the prayer and inspiration of the Rule right into lay life to create a cloister in the world. Thus the ancient tradition of Benedictine Oblates, who are so diverse both in prayer and in work, formed for the Manquehue Movement an example of how Benedictines have always influenced lay life and how lay life has often been enriched and influenced by the Rule.

It was, however, a particular tradition of Benedictinism, in which the apostolate had always been valued through the centuries, to which José Manuel turned at an early stage. This was the tradition of the English Benedictine Congregation. He turned to it first of all when he was founding his first school. He was attracted initially because of its active educational tradition and because for many centuries it had in various different ways followed a monastic path which was also apostolic. A brief summary of some of the highlights of history of the English Benedictines will help this account of the Movement by illustrating how from a very early stage the apostolate and evangelization were integrated within the Benedictine vocation. This is important to the Manquehue claim to Benedictine inspiration.

On his early visits to Ampleforth Abbey in England José Manuel found a Benedictine tradition which was different from the one he had known in Santiago, yet it was strangely and profoundly similar. The

English Benedictine tradition goes back many centuries. Gradually he learnt the reason for this and understood through his contacts in England, Europe, South America and Rome that the Rule, although it is old, is not a mere relic of the past but has some precious things to contribute to the Church today. How the Rule came to be and developed with the growing, developing Church is important for this understanding. It is important also for the understanding of the Benedictine character of the Manquehue Movement and the riches of the past on which it draws.

From St Benedict to Anglo Saxon England

What we know about St Benedict is not very extensive, but it is very precious. He was born in the remote hill country town of Nursia north of Rome and well off the beaten track. His family sent him as a young man for higher studies in Rome. There he was plunged into the mainstream of contemporary life – and student life at that - and he did not like it. Rome and Italy at the time were under the usurping power of the Gothic King Theodoric. The Goths, besides being barbarians to Roman eyes, were heretical Arians to the Pope and the Catholics like Benedict. The Romans despised them but were subject to them. The Senate was allowed to retain its status for show but it was without power except by courtesy of the occupying Goths. The undercurrents and crosscurrents of such a situation can be imagined. Benedict did not like what he saw and experienced in Rome. Like many of the young in the 20th and 21st centuries he wanted something deeper. He wanted prayer and solitude with God. He wanted to give his life to God.

At Subiaco in the hills forty miles from Rome he took refuge in a remote cave to live the life of a hermit. He became known and admired in the countryside and people sought him out. A local community of monks begged him to become their Abbot but, when they discovered that his ideals were too strong for them, they repudiated him by attempting to poison him. He went quietly and sadly back to his cave. It is perhaps a surprise that a little later he was willing to respond to a second request and once again became Abbot of a monastery at Subiaco.

After a time he moved to Monte Cassino where he wrote his Rule and founded the great monastery there. Monasticism was already strongly established in the West under a variety of monastic Rules. St Benedict's Rule came to be recognized as outstanding for its great human understanding, wisdom and spiritual depth. However little we know about him otherwise, we may safely see St Benedict himself in the luminous balance, wisdom and spirituality of his Rule.

During Benedict's lifetime Italy was subjected to war, famine and persecution. The Greeks of Byzantium tried to re-conquer Rome in a war which subjected Italy to terrible suffering and left it devastated and powerless before another barbarian invasion of the Lombards. This was the civil/political background to St Benedict's peaceful rule of life. After St.Benedict's death his own monastery of Monte Cassino was destroyed by the savage Lombards. The monks escaped to Rome and took with them Benedict's own copy of the Rule. Thus Benedictine monasticism came to Rome

At the end of the century in 597 Pope St Gregory the Great sent Augustine of Canterbury with a group of forty monks to England to convert the people to Christianity. There had been an earlier Christian Church in England under the Roman power but it had been swept away by barbarian invasions except for some remnants in Wales and the west. Now Gregory, who was himself a monk, wanted not a reconquest but conversion of the barbarians to the Christian faith by a group of monks. This was a new style of mission for monks which needed so great a man as Gregory to justify and follow up. Monks now moved into an active apostolate but with a difference. St Gregory was explicit in his instructions. Their life in community was to continue unimpaired. Their life of common prayer in their choir was to be preserved intact. Their apostolate was to develop principally through example. They were to be a light in darkness, a witness by their example to Christ and his salvation. St Bede records how Augustine and his forty monks began their apostolate in England:

> They were constantly at prayer; they fasted and kept vigils; they preached the word of life to whomsoever they could...they practiced what they preached.[2]

Augustine and his monks soon began to have encouraging success in the southern regions of Britain. They discovered also that they were not so alone in this monastic apostolate as they may have thought. In the seventh century up in the north of England and in Scotland there were other monks from Ireland who brought the message of Christ to the people and established monasteries to support, develop and strengthen the faith. Outstanding among these missionary monks, who converted Scotland and the north of England were Aidan and Cuthbert. Bede tells how Aidan, when he was sent to northern England from the Celtic monastery of Iona, rejected the severe methods attempted by another monk. He gave expression to the monastic approach to evangelization:

> Brother, it seems to me that you were too severe on your ignorant hearers. You should have followed the practice of the Apostles and begun by giving them the milk of simple teaching, and gradually nourished them with the word of God until they were capable of greater perfection and able to follow the loftier precepts of Christ.[3]

Aidan's gentle methods were successful. Cuthbert, who followed Aidan, was at first a monk at Melrose[4], where be became Prior. He became a great ascetic and mystic but he was a great preacher also. Bede writes of him:

> He did not restrict his teaching and influence to the monastery, but worked to rouse the ordinary folk, far and near, to exchange their foolish customs for heavenly joys...He often used to leave the monastery....and visit the neighboring towns where he preached the way of truth to those who had gone astray.[5]

The Celtic monks also penetrated with their apostolate into post-Roman Gaul and Italy bringing with them the gospel and their formidable tradition of monastic learning. It began when St Columbanus[6] set out some time around 585 to 590 (before Augustine arrived in Britain) with twelve companions to found monasteries in the pagan melting pot of post Roman Europe. He founded two monasteries in Burgundy – Annegray and the great monastery of Luxeuil. Like Aidan and Cuthbert in Northumbria he went to the ordinary people of the land in the wild countryside which he loved. When he was driven out his monasteries remained because they were already native and of the people. He went to Switzerland where his disciple St Gall gave his name to another great monastery while Columbanus went to Italy to found Bobbio. These monasteries became large and strong and later they adopted St Benedict's Rule and became Benedictine so that their Celtic origin and the continuity of their mission was forgotten by many. Earlier in the sixth century Scotland was evangelized by St Columba from his monastery in Iona – an island which is still called Holy Island. It was from there that later Aidan came to England to found the monastery/bishopric of Lindisfarne off the east coast of Northumbria. That also is an island and still called Holy Island.

It was thus that the two monastic traditions from Rome and Ireland, having arisen independently in the sixth century came together in England during the seventh in the great flowering of Anglo Saxon Christianity in Northumbria. The Rule of St Benedict was among them early on, perhaps in Augustine's mission from the beginning and certainly after St Wilfrid, who was a monk of Lindisfarne and a great missioner n the generation after Augustine. He traveled to Rome and embraced the Roman traditions together with the Rule of St Benedict which he took with him everywhere. Already the Rule of St Benedict was becoming dominant in western monasticism. This can be seen in the beauty and majesty of the earliest copy of the Rule which is preserved in the Bodleian Library in Oxford.[7]

From among the court nobles of Aidan's converts in Northumbria came Benet Biscop, who traveled three times to Rome and brought back countless books, a teacher of Roman chant and craftsmen in stone and stained glass to build his Benedictine monastic Church which still stands in Jarrow. From that monastery of Benet Biscop came St Bede – scholar and historian of unique stature.

That same Anglo Saxon tradition was itself eager for missionary work when needed among the still pagan invaders of the continent of Europe. From south west England came St Boniface bringing a new monastic mission as the apostle of Germany, where he founded the Abbey of Fulda and, as legate of the Pope, established the Catholic Church of Germany. From Anglo-Saxon England also came St Willibrord, who converted Frisia, and St Willibald who went to evangelize Germany after a period of quiet at Monte Cassino. They and many others were monks and monasticism was their main instrument in spreading the faith and keeping it alive.

Evidently for such great Benedictine monks their stability was not a rigid concept defined by locality but a radical fidelity to their monastic vocation, wherever that was needed by the Catholic Church. Their work of evangelization was always based on the strong centers of the monasteries and communities they founded among the people and on the prayer and community life of the monks.

Extermination by the Vikings and revival under Charlemagne

In the second half of the 8th century and through the 9th the peace, the Christianity and the monasticism of the British Isles was shattered by a wave of sea-born invaders from Scandinavia. They were known generically as the Vikings. These tough and adventurous seafarers reached Iceland and perhaps even the coast of North America. They penetrated down the rivers of Eastern Europe reaching even the Black Sea. At first they were raiders for loot but eventually settled especially in Ireland, eastern England and finally Normandy. They knew nothing of Christianity. They plundered and exterminated the monasteries and killed the monks indiscriminately. The tide was turned by Brian Boru in Ireland and by Alfred in England, who, having stemmed the tide of invasion, began the work of Christianizing the invaders who had settled and made England their home.

Alfred longed for monks to help him to educate and preach the gospel to the people he had rescued from the invaders, but the Vikings had left none in England. The continent of Europe had fared better under Charlemagne (742 – 814) and his immediate successors. They succeeded in establishing the first strong state to succeed the Romans and so created a defensive basis for peace in Europe. They defeated the Muslim invasion from Spain and promoted the work of monasteries in preserving and passing on not only the learning and culture of the Christian past but also they rescued and copied the remnants of Classical learning which Christianity had inherited from Greece and Rome. Their success in maintaining civilization was a close run thing, because the layer of literacy among the peoples of Europe at that time was perilously thin.

It was the monks and monasteries that made possible the survival and revival of literacy and learning in Europe.

In this great work there was vital contribution also from the northern islands through the scholar, Alcuin of York, who later became a Benedictine monk and was Charlemagne's chief advisor in the promotion of monastic reform, educational work and the vital production of manuscripts, which were the only vehicle for the preservation of knowledge and learning. It was at this time under Charlemagne and his advisor Alcuin that the Carolingian Minuscule[8] was established.

There was contribution from Ireland also through the scholars who brought back to Europe the learning they had preserved in the Celtic monasteries. Charlemagne gave strong support to monks and monasteries. He made sure that all the monasteries in his empire adopted St Benedict's Rule. He arranged for the original MS of the Rule, preserved still at that time in Monte Cassino, to be copied very carefully to provide an authentic text for the future. The copy made for him is still preserved in the monastery of St Gall in Switzerland which was originally Celtic but by that time had become Benedictine. Scholars recognize in it the most authentic text of the Rule. It was from this time that all monasteries in Europe adopted the Rule of S Benedict.

Cluny

Among the developments of the 10th century in western Europe there was a widespread revival of monasticism. The most impressive example was the foundation of the Abbey of Cluny in 909 in southeast France. From the first it was an Abbey of high ideals and strict standards and it was strong in support for the Papal reforms of that century. It had been the habit for Abbeys to be founded by regional Kings or local nobility who often, as time went on, plundered its revenues and secured the appointment of unsuitable Abbots. To avoid all such abuses Cluny was founded under the exclusive patronage of the Holy See. The effectiveness of this was demonstrated by the election of a succession of four outstanding Abbots who ruled the monastery for two hundred years.

Cluny was in many respects different from other Benedictine Abbeys before or since. After the upheavals of the previous century many of the monasteries of Europe were in need of reform. Cluny became so strong as a promoter of reform that it was invited to monitor the reform of other monasteries. Some of the reformed monasteries and other new ones that Cluny founded became part of an extensive network of Priories under the rule of the Abbot of Cluny. The fact that they were all made dependent monasteries under the Abbot of Cluny cut across the Benedictine principle of independence, but it was an effective arrangement at the time and had a powerful influence on the whole Church – especially in liturgy. In fact liturgy became so dominant at Cluny that many other aspects of Benedictine life were neglected or undervalued so that the many monks living under that regime had little time in the day for anything but liturgical prayer. Cluny's greatest days lasted for 200 years. After that its influence dwindled but it went on through the Middle Ages and came to a violent end only with the French Revolution and Napoleon, when the Abbot of Cluny was guillotined for offering Mass and the great buildings were contemptuously blown up with gunpowder by those revolutionary prophets of the future.

Norman monasticism & England
Important as Cluny was, it was not the whole story of monastic development at the time. The Benedictine tradition was so strong and pervasive that there were other strong monastic renewals with a different emphasis from the 10th to 12th centuries. Abbot William of Dijon knew Cluny well but had different and perhaps more balanced ideas about Benedictine monastic life. When beyond all expectation the Normans were converted from their Viking life of raiding and plunder and murder they settled in a desolate part of northern France which we now call Normandy. Rather suddenly, but apparently quite freely they became Catholics with formidable commitment and a sudden desire to lead the Church. The Dukes invited William of Dijon to renew the Abbey of Fécamp on the channel coast. He did that and founded many other monasteries in Normandy.

Quite independent of his reforms there was another Abbey in Norman lands founded in isolation by an ex-soldier named Herluin who renounced soldiering and embarked on a solitary search for God. He founded an Abbey called Bec which might never have been heard of, if it had not been for a wandering scholar from Lombardy who arrived by chance to join Herluin. His name was Lanfranc. He founded a school there that soon became one of the most famous of Benedictine schools.

Lanfranc was followed some years later by another young man called Anselm. He had wandered from his home, also in Lombardy, in search of - he knew not what. He rejected the pull of Cluny in the south. There was not enough scope for study there, so he went north and joined Lanfranc – attracted by his brilliance as a scholar. He stayed to study with Lanframc and, to Anselm's surprise, Lanfranc enticed him into the monastery at Bec where Anselm turned out to be a holy monk, a great thinker and writer and a great teacher who listened to and befriended his students, so that they loved him and never wanted to lose him. He was one of the greatest of Benedictine educators.

Between them Lanfranc and Anselm made Bec one of the greatest of Abbeys - an outstanding center of learning and education. One after the other Lanfranc and Anselm were called to England by Duke William the Conqueror and his successor to be Archbishop of Canterbury. In England they found a strong Benedictine tradition in the south which had achieved in the tenth century what King Alfred had so much hoped for when he re-established English power against the Danish invaders.

In the century before the Norman invasion Dunstan, with Oswald and Ethelwold, had revived and renewed many of the ancient Abbeys starting with Dunstan's own Abbey of Glastonbury. In the end he was made Archbishop of Canterbury. He revived the monastic tradition there, but perhaps his greatest gift was his ability to earn the love and gratitude of the young through his way of teaching them. He and Anselm were certainly two Benedictine teachers who were many centuries ahead of their times in their pedagogy.

When the Normans conquered England in 1066 they began a great Benedictine revival through the whole country. They themselves did not think much of the Anglo Saxon Benedictines who followed Dunstan in Glastonbury, Canterbury, Worcester, Abingdon, Winchester and Westminster and many other great Abbeys. Historians on the whole have accepted – probably mistakenly – the Norman conquerors' assessment and seem to think well of the ruthless Normanization of monastic life which occurred in the late 11th century. It was a cultural clash which swept many precious things away as well as creating something new.

In the north of England at the time of the conquest nothing was left of the great Anglo-Saxon monastic past. It had been left desolate by the Vikings and was further ravaged (as part of his conquest) by William the Conqueror. However, once his power was assured, a restoration began. Lanfranc of Canterbury was in charge with the support of King William and his was so dominant a power both in the whole Church in England and among the Benedictines that his influence was greater than that of any Archbishop before or since. He increased the number of monastic sees[9] establishing nine of them in England – an arrangement which was absolutely unique in Europe and survived until the Reformation. This cathedral monasticism ultimately left a strong imprint on the liturgy of the Anglican Church which is still observable and now at last recognized by Anglicans and Catholics in the age of ecumenism. It must be added that Norman feudalism had a terrible effect on monasticism which led to many corruptions of the Benedictine ideals.

The Cistercians

On the continent there was a strong monastic reaction against what some considered to be an excessive emphasis on liturgy in the Cluniac reform. This reaction was led by the Cistercian reform which started early in the 12th century. It came quickly and swept through Europe under the dynamic inspiration of St Bernard of Clairvaux. The Cistercians turned emphatically from Cluniac grandeur to a simplification of liturgy and monastic life. They introduced a stricter interpretation of St Benedict's Rule. They favored for their monasteries remote and desolate places with more time for silence and a greater emphasis on manual labor. The Cistercians came to England in 1128 and were soon very strong there. However the great Cistercian abbeys which were established then and grew rapidly in that and succeeding centuries suffered like the Benedictines themselves from the influences of feudalism and from their own success in cultivating the land, which made them strong and rich. Their Abbots, like the Black Benedictine Abbots as they were called, became secular Lords in the Feudal style. Their farming was so successful that they became rich on it, as they transformed desolate land into rich pasture.

During all this time in the Dark Ages and early Middle Ages the layer of literacy in Europe remained thin and vulnerable and wherever monasteries were renewed and strengthened then literacy and learning and the hope of human development were revived. However a change was gradually taking place in society. As these post-Roman ages developed into the High Middle Ages the centers of preservation and creation (in literary and human learning as well as in theology) moved gradually away from the monasteries into the cathedral schools and the new institutions called Universities which grew so rapidly in the 13th century. As this happened and the Orders of Friars – especially the Franciscans and Dominicans – were founded the influence and importance of the monasteries began to fade. A new age had begun and the Benedictines had to learn how to adjust to their changing role within the Church.

The Universities & the Friars

The Fourth Lateran Council of 1215 under the great Pope Innocent III was a key event in this age of development. A new concept was introduced to the Church by that Council – the concept of the centralized Orders of Friars in which all the Houses and each individual member came under the central authority of one Superior who was assisted by local superiors but whose authority was above theirs. Moreover the members of the Order could be moved at will from house to house and from country to country. Their profession was to the whole order and not, as with the Benedictines, to the spiritual family of one individual Abbey. Both the Franciscan and Dominican friars were first approved by Innocent III at this time. The Council also required the Benedictines to form Congregations of Abbeys in each country, which would introduce regular visitations and establish some co-operation between the Abbeys without infringing the independence of each Abbey.

Although most Benedictines of the continent were slow to respond to the Council, the Benedictines in England were very prompt so that they were the first to set up the federal organization which became the English Benedictine Congregation. They also moved into the new world by founding monastic houses of study at Oxford so that monks could be sent from individual monasteries to get degree.

The Black Death and Dissolution of the Monasteries

It was during the year 1348 that the Black Death came to England. The monastic communities suffered terribly from this sudden and mysterious plague. They were particularly vulnerable because of the community life which they led together. A typical example was the great Abbey of St Alban's from which in a few days the Abbot, Prior and Subprior and 46 members of the community died of the plague. Suddenly, unexpectedly, in so short a time it left the community at little more than half strength with its experienced leaders gone. The larger and stronger communities managed to struggle back slowly to something like normality, but they were all permanently weakened and many smaller communities never recovered at all. Even for the larger monasteries nothing could ever be quite the same, and from the mid 14th century there were regular recurrences of the plague, although none were so virulent as the first. The plague left the whole monastic Benedictine Congregation much weaker and in great need of radical reform and reorganization which never came.

After another difficult century in which with the rest of the nation the Benedictines suffered from the divisive horrors of the dynastic Wars of the Roses, the Benedictines were fated to meet not with the reform and reorganization they desperately needed but with sudden and catastrophic dissolution at the hands Henry VIII and his ruthless Chancellor, Thomas Cromwell, who was carefully chosen for the purpose of plundering every one of the religious houses of England. By the new masters of England everything Benedictine was discarded with contempt and cruelty.

Continuity & renewal on the continent

During the brief reign of Mary (1553 to 1559) there was an attempt at the restoration of monasticism in England in response to a plea made to the Queen by forty of the old monks who twenty years previously had been turned out of their Abbeys. It led to the refounding of the Abbey of Westminster with a community of monks led by Abbot Feckenham. The monks returning to the monastic life of which they had been deprived were joined by a number of young novices. Full monastic life was restored in Westminster Abbey. It lasted for only two years when Mary died and with the accession of Elizabeth Westminster Abbey was again dissolved. Abbot Feckenham was imprisoned in the Tower and most of the community suffered similarly for their unshaken faith.

In the next century under James I (1603 – 1625) there was a new development. Many young Catholics from England went to the continent to look for ways of becoming Benedictines. It was the powerful memory of the Benedictine tradition in the English Church from Anglo-Saxon to Tudor times that inspired them. In 1607 they met in secret in London an old monk of Marian Westminster who had spent much of his life in prison for his faith. His name was Dom Sigebert Buckley. He was the sole surviving member of the old English Benedictine Congregation. There in secret he passed on to these young Catholics the Benedictine habit he had himself received in Westminster Abbey. Together with the Benedictine habit[10] he explicitly and deliberately passed on to them all the rights and privileges and all the spiritual tradition of the old English Congregation. What was so carefully accomplished in London was later approved and validated by the Pope with the intention of officially recognizing and confirming that continuity. Accordingly the revived and renewed English Benedictine Congregation was officially established by a Papal Brief in 1617 and this act was later confirmed by a Papal Bull in 1630. Three English Benedictine monasteries were now set up on the continent: St Gregory's at Douai, which is now at Downside in Somerset, St Laurence's at Dieulouard in Lorraine, which is now at Ampleforth in Yorkshire and St Edmund's in Paris, which is now at Woolhampton in Berkshire.

French Revolution and after

From this time until the French Revolution the three small monasteries on the continent continued their Benedictine life of prayer and study. They educated young Catholics who came over from England and prepared them to be monks and priests. Most of them were sent back secretly to England to bring the Mass and sacraments to the persecuted Catholics there. The great difficulties of the times and the demanding mission of these monks to serve the laity in England had called for a centralized organization in which the President had supreme authority. After the French Revolution they came back to England. They continued their pastoral mission in England during the nineteenth century with the center of their interest in the missions or parishes, which were predominantly in poor industrialized areas. These missionary monks were faithful and much loved in their service of the poor Catholics but the monasteries, still only Priories, remained small. They ran Catholic schools which were proudly conscious of their ancient tradition but they were small and in need of development. There was need for reform and a reluctance to face it because of the monks love of pastoral work among the poor.

In the end reform was achieved through the intervention of the great Pope Leo XIII. The three monasteries, which had been founded in France and returned to England in the aftermath of the French Revolution, were made the Abbeys of Downside, Ampleforth and Douai. The fullness of Benedictine life had been restored to England by the Pope.

The Monastery of the Holy Trinity in Las Condes

What has been said so far gives a brief outline of the long and diverse Benedictine tradition which José Manuel encountered on his first visit to Ampleforth Abbey in 1981. What he found there was different from the Benedictine tradition which he knew already in Santiago. There was a difference and yet there was a deep spiritual identity. The Monastery of the Holy Trinity in Las Condes was inspired by a different Benedictine source in Europe.

During the 19th century Ampleforth and the whole of the English Benedictine Congregation were struggling to establish themselves again in England. At the same time in France an almost miraculous Benedictine revival was taking place. After the Revolution and Napoleon there were no Benedictines left. The dominant atmosphere of the country was secular and anti-Catholic and the Church had largely forgotten monasticism. In spite of this it happened that in 1832 a young diocesan priest named Prosper Guéranger, who had a scholarly understanding of the Catholic tradition, yearned for a Benedictine revival. He collected enough local support to buy the buildings and site of the former Benedictine Priory of Solesmes in northern France. In the next year he began community life there under the Rule of Saint Benedict with five other priests of like mind. The Pope approved their onstitutions and made this new house a Benedictine Abbey with Dom Prosper Guéranger as their Abbot. That was the beginning of the great Abbey of Solesmes.

From Solesmes at the beginning of the twentieth century Quarr Abbey was founded in the Isle of Wight in England and from Quarr, through the initiative of Dom Peter Subercaseaux, the monastery of the Holy Trinity was founded in Santiago of Chile. However Solemnes found the distance too great for their oversight and withdrew, leaving a group of Chilean monks without support. It was then that the German monastery of Beuron, founded by the brothers Wolter in the revival of the nineteenth century, took over the little community in Santiago and made it one of theirs. Later it was aggregated into a new Benedictine Congregation of South America called Cono Sur.

That was the Abbey in the district of Las Condes to which Abbot Gabriel Guarda invited José Manuel at his moment of deep spiritual crisis in 1974. It was an invitation which led to three years of sharing *lectio divina* with him. This was the real source of the Movement and the first act of formation which shaped it. It was in a Benedictine Abbey. It was under the shadow of the Rule, to which Abbot Gabriel gently and gradually introduced José Manuel. When three years later the young began their vocation of prayer and work with José Manuel, Abbot Gabriel was always on hand and they often looked to him and to the Abbey for support and guidance. When Cardinal Silva directed them towards Catholic education it was Abbot Gabriel who encouraged José Manuel to think of it in Benedictine terms and gave him his first introduction to Ampleforth because of their educational work. Everything that followed flowed from those early Benedictine encounters in Las Condes and the union of the two streams of Benedictine tradition from Ampleforth and Solesmes.

Ampleforth Abbey
It all happened step by step, as the Holy Spirit usually works. It was in 1974 that Abbot Gabriel gave José Manuel a copy of St Benedict's Rule

as a present. This was the sowing of the seed. A few years later in 1979 there were about 20 active young members of the Movement. The growth of their inner life had matched the growth of their work and José Manuel got copies of the Rule from Argentina so that each of them might have one. These copies were solemnly presented to the young members in a ceremony in the Monastery in Las Condes in the presence of Abbot Gabriel. They were reverently received and kept, and the following year they used chapter 4 on The Tools for Good Works as the basis of their scripture meditation, although the full text had yet to make an impact.

It was in the next year, 1980 that Abbot Gabriel put José Manuel in touch with Fr Dominic Milroy of Ampleforth. In an article, which Fr Dominic had written for the centenary of St Benedict's birth in that same year José Manuel read a comment about how St Benedict's wisdom is still relevant today. This idea stayed with him and impressed him strongly. It began to shed a new light on the possibility of the Rule being important for the spiritual development of the Movement and gave a new purpose and point to his first visit to Ampleforth.

That visit took place in 1981. He remembers it as having made a deep impression on him because he saw there the Rule in action in a monastery that was deeply involved in education. He began to understand it in a new way. The school, to which Fr Dominic introduced him, came into this, but is was the Abbey Church, the monastic community working in the school, the prayer life of the community in the Church that influenced him most deeply. On subsequent visits he came to know Fr Columba Cary-Elwes, who spoke Spanish and had much to say about the spirituality of the Rule and its relevance to the laity today. It was the beginning of a friendship which became very influential both in England and in Chile when Father Columba later visited the Movement there. He was introduced at Ampleforth to Cardinal Basil Hume's book "Searching for God", which became and still is a valued source book for the formation in Benedictine spirituality among members of the Movement in Chile.

Those first visits by José Manuel and by other Oblates became, as time went on, an important factor in the Benedictine growth and development of the Movement. There were other vitally important visits to Rome to the Holy See's 'Council for the Laity', whose President Cardinal Eduardo Pironio was a friend of Fr.Dominic Milroy. Fr. Dominic assisted José Manuel on three of his visits and Abbot Patrick on a later one to the following President, Cardinal Stafford. It was on José Manuel's fifth visit to the Council for the Laity in 1993 that the Movement was issued an official 'Laudatio'. This was a note of approval and encouragement from the Holy See and contained a message that confirmed the course to which the Movement was committed, once more urging the Movement to be ecclesial, lay and Benedictine. Cardinal Pironio had pointed the Movement along this path for the first time in 1986 and on other occasions also always repeating the same words, *ecclesial, lay* and *Benedictine*. These words were remembered and cherished making the Movement all the more anxious to discover how to be more genuinely Benedictine in the context of their lay, ecclesial life. It became ever more clear to them that it was not enough simply to use bits and pieces of the Rule to fit into their lives but they must find a way of forming their life and work together as laity in the spirituality of the Rule. In this context they were also encouraged by Cardinal Pironio in the Laudatio to develop their relationship with Ampleforth and extend it to other Benedictine communities. Cardinal Pironio's successor, Cardinal Stafford, went further and looked forward to the day when the Movement's Benedictine and lay presence in evangelization would be carried from Chile to other countries also.

The Gringos

One of the most striking ways in which the strong Benedictine roots of the Movement have become apparent is to be seen in the story of the Gringos. It is a story which, as already recorded, began with José Manuel's second visit to Ampleforth in 1982. These visits still continue today. Over the years more than a hundred of these young men have spent months or years working with and learning from the Movement.

For the Ampleforth Benedictine cocmmunity itself the new association with the lay Benedictines of the Manquehue Movement in Chile brought an inspiration and new openings in the same tradition which proved to be full of hope for both communities. From the early days a strong empathy grew up between the two communities – the

English Benedictines of Ampleforth and the new Lay Benedictines of Chile. This understanding was centered on the life of prayer and work of St Benedict's Rule and the Benedictine apostolate which had come down from the earliest days and was cherished through the varied history of Ampleforth. The link was sealed on both sides by their mutual recognition as confraters, through which the differences and independence of both communities are recognized.

EMLA[11] & other Abbeys

Cardinal Pironio's encouragement of contact with other Benedictines took the Movement a step further in 1994 when, to their great delight, José Manuel and one of the Oblates Manuel José Echenique were invited to attend the meeting of EMLA in Sao Paulo in Brazil. The welcome they received and the help and advice they were given by all those South American Abbots gave them confidence in their Benedictine development. They were impressed by the variety of participants in EMLA. The false idea of Benedictines as a unified Order faded further into the background. They came away with a new view of the flexibility and adaptability of the Rule in their new lay Benedictine apostolate. This gave José Manuel the confidence in 1995 to produce the first version of the "Minima Regla"[12] which was the name they gave the Rule of life for the Oblates the first edition of which José Manuel produced in that year. They began to talk with greater assurance of "an extended monastery" or "extended Benedictine community" *Communidad Benedictina extendida.*[13] Once conceived and put into practice this way of describing their community life – for both celibate and married Oblates – had two Benedictine qualities – simplicity and strength. Their lay cloister was defined by their houses of residence, where the Rule was strictly kept, and their places of work, that is the schools or other sites of the Movement's work. After work they return to their house of residence and always make the journey together so as to avoid distraction and help each other to keep focused on their shared undertaking. Their prayer, *lectio*, meals are taken together in one or other location. They can and do keep the Rule within that framework. For the liturgy – and especially for major liturgical celebrations – they have a simple Habit, worn alike by men and women which helps their sense of community prayer and is a visible affirmation in a liturgical context of their dedication and their witness. It is important both for themselves and for others, making it clear that, although they are authentically lay, it is with a difference – they are lay Benedictines.

The testimony of Fr Geraldo Gonzalez OSB

Other Benedictine connections began to grow and are still growing. In 1990 a friendship grew up between José Manuel and Fr Geraldo Gonzalez y Lima OSB of the Abbey of Sao Geraldo in Sao Paolo in Brazil. In that year Fr Geraldo visited the Movement and was so impressed by the dedicated Benedictine-style life they were leading that he arranged for exchanges of pupils and staff between the Movement and the Abbey School of Sao America. He even invited a small group of Oblates to come to Brazil to work on catechesis of the young in the Abbey school. This lasted for two years to the great benefit of all involved. Fr Geraldo made further visits and finally in 1996 it was arranged that he should spend a full year in Santiago living fully the life of the celibate Oblates in all its aspects. It might have been thought that he, an experienced Benedictine, might have come to teach them something. In fact he writes that it was "an enormous surprise to find myself experiencing a renewal in many different areas of my monastic life." He found that the 'extended community' and the 'extended cloister' were no mere airy ideal but very real and formative:

> each one of us has our cloister defined according to our particular work or service. My cloister, for instance, is restricted to Casa Santa Francisca Romana (the residence of the celibate Oblates) Colegio San Benito, José Manuel's houses in Santiago and in Leyda in the countryside. If we have to go out of our extended cloister we do so in groups or as an entire community; rarely do we go anywhere alone.

He describes the community's practice of shared *lectio divina*:

> A precious and vital aspect of the Oblates' life is the profound encounter they have as a community with the Word of God......The process of doing *lectio,* whether in pairs or in groups, puts those who

312

participate directly into the presence of Christ and as a result creates deep bonds of friendship between them.

Fr Geraldo speaks of his great surprise at discovering the modern benefits of the ancient practice of 'fraternal correction' not only as a way of maintaining discipline but as an expression of love:

> it helps to lead us to truth and to spiritual richness. It is something very precious and liberating and is practised by all members of the community.

Equally Fr Geraldo was impressed by the frugality of the community, by the system of mutual service on which the household was run and he makes the comment that "in many ways I live in greater frugality here than in my community in Sao Paolo."

During his time in Santiago Fr Geraldo experienced the reality of living as an experienced priest in a lay community in which he was the only priest. It is worth quoting fully his reflection on this experience in view of contemporary concerns in the whole Church about the present and future role of the laity and the status of priesthood in the Body of Christ:

> Rather than highlighting the differences between laity, monks and priests, it is important that we seek out the areas of common ground. These can be found in our common baptism and in our shared Benedictine spirituality. From this point of view I lead a life which is identical to that of the celibate Oblates, as I am subject to the same discipline and obedience. The only difference is that I am able to serve them through my ministry as a priest. Far from degrading my role as a priest by serving the community in this capacity I have been able to rediscover my calling to be priest and monk. Being freed from other responsibilities I am able to devote myself more completely and more attentively to sacramental service and towards giving time to specific individuals. In this community, the laity carry out all the tasks that the Church permits them with the result that my role is purely priestly, centered on saying Mass and hearing confessions. The process of relearning has been very moving for me and has come as another quite unexpected benefit of staying here, at

the same time this new understanding of the role of the monk and priest contains nothing that cannot be found in chapters 60, 61 and 62 of the Rule of St Benedict.

One final comment of Father Geraldo is worth quoting. He says

> In all that I have written about here, the truth of my own experience and witness, I see how an exchange and integration of life between the Benedictine monks and nuns and the laity is perfectly possible. I feel that new perspectives are being forged and that there is a great deal we can share.

Worth Abbey and 'Cunaco'

Then there was Worth Abbey in Sussex, where José Manuel was invited to speak at the World Conference of Benedictine Educators. José Manuel gave a strong and lucid exposition of the Movement's educational vision and experience. The overall question was about what Benedictines could and should aim at in education in the light of the spiritual vision of the Rule. It was there that he met Fr Christopher Jamison, Headmaster of Worth School (now Abbot of Worth Abbey). Together with Fr Gregory Mohrman of St. Louis they agreed to start a small group to develop ideas which had emerged in the Conference .

The first encounter of this group took place in Chile in March 2000. They met in a house in the country, which is owned by a member of the Movement. The house is called 'Cunaco' and this name was adopted for the meetings. It is intentionally a small group and the members taking part were from the Manquhue Movement, Ampleforth Abbey, the Abbey of Sao Geraldo in Brazil, Worth Abbey and the Abbey of St Mary & St Louis in USA (founded from Ampleforth in 1955). There have been four subsequent meetings in Sao Paolo, in St Louis, in Rapel in Chile and in Worth. The intention is that it should remain a small group with limited and practical objectives.

Saint Louis Abbey

The first meeting of the Cunaco group in 2000 co-incided with a visit to the Movement by Abbot Thomas Frerking, Abbot of St Louis Abbey who came with his Headmaster, Fr Gregory Mohrman. St Louis Abbey had been founded by Ampleforth Abbey in 1955. Already Fr Gregory had paid an extended visit to the Movement and its schools and it seemed natural that these North American Benedictines engaged in education should be invited to take part in the Cunaco meetings with the South American Benedictine Movement. Exchanges between the pupils of the two schools and visits from other members of the community have followed. The developing relationship is very much in line with Pope John Paul's appeal for greater unity and more sharing between North and South America. Exchange visits between the communities and the schools have continued and are strongly encouraged by a sense of empathy and understanding which is rapidly growing.

Reflections of Abbot Gabriel of Las Condes
Looking back on the beginnings of José Manuel's first contacts with the Benedictines during his three years of daily visits to Las Condes monastery, Abbot Gabriel reflects on the Benedictine connection and how it may develop:

I cannot say how it will develop - in what degree the Movement can become affiliated to the Confederation. It is clear that José Manuel has received a very warm welcome whenever he has had contact with monasteries or superiors anywhere. This is because they see something which is very much of our age - post conciliar - like so many other Movements which are new realities in the Church inspired by the Holy Spirit. And the structure and insertion of these realities within Canon Law and the actual structure of the Church is not clear yet. But, just as it has been approved by the Holy See with the *Laudatio* and Cardinal Pironio's support - all these are signs that the Church is welcoming this thing, and we Benedictines are part of the Church.

Let us think about the history of monasticism. There have been examples of cyclical progress in it, of things that were not there in the beginning and things that were not there a thousand years later. That explains the growth of the Benedictine world and its expansion, which has embraced new realities - geographical, cultural or belonging to one specific age. In that sense maybe something very curious is being written and I don't know how it will develop. It is in the hands of the Holy Spirit.

These comments of Abbot Gabriel are important for any assessment of the Manquehue Movement. Both in its relationship to the Church and to the Benedictines the Movement is in a state of transitional development. Its roots in the Church, through the Archdiocese of Santiago and the Council for the Laity in Rome are both positive and strong. They are full of hope, being founded on the theology of Vatican II. Yet it is not yet possible to predict its future development. Similarly its relationship with the Benedictine Confederation is firmly founded on the following of St Benedict's Rule and the Movement's growing fraternal association with Benedictines. It is inconceivable that this relationship should not continue but it is not yet possible, as Abbot Gabriel perceives, to predict exactly its final development in the context of the worldwide Benedictine Confederation.

Summary & Conclusion

This chapter has attempted the difficult task of explaining the Benedictine dimension of the Cloister in the World as it grew from small, unnoticed beginnings in Santiago.

The diversity of the Benedictines in their history and its reflection in contemporary monasticism is one of the factors that makes such a new development as the Cloister in the World plausible. Such arguments might remain interesting but marginal were it not for broader and more fundamental developments in the Church, which call for the awakening of lay Catholics to the full realisation of their evangelical and apostolic role in the life of the Church. The laity may be described in Pope John Paul II's words as 'the sleeping giant' and the question, which has been hovering over the Church since Vatican II is 'what will happen when the giant awakes?' It is important in attempting to answer this question to avoid the sterile attempt to turn it into one about power and see it instead as an insistent spiritual question for everyone. That is just what the Movement has done and in doing so has found the true road to liberation. Whatever the future may hold the first twenty-five years of this Ecclesial, Lay, Benedictine Movement have been both inspiring and prophetic of renewed lay Catholic life.

ରେ

Notes for Chapter 15

[1] See the next paragraph for an explanation of the meaning of Constitutions.

[2] see Bede, History of English People I, 26

[3] Bede History Bk 3, ch 5

[4] an originally Celtic monastery in the border land between England & Scotland

[5] Bede, History Bk 4, ch 27

[6] The Latin form of his name is retained to distinguish him from his predecessor St Columba (or Columcille) who took the gospel to Scotland and founded the monastery of Iona.

[7] It is an English uncial manuscript, perhaps from Canterbury – the oldest extant manuscript of the Rule, although the text of the manuscript of St Gall, copied in Charlemagne's time, comes from the Monte Cassino text of St Benedict.   Naturally there is disagreement about the date of the Oxford manuscript, as there always is when so little evidence is available. A plausible date would be around 700, although some might want with little evidence to put it later. Either way it is eloquent evidence of the great importance of the Rule in Anglo-Saxon Christianity.

[8] The name given to a beautiful alphabet developed in Charlemagne's time for the copying of Manuscripts. The heavier Black Letter took over in the later Middle Ages but the Carolingian Minuscule was rediscovered by the Renaissance Humanists and copied by the early Italian printers. This was the model of the printed alphabet we use today.

[9] In a monastic see a resident community of Benedictine monks formed the chapter and choir of the Cathedral. The monks were ruled by a Cathedral Prior. The arrangement worked best when the Bishop was himself a monk, like Lanfranc, but this became more rare and difficulties multiplied when the bishop was not a monk.

[10] The ceremonial act of passing on the Benedictine habit by clothing a new monk in it during a formal ceremony was an act of great importance. It was a sign of the acceptance of a new member into a monastic family and marked the beginning of monastic life for that new monk. When St Benedict took refuge from the confusions of the world in the solitude of Subiaco his act was given a sort of validation by a neighboring monk named Romanus who gave him a monastic habit. The same act became and still is the normal way in which a new candidate is accepted into a monastic family.

[11] Encuentro Monastico LatinoAmericano ~ Latin American Monastic Conference

[12] The Little Rule for Oblates of the Manquehue Movement

[13] *The Movement's Rule (Minima Regla) describes the Extended Benedictine Community as follows:*

[1]A Benedictine monastery is formed by a community which serves under a rule and an abbot. [2]In a way which is analogous to this the community of the Manquehue Oblates is formed by a group which serves under the Rule of St Benedict and a Principal who presides over them. [3]However the monastery described by St Benedict in his rule had everything in place for the monks within a defined area. By contrast the community of the Manquehue Oblates is a center of unity for people leading a lay life and so, although it does maintain private establishments for its own purposes, it reaches out into different neighborhoods and centers of life and work and relaxation to which Oblates' duties will take them. [4]It is for that reason that it is called an extended Benedictine community.

[5]The style of life of this extended Benedictine community is just like that of a Benedictine monastery in that it offers the framework of an alternative society. [6]It takes the gospel as its guiding light and [7]the principal pillars on which it is built are: listening to the Word of God in *lectio divina*, [8]a life in community based on the rule of St Benedict, [9]the celebration of the liturgy of the hours and [10]community work. [11]The purpose of this way of life is to create a union between faith and life which is both intimate and realistic. It is indeed an alternative way of life, but it is set within the context of civil society and not outside it, observing civil law and respecting civil authority. [12]It is called to act on civil society from within, just like yeast in dough (Lk 13, 20-21) and to influence the way temporal order is built up so as to help towards its ultimate fulfillment in the light of Christ.

Chapter 16 ~ Structure & Spirituality of the Movement

The structure of the Manquehue Movement

The beginnings of the Manquehue Movement arose, as we have seen, from personal conversion through *lectio divina*. That awakening to the word of God brought the first young members of the Movement together under the personal influence of José Manuel Eguiguren. It became a corporate reality for them through praying and working together in community. It was all very simple to start with, but it was not possible to continue in this prayer and work together without a clear structure and a practical purpose which could be understood and accepted. Gradually in the early years that structure was worked out by José Manuel in dialogue with his followers. The time came when some codification was needed and the result was the document which is known as 'The Little Rule for the Oblates'. It echoed St Benedict's own description of his Rule in Chapter 73[1]. It opens with a simple statement of what the Movement is and what it is for:

> The Manquehue Apostolic Movement is a Private Association of Faithful Catholics from among the laity. The aim of its members is to bring the sacrament of baptism to its fullest and deepest meaning in their lives with inspiration from the spirituality of the Rule of St Benedict and in filial communion with the bishop of their diocese. To achieve this, its members are organized in concentric circles so that each circle represents a different level of participation and commitment within the Movement.

The striking thing about this statement of purpose for a lay Movement engaged in an active apostolate is that its first focus is not on external achievement but on personal holiness through the fulfilment of their baptism in the spirit of St Benedict.[2] There were, of course, plenty of practical aims to come for the Movement, but they depended on that first aim of baptismal fidelity. After that comes the simple structure of the Movement:

> There is one community at the center, formed of the members of the Manquehue Apostolic Movement who have made a life-promise of indefinite duration. This community is called the Community of the Manquehue Oblates and it is the community to which this Little Rule applies. The community of the Oblates is the heart of the Movement and the whole life of the Movement flows from it.[3]

The Oblates, who have made life-promises and form the community at the center follow a way of life which is set out in the Little Rule. The Little Rule is not so much an instrument of legislation as an agreed expression of a set of principles and spiritual aims and ideals to which they are committed. These principles, aims and ideals seek to draw out the full spiritual meaning of the basic commitment of baptism, understood in its fullest sense, both for the celibate and the married Oblates.

The Oblates do not take formal vows as do the Religious Orders of Consecrated Life. They take promises using the monastic formula of St Benedict. These monastic vows commit monks to *Stability, Obedience and Conversion of Life.* The Oblates take these, not as solemn vows, but as promises of indefinite duration. The duration is indefinite, because these promises are essentially a renewal of their own baptismal promises which, once they are fully recognized and accepted by the individual, are of their very nature a commitment for ever. There is no such thing as a temporary or provisional baptismal commitment and so, without bringing in any other consideration, the Oblates see their promises also as being in the baptismal sense - forever. Where they involve certain practices which are special to the Oblates these exist and are accepted and cherished, not as impositions from authority, but because they are understood as ways of bringing the meaning of being baptized into Christ to bear on the realities of contemporary lay life. As such they are accepted by the Oblates and put into practice in obedience to that Christ-given aim.

The core group of the Oblates is surrounded by the other members in concentric circles. Those who join these concentric circles have not made any formal promises and their commitment is conditional on their discerning in this way of life God's call for them in their lay state. As *El Camino Manquehino*[4] puts it, they are at different levels of participation and commitment. The one structural element which identifies and gives them life and creates physical coherence is that they are organized into small Manquehue communities or *lectio* groups under a leader. These *lectio* groups are arranged into Ramas or Branches.

There are separate communities for men and women and for boys and girls over fifteen. Each of these communities has a patron saint and they are committed to meet at least once a week for shared *lectio*. These groups also meet once a month for *convivencia*,[5] attend General Retreats, which happen every year and General Vespers which are celebrated once a month at one of the Schools of the Movement. Both General Retreats and General Vespers are celebrated by the Oblates and all the members who can attend. They are welcomed to the Liturgies of the Movement for Holy Week and Easter and the great feasts of the Liturgical Year. The organization and encouragement and continuing motivation of these communities, or Ramas, is managed by one of the Oblates, who is called Dean of the Ramas and who reports to José Manuel.

The ordinary members of the Movement of all ages, who are thus spread out through the city (there are currently nearly 1,000 of them), do not make any formal commitment. Their membership is realized and encouraged and enabled to grow by attendance at their own group for *lectio* and at the liturgy of the Divine Office and of Eucharistic celebrations, at Retreats and the solemn celebration of the Liturgy on the great feasts and at many other activities of the Movement. Their sense of belonging is strengthened by these communal events and by mutual *acogida* expressed in many meetings, which build up human contact and mutual affirmation. Some of them may be involved in the various works of the Movement, to which the Oblates themselves are committed. If so, this will be a powerful bond. Their work may on the other hand be quite outside the Movement. In fact their work is very diverse and covers many different professions and occupations.

The Ramas include groups of students, who have their own communities, and there are also older people who are retired and find in their Manquehue communities new life and inspiration. The fundamental bond is that they are all engaged in the search for God through the Benedictine spirit newly realized in a style of life which is uncompromisingly lay but radically Christ-centered. It is a very open search. They may stay with the Movement for a time and then leave and then come back again.

There are always some of those who begin their association with the Movement through the Ramas and then find that their experience in their community deepens their readiness for further commitment. That may lead them to ask to become Oblates. If their request is accepted they become 'aspirants' to become Oblates. They will be aspirants in the state of life - celibate or married - in which they have seen that God has called them. They will be tested and guided for a period of years by one of the Oblates, who will arrange for their formation, for retreats and for other aspects of their preparation and instruction before they can be accepted to make their promises. During this time as aspirants they will have close contacts personally with José Manuel. Then, if at the end of their probation they still want to commit themselves to this way of life they must be formally accepted by the Chapter of Oblates. They will then make their promises to become Oblates in their chosen state – celibate or married in an impressive ceremony before all the Oblates in which they are welcomed into permanent commitment to the Movement.

In all this process the formal, semi-legal stages are of less importance than the inner spiritual growth that accompanies them. This growth comes about not through the acquisition of status but through the personal relationships and spiritual companionship that are always developing in the community life of the Movement. It is above all the welcome (*acogida*) centered in Christ, with which they meet from the first in their communities and in all the Movement gatherings, that matters most and is most valued. It is that ongoing welcome, which is so characteristic of the Movement. It owes much to St Benedict's brief but moving description of the spirit which should inspire monasticism.[6] That spirit is always in the Movement the formative influence leading to growth and spiritual progress in community and giving it in the midst of lay life the indelible stamp of St Benedict. It is significant that in dealing with the Responsable (who is at present José Manuel the Founder) the Little Rule singles out the encouragement of this spirit of *acogida*, expressed through spiritual companionship, as the most important duty of the Responsable:

> The most important office of the Responsable is the exercise of spiritual companionship, that means being available to the brethren with encouragement, directing their attention to the word of God and guiding them lovingly towards Christ to becoming more truly the Church in the way of the Movement.[7]

When it comes to the principles and practices of spirituality the Oblates live out the spirituality and practice of the Minima Regla more intensely than non-Oblates (praying the full Office according to the Roman Rite, daily *lectio*, working together, shared daily meals, etc). The other members of the Movement follow the same ideals in a less structured way, seeking to live out the true meaning of their baptism in their *lectio* groups and communities, and by doing so to revive in the contemporary Church in appropriate ways the idealism, generosity, mutual love and support and utter devotion to the Risen Lord of the first Christians after Pentecost[8].

Roots of a lay spirituality

As we have seen already, the beginning of the Movement's spirituality came to birth in José Manuel himself. It was when his experience of conflict and chaos about life and its meaning in a troubled and divided world met with a new spiritual vision which he learnt through *lectio divina* from Fr Gabriel Guarda at the monastery of Las Condes. It was providential that at this moment he found his way to one who was able to lead him gently to conversion of heart and mind through the word of God. It took three years of intense daily searching in the Holy Scriptures with the help of Father Gabriel in the stillness of the Benedictine monastery of the Holy Trinity at Las Condes. The monastery is high on a mountainside – a landmark overlooking part of Santiago. It created for him at that time an ambience remote from the turmoil of the university and the city but close enough to be available. It was important that the monastery was outside the conflicts of the time - political and academic - standing for values that transcended them. As Abbot Gabriel put it:

the monastery was not against anyone but it was always faithful to the Church.

It was during these long hours of quiet in the monastery that José Manuel discovered a world of spirituality more real than the turmoil of the campus and the city he had left behind. With that discovery came not only his own healing but also the primary inspiration of the Movement, which he later founded.

Fr Gabriel, as Guestmaster in the monastery, was used to spending time with people and helping them to untie knots. He found that José Manuel's problems, as they unfolded day by day, were in themselves not untypical of the youth of the day. But the man himself was exceptional, because he was very bright with a very special personality.[9]

> In José Manuel's case the process was long – terribly long.... Today I realize it was something from God...Think of it. It was not one hour. It was two hours every day and it went on and on for three years. Nevertheless there was something that pushed me ahead and made me understand that I must go on....It was like this. We would start from any topic of conflict for him and I would answer with some passage from scripture. This procedure, he told me later, was very important for him, because it meant that he was not putting his faith in me but in the quotations from scripture to which I pointed him as the pure and holy source of truth. That is something that comes from the monastic tradition of *lectio*. I did not come to him with prepared passages of scripture, but a passage came to my mind in response to his difficulties and then we would go and look for it together. That would satisfy his question because it was not I who was saying something but the word of scripture speaking to him without intermediary. I myself received a lot from this process as well, so there was mutual enrichment.[10]

The political, social and religious divisions and conflicts in Chile at the time could not be ignored.

> His family was on one side of the divisions in society and his university was on the other and he himself was right in the middle. He suffered and was attacked from both sides. I don't think his

family was really explicit in its attacks, but even silence must have been very eloquent. He lived at the same time in two fields which were at war with each other. I was explicit about fidelity to the Church. Later he developed on his own a fantastic fidelity to the Church to the point that Cristian Precht[11] mentioned it in a letter but the families of his followers were very critical of the Church at that time.[12]

In spite of all these difficulties Abbot Gabriel's perseverance and José Manuel's integrity were blessed with an outcome that few could have anticipated. At the end of the three years he came from the monastery with something to give. It was a simple but compelling memory, that never left him, of a unique experience of the word of God in scripture. It touched every aspect of his life. He had learnt that Christ spoke to him through the word of scripture with the inspiration and guidance he needed at that moment.

Very soon after his experience in the monastery he began to help the young who came to him for the same kind of help he had received from Father Gabriel. That was how *lectio* was the beginning of the little community that later became the Movement. *Lectio* became and has ever remained its principal spiritual mainstay. The circumstances of his work with the young changed and kept on developing yet always at its core was the word of God in the text of the Bible and the sharing of that word through *lectio*. He gently led others to hear the same gospel summons to conversion "repent and believe"[13], which comes from Christ to everyone who will listen.

Lectio in the Movement today

The experience of *lectio* as a foundation has led to certain practices in the Movement which are now commonplace. In the first place it is around *lectio* of the word of scripture that all the Manquehue communities, of whatever degree of commitment, are formed. They meet weekly to read and meditate and pray on the word.

Then also it is normal in the communities and among individuals in the Movement to read carefully the gospel of the day every day, seeking its meaning here and now for each one individually. Through these daily readings their individual search is linked to the daily liturgy of the church. They also use brief *lectio* regularly at the beginning of any task or meeting - consciously following St Benedict's recommendation in the Prologue that everything should start with prayer:

> This, then, is the beginning of my advice: make prayer the first step in anything worthwhile that you attempt. Persevere and do not weaken in that prayer. Pray with confidence, because God, in his love and forgiveness, has counted us as his own sons and daughters[14].

In following this advice they may use the gospel of the day before a meeting or class or conference, or they may use some other text, or they may open the Bible at random to inspire a moment of prayer. In whatever way it is done, it is an expression of faith in the presence of Christ in the word as taught by Vatican II, reviving at the same time an ancient monastic practice in the ordinary lay life of today. It may indeed be seen as modeled ultimately on what Christ did in the synagogue at Nazareth[15]. The text of the word leads to a brief reflection, meditation or prayer which serves to bring the work to be done into the presence of the Lord. This practice is an ordinary, every-day habit.

In their use of *lectio* there is a strong awareness in the Movement also of the traditional progression of *lectio – meditation – prayer – contemplation*. However any such analytic scheme can easily become rigid and involve an attempt to 'manage' our prayer, as we may manage our diet and its results. If that happens inspiration is obscured by method which is disastrous. It is of the very nature of the prayer that comes from *lectio* that there is no question of such management. When prayer comes alive and we are held by it, it is spontaneous and not at our command since it is recognized as given entirely by the gift of God.

In everything to do with *lectio* this for the Movement is a golden rule to remember. It is for us to open our hearts to God through the word and to accept whatever he sends us. That it should be a matter primarily of heart and not of intellect and that the 'opening' and the 'accepting' should be the whole of our contribution – that is the very essence of the prayer and meditation which is his gift to us through *lectio*.

As to contemplation – that is the ultimate gift which is not at all amenable to 'management' or the effects of special training or method or formation processes. It is a gift and the only preparation for it is fidelity. Learning to wait patiently on the word during *lectio* and not force a response and fit it into any pre-arranged concepts – that is a better preparation for contemplation than any man-contrived regime – whether physical or spiritual or both. In the psalms our part is well expressed in a way we should remember: "Be still – and know that I am God"[16]. "Be still before the Lord and wait patiently for him"[17] Turning to the word of God in *lectio* is an adventure which only begins effectively with the utter abandonment from the beginning of self-centered expectations and human contrivance.

In this practice there is for the Movement no claim to 'inner light'. The only inner light that is involved is the light of that faith in his word which Christ demanded in the gospel and always still inspires in those who are faithful to him. Nor does *lectio* attempt to separate the private use of scripture from the tradition of the Church. The Manquehue practice is wholly in accord with Vatican II:

> The Church has always venerated the divine Scriptures just as she venerates the body of the Lord, since, especially in the sacred liturgy, she unceasingly receives and offers to the faithful the bread of life from the table both of God's word and of Christ's body. She has always maintained them, and continues to do so, together with sacred tradition, as the supreme rule of faith, since, as inspired by God and committed once and for all to writing, they impart the word of God Himself without change, and make the voice of the Holy Spirit resound in the words of the prophets and Apostles. Therefore, like the Christian religion itself, all the preaching of the Church must be nourished and regulated by Sacred Scripture. For in the sacred books, the Father who is in heaven meets His children with great love and speaks with them; and the force and power in the word of God is so great that it stands as the support and energy of the Church, the strength of faith for her sons, the food of the soul, the pure and everlasting source of spiritual life. Consequently these words are perfectly applicable to Sacred Scripture: "For the word of God is living and active"[18] and "it has power to build you up and give you your heritage among all those who are sanctified"[19]

329

As a faithful ecclesial Movement they accept also the relationship between scripture, tradition and the teaching *magisterium* of the Church so clearly expressed in Vatican II:

> It is not from Sacred Scripture alone that the Church draws her certainty about everything which has been revealed. Therefore both sacred tradition and Sacred Scripture are to be accepted and venerated with the same sense of loyalty and reverence. Sacred tradition and Sacred Scripture form one sacred deposit of the word of God, committed to the Church. Holding fast to this deposit the entire holy people united with their shepherds remain always steadfast in the teaching of the Apostles, in the common life, in the breaking of the bread and in prayers, so that holding to, practicing and professing the heritage of the faith, it becomes on the part of the bishops and faithful a single common effort.[20]

All this approach to the word of God and to the prayer to which it leads is, in the hands of tutors, parents and sympathetic teachers, a strong and effective way of teaching the young. As such it is a fundamental spiritual resource of the Movement both in the personal lives of the members and in their work of evangelization. Among the most important aspects of sharing *lectio* in Manquehue communities is the *echo*. An *echo* expresses the resonance in an individual life of a particular word of scripture. It must be expressed in quite specific terms in the first person singular or in a personal prayer. This is something essential to the spirituality of the Movement.[21]

The young themselves are often quickly aware of the significance of *lectio* and prayer in their own lives so that *lectio* becomes a personal resource of their own. Sharing the word with them becomes real and unaffected as they grow up with it and learn that the word of God in scripture is integral to their lives and destiny. They can often respond with an spontaneous ability to go straight to the essential meaning of the word for them. In the Movement the power of *lectio* in the home and school is recognized as a wonderful gift both for parents and children, teachers and students.

It is noticeable that the Oblates themselves, as they move around the extended monastery during the day, always have a Bible with them in a shoulder bag and they frequently use it in their pastoral work. It is an eloquent expression of their faith, but it is important to recognize that it is neither an empty show nor a weapon of controversy. They carry their Bibles so that in their daily work of education and evangelization the word of God may provide the source of their inspiration and solution of their problems. They do not use the text to clinch arguments or settle controversial points of doctrine. They use it to share the word and to invite others - both the young and adults - to listen to it and test what the risen Lord, who is present in his word, is saying to them in the various crossroads and currents of their lives.

Lectio has thus a very special place in the spirituality of the Movement. The most important messages it conveys in everyday life are: the presence of the risen Christ in the word of scripture - the power of the word to convert and renew us through careful, attentive, meditative reading - the power of shared *lectio* in communities through which 'echoes' are shared - its power to build and strengthen communities, its power as an instrument of catechesis to confirm faith, and effectiveness as an instrument of evangelization to awaken the faith in others. All these uses of *lectio* are alive and active in the Movement. That is why *lectio* is so vital and fundamental to its mission.

The Liturgy of the Hours & St Benedict's Rule

The participation of young boys and girls in the Liturgy of the Hours is a practice of the Movement which greatly helps their growth in faith and holiness. The young are always welcomed to join the adults in the daily celebration of this Liturgy. It is not achieved by the imposition of a rigid regime. Their participation is best if, as is the custom of the Movement, it is free and spontaneous and seen not as an imposition but as a privilege.

It is part of the Benedictine charism of the Movement that the Liturgy of the Hours is always a part of the day at school and at home (for those who are members of the Movement). Through this custom they grow up in the awareness of the prayer of Christ in his faithful (the Church) as a normal part of lay life in school and home. Their attendance and participation depends on their understanding and readiness, although that will grow more quickly when there is a warm welcome (*acogida*) for them in such important occasions in the day. In the homes of Manquehue Oblates the singing of the office of Compline in the family has often been a strong attraction for children ending with the Marian antiphon as a last moment before bed.

The adoption of St Benedict's Rule has been another great source of spiritual strength in the development of the Movement. It is always available and frequently used as an inspiration, with its wisdom and guidance in life, at all levels of the Movement.

The Rule became a strong influence in José Manuel's life and work with the young at an early stage. Although his experience at the monastery had been under the overall influence of St Benedict and the Rule had come into his conversations with Fr Gabriel, the formal adoption of the Rule for his new lay Movement was a more gradual process. It was in the midst of great troubles and problems about many things - about his marriage and the baffling illness of his children, about the founding of Colegio San Benito, about the interminable difficulties which beset the beginnings of Colegio San Lorenzo, about the responsibility for so many young people which fell heavily on his shoulders at that time - that the Rule began to have a formative influence on his life and that of his followers in the Movement.

All the difficulties of that period might well have put an end to his dreams and plans through the sheer pressure of inexorable demands, but he turned at that time to the Rule of St Benedict and quietly but emphatically adopted it for the building up of both communities and schools. It is important to recognize that he adopted it as a guide to lay life in the ordinary circumstances of the laity. He did so because he and the young people working with him came to see the Rule not as essentially clerical but as an application of the wisdom of the New Testament to the lay life of a committed Christian. It became a new source of great strength which was greatly needed at the time. Perhaps he was led to this perception by such words as those in the Prologue, which are almost equally applicable to the lay pilgrimage of a committed Christian as they are to monastic life:

> as we progress in this monastic way of life and in faith, our hearts will warm to its vision and with a love full of delight that cannot be put

into words we shall go forward on the way of God's commandments. Then we shall never think of deserting his guidance; we shall persevere in fidelity to his teaching in the monastery until death and so through our patience we shall share in the passion of Christ so that in the end we may receive also a share in his kingdom.[22]

José Manuel needed at the time all the support that the Rule could give him. There can be no question about how much José Manuel had to suffer. Fr Gabriel had got to know José Manuel very well and he remembers those days of trial and difficulty and creativity:

It happened (the founding of the Movement and the Schools) in the midst of very big difficulties. One of the things I really admire in José Manuel is that, if you look at his life, it is all full of trouble. He has always been in difficulties but he never makes much of them. If you look around you will not easily find someone with more problems than José Manuel....and about the big problems - they don't get him down.[23]

José Manuel realized that what he needed – what the young Movement needed – to give them strength and coherence in dealing with all those early difficulties and to give the Movement a way which it could follow was a life-structure of spiritual depth. It must be a structure which would not "quench the spirit"[24] but would reinforce and carry forward the early experiences of *lectio* that had formed the Movement so far. In the Rule of St Benedict he found what he needed and adapted it to the needs of the laity who would always be living, praying and working in the world while always remaining authentically lay – as lay as the early monks had also been.

Having accepted in general that the laity must be authentically lay and involved in the world, it was paradoxical that the monastic Rule of St Benedict should provide the means of putting the Movement's vision into practice in the world. This adoption of the Rule was not a matter of dreaming idealism but of daily application to the mundane problems of life. After an initial period in which they had accepted the Rule but hardly quite knew what to do with it, they began to take it very seriously indeed and to consult it for practical guidance in their everyday life and work. That was a turning point. Perhaps they were surprised at what they discovered, but certainly it greatly surprised experienced Benedictine monks who came to know them, to see how they referred to this monastic Rule for concrete guidance in the problems and perplexities of their lay lives. Perhaps we should not be too surprised. It was, after all, to laity in a world as alien to God as ours is becoming that St Paul addressed his earnest appeal:

> Do not be conformed to this world but be transformed by the renewal of your mind that you may prove what is the will of God, what is good and acceptable and perfect.[25]

The earliest Christians were called to go on living in the world, from which they could not escape, but to reject its false values and to transform themselves and it through the renewal of their minds by embracing the alternative of Christ. The Rule of St Benedict became the catalytic agent which enabled the Movement to follow in the same way, because it gave them a structure of life and ideals which gave an inner meaning to all they attempted to do.

The Extended Benedictine Community

That was how it came about that this very modern lay Movement in South America began to see themselves as an *Extended Benedictine Community* or *A Cloister in the World*. It was in the Rule of St Benedict that José Manuel found the pattern of living that he looked for. It was not simply a matter of borrowing a few spiritual principles of monasticism and applying them to lay life. At a time of profound difficulty and uncertainty about the future José Manuel accepted the Rule in its entirety as the spiritual way forward for the whole Movement. He published for their daily use copies of the Rule in its entirety. He gave them their own Rule, the *Minima Regla*[26], which is nothing but an application of the spiritual vision of St Benedict's Rule to their lay lives - the married as well as the celibate. They began themselves to use it to their own lives for guiding the young and so discovered what adaptations were necessary to make it fully applicable to the lay mission in the world. It was that mission - to bring the Kingdom of God to the lay world - which had already become the clear commitment of their lives in the Church even before the publication of *Christifideles Laici* in 1988.[27]

This adoption of the Rule made the Movement authentically Benedictine and governed its spiritual development, together with *lectio divina,* from that point onwards. In their own printed version of the Rule they marked passages to be read at Lauds every day, wherever that Office was celebrated. They included in it an index of topics for easy reference to be used constantly in their own community lives, in their families and in their educational and other work. The self-understanding of the Movement and of each individual member took a great step forward with the making and implementation of this decision. From then on they saw themselves – celibate and married Oblates alike – as truly monastic as well as lay. They saw their monastic commitment as fidelity to the teaching of St Benedict with these principal differences – that it includes married Oblates and their families and that the cloister in which they live is determined not by the physical encirclement of walls but by the defined locations of their prayer together and their work together in the world. Within this ambience they are faithful to the common ownership, humility, obedience and community living of Benedictines as laity in new ways dictated by new circumstances.

They see this Cloister in the World as a lay instrument of proclamation and testimony to the world, affirming Christ and his Church through their absolute fidelity to both. St Benedict had said that everything in the monastery must be done within the walls. The monastic space enclosed by the walls later came to be known as the enclosure. José Manuel and his followers adapted this to mean that everything must be done, never alone, but always together in community and within the houses and locations of the Movement's work. Within this extended Benedictine cloister their prayer and work must be community prayer and community work. In this way they were simply giving the Benedictine reality a new dimension whereby it invades the world instead of withdrawing from it. Such was this new vision of an extended Benedictine community of lay men and women.

A few years after the beginnings, when the Manquehue understanding of the Rule was given full contemporary expression for the laity by the publication of *The Little Rule* and *The Way of the Manquehue Movement,* this second great formative influence on the spirituality of Manquehue Movement was fully in place. Neither in the case of *lectio divina* nor in the use of the Rule to shape the Movement was it a question of rigid principles being adopted and carried through to a logical conclusion. The process was much more like José Manuel's own experience during those three years at the monastery of Las Condes - a gradual enlightenment through the mists of confusion and contradiction leading to practical conclusions, which unmistakably pointed the way of a vocation which was to be both lay and Benedictine. The test was always that it led to a peace which is not the result of argument or management or human contrivance – still less of the restless dominance of an entrepreneur - but can always be recognized as a direct and unmistakable gift from Christ himself.

Baptismal grace, baptismal vocation, baptismal mission

With the full adoption of St Benedict's Rule and the more specific development of the Oblates' life in accordance with the Rule, the overall picture of the Movement took definitive shape. The Movement's specific vocation and mission within the Church has its roots as we have seen in the fullest possible realization of baptism in daily life.

The educational work of the Movement, therefore, does not define its fundamental nature. It was undertaken at the request of Cardinal Silva Henriquez and became in the early stages the predominant work of the Movement. However the primary aim of the Movement is not educational work nor any other particular service to the Church. The aim of the Movement is to live out in their lay lives the full meaning of their baptism. This means that, if their educational work or any other work they may undertake should fail, the main spiritual purpose of this Movement among the laity would still remain. Educational work may well continue to be a major commitment but it will never be the only or the overriding commitment. The members of the Movement, like all the laity, are called first of all to holiness.

For the young people themselves the process of learning this new way was a gradual one. They probably hardly noticed or understood at first the reality of where it was truly leading. When in fact the first group came together their way of living was not in itself so very remarkable. It must even have appeared to be normal in the sense that the aspirations and ideals of the young involved were not much different from those of

336

many small groups of ardent young people at that time in the Catholic Church.

They valued the experience of community and of working together in community and that was common enough at the time. They prayed together perhaps at first simply because they liked doing things together as happens quite often with the young. They worked together to meet the needs of others which was not unusual for students whose idealism and generosity led them to help others. They responded to the lead given them by the man whose inspiration had brought them together and opened up new perspectives in life for them. As with many others in those days it might all have been for them a wonderful but passing experience in life for which they would be grateful as they moved on out of the student world to other things and to lives structured in a different way. In fact that was just what happened to some of those who originally fell under José Manuel's influence. But the core of his followers who stayed with him by their own choice were different.

They often spoke of their vocation as baptized laity in the world. They needed no other vocation. It was for them the supreme vocation calling them to witness to the risen Christ in a secularized world simply because they were baptized into the risen Christ and belong to him even in this life. This perception gradually emerged in the Movement not only in the sense of a principle to live by. It is more than that. It is a vivid continuing experience through their *lectio*, prayer, sacramental life and their work together to realize the kindgom of God in lay life.

This status as baptized laity is not conferred on them by ecclesiastical authority. It is the unmediated gift of Christ. It was not, they found in the Movement, possible to read seriously in *lectio* St Paul's comment on baptism

> Do you not know that all of us who have been baptized into Christ Jesus were baptized into his death? We were buried therefore with him by baptism into death, so that as Christ was raised from the dead by the glory of the Father, we too might walk in newness of life.[28]

without seeing oneself, one's life, one's lay vocation in a new light. This perception was strengthened by reading about the first days of the ordinary laity of the Church in Acts[29]. When they turned to St Benedict's

Rule it was not possible for them to read the third paragraph of the Prologue without seeing that what St Benedict described with such economy and precision was an urgent call to take seriously the vocation through baptism of ordinary laity:

> However late, then, it may seem, let us rouse ourselves from lethargy. That is what scripture urges on us when it says: The time has come for us to rouse ourselves from sleep. Let us open our eyes to the light that can change us into the likeness of God. Let our ears be alert to the stirring call of his voice crying to us every day: Today, if you should hear his voice, do not harden your hearts. And again: Let anyone with ears to hear listen to what the Spirit says to the churches. And this is what the Spirit says: Come my children, hear me, and I shall teach you the fear of the Lord. Run, while you have the light of life, before the darkness of death overtakes you.[30]

This they recognize as a text of essential Christianity. Vocation means 'call'. This text is a call to every sort of Christian to be what they are called - Christ centered. Monk or nun, layman or laywoman, married or single - all are called to find themselves and the real meaning of their lives through utter fidelity to the call of Christ made actual primarily in their baptism.

Thus it came about that for all who followed the Manquehue way in any depth and with any seriousness it was – after conversion - the meaning of baptism in their daily lives that became the indispensable focus of their growth in spirituality and a constant theme of reflection and self-awareness in their community life and in their understanding of the mission to which they are called in their lay life. It became a well-remembered key to their lay spirituality to which they always reverted. It is not surprising that it was the first message of *El Camino Manquehino* when later José Manuel began to sum up their spirit:

> On receiving the proclamation of the Resurrection the first Christians gave themselves to be baptized in the name of Jesus Christ. Etymologically this reception of baptism in Christ means to be 'submerged' in Christ. It was for them a moment of conversion, of change which influenced every moment of their lives. The book of the Acts of the Apostles shows us the fruits of baptism in the life of

these men and women: they lived in unity, they remained faithful to the teaching of the apostles, to the brotherhood, to the breaking of bread and to the prayers and the praise of God, they owned everything in common, they sold their goods and possessions and distributed the proceeds among themselves according to what each one needed. The first Christians did not break away from the society of their times but they set up a form of life which was different and which was recognized as such by the rest of the people with sympathetic wonder.

The members of the Manquehue Apostolic Movement have also received the proclamation of the Resurrection of the Lord and through *lectio divina* or prayerful reading of the sacred scriptures they have learnt by experience that Jesus Christ is alive and that he speaks to them and intervenes in their lives by enlightening them and by filling them with a purpose in life. The gospel proclamation has also brought them to be baptized or, a thing which is equivalent to this and applies in the majority of cases, it brings them to take full account of their own baptism received in their infancy which involved a true consecration to the Lord, living in the presence of God in Christ Jesus, accepting Jesus Christ as their own personal saviour and as Lord and King of every one of their actions and decisions.[31]

Acogida & personal relationships

When José Manuel, after his three years with Father Gabriel, found himself unexpectedly committed to teaching the good news of the gospel to a group of eighteen year olds, largely unmotivated and indifferent in their faith he broke through their defences with the help of *lectio divina*. This break-through paved the way in the end for the creation of the Movement. However there was - there must have been - more to be said than that about it. *Lectio divina* is not a spiritual battering ram and its success with these young people, and many others later, owed a lot to the very special way in which it was used. That brings us to another vital factor about the Movement.

When he entered that classroom José Manuel had himself come to a profound realisation of the presence of the risen Lord in his life. When he turned to *lectio divina* to teach those boys it was with the purpose of bringing to life that same realisation in their minds and hearts. He saw Christ as present in them and sought to awaken them to a new awareness of that presence in their own lives and in each other. Such things cannot be done in the context of a cold, detached relationship at arm's length nor by means of a clever technique, however strong and effective it may be. It was with real personal warmth, founded on living faith in the risen Christ, that José Manuel welcomed them. That was what above all melted the ice-bound atmosphere and taught them through his personal self-giving how to recognize Christ in the unpromising context of their own lives as rich young men in a state of confusion. It was the warmth of the relationship they first met with in him that counted.

The young who worked with him soon began to learn the same lesson. They became aware of the risen Christ in their lives, they recognized him in each other, they began to see him in those they served in his name. It created a new atmosphere in the group. They used the Spanish word *acogida* to express this mutual relationship - mutual in the longrun although it might have to start by being one-sided. As to its meaning - it is best to keep the Spanish word *acogida* because there is no adequate English equivalent - at least in the rich sense in which it came to be used universally in the Manquehue Movement.

The surface idea is that of welcome. Beneath the surface is the idea of personal affirmation, support, encouragement, love. Bound up in this is the recognition of the truly personal quality of the relationship which the word expresses and the love combined with deep respect which is inseparable from that relationship. Finally there is a transcendental quality beneath the surface of every act that it inspires because it is founded on the recognition through faith of the risen Christ in the other. A human relationship is transformed by the eternal fire which Christ came to kindle on earth.[32]

On this basis and because of the supreme importance of *acogida* in the growing spirituality of the Movement it had another practical consequence. It implied and demanded a readiness to make time and space for other people - to be available - even to waste time with them. From the first beginnings of the Movement *acogida,* thus understood, was a lesson in the spirituality of the Movement which all had to learn.

More, perhaps, than any other particular aspect of Manquehue spirituality it has been responsible for its rapid growth and cohesion and educational success. The strength of Manquehue *acogida* is that it draws all together into unity in Christ. It is the full application in modern life and in modern terms of St Benedict's precept to his monks: "to put nothing whatever before the love of Christ."

José Manuel himself was personally involved at this level of inter-personal relationships not only with his original followers but with everyone in the early stages of San Benito, and everyone was amazed at what they saw and experienced. He always made time for anyone who came to him. It was very far from the availability of a politician working the crowds at the time of election. It was the ability he had of deep personal communication that was remembered. During the moment he was with them all that existed for him was what each one wanted of him. For the Oblates, for the children, for the parents and for the staff his availability was the same and when he called it *acogida* he gave the word a depth of his own. He taught them to treat each other and to treat the children they taught as he treated them.

Tutorías

In the spirituality of the Movement the development of *tutorías* in the schools was in direct line with spiritual significance of *acogida* in the life of the members. In San Benito and the other schools *tutorías* began as the answer to a need. How were children in these lay Benedictine schools to be brought to welcome, appreciate and live in their own lives the scriptural relationship with Christ which was at the center of the Manquehue vocation? The answer was that the relationship of *acogida* should be carefully cultivated in the school and, so far as possible, made the basis of both teaching and learning. The formal teaching of academic subjects was essential, but everyone needed a different approach in learning how to lead one's life and meet its difficulties and troubles. So José Manuel introduced *tutorías* in which the older pupils or alumni from the Universities taught the younger ones through the eyes of the gospel by means of *lectio* how to meet the joys and fears and problems of their lives – however big or however small.

In this work of evangelization the young tutors drew upon the wealth of empathy and instinctive understanding which the young have for the young. This gave them the unique power of sharing the gospel message through *lectio* in ways that could be understood by the youngsters. However, they did not come to *tutorías* as mavericks acting on their own account. There was always one of the senior and more experienced members of the Movement to organize their meetings, suggest parameters, encourage them and monitor their progress. They kept their natural spontaneity but worked within guidelines. *Tutorías* came to be more organized, as the schools grew, but always in a way that preserved that original spontaneity.

Friendship in Jesus Christ

Both *acogida* and *tutorías* touch on the theme of friendship in Christ which is another strong element in the spirituality of the Movement. From the first it was founded firmly on the new commandment of Christ: 'this is my commandment, that you love one another as I have loved you. No one has greater love than to lay down his life for his friends. You are my friends, if you do what I command you.'[133] From a very early stage of their evangelizing work together José Manuel and his young followers were inspired by these quotations to choose St John the Evangelist as their special patron. Later, when they adopted St Benedict's Rule, they found in Chapter 72[34] further support for their vision of deep friendship in Christ as a vital element in the growing spirituality of the Movement. St John's gospel was the first inspiration and at an early stage José Manuel was introduced by Abbot Gabriel to St Aelred of Rievaulx's writing on Spiritual Friendship within the context of St Benedict's Rule.

José Manuel himself has written a summary of Manquehue belief and practice[35]. The main points he makes about it are: first, that in a really Christian friendship two people are never alone because Christ is always truly present in their friendship. Secondly for friendship to be real it must be expressed and the love which it expresses is the love of God. Thirdly fraternal correction in community is a healthy expression of the love of friendship. It is concerned not with personal reactions but with helping each other to be faithful to the gospel and the Rule of St Benedict. Its purpose is to achieve harmony and reconciliation. Fourthly all friendships in community must be open to community. They are never exclusive. Friendship enriches a community by radiating love. Fifthly, since friendship is 'in Christ' it enables and encourages friends to give themselves to the Kingdom through evangelization and the service of others.

What Manquehue spirituality means and does not mean

As the Council and Pope John Paul II have constantly reminded them the laity are called to holiness. That does not mean that they should model their lives on consecrated religious lives. It does not mean that they are called to be pseudo-religious. It means that all the elements of their spirituality should belong to their lives as Christian laity. As we have seen the most vital element in this is the full living out of their baptism in the circumstances of their lay lives. Such is the spirituality of the Manquehue Movement.

It may seem that this principle is changed by the Benedictine element in the Movement and the following of a monastic Rule. Here the important truth is that essentially the Rule of St Benedict is not a clerical Rule and it is in great part applicable to lay life. It is concerned for the most part precisely with the full living out of our baptism and the conformity to Christ that it implies. Its use by the Movement, therefore, does not infringe the principle of laicism. It does not make of the members of the Movement a separate class within the Church, although it does bring out the holiness of their lay status. In conformity with these general principles the members of the Movement are members of their parishes and take an active part in ordinary parish and diocesan life - as laity. They have their special celebrations and special occasions (like the Oblates making their promises) but in general they are available as committed laity to diocesan and parish life and activities. The ordinary members continue to lead ordinary lives in ordinary lay occupations and careers and they mingle with others as ordinary lay men and women. The difference is in their fidelity to the following of Christ in these ordinary lives so as to make them extraordinary in their deeper, largely hidden spiritual meaning.

℘

343

Notes for Chapter 16

[1] St Benedict in Chapter 73 describes his own Rule as: "this little Rule which is only a beginning"

[2] José Manuel's words, although he cannot have known it at the time, almost echoed the words of Pope Leo XIII in his Apostolic letter *Religiosus Ordo* through which in 1890 he began the renewal and the introduction of new Constitutions for the English Benedictine Congregation. Leo XIII began by insisting that the Congregation is in its essential nature monastic, its primary end being the sanctification of its members in the observance of the Rule of St Benedict.

[3] Minima Regla ch. 1

[4] 'The Way of the Manquehue Movement' – A later document explanatory of the Little Rule.

[5] This a word of strong significance in the communities of the Movement. It refers to an occasional meal for each community. It is a way of strengthening their bonds of Christian friendship, mutual understanding and mutual support. In *convivencia* the members of these communities meet one another not directly for prayer or work but simply to deepen their personal relationship with each other in Christ in the context of sharing a simple celebratory meal together.

[6] See St Benedict's Rule Chapter 72

[7] See Little Rule 6, 5-6

[8] See Acts of the Apostles 4, 32 - 35

[9] Interview with Abbot Gabriel 1.

[10] Interview with Abbot Gabriel 2

[11] Mgr Cristian Precht, Vicar General of the diocese at the time of the founding of the Movement and always a strong and understanding supporter of José Manuel.

[12] Interview with Abbot Gabriel 2

[13] Mark 1.14

[14] Prologue of Rule para 2.

[15] He went to the synagogue on the Sabbath day. And he stood up to read; and there was given to him the book of the Prophet Isaiah. He opened the book and found the place where it was written: the Spirit of the Lord is upon me because he has anointed me to preach good news to the poor.'

[16] Psalm 45 (46) 10

[17] Psalm 36 (37) 7

[18] Hb 4.12

[19] Documents of Vatican II - Dei Verbum n. 21

[20] Documents of Vatican II - Dei Verbum n. 9-1

[21] "A (Manquehue) communty is born through the sharing of echos, it grows through friendship in Christ and serves in the army of the Lord Christ, the true King, through life under a rule (the Rule of St Benedict) and an abbot." *José Manuel, speaking to the Oblates in 2003*

[22] Prologue to the Rule paragraph 8 (final para)

[23] Interview with Abbot Gabriel.

[24] 1 Thessalonians 5.19 "do not quench the spirit; do not despise prophesying."

[25] Rom. 12,2

[26] See Appendix 3, Section 19 – The Cloister of the Oblates

[27] Chrstifideles Laici – an Apostolic Exhortation on the Vocation and Mission of the Lay Faithful in the Church and in the World published in 1988 as a result of the Synod of Bishops on the Laity in 1987

[28] Romans 6. 4

[29] Acts 2.44-47 "And all who believed were together and had all things in common; and they sold their goods and possessions and distributed them to all, as they had need. And day by day, attending the Temple together and breaking bread in their homes, they partook of food with glad and generous hearts, praising God and having favor with all the people."

[30] Benedict's Rule - Prologue para. 3

[31] *El Camino* - The Way of the Manquehue Movement - Introduction

[32] Luke 12, 49: I came to cast fire upon the earth.

[33] Jn 15, 12 - 14

[34] "they try to be first to show respect to one another with the greatest patience in tolerating weaknesses of body or character. They should even be ready to outdo each other in mutual obedience so that no one in the monastery aims at personal advantage but is rather concerned for the good of others.[34] Thus the pure love of one another as belonging to one family should be their ideal." Rule chap 72

[35] see Appendix 5

Chapter 17 ~ Witness of the Laity

Introduction

The story of the founding of the Manquehue Apostolic Movement and the first quarter of a century of its apostolate in Chile would not be complete without some evidence of how it was experienced by the Catholic men and women to whom it came to mean so much. To help in this direction, therefore, this chapter consists of extracts from interviews and testimonies given to me over the last few years by Oblates of the Movement and by other men and women in various stages of membership. They include contributions by young people at university or already earning their living.

One of the strong characteristics of the Movement is the way it encourages among its members an ability to speak in open and simple language about God and our relationship with Jesus Christ. They do this without any of the inhibitions and artificiality which are generally imposed on Christians in the western world by western society's ambience of rationalism and secularism. In the Manquehue Movement they sincerely and openly believe in the presence among us of the risen Christ and they take seriously the words of St Peter:

> that you may declare the wonderful deeds of him who called you out of darkness into his marvelous light.[1]

That text is in some ways the key to this chapter. These members of the Movement are always ready to share the peace and happiness they have learnt from the risen Christ himself. They speak very openly, therefore, about their own experiences - both negative and positive - always in the hope that it will help others. Since their spirituality is firmly based on the word of scripture, their message is easily understood by all Christians. When speaking about God and their experiences of conversion and the love of God and prayer and community living and our need for each other in Christ, they do not rely on emotionalism and it is not part of their charism to dominate and threaten and demand response. They rely rather on the simple recognition of their own inadequacy and the wonder of the grace of God. It is in this spirit that their message is conveyed in the following extracts.

THE EGUIGUREN FAMILY
From an interview with José Manuel Eguiguren senior

1 - Three years with Fr Gabriel

I left everything and spent almost three years going in the morning to the monastery and in the evening staying at home and reading the Bible and praying. I decided to leave the university because I was not able to go on, and now I had found a new way. The first meeting was very powerful and there was something special about it because I was accepted by Fr Gabriel without any judgment about myself. He only gave me the word of God and spent the time with me; and he was very liberal. Through *lectio* I realized that my whole approach to the Bible before was wrong.

In the past I had experienced that when I approached the Church there was some sort of duty involved which would mean I had to change because of the commandments or something like that. Fr Gabriel was not demanding in that way, but afterwards I understood how important everything is. But at the time nothing like that (about obligations) was said.- only what was in the word of scripture. There were times when Fr Gabriel invited me into the monastic choir with the monks, but I didn't want to go because I thought at the time it was too much. I was very nervous and on edge. I once said to him: I am very happy how things are going but I am not ready to make a confession. He hadn't said anything about it and he replied: 'No, that is your problem. When you are ready you can confess but there isn't any hurry.' Sometimes I felt the pain but I wasn't ready to make a confession. It doesn't matter, he said, but remember that the sacraments are also spiritual food. Then the time came when I got over my difficulty and it was time for me to go to confession and receive communion in the little chapel in the monastery. It took a long time.

2 - *The first class with the young*

And so I started there in the year 1976. My brother and about 22 others were the confirmation class - all 18 years old and all in their last year at school. It was very difficult to start with. They wanted to be confirmed because that was the normal accepted thing and paved the way to get married. I realized all that and I suddenly started speaking about what had happened to me - but with the Bible. One of them came to me and said it had been very helpful and he told me what had happened to him. And from that little by little the community started and I changed the normal preparation through the texts they had by reading them the Bible. I had destroyed all that I believed before and now the only thing I believed was the word of God and so my answer was always the word of God.

3 - *Visit to Ampleforth Abbey*

When originally I had gone to Fr Gabriel what attracted me was that he was very open minded. And this was much broader at Ampleforth. Not only the spirit but also the mind of Ampleforth was very probably made for me and that was why I felt very, very much at home with a deep spiritual experience and I felt also that this was the way I should go but without knowing how. I saw Ampleforth as the Church in miniature so it was a big experience

4 - *St John the Apostle*

My own reflection led me to see that St John was very near the heart of Christ, as human being and Lord. John followed him in everything to the cross. To him also Christ gave his Mother, so he was very near also to Mary's heart. I was impressed also with St John's words about love, about driving out fear and especially about friendship and about the greatest love of giving one's life for one's friend. We wanted to have this great love. So we took his letters and his gospel and found in it great love of the hearts of Jesus and Mary. We discovered the heart of Jesus in *lectio divina*. And we prayed to Mary in the rosary. Thus all things came together. And devotion to John brought a strong sense of community. Christ's words in St John were important: 'by this will they know that you are my disciples if you have love for each other.' Then in St John there was

349

the phrase, which Fr Gabriel had pointed out to me: 'You have not chosen me, but I have chosen you.' This gave a sense of liberation, and also of mission - of going out to be brave in carrying the cross. It meant being intimate as in the last supper but also to learn the language of love. Then when John saw the Holy Sepulchre completely empty he at once believed. He didn't need to see; he had the language of love. As Fr Dominic had pointed out we saw the influence of St John in St Benedict's idea of discipleship.

5 - St Aelred of Rievaulx

As to St Aelred - I had visited Rievaulx when at Ampleforth, when I didn't know St Aelred and I didn't know his writings. What happened was that I saw a very strong kind of friendship developing among us and I asked myself if this was all right, because love was good but it was also very dangerous. So I took the problem to Fr Gabriel; he was always there. He said, well why don't you read St Aelred. So I read his writing and it gave me a sense of development - horizontal rather than vertical as we had before. Now with the years I have more experience and St Aelred comes to us through St Benedict.

From interview with Señora Luz Guzman, José Manuel's mother.

José Manuel as a boy never said anything about his lameness. He never asked why do I have this. It seems that he always accepted it. He was never jealous or envious of his brothers. On the contrary he was very proud and very happy to go out with his brother anywhere. Maybe he might have been envious but he wasn't and that was very good, I think.

Later at the university he changed a lot and became terrible. I don't know if it was that he got into university at a moment of terrible political problems or maybe it was a crisis for his legs; I don't know. He was very much into politics and he was always changing. One day he was for Che Guevara; then he was a socialist. That was what JM was like.

Then suddenly - I don't know what happened. Thank God it happened. It was a gift of the Lord. He suddenly started going to the monastery and there he met Fr Gabriel Guarda. And he also met somehow Fr Alfonzo Puelma. The two of them made him change. He didn't care any more about going out and parties and all that life he had been leading and he became a different person. That is what I can say.

The change was very sudden. When Vicente[2] made his first Communion José Manuel didn't want to go to the Mass, and all the family was very upset about it. Juan Eduardo was the religious boy of the family. They slept in the same room and Eduardo's side was full of holy pictures and on José Manuel's side there was nothing, and he would say: 'this is my half of the room and please keep your saints on the other side'. And José Manuel rebuked Eduardo and said: 'are you going to be a bishop?' And then he changed.

He was always very good in his relations with people, despite his problem about walking. He never lacked people that would pick him up and take him to places. He was very good at amusing people. Well, he still is. When they say to me that he is a holy man now, I say: well, you may say that, but I know him from before. The miracle was not only for him, but it was for all of us. Now everyone congratulates me on José Manuel. I say: 'thank you; but I cannot forget all the things that we went through.'

José Manuel had a manual printing press and, when Pinochet came to power, he was worried and sent it away into the country. Once a soldier came to look in our house and thank God we had nothing suspicious. José Manuel was very worried at the time because practically all his teachers and classmates at University were active socialists and many of them were sent into exile. When the soldier came he asked both José Manuel and Juan Eduardo if they knew any communist people and if they would help to find them. But neither of them said anything. Actually they helped some friends out of the country.

I was a bit worried when the Oblates started - especially when Luté (her daughter) joined in. But then I thought that the Benedictines were behind everything and so it had to be all right. With that support I knew JM was not founding a sect.

I don't want to say that he is more than he really is, but he certainly had enormous attraction for people. At university and everywhere - I don't know why. People would follow him and so he definitely needed something behind him - something that would give everything a firm foundation and that was the Benedictines. I love to see him off to Ampleforth every year. The first time was terrible for him. I didn't think he had gone mad; I thought it was salvation. Rafael Valdevieso said 'he is mad'. But despite that he supported him. But I thought it was great because I knew he would be given a way to follow and so he would not have to invent one.

From conversation with José Manuel's wife, Luz Cosmelli

Luz said that she was born and brought up in Chile Chico in Chilean Patagonia, where her father was Governor. She went to school at the convent there. Her mother was Catholic. Her father was Catholic but too busy traveling the province to be often in Church. Luz had five sisters and two brothers.

By the time she had grown up they had moved to Santiago in the house in Las Condes. Luz got a secretarial job in a small firm in Santiago. That was the situation when the accident occurred. She was 22 at the time; already she was feeling something of a crisis of identity in life.

She thinks that others suffered more than she from the actual accident. She was unconscious and unaware of anything. When she came to in the hospital she found it difficult to grasp what had happened. She remembers that she just lay there completely passive, while they did things to her - with her legs under traction while the fractures healed. She was there for two years.

In the end they said that she could go home but would have to learn to walk etc all over again. Her reaction to this deep inside was to ask 'why?' Why should she bother to start again and learn again. She felt that she had been completely emptied out and left with no notion of what life was for or why she should start again. It was a real existential crisis and she couldn't find any motivation or will to start again. Nevertheless she did make the very painful and difficult (and to her pointless) effort to go through the rehabilitation and physio-therapy. Luz fought her way through but she says that, when she had returned to more or less normal life, she was still without any vision of what it was all for. Her experience was one of complete emptiness and she could see no point in life at all.

Luz says that she never gave up being a Catholic and after the accident she still went from habit to Mass every Sunday. It was at a Sunday Mass at her parish that she heard an invitation to a meeting with the Catechumenist community of the parish. At home she said she thought she would go and a brother and sister went along with her for company. When she arrived at the meeting, almost at once she felt strongly that God had sent this to her and that it was meant for her. She went to all the meetings for catechesis and at the end of each felt it was terrible that she should have to wait several days until the next meeting. She was soon made head of one of the communities and has remained so ever since - integrating it most remarkably with her marriage and with the Movement.

Luz remembers that she had been already three years into this new life as a Neo-Catechumenist when she first met José Manuel. She was in fact often out of Santiago at that time on 'missionary' work, setting up new Catechumenist communities elsewhere. Her meetings, therefore, with José Manuel were not all that frequent. They both felt that they had a mission for the Lord into which they could not easily fit this new relationship. At Christmas 1978 they agreed not to go on meeting each other. Luz, by then full of vision and commitment, says that she was fulfilled and sought only peace and her community and she didn't need anything else - not even José Manuel. Thus they went off on their summer holiday. But at the end of it, in March, they met again and decided to marry.

Luz recalls that she has continued throughout her marriage with her Catechumenist community, which is now 60 strong. She has supported and helped the Movement and many of the Oblates have become almost part of the family, but she has remained faithful to the Catechumenists and her community. There have been problems about the way she and

José Manuel have each had a special but different call from the Lord, but in many ways, she says, it has been wonderful.

Testimony of Joselo Eguiguren, eldest son of José Manuel Eguiguren

The relationship we had in the family with the Oblates began before I was born. The truth is that I have no recollection of getting to know them; they were simply always there. Always when I was little they carried me everywhere.

The Oblates were always like parents to me. Then, as I grew up, this relationship gradually changed from a filial relationship to one of friendship, and this happened as I began to be interested and involved in the same things that interested them. I think that the reason why I grew into this relationship was the wonderfully close relationship my father had with the celibate Oblates.

Sometimes I think that this very close relationship was due to the presence of Ignacio. To some extent that is true because Ignacio's presence among us confirmed and strengthened it. We were five (four brothers and one sister) with not more than five years between us and we were mere children looked after by our mother and a father, who was always helpful but not able to do much in practical matters because of his disability. We could not even have managed a summer holiday together without the Oblates. We should never have been able to spend the summer at San José in Patagonia or go on longer journeys if they had not been with us.

Now even today the needs of the family are great although we children have all grown up. My mother cannot by herself manage Ignacio and needs much help and we provide the help - that is the community of the Oblates together with his brothers and sister. That is what makes Ignacio a unifying influence extending and strengthening our friendship.

Little by little our mutual love grew. I myself had a great affection for all the Oblates and I know that the same is true of my brothers and sister. Perhaps one or other of them might have a special place in our affection, but nevertheless we had the same deep attachment for all of them. Now that we are adults our relationship with some of the Oblates naturally is less close, but, thanks be to God, we still have the opportunity of being all together for the summer holiday which brings occasions in which we can renew the bonds of friendship which draw us together.

It was when I was 21 years old that, just like all of them, I experienced my encounter with Jesus Christ. It was at this late age that I came to realize that there is a God who loves and who actually loves me personally, who knows me and has a living relationship with me which up until now I had not been able to see. This encounter brought me to my senses so that I became involved more every day in the Movement. It made me see the whole of this story of the Oblates and my family from another point of view. It made me realize the privilege I had enjoyed of being able to live close to this community of friends. Moreover as a result of this conversion I became more involved in the Movement and my friendship with the Oblates grew so as to embrace also all the rest of the men and women Oblates. From the early days I had come to know all that concerned them with the exception of the married Oblates who for obvious reasons spent less time with my family.

In recent years I have been able to get to know the married Oblates better. The truth is that the more I have got involved in the Movement I have increasingly realized that we have a common mission, but this arises not so much from the family but it comes home to me more as a member of the Movement.

To have grown up in the midst of a Benedictine community has been something which is really different from the experience of my other friends. The truth is that there have been for me distinct shades of meaning, which became stronger with the knowledge of the Rule and the ability to see things in the light of the risen Lord. It has enabled me to understand how much the Rule has influenced my life. There are topics from the Rule like: what sort of person the abbot should be; like the order of the community; like obedience. They are things which have really affected my life both in my way of thinking and in my way of acting. It has meant that when I read the books 'Seeking for God' or 'Spiritual Friendship' they have not taught me anything new apart from giving a really good expression to a way of life I was to some extent already living.

A testimony by Pedro, José Manuel's second son has already been given in Chapter 4. His third son and daughter also contributed to Chapter 4

THE MARRIED OBLATES

Alejandro Allende - one of the first Confirmation group

When José Manuel arrived to speak to our class, which was a group of about twenty or thirty, he was very open with us. I would sum it up by saying that from the first moment he opened himself up to us a lot, in spite of how difficult that was. He opened himself up in the sense that he gave us a lot of himself. He liked what he did, the meditations, the preparation for the confirmation. He was a person besides that who transmitted a lot of love, a lot of friendship. He was a person who was capable of maintaining within the group a very great friendship. Now I think back, he was a person who liked to show friendship. He caused, he provoked friendship. He made us meditate; he made us participate; he made us speak.

To the question: what has lectio and the scriptures meant to you in life?

Everything - yes everything. When we began to do *lectio,* to meditate the word of God, for a long time I said nothing. But in spite of this something remained within me and left a mark. The impact *lectio divina* had on me was that it made me understand the love of God. I used to speak very little, but the word of God penetrated with great force in me. José Manuel also gave a lot of love. I began to understand as I went along the love that existed among us.

José Manual in the early days used to like very much to receive people and to speak with them. Some of us were already university students and he used to speak to us simply about the things of God - this was very important at that time when nobody spoke about the things of God. God was forgotten.

What does the Rule of St Benedict mean for you?

I would like to say something that I have always felt - that before getting to know the Benedictine spirituality somehow it was already in me. I don't know why or how, but when José Manuel began to transmit the Rule in the Movement I found myself saying that I had heard this before. In one way or another the Benedictine spirituality went along dovetailing with my life without my knowing how. In this development of the Movement and the development of my life there were elements that had already happened before.

For instance there was the importance that St Benedict gives to freedom in doing things not so much because of rules but through entering into the lives of people. This was something that I had always thought about; not living in a world with so much rigidity but rather with a desire to have God closer to me - not so distant - who could understand what was going on inside me - sometimes rebelliousness, sometimes sin, sometimes pain, sometimes unfaithfulness. That is a God who shows mercy and forgiveness. As I meditated and thought about this with St Benedict, it became clear that God accepted anybody. He didn't have restrictions. He that wished to follow him could do so. It was for those who really wanted to search for God. That was it - not more than that.

Life in the Movement made me think about, meditate on and really value married life. For me in our courtship and married life the Movement was a very important factor. It was never a separate issue. When I had doubts about my vocation to marriage, we decided to leave a certain time to think each one about their respective situation, and whether our vocation really was marriage, and let God decide. And in this way by an apparent coincidence he brought us back together again and to married life together. The presence of God, the presence of José Manuel, and the presence of the Movement were very closely related to my marriage.

One other thing which has been most striking for me was José Manuel's decision to dedicate himself one hundred per cent to the Movement once we had left the Manquehue school. We had to go and ask for money so that the Movement could survive and José Manuel could live. We were quite revolutionary for that time and not at all understood in our social milieu. It was quite striking and unusual that one could be dedicated to evangelizing and at the same time raise a family. For me this has been very useful in order to understand the development of the Movement. Our lay spirituality in no way inhibits our evangelizing and our being able to have a family. It is not necessary to leave things spiritual to certain periods of spare time. This has also been part of the path I have found in the Movement.

Mario Canales and Alejandro Allende

ALEJANDRO said that throughout his married life, and even before he was married he has been inside the Movement. That is important because the Rule of St Benedict was not a theoretical thing brought into his life but it was a natural thing that became more and more important to his own life. He never follows literally the whole Rule in family life, but it is very important in his way of thinking, for example in authority, community life, prayer and other things. The importance of the Rule for family life is its way of understanding authority, of living love, understanding the role of the abbot as service and this is applied to the family and also to the relationship between Alejandro and his wife. All these points of the Rule have something to say to him about how to face the different matters of family life. He thinks that on any page of the Rule there is something which could be applied to his family life. If he opens the Rule he finds how God is present in everything in life.

Alejandro said that when he got married it was just at the moment when the first Oblates went to live together and he felt very deeply that he had two choices: one was marriage, and I was very afraid of marriage at that moment, and the other way was community. I felt that love was present in both - I felt that I had a real choice between them because I was not pressurized by anything. I didn't get married because I wanted to be loved by someone because in the community I had found the same. It made me more clear that marriage is a vocation from God and not just a lay alternative. It really is a vocation to find God. Besides that I felt that nobody was showing me the way of being married. I felt from the beginning strongly called to marriage as the way of living a vocation from God and following the way of St Benedict. I was very fond of the monastery[3];

I was one of the members who used to go there and I liked it very much; I was attracted to that life also and was completely confused about how to achieve it.

The Movement makes it much easier to bring up children. Our children belong to our school and what they see in the family they see also in the school and what they see in the school they see also in the family; and so it is all easier to understand. Each of the children is different. The older boy understands very well what the Movement means and what Alejandro is involved in; he wants to pray; and he understands what it is; he asks sometimes to go to Lauds and to wake up early in the morning to do so; and every night he prays Compline on his own; he understands it all well. But the children are not all the same. For them spirituality has been a normal and natural thing; they are involved in a natural way in a situation where prayer is accepted, where having the tradition of the Movement is normal and they get involved in the school activities in a very natural way. You see there children, praying, reading lessons and singing and it is a normal activity for them. Thus children learn - not through words - but more simply and naturally through the way they live at school and home.

MARIO agreed with Alejandro that teaching the children the Rule of St Benedict is not a problem - they just find themselves in a family where everyone, judging by the way the world thinks, 'is mad' - so we have to be very careful with that. In a family it is different from a celibate community of Oblates; the celibate Oblates are together because they have chosen that way. A family also is a community but some of them - the children - have not chosen to live like that. They have been projected into it and have to live there. So we have to be very careful and show great respect for them. We have not been 'training' them or pushing them into the Movement. I am free in my vocation and all vocations have to be free. That doesn't mean that I don't have to show them the way; for example, when I chose to give them baptism, I didn't ask them first, I just gave them baptism when they were babies. So I make some choices for them. So there must be a balance between two things: the choices that I make for them and the choices I have to leave them to make themselves.

The Rule, then, is not a training for the children. The only way to look on it is that it is a gift. Like Alejandro I think that having our children in the Movement schools makes it much easier. Sometimes, in fact, they push the Rule to me, because they are living the Rule also at school. They learn praying before meals, for example, at home and at school also; and they would sing it at home because they learnt that at school. In these things I give them support and then leave it to their will.

Mario thinks there are several ways in which the Rule applies to families. The way of exercising authority is very important and the way of punishing and of giving prizes; this is all very simple and also very complex because we are always learning how to apply rules in the family; there is not one way only of doing so; there are a lot of small details that can bring things home to them.

As to prayer, I think that our children live in an environment of prayer - a life of prayer. I had an experience about that which touched me very deeply. My experience in my own family with my parents and my in-laws was that I had to be very careful because I didn't want to force anything on them. So my spiritual life is a matter for our own family and I don't reveal it to them. And my children during the summer told their grandfathers that they used to pray Compline every night. My mother-in-law was very interested in that and my father-in-law's brother who is a priest asked about it. As a result of that for the whole holidays we prayed Compline together with all the cousins and the whole family. That was the achievement of the children; they had no fear about it and they think that praying is very natural.

One of them, for instance, is four years old and he takes a bell with him at night and wakes up his brothers and sisters to come together to pray. It is not monastic prayer - it is very different; they want to light the candles; they want to sing; it is all very mixed like wheat and tares - both grow together. But they love the experience of praying together and that is fantastic. The Divine Office gives you a way to do that in the family. Also when we get different families together we have a fantastic experience of prayer. In praying together and eating together we have God to join us in the countryside - far from shops and city life. This kind of life has brought a great presence of God to us.

ALEJANDRO has a special point of view about this because he lived away from the Movement with his family for six years working right out of Santiago. It made him realize how important the Movement was for his own life but also for his family life. It was not just a question of praying in accordance with the Rule of St Benedict but also of living a community life together. The Movement gives us a community that supports us for the whole of our lives. Alejandro in his own family is like an Abbot and as Abbot gives a testimony to his children and it is a testimony which is linked with a life seeking God; and that gives it strength because without it his testimony is just talking about and not living what he believes.

They learn through objective deeds and acts more than through words alone - it is the daily experience that we came to live not our own will but God's will. The Movement is the community and the community - the other members of the community - have the same problems, the same lives and they share this life, not in a communistic way, but in the meeting with Christ; that is what teaches you and allows you to live not only for yourself but also for the others - first for Christ but also for the others and with the others. And so this community life fits into family life with the real experience of living together and praying together. At this point meeting at the right time to pray the Office together is very important because it gives you strength and it gives you a way and to bring it to your own cloister, which is your family. It is also in community that you learn to obey.

Carolina Dominguez and Isabel Perez

To begin with CAROLINA said that from her experience and for the other women Oblates that in her life and her search of God she has found in the Movement an encounter which is very profound and very deep in community; and she has found a way in which that experience has been intensified along a very defined path in which she could follow that commitment.

ISABEL said that she was very much attracted to the Movement in the first place because of the community life. She found it very difficult praying alone and having a relationship with God on her own. One of the great impacts for her in the Benedictine life is that God took her for what she is; God loved her and loves us for what we are. She went to a very Catholic school; she was brought up in a very Catholic family; and all the way through her life when she left school and went to University, she never left going to Mass; but God for her was someone for whom she had to be very good; she couldn't be herself; she had different image of who God wanted her to be. But in the Movement all this has changed. She discovered a place and she discovered a way in which she could be herself. She found that she didn't have to be a perfect person; she didn't have to be all good. God could love her with all her weaknesses exactly as she was. It was only through being in community and the Movement that she had found that relationship with God. It was exactly because she was like that that God loves her as she is; and she has discovered how much she needs him.

CAROLINA said that she always looked very deeply for a path within the Church and she has found it in the Movement in three areas: the first is in the resurrection of Jesus Christ in the Holy Scriptures - the second in the very welcoming attitude of the Benedictine family - and third in the need for correction. It is these three elements that have sustained her faith and have enabled her to transmit it to her family. One very important aspect in Carolina's life is the rediscovery of her baptism and the conscious realization of what it is to be baptized - that being baptized is being consecrated in Christ and to God. The oblation[4] for her is a confirmation of this commitment.

CAROLINA AND ISABEL both commented that in their lives they have been invited to join many different types of paths within the Catholic Church - the Jesuits, Schoenstadt, the spiritual exercises of St Ignatius, Opus Dei. They have had many different options to find Christ. But there is one thing they have both learnt from the Benedictine life is that wherever you find Christ, it is there that you have to advance. The path is difficult; it is not easy. As they say, when they make their oblation the response in the Suscipe is 'O God, do not frustrate my hopes'.

CAROLINA AND ISABEL said that what they find in the Rule of St Benedict is great wisdom about life. It is a Rule for life and Saint Benedict knows exactly what it is to be human and they have often joked at school about how he is the first psychologist. He knows human weakness - he knows what it is to order - he knows what it is to give discipline - he knows how to be kind - how to deal with people of different temperaments - how to give permission - when to give permission - how to treat those who need a stronger hand and with those who are weaker give a gentler hand - with those who need words to give them words and for those who need acts to give them acts - and so the Rule caters for all different kinds of personalities and different characteristics. There are so many different chapters of the Rule; it is very apparent that St Benedict knows exactly what it is to be human. They personally have found it an enormous benefit in their lives, not only in how to differentiate the different criteria needed in different situations but also in the way they deal in their marriages with their husbands and children, with people they work with. It is basically a rule for life and it has given them a way to be concrete about the decisions they take.

They say that one aspect which is very important in the Movement is spiritual friendship. They both commented that in the world there are lots of different types of friends that one may have - even a friendship within the family. But they both agree that the friendship that is there between the Oblates is much truer and much more profound than any other love connections anyone may have. It is a friendship in Christ; it is an unconditional love that is expressed in a deep communion in prayer and in love which goes beyond any other type of friendship one may have that doesn't include Christ.

ISABEL said that, when she joined the Movement, it wasn't very difficult because all her four children were actually in San Benito. When she became an Oblate and made the promise for life, her children were little and they were very happy about it. With her husband she had a few more problems because he didn't really understand what she was doing. However over the years that has changed and he has now entered the community of the Movement.

With her in-laws, cousins & sisters - in the beginning they didn't very much understand what Isabel was doing; they were scared for her and for the commitment she was making because they didn't know what she was committing herself to. They were worried that she was becoming fanatic and getting involved in something strange - they didn't know where it would lead her to or where it would stop. However over the years they have seen that it has brought her and the family stability. Because they see that, they are now much happier and not so much questioning.

CAROLINA said that her experience with her family of being an Oblate has been quite different. As her husband is not a Catholic - he has his own spiritual life and is very respectful of the spiritual life that Carolina has. In that way he is a great support. He believes that every person has to develop their own spirituality and in this way it helps her to develop her commitment to the spirituality of the Movement. He is very happy that she has her own path. The children are also very happy with her decision - and even happier that her decision is radical, because they can see that she is sure in the path that she has chosen - or that God has chosen for her - and that she is happy not only in what she does but in who she is, the work that she does and the type of life that she leads. They see that she is happy and that she can transmit this happiness and the joy in life that she receives from being an Oblate in the Movement. They like to share what is going on - they like to pray with her - they like to participate in the general activities. Out of the six children only one goes to a *lectio* group - but there are also some who are very little. There haven't been any problems or friction at all.

To a question about the attitude to the Movement of parents who have children in the schools ISABEL replied that there are three typical reactions. In her experience she had four children in the school - the youngest left only two years ago. Through that period of time in contact with the school she found that there is a group of parents who are very happy that their children are in the Movement and in groups of *lectio*. They themselves may not have a very full spiritual life - they go to Mass - they fulfill the conditions of being practicing Catholics; but they are very happy that their children have a greater contact with the Word of God, have the experience of going to retreats, having day workshops, getting involved in the social action of the Movement because it enriches their lives.

Then there are parents who are less happy; they are scared that the Movement may be taking their children away from them; they are scared that the Movement is trying to make their children Oblates and using up all their free time to become professionals; they see their children becoming very involved in all activities in all different types of levels and they begin to resent the Movement so that their children may say to friends who are going to meet their family: 'don't say you are from the Movement, because my parents won't let me speak to you'. They are the other camp, who are completely extremist.

The third kind of parents is completely indifferent - they don't really mind. CAROLINA added that she believes very strongly having parents who are involved in the same spiritual path as that of the school because this affects the children deeply.

Fr Patrick spoke about conversations he had with groups of university students and students of San Lorenzo and how they talked very openly about spiritual companionship and the reality of *acogida* and the love they have for their classmates; he said that in England and US it would be difficult to write about this love without overtones of sentimentality or sexuality and asked for their assessment from Isabel and Carolina.

ISABEL AND CAROLINA both commented that it is only within the Movement and in the School founded by the Movement that this love is understood. Outside this circle in Chile there would also be suspicion of sentimentality and sexual element. The love these young people talked of, therefore, is not something characteristic of Chile but it is particularly characteristic of the Movement and of Benedictine spirituality. Isabel said that she thinks it would be terribly difficult to write about this love; it is much easier to experience and to live it. However, she said, she changed schools for her elder child when he was about 11 years old, and the change in him was incredible because he felt in San Benito that he was loved as he was. He felt that he didn't have to be good at football to be loved; he didn't have to have the biggest power? or the best shoes to be loved; he relaxed in himself and began to take himself for who he was. He felt loved by God and by everyone around him. He didn't have to pretend - to have an image of someone he should have been. So, when he arrived at San Benito he found that he had arrived to find out who he was

CAROLINA said it is difficult to write about this love but what she suggests is that you should write about what you see, about how you see them with their children, about how they look after each other, how they respect each other in the places where they were, the places where they live, the relationship with their husbands/wives, with their children, with their friends and with members of the community. Only by writing in that way will this love be able to be expressed.

About the importance of St John the Apostle and the Movement theme 'No-one has greater love than to lay down his life for his friends' they replied:

ISABEL said that here is the whole origin of the encounter of Christ in his Word enabling us to love and to be loved in the way in which Christ loved St John, making him feel loved by God and by Jesus; it is a very real expression of love. CAROLINA said that the love between Christ and his disciple had particularly helped her to feel how Christ loved her. Isabel mentioned the aspect of seeing, when she first entered the Movement, among the people already in the Movement the love that existed between them - how it created an atmosphere of love which filtered through and how that way of living and that act of love was transmitted.

THE CELIBATE MEN OBLATES
Manuel José Echenique

One aspect which marks the early period of San Benito was a very strong emphasis on conversations with the children with the help of the Word of God in the Bible. The tutors at this time were members of the Movement working in the school. They were quite happy to take children out of classes without asking anyone's permission; they would just go off and read the Bible with them and talk with them. This obviously would have an impact on any child, but especially more so because many of the children had come to San Benito at this stage from other schools. They already had experience of school and arrived at San Benito and discovered that the whole concept of what a school was - what it was for and what the important things were at a school - was completely different. And so the impact was stronger because they could contrast it with what they had known before. A lot of these ex-pupils now would say that it was as San Benito that they discovered that there is a God who loves them. They discovered that through the *acogida* of a person who brought them to that realization.

The experience of the time for the tutors involved a sense of fear, not so much of what the future might hold, nor necessarily of the weight of responsibility for the school on their shoulders, but a much more immediate fear of facing the parents of the children. Although some of them had a natural inclination towards working with young people, not all of them did by any means. They learnt in the process of becoming accustomed and conquering disinclination or fear or trepidation in the relationship with parents or pupils in the classroom.

At that time there wasn't really any division between the Movement and the School. If you wanted to join the Movement, the school was what you did. Noone asked you if the school was what you would like to do. Working in the Movement meant working with children. And so, you could say that at this stage, very early on, the educational character of the Movement was put to the test. It was under these circumstances that the seeds were laid for opting to work with the young.

What is also surprising and certainly very impressive is that José Manuel was able to inspire great confidence - especially in dealing with the parents. He was able to transmit to them that this was an educational project which really was getting somewhere. His role at this stage was interesting in that respect. On the one hand you can see that there was a loneliness which he must have experienced at this time and also very great faith. He was building a school on friendships and searching for God but not on a clearly defined professional project. For example one can look at the emergence of the relationship with Ampleforth at this stage. It was the first years of the relationship with Ampleforth. José Manuel was going every year himself - not really knowing quite why he was going. Those he was working with in Chile were even less clear about it. Gringos were coming from England and people were saying: well, what are they here for. On one level having English people working directly in the school could be perceived as lending a certain prestige to San Benito - more so then than now.

It is easy to look back now and see that all these initiatives of José Manuel have ended up leading where they have led, but at that time the people he was working with certainly had no understanding of some of his schemes and priorities. He himself was intuitive, so he was largely living by faith and intuition, which is an unusual position from which to be building such a large and complicated project. Manuel José thinks that it was probably just as well that he himself didn't speak English well when he accompanied José Manuel to Ampleforth, because he only half understood what was going on and how much things changed from visit to visit. If he had understood more, he would have been terrified.

Retreats

The school retreats certainly set San Benito apart from other schools in which retreats were not part of the requirement of being at the school. José Manuel always accompanied them and a lot of the talks were given by him. It was an experience that marked the pupils very strongly that their first big group event outside the school should be a spiritual one. It is surprising, looking back on it, that there was not more resistance and trouble in the school from the parents, because the laity were giving the talks in the retreats and because young people were in charge of such an important area of their children's education. On retreats there were occasionally comments saying: wouldn't it be good if a priest went along with you? But there was surprisingly little of this. The tutors themselves never even thought it strange that they should be giving talks on spiritual matters instead of a priest; they just got on with it; they were anyway quite used to being in spiritual contact with the pupils. That goes also for the scouts. Certainly it is surprising that parents were prepared to entrust their children to young people who were in their early twenties. They were in authority and in charge at such a young age.

José Miguel Navarro
Early days and the founding of the house for celibate Oblates
When San Benito was in the early stages there was an apostolic spirit among the young people living very closely together; they spent a lot of time together. I used to spend all the day in the school with this group, leaving everything to live with them. The only thing I was doing at my parents' house was sleeping. On the old site in 1984 we started saying Midday Office; it was our first Office; we read it together every day. When we moved to the present San Benito in 1985, the Divine Office was already in place in the curriculum; it was part of the day. We took our promise in 1986 and the House for Oblates was started in 1987.

In the summer of 1987 the five of us who were to found the Oblates House decided to spend the holidays together. That experience, although it was difficult, was very important. It was the first time that we spent a long time together. Also it was our first time without José Manuel, who was for us like both mother and father.

It was in that summer that Ignacio Eguiguren got sick. That situation had a big effect in uniting the community. We all drew close to each other in our support of José Manuel. For me this bonding together was especially strong with Manuel José during those days. Ignacio was a completely normal baby. José Miguel remembers going to see Ignacio with his fists clenched, with his head swollen - he was a baby that was suffering and seemed to be dying.

By the middle of August one day José Manuel took me to his house after work in the school to speak about founding the Oblates house. José Manuel said 'look, the house is there. Now we only need the people. If people want to go, then we start'. I replied: 'I want to'. We had a ceremony for beginning the House on the thirteenth of September on a weekend - either Saturday or Sunday. I was very happy.

At the beginning of 1988 for the first time we spent the summer with José Manuel and his family. That was again a new experience. Also it started a special relationship with Luz (José Manuel's wife), who joined us in all kinds of sports - going out running or swimming. She not only joined us in sports but also in prayer.

We had a very strong cloister in the Oblates' House from the beginning. We didn't let anyone into our House, nor give our telephone number to anybody. For Holy Week we used to go out on retreat and José Manuel usually used those retreats to incorporate some new element into community life. It was on one of these retreats that we started reading at mealtimes the Letters of St Teresa de los Andes.[5] From then on we had reading with the meals. The year after that I remember that we went to stay for Holy Week and Easter at the monastery here in Las Condes. I remember that one day Abbot Gabriel came down to the Guest House and said to us "I have seen Scripture fulfilled in you, because I see how you love each other."

In the summer of 1990 it was the first time we went to Cohaique and to San José in Mallin Grande in Patagonia. That summer was very, very important. All the summers have been important, because they all involve traveling down there together and the kind of life we live down there in community. That is very important and 1990 was the first summer we spent there. In the community in Santiago we had the work, the apostolic work, the retreats, the camps and everything - we were always involved in heavy work. That meant that, even though we lived together, often we didn't spend much time with each other; so the times when the community has really been built has been on those holiday experiences in the summers, when we were always together. The community has been built in the summers.

Another strong moment was when José Antonio and Rodrigo Vidal (both members of the celibate Oblates House) went to Brazil in March 1995. It was very challenging to lose them from the community. We didn't know how long they would be away and it involved a long distance between us. At that time I was surprised to discover that for me it was more difficult that Rodrigo Vidal was leaving than my brother, José Antonio. When I had to write a letter or something like that I was more moved by the fact that Rodrigo was away in Brazil than for José Antonio.

Juan Pablo Moran

I grew up in a traditional religion - a religion in which you do something and you receive something for doing that - you do something good and you receive from God - it is like a form of trade. All that for me at the time was very good. I was good at school - I went to Mass almost daily - and it felt that God was good for me, because I was doing that. At school I was a good boy and God was giving me things that I deserved for being a good boy. I was good at praying & going to Mass & used to like it, and I was really good at controlling my life in the way they taught us to do.

So I went to University to study law feeling that I was doing what God wanted me to do. Then suddenly in the beginning of the second year I fell into a strong depression. I discovered that I wasn't going to be happy being a lawyer - or in being anything, being a professional. I discovered that professional life was not what I wanted from life; I was not going to be happy just being a professional. I used to think that life was that - you have to be the best in what you do, and if you do it and you are the best you feel completely happy; and that is life and that is what you can get from life. But in the second year at University I got to the point that I realized that no matter how hard I tried to be the best lawyer I wasn't going to be happy doing just that; and at the same time I fell into a strong depression.

So I spent two or three years seeing doctors and taking almost endless medicines that were available in the market. But I was not getting any better; I was getting worse and worse and worse. During that time I just tried to carry on with University, doing the best I could, attending classes and studying for the exam. I was beginning to develop a deep feeling of anger against God with the sense that I didn't deserve this - didn't God want me to be a good lawyer - didn't he want me to be a good father? So I left the Church almost completely.

I began to drink. If God didn't care about me, I was just going to do whatever I wanted to do. I felt free to do that. I stopped the way of life in which I controlled everything and I started to do anything - drink, live a wild life; it was not because of the pleasure but because I felt I was free to do things. In some ways I felt the presence of God telling me 'I love you no matter what you do. It's not important what you do. I love you'. I felt that all the time while this was happening. But that encouraged me to get more involved in dangerous things, because I thought it would be all right - I could do anything. So I began to live a double life - a life by day and a life by night.

At that time I finished University at the right time and got a good degree. So I had the question: 'what am I going to do now?' I didn't want to work and get into the system; I didn't feel that was for me; but I felt the pressure, because when you finish University you have to start working immediately. You cannot live for two or three years traveling, for example. Lawyers have to be very conservative and they don't trust people who are not consistent and want to do other things. So I felt the pressure that I had to decide what I was going to do now.

So I started to ask people, because I didn't know what to do. Then suddenly I remembered one classmate; he wasn't at that time a friend of mine; but I knew he was involved in something different. He had studied Economics in the University, but he wasn't working in a company. He was working in a School. So I thought I shall go and talk to him and see if he can say something to me and give me a piece of advice. So I went to San Benito and talked to Cristobal Valdes who had been a classmate of mine. I just went there; there was nothing to do with religion in my decision - it was just a professional decision about whether to keep on studying or something else.

372

Well, I talked with Cristobal and told him all the problems. There were two things that gave me a shock in his response; the first was that he did a couple of readings from the Bible with me - that gave me a shock; and the second thing was the most important, I think: he said 'I can't give you any piece of advice; I cannot tell you what to do; the only thing I can tell you is that I am here; this is my office and I am going to be here any time you want to talk or just be here; come, just come and be here and talk or do nothing.' That really gave me a shock and from that time I just began to go there. What impressed me was that I felt someone really cared about me; I felt a sort of connection because he did care about me.

So I began to go to San Benito and be there and just talk and do some reading and I began to develop a strong relationship with him. I began to discover the Bible and I began to read the psalms; I could stay there two hours just reading the psalms - reading, reading, reading. As I read I could say 'this is for me - this is what I feel - this is what I want to stress'. Then suddenly, without noticing it, I began to forget about depression or about working; it all just disappeared. And I felt strongly that this was the place for me and I went to San Benito any time I could. On the weekends I really suffered - I really looked forward to Monday just to go and see Cristobal.

I began to drink less, to have less nightlife. I think I must have driven Cristobal mad because I was his shadow. I was the whole time with him; I was talking and talking and talking and listening and he almost couldn't do anything; he couldn't work or anything. I didn't attend office; I didn't want to. Cristobal would stand up and go to Vespers and I just waited for him to come back. This went on for almost a year and a half - this relationship.

I attended the first Formation House in Santiago. It was a good personal experience. At that time I didn't want to pray. I didn't like the Office. I just went to it because I had to do it, because I was in the Formation House; I didn't want to know anything about prayer. But the Bible was different; the Bible wasn't prayer; for me the Bible was life. I began to discover the Old Testament and then to discover the New Testament and I loved it.

Then suddenly Cristobal said to me 'well, why don't you work in the Movement? Since you have all these doubts about working outside, why don't you work inside - why don't you go to San Lorenzo - to a project we had in San Lorenzo to develop a printing workshop - why don't you go there and take care of it?' So I said I don't know anything about printing. But I went there and did some training in the printing workshop; and when I began to work there I began to love it. I found what I didn't find in Law - I began to love what I was doing. For me it was excellent to be able to do that - so that I couldn't believe it. I went there and worked on Saturdays and Sundays and really loved my work. It was wonderful being at San Lorenzo. And then I began to attend the Office and I began to like it.

I kept on with Cristobal and I stayed on at work in San Lorenzo for two years or so. It was nice; I didn't have any life outside the Movement. At first I used to go out with some friends; but it was so boring to go to parties. The music was loud; the conversation was so poor; it wasn't for me. I learnt to make up stories to tell them why I didn't go out with them - I was in trouble - I had to do something in the house - I used to invent things to tell them just to avoid going out.

At that time I began to worry about my vocation. After I had discovered the Office, I began to feel very strongly the presence of God in my life. I felt like a train keeping going all the time inside, getting wood in it to keep the fire going and growing stronger; every day this thing was going harder and harder and I was feeling it in the Office and in the Bible and in community and in the work I was doing in San Lorenzo.

At the beginning of the next year I went to San José with the Oblates and that was wonderful; that was my ideal - the relationship between the people was so good. I felt so 'in place'; I really wanted to be there - in that community - to be in that community, with those people.

Then Cristobal told me about a Movement House that was beginning in March for people to just live there. There were only two Oblates there and the others were people who were looking for something else. So I stayed there the whole year. In the middle of the year the presence of God was so strong that I went to talk with José Manuel. At that time the readings were from St John - they were about life - if you want life, come to me, and the truth. I kept on reading John, when I went to talk to José Manuel and I told him "I want life - I want life now. I can't wait and I have to commit myself." So he said "you can write a letter to apply to be an aspirant"[6].

He said that to me one Wednesday and he thought it would take me two or three months to think about it. But the next day, Thursday, I couldn't work, I couldn't do anything if I didn't write that letter. I couldn't work, I couldn't sleep. I had to write the letter. So on Friday I wrote it and gave it to José Manuel on retreat on Saturday. Then, when I had done it, I was really shocked; I said 'Oh, what have I done with my life? I am going to spend the rest of my days in retreats and working with children.' That lasted really strongly for three or four days; I couldn't sleep. I realized I was doing something very important. Before I talked with José Manuel I felt I needed to die. Afterwards I felt - well, this is dying; I felt like a corpse. Then I began to get more calm; I began to develop a feeling that this is my place. So I kept on being in the House and I began to develop a doubt that maybe I had a vocation to be a married Oblate and not a celibate one and I used to say this to Cristobal.

Then at the end of the year Cristobal said: "I am not sure about your vocation - maybe you have a vocation for a married life, not a celibate one. Why don't you go and have a vacation outside the Movement and go to Europe or something. And why don't you spend some months in your parents' house and see if you have a celibate vocation or a married one?"

I went to Europe; I went to Ampleforth. It was hard for me; I went to Ampleforth and my heart was pounding. I felt somehow inside the Movement.

I was in Europe - I was thousands of kilometers away but I was in the Movement. Cristobal arranged the whole trip for me in England so they were expecting me and I felt a kind of vocation inside the

Movement - not outside it. I met Chad & Fr Anselm and I felt so at home at Ampleforth. And I felt I loved it.

I could stay there for a year at the Office and reading and working round and to the village and I went to Rievaulx where St Aelred was a monk - walking and it was wonderful, wonderful.

Then I went to Italy; and I thought: now, I am going to meet some girls and try my vocation for a married Oblate; this is my opportunity. Then something really strange happened to me. Married couples appeared everywhere - everywhere - everywhere I looked there was a married couple. I went to Rome - to Naples and other places. Everywhere I just couldn't see anything but married couples. I was trying to concentrate on buildings and landscape but I was seeing married couples all the time. And I said 'this is not for me'. I felt like it was prison to me. I thought 'I can't do that for the rest of my life'. If I do that it is going to be crippling.

I went to Subiaco[7]; it was wonderful. At Subiaco at Santa Scholastica monastery one monk said to me: "well, you could stay here; we have a place where you could stay for a couple of days." That was for me a complete relief. I couldn't communicate with the monk who was in charge, but I really felt that I just didn't want to be traveling any more. It was wonderful there and I felt I just want to be in a monastery. I wanted to rest - I wanted to rest from everything. So I went back to Cristobal and said: "Look, I was completely wrong. You must take me back in Chile. I know I have a celibate vocation. I don't want more going around." And he said to me "no, you are going to have to wait and stay in your parents' house." That for me meant suffering; it was really hard.

So after two month living in my parents' house and trying to be a commuter to the other house – it was almost impossible reading the Office in my house; it is not the same as praying the Office here or in the School. But Cristobal said I would have to wait until the end of the year. Then suddenly after two months a new house was beginning in the middle of August, and Rodrigo said "you have to be back in community", so I said 'OK', and I just almost jumped in like into a pool and I really love it. I have terrible problems with community life; I have bad moods; and I have problems with obedience. José Manuel did not reply to my letter at once, but now he has replied and so I am finally an aspirant.

Eventually in 2002 Jan Pablo made his promises before all the Oblates and was received as one of them

Cristobal Valdes

Extract from an address at a General Retreat 2002 for members of the Movement

Listen carefully: today Jesus Christ comes into your life to fulfill all God's promises in you. Jesus Christ comes into the story of your own life, just as he came into the lives of those who heard him in Galilee. He comes into your class, he comes into your *lectio* group, he comes into your family - whatever the problems involved - he comes to share your sickness, your work, your friendship, he comes to fulfill completely the destiny which God has had for you from all eternity. He is the Word of God, who has been with God from all eternity, the true light which enlightens every man that comes into this world. He is all that you are searching for - all that your heart desires. God has sent him onto the earth so that you may hear him, so that you may see him, so that you may touch him with your hands and learn by experience that the kingdom of heaven has come even to you.[8]

Do you know what the kingdom of God consists in? The kingdom of God is a new reality - a new creation - into which we are carried or born through the power of faith. That is what St Paul says in the Letter to the Colossians: "He has delivered us from the power of darkness and delivered us into the kingdom of his beloved Son in whom we have redemption and the forgiveness of sins"[9] We enter this new reality like a new dimension by means of conversion, which is a change in our minds, an alteration in our mental outlook which grows from our faith in the word of Christ and which enables us to see things in a new and different way. It is just as the Letter to the Romans says: "Do not be conformed to this present world, but be transformed by the renewal of your mind"[10]. This is the conversion which leads us to Baptism - or for the majority of us - to become aware of the meaning of our Baptism. This is the new birth which Jesus proclaimed to Nicodemus: "Truly, truly I say to you unless one is born anew he cannot see the kingdom of God"[11] This is the new creation of which we sing on the night vigil of Easter and of which the Lord speaks in the Apocalypse: "Behold I make all things new."[12]

Do you know what the kingdom of God is? The kingdom is a word, which when you hear it and welcome it in your heart, frees you from fear of death[13], because death has been destroyed by the death of Christ as the Easter *Exultet* proclaims. That is why the martyrs died. That is why they despised death.

Do you understand now why Jesus Christ became man and why he gave himself up to death? It was so as to manifest more clearly that he is able to care for you, that he loves you, and so that you should never again have doubts about this love of his. Believe in this love of God and then you will be free to love your brothers and sisters as St John puts it: "Beloved, if God has loved us in this way, we also ought to love one another."[14] Then you will no longer seek to be called the master or director so that others should serve and praise you. You will be free to be the last of all and become poor so as to let nothing get in the way of your serving others.

Jesus Christ is King but his kingdom is not imposed by force but by love. He does not allow his disciples to defend him with the sword......Nevertheless he is a King who after his resurrection asks for the love of men - yours and mine. "Simon, son of John, do you love me?"[15] he asked Peter three times. Jesus Christ is King, but he does not seek to reign except through humiliation and suffering, through complete identification with all the grief of men - of yours and mine - of all the generations that have been and will be in the world - through identifying with the grief you have brought on yourself through your sin. On mounting the cross this King ascended his throne, because the cross is for each one of us a definitive declaration of love. It is the strongest invitation to surrender, to self-giving, to love which cannot be more intense. For this reason in St John's gospel he said: "when I am lifted up from the earth - that is when I am crucified - I shall draw all to myself."[16]

Paul VI coined the expression 'civilization of love' and John Paul II never ceases to repeat it to young people whenever he meets them. In a recent visit to Poland he again insisted on it. The civilization of love is the building of this present world with our sights set on the Kingdom, with the values of the Kingdom, while measuring progress by what people can come to be, not by how much they can possess, by what relationships of friendship they can achieve, by their solidarity with each other, by the way their love grows, by the communication and mutual concern for each other they can experience, by the stability with which they can build up a family or a local community, by the meaning they can bring to their lives, by the dignity of their work measured not only by earnings but by what service their work performs and what their work achieves and contributes to society. It is to measure progress by the support given to youth to save them from abandoning their ideals so that they may devote themselves and devote their lives with real enthusiasm in things that are worthwhile.

Let us read the word of God each day, bending the ear of our hearts, as St Benedict says, and let us prepare ourselves to serve as soldiers of the Lord Christ, the true King. Those who believe in Jesus unite in Him to form the Church, which is the assembly of those who believe and a foretaste of the Kingdom of God among us. Then there is our Sunday Eucharist also which is the moment to renew each week our living faith in Jesus - Jesus who is the Messiah and the Son of God, and it is the moment also to relive the experience of his declaration of his love for us.

This is the Movement - a manifestation of the Church and first fruits of the Kingdom - in spite of all our weakness and all our sin. It is a community enriched through the Holy Spirit by a special way of building up the Kingdom which is the Rule of St Benedict. It is a way which is profoundly human through which ordinary people can live a life in community while putting absolutely nothing before the love of Christ so as not only to build the Kingdom of God on this earth but also come all together to eternal life.[17] This little community united through the bishop to all the believing communities of the whole world, united to the Universal Church, is truly like a grain of mustard seed which a man took and planted in his field.

THE CELIBATE WOMEN OBLATES
These testimonies were all made while they were preparing to become Oblates. Since that time they have all made their oblation and have been formally received as Oblates

Consuelo Braun

In the spirituality of the Movement there are several things that attract me: the first one is the divine Office. I like singing very much and to pray in groups and to praise the Lord during the day; I thought it was a very special thing when I discovered this. Also the Rule means a lot. I think that all the guidance that St Benedict gives to us there day to day - how to work, to take decisions, to pray, to organize the monastery is something I can use when I am at home with my family, when I am working in the School in the Movement. I recognize that in the Benedictine way of doing things everything is organized to thank God. Through the scriptures, through the Bible, through our work and *lectio divina* I have discovered all the life, all the light, all the truth for which I was searching in other places, in other things, in other people.

For me also it is very, very important to live in a community; I don't like to be alone. For me community life is also one of the things that make me realize that I am called to this vocation. I have a very strong feeling for living very deeply all the fraternity of the Movement - with the Little Rule, with the Oblates, with all the life that we lead there.

Alejandra Valle

I feel that I have been part of Benedictine life all my life. The Rule, the Office, the *lectio* have been my life since I was 11 years - since I entered San Benito School. I don't know if I discovered something new some day; it seemed to be in my life always. The School was very important for me but when I left the school I went away from the Movement. I got very accustomed to University with my friends and everything but then I came back and started to do *lectio* again. It was a very important time and a very important step for me. I live something now that I used to live first when at School at San Benito - the community life.

We had the opportunity to have this formation house for women. After a visit to Europe I went into the formation house. My family was in the Movement but they didn't support my decision very much, so things were difficult but it gave me more strength to go through this, although I didn't know how it was going to end. The same happened to me when I decided to go to Brazil; I was very conscious of my decision. I didn't look to the future. The only thing is that it makes me very happy and I feel close to God. That is the most important for me.

Cecilia Bernales

My first experience of community life was when I was in School at San Benito during the Missions organized in rural places in Chile. That was very important for me because it was the first time I had an experience of praying together, working together, doing *lectio*. That experience during the holidays of winter and summer made me realize that this activity of the Movement was for me. I discovered there was space. I could work. I could pray with other people that were seeking the same things as I was. But that was only for a short period. It did not affect my entire life.

Then I went to Brazil seeking again the things that I had discovered in the missions; and I realized there that I could live this community life, working together, praying together not only for a time, but it was real. It was the first time I was living with the Oblates and discovering that they lived always the life I was seeking - the experience of friendship, of praying, of working together. It was very, very important for me, but I thought that it was a passing experience and that I would return to my normal life back in Chile.

However I couldn't just go back. The Brazil experience was my first love, and I wanted to continue even back here. That is why I entered the Formation House. But when I told my mother, I said it was only for one semester to prove if the vocation was for me or not. Well, I came here working in the School and it meant a lot for me. When that period in the Formation House finished I went out from the house and I knew that this was my vocation - that I found peace here and love. I discovered that I can live the Rule.

I think the thing I liked most was the recognition that every person is different and weak and a sinner. I was attracted also by the teaching of St John, leading us to rely on the heart, trusting in the mercy of God; but it was a fight with myself because I never thought that God could call me to give my life to him. So that period when I left the Formation House was very difficult for me, because it was a fight with God. I didn't want to be consecrated but I knew still that this was my vocation and I wanted to live here with the community, working and living in the Movement. So I decided to return and to live in this community until I will be convinced that I should be an Oblate. I am waiting for that conviction - and in some way I know it is here.

Consuelo Verdugo

I think I have been hearing about God since I entered San Benito when I was ten, but I think everything really started when I was fifteen. I remember we had a retreat once a year and there was someone talking to us. I cannot explain it very well but I saw all the majesty of God and I felt a great difference - I cannot explain this - and in that moment I knew that I wanted to become an Oblate. I don't know why; I don't remember what did it, but I do remember that feeling - a strong feeling. It was the greatest thing I ever experienced.

Well, I came back to Santiago and I started living a very committed life - as well as I could for my age - in the Movement. Then time passed and I started forgetting that feeling. I hardened myself to what I felt that day. I even left the Movement when I was seventeen or eighteen.

And then I was knocked down by a car. That was the beginning of my conversion; I had broken my leg. I had always been a very self-sufficient person and from this point I needed a lot of help from every body else. The point of that experience was like confronting me with death; for the first time I was asking myself what was the meaning of all this - why I didn't die there and then - things like that. So I started coming back and my reception of the sacrament of Confirmation involved for me a very important decision about coming back. Yet much of the meaning of this was subconscious.

I went to Brazil, not quite knowing why. I didn't have a clear purpose but I do remember in Brazil how I felt that something big was behind all that was going on in my life - all this life in community and *lectio* and the Office and everything else, but I couldn't say what it was. It was just like an intuition - like a feeling. But I couldn't explain it.

I came back to Santiago and that year there was a possibility to form a House for Women, but I didn't want to be there. Yet somehow, when the time came in March, I was there. At the end of the period I was living with all this stowed away in my subconscious and I went traveling with my parents. When I came back I remember that Cecilia and Allejandra wanted me to join them in the House but I told myself all the reasons why I didn't want to be there.

I remember one day I was doing *lectio* on the Transfiguration but I didn't pay attention. And I looked on the page on the left and it was about the conditions to follow Christ; and there was a phrase: "the one who loses his life will win it"; and in that moment I felt again the same thing I experienced when I was fifteen and I knew that I had to come back. That is why I am here.

OTHER MEMBERS OF THE MOVEMENT

Rafael Carvallo, when he was still at university
I began as a member of the Movement when I was sixteen. I was at San Benito when they gave us the opportunity to become part of the Movement in a community. The invitation was open and I went in

383

with some of my classmates. I think about 90% of the boys joined the community. Its name was St Pancras and Manuel José Echenique was the leader of the community. The names and character of the group changed through the years. I joined the group because lots of my friends did and at the beginning I wasn't really searching for God. I was curious about this experience and good friends with many of the others and I really liked San Benito. I felt comfortable at San Benito - I think they were my happiest years - and still my closest friends are from San Benito. So the members of my community are my best friends. Well, at the beginning just because my friends were there it was a great experience - that continued until I was in my last year at school.

In my first year out of school I went to study at a place that is 120 kilometers from Santiago. I spent a year there studying economics and I didn't like it so I came back and entered for Law. Because I and other members of the community were going outside Santiago we started meditating on Saturdays. When you are 19 Saturday is like a sacred day & it is quite difficult to go to a meeting, because your friends are going to do sport and other things, and it is quite difficult. But the main reason for the difficulty is this new experience of going to university. You feel like you were born again. You have got more liberty. You meet people who think very differently in a very different world. It is great; but it makes your fervor die down and it weakens the will of members to go to community meetings and serve the community so that we began to lose members.

When I was fifteen we were 20 in our community; then when we left school we were 14; after one or two years in university we were 6. The community of S.Pancras joined with another and formed a new community with people who were more stable. As the years passed changes were made. The communities below mine had the same story to tell. After two or three years of university many members left the community.

What did the community mean to me? At first in school I was there because of my friends. There was a kind of searching for God. I could see that many - like the Oblates - were very happy in living that life. That is quite difficult to understand because usually when you look forward in life with faith in the future you think of happiness as getting to.know a woman, marrying her and having lots of kids and achieving economic stability and you think of that as happiness.

On the other hand I saw these young men of 29 or 30 and they were all very happy and they expressed more happiness than people in the world who had got married and had children. So I was quite curious about that. The conclusion for me was that happiness has nothing to do with what the world thinks happiness is. I think I was searching for their happiness, because I saw in them a madness for God and there had to be something behind that. That was the beginning.

In university you get to know many people, you get to know different ideas, different thoughts. At university, among other things, they train you to search. With my friends in the community it was always that way - searching, searching, searching - searching for happiness - for joy maybe, for God.

That went on until I was in third year in law. Then José Antonio told me about this experience in Brazil and asked if I wanted to join them. I said 'yes'. So for a free year I went to Brazil. It was a great experience, but a bit tough. I think I grew a lot during that year in Brazil. I came back and they put me in a new community which was being founded with some members who were not at San Benito and some who were one or two years below me, when they were at school. It was quite a mixture and seemed odd, I thought, at the beginning. Some did not last very long, but that community is where I have experienced most of God's love.

I must say that I have never been a very spiritual person. I have never had this joy of reading the gospel and feeling absolutely in heaven or stepping into the clouds. I think my faith is quite rational. But all this year in community and basically in the last three or four years it has been love that I have really experienced. The members in my community, as I was saying in the beginning, are more than my friends. I realize that everything I have done in my life, every person I have met in my life, I have been consciously or unconsciously asking for love and always searching for love, and I think in this community, apart from my family, is the only place I really feel loved because of who I am more than because of what I can do or because of the goals I have in my life. I feel really comfortable with them. I have been always trying to pretend to be more of a cool person or to be funny or to appear intelligent. But here I don't need to do that. I can be completely relaxed; it is great; It's amazing, and I have felt God's love through them. I know that God is here and I feel it. In some mysterious way I know that this is my community. It has something to do with the love of God.

My faith is not like my mother's which is very spiritual. But I know that prayer has been the center of that union and prayer has been where love has arisen. In fact every time we happen to meet and we go out together and have been to vacations, prayer has been the center of the life and of the things we do during the day. And that is not only because Cristobal was with us, because many times he has not been there. Although our love has been the reason and the center of why we are there it has been only the tail of our greater love of God. Prayer has been the way of remembering that we are there because our love is part of a greater love in our mission. It is not only to preserve it among ourselves but to make it grow among others.

Nicolas Meneghello & Ignacio Hertz - when they were still at University

They were both in the same year and they remember how they changed school in 1985 when they moved to the new site of San Benito. There was building going on there all the time. There were new houses going up around and they remember playing with the building site materials and the builders' helmets; it was part of life. We felt that the school was ours - like our house. It was very much a sense of beginning something new and the school was being founded and built around us so that we were part of a new project.

IGNACIO remembers how, when his younger sister began in the school, the whole family became involved in the school with younger brothers and sisters, so that their home became involved in the school.

NICHOLAS remembers how one year, when they came back, the teachers they knew came as Oblates and they were wearing jackets and ties; and it seemed that 'this is serious'. It was in 87 when the first Oblates took their promises. They remember the *tutorías* and that they didn't quite know what the Movement was about at that stage.

NICHOLAS remembers having academic problems over which he needed and received a lot of help and a lot of personal attention. Now as a University student, Nicholas says: 'looking back on my time in San Benito my memories are very different from those of boys from other schools. I have retained a certain way of being that I lived in the school. I have continued to pray; and there is another aspect of life which I learnt here and which I have carried on into University life, which is the ability to share with people, to get close to people, and even to be able to pray with my friends as well, achieving some sort of closeness and capacity for friendship; I have been able to continue this in the University with the people there.

NICHOLAS said that he is at present working here in San Benito, when he is not at University; he works in the *tutorías* and he is a member of the Movement as well. In many ways that is a reflection of his formation in the school. He does *tutorías* now because *tutorías* were a part of him when he was here; he has developed a love of the Divine Office, because that was what he began discovering through the school. In the retreats which Nicholas is sometimes in charge of - he is prolonging and developing what was initiated for him in the School; he feels that it is very much a part of him.

They said that having lay people in charge of religion - the tutors and Oblates - was good because it meant that they were much closer. It would have been very different having them dressed as priests or monks because there is a distance produced by clerical dress. There was a closer feel in the education at San Benito. Nicholas felt much closer to Monato, for instance, than he could have done with a priest.

જી

Notes for Chapter 17

[1] 1 Peter 2, 9

[2] Younger brother of José Manuel

[3] The monastery of the Holy Trinity in Las Condes, Santiago

[4] That is the promises the Oblates make in their formal reception.

[5] A young Carmelite saint of Chile, who lived in Santiago in the early twentieth century and whose shrine at Los Andes is a center of pilgrimage especially for youth.

[6] an aspirant is a member of the Movement who wants to become an Oblate and whose request is under consideration while he or she is being tested.

[7] where St Benedict was a hermit and founded his first monastery

[8] cf 1 Jn, 1, 1-4

[9] Col 1. 13-14

[10] Rom. 12,2

[11] Jn. 3, 3

[12] Rev 21, 5

[13] Hb 2. 15

[14] 1Jn. 4, 11

[15] Jn 21, 16

[16] Jn 12, 32

[17] see Rule of St Benedict chap 72

Chapter 18 ~ Witness of English Oblates

Introduction

The connection between the Movement and Ampleforth Abbey and College in England began when the Movement was already four years old and making a start on the great venture of Colegio San Benito, their first school . Subsequently the connection developed and led to yearly visits by Ampleforth students before or after University. While in Chile these students entered into the life of the Movement and shared its prayer and activities. Almost invariably their faith was deepened and they were inspired by what they saw and learnt. Some of them stayed longer than a year. Some of them went home to University or work and then paid another visit. Some were so profoundly affected that they stayed on longer to consider seeking acceptance as Oblates of the Manquehue Movement and giving their whole lives to share in its life and lay apostolate. Their reasons for so important a decision were individual and complex, but the following testimonies will give some idea, in the case of three of them, of the sort of reasons that inspired them.

Jonathan Perry

Mine was a traditional and very "English" upbringing. My parents sent me away to boarding school at 8: a large, old country house in the midst of some glorious Hampshire countryside. The school was Catholic which meant that in between classes and acquiring a great love of every type of sport, I learnt my prayers and sang hymns along with the other boys, went to Mass and Benediction on Sunday and took part in the occasional retreat given by a friendly priest together with the rest of my friends and classmates.

At the age of 13, recently confirmed, I made my next step up the private school ladder when I was sent to Ampleforth, then and still the country's figurehead Catholic senior school. Ampleforth is Catholic education at its most impressive: set in a beautiful valley in North Yorkshire, imposing buildings, acres of sports fields and a large monastery home to a community of a 100 Benedictine monks. There I was fed on much the same privileged diet of study, plenty of sport, country pursuits, morning prayers and Sunday Mass and the yearly retreat. Friendship meant everything. We had a lot of fun. The general atmosphere was religious of course, but somehow the role models and dreams I aspired to were definitely secular. Throughout my five years there Catholicism was to me a gentle backdrop to the real world of getting on with being successful and getting abreast of the competition.

So it was that I gained a place at Cambridge to read history, at Trinity College, where consciously or not I ended up by dedicating my energies to the pursuit of more fun, prestige and achievement, be it academic, sporting or social. I did pretty well, traveled a great deal in the holidays, made many friends and at the end of three years accompanied my contemporaries in the search for good money and careers.

I joined British Petroleum and began working in their international trading business in London in the hope of some attractive foreign postings and a solid grounding in industry on what I hoped would be my way up and up the executive ladder. I worked hard and played hard, but despite my Catholic schooling, my behavior and aims were sadly those of thousands of other people of my generation, amounting to little more than planning as successful, cultured, traveled, comfortable and pleasure-filled life as possible.

Things began to change. There were no blinding flashes, just a growing sense of unease with what I was doing. I started to question the path along which I was walking and the cosy self-centeredness of my life goals. God became an issue. I began looking for somewhere to start, some sort of guidance and was invited by a friend to go back to Ampleforth for an Easter retreat which I accepted and then, once back in London, I summoned up the courage to begin going along to a group that met up once a week to read the Bible and share what each person felt God was saying to them through the text.

This contact with Scripture was strange to start with, but I persevered because here was something new. I relished the company of other young stumblers like me looking for a meaning to life that might be God and, secondly, there was the very gradual awareness that Scripture speaks – even to cautious cynics like me. Without knowing it, I was discovering *lectio divina*. God was becoming something important. I began to read the Bible more and more and began to pray and go to Mass on Sundays once again. It was an unhinging process, full of contradictions that eventually led me to do something utterly unexpected in my increasing search for silence, space and answers.

The *lectio divina* group I belonged to in London formed part of a Catholic organization called the Manquehue Apostolic Movement, which came from Chile, and at that time had a small branch in England. I'd been a member of the group for a few months and was introduced to the Movement's founder, José Manuel Eguiguren, who was on a visit to the country from South America. During the course of the conversation I surprised myself by asking if I could go to Chile to find out more about *lectio*. On my various travels I had come into contact with Buddhism after an audience with the Dalai Lama in India and a meeting of monks in Thailand. I had dipped into Christian orthodox writings after meeting the Patriarch of the Greek Orthodox Church in his offices in Istanbul. And in Turkey the minarets and Moslem call to pray left a deep impression on me, but this experience of *lectio divina* was different. I appeared to be coming full circle, back to my Christian, Roman Catholic roots, and if it meant going to Chile to find out more then, so be it.

I wanted time to be alone and read the Bible, as my London life seemed too busy and intense for the serious spiritual search I was increasingly intent on. I dithered and doubted of course, but there was no way back on my plans for Chile once BP, to my astonishment, said they'd happily have me back if I were to head off to Chile for a year or two. God's hand was clearly at work and by the end of the year I was on a plane heading across the Atlantic to South America.

I threw myself into the community life that greeted me there. I was invited to live in a house along with the "Oblates". What struck me immediately was the way in which this group of young men did not seem to feel that God was calling them to the priesthood or the religious life, rather they appeared to be convinced that Christ was telling them to follow him in all seriousness in the Church, but as lay people: militantly Christian, obedient to the local bishop, inspired by the community vision contained in the Rule of St. Benedict, but lay. This came as something utterly novel.

All the way along my short but intense process of spiritual awakening I had presumed that taking God seriously, feeling the niggle of a vocation would inevitably imply becoming a priest or a monk. I had seen when younger how people in Church prayed for vocations, but the common assumption was that they were referring to priestly and religious vocations. The implication had always been for me that the lay state was a second rate option, for those who didn't feel the call to go the whole way. Yet here I was living in a community in Chile with a group of young lay people whose understanding of vocation was something very different. The important thing, I soon picked up was to be Christian, to follow Christ and live the Gospel. I was astonished to hear that to be lay, religious or a priest were just different ways of following Christ and living one's Baptism. What's more, I was amazed to discover that this radical, lay vocation had been encouraged by successive Archbishops of Santiago and received heartfelt encouragement from the Vatican. This reassured me that what I was involved in was not some overenthusiastic sect, but something authentically Catholic and "safe". Despite all my harsh criticisms of the institutional Church and it's doctrines as a school and university student, in my newfound desire to give myself over to this God of love I had encountered through Scripture, I gradually found myself rejoicing in being Catholic. For the Oblates' loyalty to the local bishop, their active participation in the local Church, my discovery of the Divine Office as the prayer of the Church, together with the hierarchy's blessing and encouragement of the Movement were all persuasive, converging factors, movings of the Spirit, intent on bringing me home to Mother Church.

I decided not to go back to BP. I had learnt a great deal in my two years with the company. They had been very generous and understanding in keeping my job open, but what I had found in Chile was deeply inspiring and fulfilling. Community life and the space for friendship and prayer that this afforded was something I was not prepared to give up, even if it meant remaining so far away from my friends, family and my whole way of life in England.

Neither was I prepared to give up my pastoral work among the young in the Manquehue schools. I had been thrown into the *Tutoría* Department in San Benito school on my arrival and soon became involved in retreats, scout camps, missions and the essential job of being with the children and making friends with them. Despite the language barrier, and to my surprise, I was gradually able to strike up a good relationship with the boys and girls. What gripped me about the school work was the way that the Oblates related to the young and sought to share their faith with the boys and girls in such a natural and convincing manner. The *Tutoría* system, whereby the Oblates and other tutors brought their fun and friendship into the lives of the students, especially in the all-important out of class moments, amazed me.

The emphasis placed on simply being available for the boys and girls, of "wasting time" as it were, in those extracurricular, informal moments meant that a good many student, seniors and juniors alike, were being provided with the sort of support the young need and that frequent, everyday contact with spiritual mentors so necessary for allowing faith to be simply picked up or breathed as naturally as the air, rather than having it taught in special classes or ceremonies. The way that the Oblates and other tutors spoke openly and convincingly about the action of the Risen Christ in our lives in addition to the chat and banter of everyday conversation made a huge impression on me. I came to see how Christ was an explicit element in the life and language of the school, not only in retreats, but in the morning assembly, individual meetings and informal conversations, wherever it be. Here in San Benito, evangelization was the essential reason for the school's existence. There was a climate of mission. And what astonished me and at the same time drew me on strangely enough was the fact that it was a lay project, fully in communion with the hierarchy, utterly Catholic, but lay.

My friends back in England couldn't quite understand what had happened to Jonathan in Chile. And my poor family had a hard time in accepting the changes in my life. It was difficult for them and for me. Nevertheless, the words of Jesus, "Come follow me", "He who looks back is not worthy of me" and countless other texts reverberated in my mind time and time again and filled me with a sense of elation and meaning that is hard to describe. When I decided to become an Oblate and commit myself for life to Christ in the Manquehue Movement with the likelihood of spending the rest of my days in far away Chile there were tears and I fear much resentment back in England, at least to start with.

Since then the years have gone by. The schools have developed. The community of Oblates has grown. The Movement has continued to learn and mature. And there are four British Oblates: two of us celibates, Anthony Dore and myself, and a married couple, Patrick and Gigi Blumer.

It was Gigi and Patrick who originally invited me to the *lectio* group in London where I first encountered the God who speaks in Scripture and came into contact with the Manquehue charism. I never imagined, of course, when I accepted their invitation to buy a Bible and meet up after work with the rest of the group, where it would all lead. I am truly thankful. Why I have had to come to Chile, half a world away, to discover my vocation as a Benedictine, celibate, layman is God's business. He does what he wants, His Spirit blows here it wills and all I know is that I am happy.

Over the years I have often been asked by Chileans how I have came to stay on in the country so long and normally they pre-empt my reply with the words: "Te gusto Chile, entonces" which translated means "You obviously like Chile then". "Yes, I do like Chile" is my reply "But there's more to it than that". And so I go on to explain as succinctly as possible that it is a matter of vocation, of somehow knowing that this is what God wants of me, that it is not a matter of liking the country, however much I have indeed come to love the landscape, the food, the climate, the culture and the people. I try not to bore people too much. I am always thankful for the question because it makes me reflect on why I am in this country, on the very nature of my vocation and indeed where I belong. For I am and remain English! I miss England, of course, and "all things English".

Yet on the other hand I have happily absorbed many attitudes, expressions, customs that are distinctly Chilean, Latin American and I have come to love the country that has been my home for so long now. Nevertheless, I can honestly say that I have come to realize that I would be happy living out my commitment to Christ, my desire to be Christian, a Roman Catholic Christian, to love the Gospel, in any part of the world. What I could not do without, however, is community life as lived in Manquehue: the shared *lectio*, the Divine Office, the emphasis on friendship and community lived out in the workplace, at home, at all times, the Rule of St. Benedict, the unassuming, unaffected lay climate, the feeling of being in permanent mission. I think that this is possible to live in any culture, any country, not something especially Chilean.

Patrick Blumer

While it would not do to take the story too far back, it would be impossible to understand why I am here now without mentioning my first visit to Chile in 1985 as a "gringo" helping out for 6 months in the English department and in *tutoría* in San Benito in my year off after leaving Ampleforth. The experience of *lectio* and spiritual friendship changed my life completely and planted in me a sense of belonging to this particular community which was deeper than I realized at the time. What has brought me back here has nothing to do with romantic hankerings after the nostalgia of past experiences, but rather with the future: the desire to throw in my lot with this particular group of people, having discovered that their way of doing things and their priorities, their accumulated wisdom and vision is how I want to live out my life. And that is not a rational decision based on pros and cons, but something of a coming home?

So, how did Manquehue become home? As I said, 1985 changed me completely. I cannot single out specific moments, but the time lavished on me by José Manuel and others is key, hours spent orientating me towards the gospels. Halfway through my stay I went so far as to broach with my parents the idea of staying out here and forgetting about University, but was dissuaded. By the time the 6 months were up, the idea had formed among our group that if we were to avoid losing what we had found, the only thing for it was to set up the movement in the UK. On my last day in Chile, walking along the corridors of the school with José Manuel talking about the challenge ahead, we popped into the chapel and opened the bible to ask for a word from the Lord. This was what we were given:

> In the church at Antioch the following were prophets and teachers: Barnabas, Simeon called Niger, and Lucius of Cyrene, Manaen, who had been brought up by Herod the tetrarch, and Saul. One day while they were offering worship to the Lord and keeping fast, the Holy Spirit said,
>
> 'I want Barnabas and Saul set apart for the work to which I have called them.' So it was that after fasting and prayer they laid their hands on them and sent them off.[1]

This gave me the conviction, which never for a moment left me, of having a definite mission – the English Branch of the Manquehue Movement. Maintaining contact with other ex-gringos we set up *lectio* communities in different universities, nourishing ourselves with two or three retreats a year thanks to the enormous generosity of the community at Ampleforth. As our members left university and got jobs the *lectio* groups started gravitating towards London, and as Chile became a more and more distant memory, which to boot was not shared by the majority of the members of the Forty Martyrs[2] Community as we were known, we experienced some difficulties of identity. New ideas came from Chile as the Movement there matured and developed (promises, fraternal correction, etc.) but it was not always clear to what extent they were charisms of the rock from which we were hewn and therefore to be embraced as God's will for us, and to what extent the funny quirks of Latin-American folk 'Was Chile really relevant? What authority did José Manuel wield with his annual visits?'

There is a sequence of events which led to my and Gigi's oblations in the Movement here, and it involves two major false starts or misinterpretations of God's will, both of which however led directly to the eventual dénouement. The sequence began in 1989-1990 when

I came to Chile with a group of members of the English Movement for a month, in order to attend the general retreat. It was the first time I had been back. I was secretly engaged to Gigi at the time and we were ecstatically happy about it. She too was now a member of the Movement.

I remember during that general retreat kneeling late one night in front of the cross in the church in Punta de Tralca, saying, "I offer you everything that stands between you and me." As I spoke the words, a leaden feeling gave me a presentiment that I had just said something a little bit rash. A few days later I had a meeting with José Manuel who, without knowing of my engagement, invited me to come to Chile for a year to live with the celibate Oblates. The awful thing was that the idea held a great deal of attraction, and I immediately felt that this was God calling me back to Chile. José Manuel's invitation was for a year, but it was clear that when answering God's call you have to be open to the possibility of a year becoming a lifetime - all the more so when the following reading popped out of the bible.

A man had a fig tree planted in his vineyard, and he came looking for fruit on it but found none. He said to his vinedresser, 'For three years now I have been coming to look for fruit on this fig tree and finding none. Cut it down: why should it be taking up the ground?' 'Sir,' the man replied, 'leave it one more year and give me time to dig round it and manure it: it may bear fruit next year; if not, then you can cut it down.[3]

What was God saying? It was difficult to be sure, but it certainly appeared to have something to do with testing for a period of at least a year. The upshot was that on my return to the UK, Gigi and I called off our engagement, and so began the most painful experience that either of us could remember, with all our hopes and dreams shattered by a God who suddenly appeared to have acquired the characteristics of a scientist experimenting with laboratory mice. But we never let go of the story of the sacrifice of Abraham and eventually, with the help of certain monks who counselled us, we became officially engaged and grateful for having lived through the enriching experience of being asked to offer up what was most dear to us.

We were married in April 1991. We were both heads of *lectio* groups in London, and actively involved in the life of the Movement in England, participating fully in all the retreats and other events which we ourselves took part in organizing. Gigi was working for a publisher and I was working as a teacher. One evening, shortly after learning that Gigi was pregnant with our first child, we suddenly found ourselves toying with the idea of taking off abroad to work for a while. We had both grown up in the far east and the British colonial longing for distant climes was definitely coursing through our veins that night. But it swiftly became clear that it wouldn't be enough just to put a pin in the map and hope for the best.

We both had a sense of contradiction that was answered by this idea of heading off overseas: our lives were becoming more and more centered around the English Movement, but we had the growing feeling that things in it weren't really moving. There was no shared apostolate, apart from isolated initiatives in sundry parishes helping with confirmation classes and such like, or the occasional foray to lend a hand in a soup kitchen. What was needed was a fresh impulse, and what better way to look for one than to spend a year in Chile, learning first hand about how things were being done there in order to return home and work in a more focused and dedicated fashion back in the UK? Our wanderlust and our dissatisfaction with the state of the English movement could be dealt with in one fell swoop.

That night I sat down and wrote to José Manuel. Little did we know that he had been thinking along similar lines, having decided that if the English movement were to establish itself properly it would need someone to spend time in Chile to live the Movement first hand from the inside – a year or so seemed about right. But there was a catch. The ideal would be a married couple, who are more stable, more of a unit than someone single, and at that point there was only one married couple in the English movement: Gigi and myself. José Manuel didn't dare ask us because the effects of his previous invitation had been so dramatic and so when our letter arrived on his desk a day or two later, everything seemed to fit into place. The parable of the barren fig tree, along with its time-scale of one year, was being fulfilled.

We arrived in February 1994 and the first months were very hard. Gigi found it especially difficult, having to make the transition from fulfilled working London mother to lonely cut off housewife in a foreign country. I frequently came home after school to find her crying and telling me that she wanted to go back to England. The language barrier was at times a real burden, and we both found that having to ask for advice on such a permanent basis left us increasingly without the ability to make our own decisions. We lived on an income which was a fraction of what we had been used to in London. Being here in these circumstances, responsible for the well-being of a wife and child, was very different from being a visiting gap-year teenager. Often it took a definite act of will to force ourselves to keep believing that this really was God's plan for us: we would remember the episode of the letters and remember that we were here with a mission. God wanted us in Chile, didn't He?

It wasn't long before we became aware that we weren't just on a visit to Chile. We now lived here, albeit with a definite view to going back one day. People who had at the beginning just been friendly little by little became real friends. The work we were involved in gradually became more than an activity to keep us occupied or earn our keep, but rather projects we cared about for their own sake. We both took promises, and to our alarm, gradually realized that the idea of ending up here was becoming less and less unthinkable. It became clear that becoming an Oblate was increasingly likely. However, the Movement's emerging self-definition was as a geographically located community. That meant that being an Oblate couldn't mean being committed conditionally to the Movement on the tacit understanding that this commitment would one day be lived out back in England, whenever the vague idea of an "English Mission" eventually materialized; being an Oblate meant embracing the idea that we would probably never go home. The terminology gradually changed when talking with our families: "when you come back" gave way to "if you come back", and even this became a less and less used phrase. This has been hard: I know very well that our being here is a source of pain for my parents especially, as my children are the sum total of their grandchildren.

So the time came for a choice: Oblate in Chile or back to England to go it on our own. I was due to make my promises as an Oblate before Gigi, and there was never any doubt that my decision to make them was effectively a decision of our whole family. There was no choice really to be made. We found we could not conceive of living our lives in any other way, and that a new type of belonging had supplanted the old, not diminishing love for our families, but transcending it:

> When his relations heard of this, they set out to take charge of him; they said, 'He is out of his mind.'... A crowd was sitting round him at the time the message was passed to him, 'Look, your mother and brothers and sisters are outside asking for you.' He replied, 'Who are my mother and my brothers?' And looking at those sitting in a circle round him, he said, 'Here are my mother and my brothers. Anyone who does the will of God, that person is my brother and sister and mother.[4]

Do I then count myself among those who have earned Jesus' approval by piously keeping his word? No I do not. But I do know that I desire to keep his word, even if I habitually fall hopelessly short of doing so. And I know that he has guided me to a group of people who also desire the same, and to share this desire with them and to tread this path together has become precious to me. Why Chile? I don't know, but it is true to say that the country itself is not relevant. Strangers often ask me when they learn I have been here for some years, "So, you like Chile, then, do you?" My reply is always yes, but really I should tell them the truth that the country isn't what matters - what I like, and, more to the point, what I need, is my community.

Anthony Dore

I was born in 1969 and grew up in Yorkshire, England, the eldest son of an Irish father and an English mother whose family also has in part Irish ancestry, with some English and some Welsh blood. Together with my brother and two sisters, my parents would take us off as often as was possible for long summer holidays to the village in County Limerick, in the south-West of Ireland where my Dad grew up in a large family. His mother lived in the village until she died in 1980. This, combined with the fact that Dad had lived in Ireland before emigrating to England in his mid-thirties, meant that the whole village knew him well and for these rural Irish people, we were just part of their extended family.

Back in England, the family always lived in and attended the same parish in Wakefield, West Yorkshire. The faith was a common subject of conversation, of stories told to us and in the reading material later available to us at home. Involvement in our parish flowed naturally from this. My First Holy Communion, aged 7, and Confirmation, aged 11, were accompanied by participation as an altar server. Later, my interest in music brought me into choirs and to play the organ at Mass. I had a happy and active childhood in the company of my three siblings. The four of us, having been born within just over four years, were like resident playmates for each other. We faced together the challenges and difficulties of growing up.

For my parents, who were both teachers working in Catholic and non-confessional schools within the State-funded sector in England, schooling for us was an issue of much interest. The lack of a catholic secondary school nearby led them to opt to make the effort to send us away to school. Together, and after visits there and elsewhere, we chose the Junior School at Ampleforth for my brother and me. We were aged 9 and 11 respectively. My sisters also spent time away at boarding school.

Ampleforth took some getting used to but, I believe, broadened my perception of the Church and helped my faith. I also had the opportunity to develop my interest in music there and to build strong friendships with some of my contemporaries. My home life however, continued to be a very necessary anchor. I was back there once every three weeks for a weekend and for the long holidays, totaling about four months a year. Ampleforth was only an hour and a half's car journey away from home and so my parents would attend concerts and rugby matches and other events my brother and I were involved in.

In terms of my life in the faith, while Ampleforth gave me another viewpoint, my home's influence was still dominant. We shared at home the ups and downs of family life with my parents and brother and sisters. I also counted on the help of others who influenced me spiritually, among them a number of priests. I felt I was able to recognize the path that God was guiding me along and to feel His presence at many, many points along the way. I always believed in God and home was always a place where family prayer was normal.

When I left school at the age of 17, I took a year out and was sponsored by an engineering company for that year to work for them, and then to study Engineering at Loughborough University. The career path I was taking, while not exactly inspired by a burning feeling of a particular vocation within, seemed to be in accordance with my view of the world. It was a path chosen to a large extent to 'keep my options open' for later. It did me a lot of good and helped me to get my feet on the ground. What I did gradually realize at school, at work and at University, was that my faith was not shared by very many people within society at large in England in the 1980's.

To speak of the Church for me still meant the parish in Wakefield, especially as my parents had never moved house. In parallel with my continued involvement in my parish during my time at University I participated in many Church activities, from those of a Catholic University Chaplaincy through to a pilgrimage to Rome for a week, which was organized by the national Catholic Newspaper 'The Universe'. One worth mentioning was when we journeyed in a mini-bus to the World Youth Day in Poland in 1991with a group of nine young people from the parish in Wakefield, plus a married couple and the Parish priest. We had a great time. On the way we found out that we were nearly all musicians and on our return we founded a folk/rock band that played several concerts - in the same old parish in Wakefield, of course!

I was thus an active member of the Church, in the normally accepted sense of the expression, long before ever knowing exactly where Chile was.

What brought me to Chile had little to do with the faith. I completed my studies at Loughborough in June 1991 and, somewhat disillusioned with my career direction in engineering and with certain aspects of factory-life, I decided to take a year out to look around over a wider horizon. Through a contact at Ampleforth my horizon stretched as far as South America!

A combination of apparently unconnected things helped me towards choosing to spend six months in Chile. I had had brief contact with two ex-pupils, three years my seniors, who had been in Chile with Manquehue in 1985 and had returned to school to help with a couple of school retreats! I hadn't really talked much to them, but, as I knew them reasonably well, I had the impression that they had lived a faith-affirming experience in Chile, while remaining the same thoroughly likeable scoundrels we had known before. I heard indirectly that it had something to do with the Bible. Seven years passed from that time before I unconsciously followed in their footsteps.

Another source of reassurance was that my brother was leaving school in 1991 and was interested in going to Chile too. We worked together in a large shop in Leeds for five months to raise the airfare. In March 1992 I climbed on a plane (for only the second time in my life) bound for 'Santiago de Chile', with five other 'gringos', plus my brother, as I thought, for six months. I really knew nothing of Manquehue when I set off as I had only read a four-page information sheet and had a fifteen-minute chat to a Chilean man who was visiting Ampleforth one weekend. He was José Manuel Eguiguren, although that name meant little to me as yet.

My aims for the time in Chile were simple- a bit of teaching experience to make it all look good on a Curriculum Vitae and, hopefully, a lot of fun: traveling, new experiences and maybe with a bit of something spiritual thrown in - the perfect cocktail for a 22 year old opening his eyes to the world beyond engineering. I think I even felt I might be helping out a bit in the third world!

What came next seemed to go by slowly, but in retrospect it was God moving and his own unobtrusively swift pace and, as ever, with perfect timing.

After settling, meeting people, taking the first few faltering steps in the Spanish (which I'd studied for two years at school) and then getting into the classroom as a teacher's assistant, I found a comfortable rhythm that consisted of working when I had to work and also relaxing and exploring. We were in a community house, with two Oblates and other young people, as guests under a very benevolent regime.

I would pray Compline together with the house and Lauds only on occasions, as attendance at the Divine Office at school was voluntary for us, as newcomers. I also recall vividly being quite exasperated when we were invited to form a *lectio divina* group. It had taken some time to get the group organized and I'd already found my routine- why complicate matters now with the bible? Sure, I'd been having the odd interesting conversation with people but it seemed that this prayer-group business was unnecessary. I thought I would find that I'd 'been there before'. I however joined in and, just as the conversations had been helping me to realize that I felt at home in Manquehue's rhythm of prayer, work and community life, so this place for *lectio divina* once a week, in English, was a time to look at scripture with new eyes, or rather to listen to it with new ears! The preparation meetings we had individually with some of the more experienced members of the group were particularly helpful.

While, contrary to my expectations, the *lectio* group was in fact something completely new to me, I felt that I still very much 'had my balance', I was still pretty much in control of what was happening and I was to some extent still in familiar territory. I recall, however, that a stronger friendship did begin to grow up among us.

God's real move came about three months into my stay and it was quick and deft. I was invited to go on retreat with a group of sixty 17 year olds from San Benito. They were friendly, I was teaching them and I got on with them, but that was not what made an impression on me that weekend. I had just enough Spanish by this time to follow what was being said and I found that, as the activities went by, slowly, gently, almost imperceptibly, God was cornering me.

The retreat was an invitation to these 17-year-old boys to accept God's love for them and the fact that He had redeemed them in Jesus Christ. The consequence of the invitation was that they could therefore forget about doing token good deeds as a half hearted way of responding to Him and somehow earning his approval, shake off apathy and 'take over' the school in their coming top-year, working for the benefit of the younger pupils in all sorts of ways. I was five years older that those to whom I thought the retreat was directed, but the talks, the message, the readings - it was all for me. I had gone on the retreat with one internal landscape. Chile was going well and my regime here of tourism with work and spirituality thrown in was comfortable and I still felt I 'had my balance'. I came back after just thirty-six hours with a new viewpoint on life and, at its center, my faith and its real meaning. I don't think I had ever experienced anything like it before. I had lived thousands of moments when I had felt close to God and I had been blessed with always having believed, but now this God who I had felt was there, I'd sometimes just hoped was there and I'd always accepted was there, was in fact speaking to me - personally, powerfully and, above all, lovingly. I sensed that I was being given the opportunity to follow some sort of path which God was inviting me to.

I asked for a meeting with and spoke to José Manuel two or three days later, telling him of what had happened to me on the retreat. He mainly just listened, but invited me to keep searching. I began to devour Scripture, by myself and with others, and God kept speaking. I began to consider seriously the idea of coming back for another year after my six months was over.

My experience on that retreat has happened to me, with admittedly rather less spectacular effects, time and time again. My extra year in Chile became many years, with visits to my family in England in between. At the beginning some of these visits were longish ones - some of up to two months or so, but I have never in my mind left Manquehue. It took time, but after a few years I asked to become an Oblate, as Manquehue was still the place for me to project my life forward, listening to this Word that gives life and feeling loved and invited to love in community life.

I have had the opportunity to work in several places within Manquehue, including each one of the three schools, San Benito, San Lorenzo and San Anselmo and I was also in the group for the first year that founded the Formation House, San José, in Mallín Grande in Chilean Patagonia. What I would conclude from the experience of living and working in these quite radically different places is that what kept me in Chile in the first place - a loving community welcome and continuing attention, the sharing of the Word of God and the friendship which grows from that sharing of the Word - are things that God has kept showing to me everywhere I have worked and in exactly the same ways.

I have worked in *tutoría* with boys aged 5-14 from all sorts of backgrounds, accompanied by fellow tutors who may be young people from age 14 upwards or may be other adults. I find that it is a humbling and awesome experience to share with all of them (children and seniors) in this work. I am not a great leader and inspirer of the young and I was concerned on beginning in *tutoría* that the children would get bored and that they would look for someone with different qualities from me. I have found that they don't and this has made me very happy in *tutoría*. They don't seem to need someone who is a gifted clown or someone with a magnetically charismatic personality. What they do need, first and foremost, is some of my time, to be with them on their own terms and that I be myself and simply be there for them. They need me to listen to them and share with them. Lastly, they need me to open the Bible and read it with them.

Apart from that, I also have to be opening the bible and reading it for myself, because *lectio* gives rise to *lectio*. In *tutoría*, whoever is involved in it and however adept they feel they are at working with other people and with the Word of God, what happens seems to me to be always the same: with anyone, from any area of Santiago or from the wilds of Patagonia, inexplicably and often even illogically, the risen Christ comes into the friendship that grows up around his Word, and that friendship is pretty much indestructible.

Although it is not something I do often, I have on the odd occasion taken a little distance, mentally, and looked at myself, thinking "well, who would have thought that a Yorkshireman with Irish ancestry who should probably be quietly trying to earn a living in a factory, or somewhere else, in England and attending his local parish, should have finished up in all this?!" While my first love is Manquehue and its people, I can also say that I like Chile - I think it reminds me of Ireland sometimes, especially in its people. Having been a home-loving person in England for 22 years I think it was a bit of a shock to find that I was growing accustomed to being so far away from my family, but God is good and makes the necessary shocks manageable. I hope and believe He has helped my family as much as he has helped me to deal with it all. They have been very supportive, which matters to me a lot. What I feel is that God has given me a home and a family here in Manquehue and has shown me that this is the place where He would have me be, and hence that it is the place where I will be happy. My search is far from over, but in my weakness I have been shown a path and am being accompanied along it, by God and by my Community, in communion with the whole Church.

I end with two readings through which the Lord has accompanied me in all this:

If you make my word your home, you will indeed be my disciples. You will come to know the truth and the truth will set you free.[5]

I am with you always, yes to the end of time.[6]

CR

Notes for Chapter 18
[1] Acts 13, 1-3.
[2] A representative group from among the many Catholics who gave their lives for their faith in England during the centuries when Catholicism was proscribed there. These forty were selected for canonization in 1970.
[3] Luke 13, 6-9
[4] Mk 3. 21, 31-35
[5] Jn 8, 31 - 32
[6] Mt 28, 20

Chapter 19 ~ EPILOGUE

I first met José Manuel on his second or third visit to Ampleforth Abbey, but that was a very brief meeting. It was a little later from 1984 onwards that, as Abbot of Ampleforth, I really got to know him. That was in the very early stages of Colegio San Benito when San Lorenzo was a hive of tiny children on the original site. There were huge question marks over the future of San Lorenzo and of the educational future of the tiny children. I went back to Chile as often as I could with a growing inner certainty that it was important to do so. I did not know at the time quite why it was so important for me to go all that way. If I had been challenged, I think I would have mentioned José Manuel, his son Ignacio and San Lorenzo. They symbolized: faith-driven love, suffering as the creative center of love and the dignity and indispensability of the poor. I was learning more and more about all three.

Then there were the former pupils from our school at Ampleforth coming back from Chile with a faith and commitment that had not been theirs before. I had to go back to Chile and try to fathom something of the mystery of the Manquehue Movement. It was a mystery in which I was myself becoming enveloped.

When I reached the age of 80 and the time came for me to withdraw from what I had thought of as my life work, I was drawn inexorably again to Chile. Now, perhaps, with nothing to distract me, I might at last be able to penetrate the mystery of this growing group of predominantly young lay men and lay women in Chile, who were living such strange and such wonderful lives as lay Catholics under the inspiration of St Benedict's Rule. They were doing what I had tried to do in education and doing it quite differently and much better. They were determined to remain authentically lay. They insisted that they were Benedictine. They received me with open arms, not as a geriatric relic, but as though I was young like they were. They forced me to act young - and I began to feel it. I was so much affected by their faith and love that, when one day José Manuel asked me if I would write the history of the

409

Movement, I knew that this was my new life and I must embrace it. I said I would try and I have been trying ever since.

For me my new life has been rewarding beyond anything I could have imagined. This book is the result. It is not worthy of the subject, and I do not know whether José Manuel will be disappointed, but for me it has been a wonderful experience for which I am grateful to God and to José Manuel, Luz and their children and the Oblates and the members who have made me feel one of them and have given me a new life while the old one was ebbing away. I spoke earlier of the mystery of the Movement. I now know better what it is; it is what St Paul would describe as the mystery of Christ within them[1].

Strangely, however, the deeper I got into the life of the Movement the more often my thoughts were turned back to England and the United States. I had lived my life in England and was now during retirement from active life resident in the United States. In Santiago my thoughts turned back to them, not in nostalgia, but because more and more I seemed in the Movement to be looking into something which must have some part in the future of Catholicism in England and the United States - if they will allow themselves to have a future at all. The Movement has taken those giant strides in the development of lay Catholic spirituality that are urgently needed and sometimes dreamt of in the west - although they seldom get further than the dreaming board. In Santiago I found the laity of the Movement in complete harmony with the clergy. I found that they were totally committed, as laity, to evangelization of the lay world. I found that they relied daily on the risen Christ, who is present in the Word of scripture as well as in the sacrament of the Eucharist. I found that they knew how to deal with the destitute, not just by giving them money, but by also by sharing their own life and faith with them. I found that they had learnt the lesson of Christ in the temple, by treating children in the process of learning as disciples with whom they share their vision of the goodness of life. And so I found that I was not too old to learn. Writing the book became, after all, not a burdensome task for me but an inspiring process of learning. I hope others can learn half as much by reading it as I have in writing it.

As I have written this story of the foundation of the Manquehue Movement and the early growth of its first 27 years, I have tried to give a faithful account of what actually happened. It is a story which could easily be looked upon as a matter which concerns only Chile and South America and has no particular message to offer to the rest of the Church in the rest of the world. Over the years, that is a reaction which I have observed quite often among visitors to the Movement from the west. It is a reaction that is rare among the young, who are open and searching, but it is quite common among the more elderly who have settled views which satisfy them so well that they are insulated from further search. However impressed they may be with what they see in the Movement, they tend to add hastily to their appreciative remarks: 'but, of course, it wouldn't work in England or the United States'.

A meeting with the members of the Movement in their everyday lives can be a strong experience for those brought up in a Catholicism which is largely private and kept in the background of their social and professional lives. Such a meeting can also be disturbing for them. They don't quite know what to make of a faith which is carried into every aspect of lay life in an unfailingly cheerful, relaxed and matter-of-fact way. Many are nervous of explicit and committed reference to that faith outside the safe walls of a church and the protecting shadow of the clergy. They tend to recoil from the prospect of inviting others to share their faith in the ordinary circumstances of lay life. In many ways this is an understandable reaction, given the ambience of an often aggressively secular culture, which cheerfully promotes every kind of liberty for its own sake - including, of course, religious liberty, provided it is kept decently out of the public eye. That sort of cautious approach and nervous reaction does not go much beneath the surface as an assessment of the Manquehue Movement.

It is, of course, true that the culture of Chile is different and has many characteristics of its own which are not and need not be shared by those who come from other cultures. There is a danger, however, that the dismissive comment that it is 'not for us', may be in truth not much more than an evasion of the real issues that have been raised by the experience of the Manquehue Movement over the course of its short life. As we have seen the real issues, which define the Movement and its mission, are not concerned with outward expression in terms of an individual culture, but with an inner reality that transcends the variations of cultures, and

411

nations. They are issues which are very much alive and relevant to Catholicism world-wide and by no means confined to the Church in Chile. They have a depth of reality which is applicable to all Catholics and to all Christians individually and to every country and culture in the world. They are issues which will be neglected at our peril.

For instance, at the root of the Manquehue experience are all the questions about the true role which the laity should have in the Church both now and in the future. They are questions which cannot be evaded anywhere. They have been on the agenda of Catholicism at least since Newman attempted to address them in 1859[2] and was rebuffed. These questions about the role of the laity in the Church were strongly revived in Vatican II and, although progress has been made since then, it can hardly be suggested that satisfactory solutions are generally in place in the western Church. It is questionable whether some of the most vocal contemporary attempts to solve the problem have been helpful. In the years since Vatican II, for instance, there have been attempts to transfer administrative and financial responsibilities to the laity or capture them for the laity. These attempts may be talked of as though they are designed to assert the rights of the laity. However, whether successful or unsuccessful, they may often turn out to be not much more than ways of clericalizing a chosen few of the laity - or giving them a role in the existing clerical structures of administration and finance.

Such efforts (whether justified or not) do not go to the root of the problem and they may in fact do nothing in the end but make the problem worse. They have not been the concern of the Manquehue Movement in Chile. The Movement has by contrast been thoroughly radical by going at once to what is really the heart of the matter. They have done so, moreover, in a way that is itself a critique of any power-struggles of a few of the laity to get a foothold in the administrative power of the clergy. The Movement has been radical by thinking and talking from the first about *all* the laity and not just a few who are fit and eager for a power-struggle. Their call has been for a very different approach to the way the laity are called to follow Christ.

This different and more radical approach is the one we have seen in action in this narrative. It consists in starting with the deep spiritual realities of the Christian vocation itself. It starts, as we have seen, with

412

the theology of baptism. There is a problem of communication in that fact. Wherever Christianity has been long accepted and influenced by the post-reformation, post-enlightenment consensus about human life - with its creeping secularization and determination to sideline all religious truth[3], baptism came to be seen as not much more than an initiation into membership of the institution of the Church - a membership which is often liable to be dominated by the clergy. Such membership is commonly seen in the west as a private choice for a private way of life. Unhappily this misinterpretation has often been accepted by Christians. It is true, of course, that baptism is an initiation into membership of the institution of the Church, but it is also much more than that. In the New Testament, where the idea of an institutional Church was at best still embryonic, it was this 'much more' about baptism that mattered. It was what mattered to the martyrs and to all the truly faithful laity throughout the ages. It never, in fact, ceased to matter in the Church, but since Vatican II, after a time in the shadows, it has again begun seriously to take center stage in Catholic thinking and teaching.

Baptism has come to be seen again, in the light especially of St Paul's teaching, as the sacrament of a union with Christ, given to all Christians with living faith, which amounts to a blessed identification with him in his roles as priest, prophet and king. It gives the baptized in their own right a share in his mission to evangelize. As we have seen in this story of the Manquehue Movement, that is where their thinking about the vocation of the laity starts. It does not only start there. That identification of all Christians with the risen Christ in his three roles is the continuing inspiration of their daily lives. This vision does not belong to any particular nation or culture. It is at the center of the post Vatican II teaching about the nature the Church. It is for everyone.

When the Movement started in its thinking about the laity from this great gospel truth of our baptismal union with Christ, they were freed at the very beginning from the idea that the laity should or could engage in any power struggle with the clergy. There is no need for that. There is no room for it, if they are serious about being Christ's laity. The laity have their own status and their own vocation which came from Christ himself, just as the clergy have theirs - also from Christ himself. The laity have their own mission to evangelize. They have their own call to be holy. It is a call and a mission strictly within the body of Christ, which is the Church, and never in separation from it. Hence communion with the bishop and with the See of Peter were for the Movement essential guarantees of unity from the start. Within that unity, and never in contention against it, their vocation is unmistakably lay, Christ-given and not dependent on a special gift or delegation from the clergy. It has no need for power-struggles. It has its own status in Christ and has no need of any other.

Having started from that radical beginning in baptismal awareness the Movement received from José Manuel their formative and continuing source of energy and vision from the word of God in scripture. They have kept it through *lectio divina* at the center of their vocation and mission. That was at first and still is the driving force behind their vision and mission. In this also they were following Vatican II, which brought definitively to an end a long period in the Church's history in which scripture had been too much the prerogative of the clergy. José Manuel's experience in the monastery had taught him and he taught his followers about the power of *lectio divina*. We have seen how it became and still is the primary instrument not only for the way they lead their own lives but also for the evangelization of all, to which they are devoted. It is an instrument which the Movement uses daily and passes on to others. This is the second point about what happened in Chile. Neither the true meaning of baptism nor the power of *lectio divina* have anything essentially to limit them to the South American culture of Chile. They are universal in the offer of spiritual freedom which they bring to all lay men and women as well as to the clergy.

The same is true of the other notable aspects of their way of life. It is true of all the ways, deriving from these two, by which the Oblates and members of the Manquehue Movement have brought the gospel to life among their followers. There is first of all their insistence on communion with the local Catholic bishop and with the Holy See. Then there is the creation of communities which are small and centered on the word of God; the Prayer of the Church which is the Divine Office and which binds them together in union with the world-wide Church; the accepted structure to hold them together in their common purpose which the Movement found in Saint Benedict's Rule; the great liberating power of friendship in Christ; the expression of that friendship in the discipline of the communities and in fraternal correction; the regular renewal of care for each other in *convivencias*; the care that no-one should be lost or forgotten or threatened by soul-less anonymity, which the Movement achieves through the Deaneries, through spiritual accompaniment and through their willingness to listen, listen, listen and even waste time with those who come to them. These are all ways of breaking down the soulless rigidity of mere secularist organization. They are all part of the universal heritage of Christianity and none of them are dependent solely on the culture of Latin America. All of them are accessible to all Catholic lay men and women and children also. Of course, different cultures develop different ways of expressing themselves but the radical roots of their faith and lives are the same.

The testimonies by the Oblates and members of the Movement of all ages given in the last two chapters, and others which have been quoted in earlier parts of this account, reveal a subtle and elusive quality in the lay spirituality of the Movement. It is a spirituality that combines the absolute confidence of faith with a realization of our personal inherent powerlessness and dependence - as creatures of a day - on the pure gift of grace from Christ. Just as this confidence is the work of grace, the other quality, which is by Saint Benedict called humility, reflects profound realism about the spiritual weakness of our human nature and its inherent spiritual limitations. There are many paradoxes in Christianity and there is a creative paradox in the combination of these two qualities - uniting the glory of grace which is given to us with the humility of spiritual emptiness which can be filled only by grace. The grace comes to nothing, if there is not spiritual space through humility to receive it. The humility remains empty, powerless, earthbound, if grace does not come to the rescue through Jesus Christ.

The two qualities come together in human living through listening to the word of God in scripture and responding by following Christ. Another way of putting it in the context of the Movement is to say that they come together through following the way of Saint Benedict, who himself follows the way of Christ. The resulting balance between absolute and unshakeable confidence in the risen Christ living among us and distrust of self in every circumstance of life except where he is present to sustain us, is peculiar to the Christian vocation both lay and clerical.

This balance is in sharp contrast to other combinations of attitudes to the two poles of our lives - God and self. It is the reverse of the distrust of God and absolute confidence in self or 'human nature'. That reversal of the Christian perspective is the driving force of much great human achievement in our western world. It is also the cause of most of its disasters and the root of the disintegration and degeneration which threatens us. The balance of Catholicism, which is the Movement's way of life is needed more urgently and more universally than many would like to think.

The way of life of the Manquehue Movement, based on these radical principles, is not, then, something only of private interest to the country in which it arose. It is significant that it in fact arose at the nadir of Chilean social and political fortunes. It was a time when all the negativities of the outer world - both from the left and from the right - burst upon this small country with destructive malevolence. It was a time when the rootless revolt of youth was being idolized and given free rein in the west. It was in that turmoil that José Manuel Eguiguren sank into the utter spiritual darkness from which he was rescued by the Benedictine way of scriptural *lectio* and the patient listening of Father Gabriel Guarda. The darkness, the turmoil, the rebellion against everything, were not peculiar to Chile. They came from outside. They are stalking the earth still - whether openly or in disguise. The spirit of the lay Movement which emerged - under the grace of God - in Chile is needed elsewhere in one form or another.

José Manuel has often spoken of the way of life of the Movement as having some of the qualities of an alternative society. In so far as it leads individuals and communities from chaos towards the kingdom of God, which Christ preached in the gospel it is indeed an alternative society. But it is not an alternative society which relies upon violence and upheaval to impose another way of life. Far from that, it is essentially an invitation to voluntary acceptance of this path of life.

It is an invitation which might even be summed up by something St Paul wrote to his beloved Philippians. The Philippians were his first converts in Europe, and a businesswoman, Lydia, was the first of the converts. The people of Philippi were on the whole a rough lot of Roman army veterans with not even a Jewish synagogue in the city. Paul did not recommend them to engage in power struggles to establish an alternative society. He was much more radical than that. He told them to start with their own inner being - to start with their own thoughts:

> whatever is true, whatever is honorable,
> whatever is just, whatever is pure,
> whatever is lovely, whatever is gracious,
> if there is any excellence,
> if there is anything worthy of praise,
> THINK ABOUT THESE THINGS.

That way of thinking starts, for the Manquehue Movement with *lectio divina*. Those who listen in this way to the word of scripture learn how to turn from evil and think about what is good, and beautiful and true. It is the first step on the 'path of life', which opens our whole being to the peace of Christ.

CR

Notes for the Epilogue
[1]   cf Col. 1, 27 'the mystery, which is Christ in you, the hope of glory.'
[2]   See Newman's 'On consulting the faithful in matters of doctrine.'
[3]   There is no clearer example of this than the contemporary determination of a few, who are in power, to exclude in the constitution of Europe any reference to the historical fact that the origins of Europe are Christian. Parallel to this is the determination of the dominant atheist interests to exclude any symbol of religion of any sort from public places.

Glossary & Other Explanatory Notes

acogida ~ a spanish word which means the act of welcoming someone. It has a special meaning and emphasis in the Manquehue Movement as the way of seeing Christ in others in accordance with the teaching of St Benedict.

Ampleforth Abbey ~ a Benedictine Abbey of the English Benedictine Congregation. José Manuel first made contact with Ampleforth at the time when he was starting his first school, San Benito. The relationship between the Movement and Ampleforth has developed strongly over the years and they recognize each other as 'confraters', which is a traditional Benedictine term of mutual fraternal charity.

Benedictine Confederation ~ the name of an overall federation of independent Benedictine monasteries of the world. It holds a Congress every 4 years for mutual support and help at the Abbey of Sant' Anselmo in Rome. It is attended by Abbots or Priors from the whole world who elect an Abbot Primate to carry forward the business of the Confederation and represent Benedictines at the Vatican.

Benedictine Congregations ~ Benedictine monasteries are grouped in Congregations which on the whole follow national lines, although some Congregations are international. Each Congregation has its own General Chapter which is attended by Abbots or Priors of the Congregation, who elect a President and agree on common Constitutions, that is interpretations of the Rule for the differing circumstances and differing work of the individual Congregations.

Benedictine nuns & sisters ~ since the beginning there have been Benedictine monasteries for women. In the early centuries they always led an enclosed life of prayer. That tradition continues to the present day, although often there is some mitigation of the enclosure to make room for some more external work. Benedictine women leading such an

419

enclosed life are usually referred to as Benedictine nuns. In recent centuries there has been a strong growth of Benedictine women leading a community life with common prayer but engaging in a great variety of apostolic works. These Benedictines are usually referred to as Benedictine sisters.

Cardinal Raúl Silva Henriquez ~ the great Cardinal Archbishop of Santiago who saw the Chilean Church through the changes after Vatican II and the political stresses of the 70's and 80's. His personal involvement in the earliest stages of the Manquehue Movement have been particularly valued.

CELAM ~ Conferencia Episcopal LatinoAmericano the Conference of Latin-American Bishops.

Chilean names ~ It is the custom in Chile that men retain as a second surname their mother's family name. Thus Eguiguren is José Manuel's father's family name and Guzman his mother's. The addition of the second surname in ordinary use is optional. A married woman will not normally take her husband's family name on marriage and will retain her parent's family names. Thus José Manuel's wife was still known as Luz Cosmelli after her marriage.

Colegio ~ a school for pupils from 4 to 18, normally used in Chile for independent schools or universities.

Conchali ~ a district in Santiago in which Colegio San Lorenzo was founded

convivencia ~ a Spanish word for 'sharing' or 'living together'. In the Manquehue Movement it is used especially for a monthly meeting to share a meal and strengthen fraternal charity between the members of a community for *lectio*.

Cunaco group ~ a small group of Manquehue Oblates and others interested and involved in their work. It was inspired by a paper written by José Manuel entitled 'Creating a new Benedictine School' for a conference on Benedictine Education held at Worth Abbey in 1999. Its first meeting was in the following year, 2000, in Chile and took place in a house there named Cunaco, from which it takes its name. The group meets privately each year in different locations to discuss ways and means of bringing the genius of the Rule to bear more strongly on Benedictine education of the young.

Deanery ~ in his Rule St Benedict proposes that, if a community became too large for a single man, the Abbot, to exercise effective care of all the monks, he should appoint Deans to act as subordinate superiors of small groups of ten. The Manquehue Movement has developed this idea, making the deaneries correspond to the work patterns of the Movement and giving them, as associates of the Responsable, a special mandate for the help and support of individuals.

DEM ~ Directorio Educational Manquehue - The Educational Directorate of the Manquehue Movement. This is a body set up under the chairmanship of one of the senior Oblates. Its regular meetings are attended by the Heads and the Deans of the different Manquehue Schools. Its purpose is to coordinate all the educational work of the Movement and above all to ensure that the inspiration of St Benedict's Rule is always reflected in the educational practice of the Movement.

Divine Office ~ this is often also referred to as the Liturgy of the Hours and in St Benedict's Rule as 'the Work of God' or *Opus Dei*. It consists of six moments of prayer during the day - Lauds, Terce, Sext, None, Vespers, Compline - and one in the night - Vigils. Among these special emphasis is set on Lauds and Vespers. It is also known as 'The Prayer of the Church', since it is universally observed throughout the Church by clergy and laity alike. It provides the framework of prayer on which the Manquehue Movement bases its works.

El Camino ~ El Camino Manquehuino or The Way of the Manquehue Movement. It is the name of a booklet explaining the way of life to be followed by members of the Movement at every level.

EMLA ~ Encuentro Monastico Latinoamericano - the Conference of Monastic Institutes in Latin America. It is a voluntary association for mutual help and discussion. It was important for the Manquehue Movement that José Manuel has been invited to attend the meetings.

evangelization ~ see Appendix 5, where the full meaning of this word is brought out by Pope John Paul II. It is sufficient here to recall what he said the the youth in Switzerland when he urged them: 'to proclaim the message of the Gospel with the testimony of your lives.'

Formation ~ this word is used in monastic circles for the process of spiritual initiation into the meaning and practice of monastic life. In monasteries it refers especially to the period candidates spend in the novitiate (normally lasting one year) but it refers also to the longer period of preparation for final profession. In recent years it has been recognized that there is an element of 'continuing formation' through which monks and nuns are open to further learning and spiritual growth throughout monastic life. For the lay members of the Manquehue Movement 'formation' is used in particular for the Houses of St Joseph and St Hilda in Patagonia. Continuing formation for them is ensured by frequent retreats, by their devotion to the Office of the Hours and daily *lectio* and the other practices outlined in Minima Regla and El Camino.

Foundation ~ a new Benedictine monastery founded by an existing Abbey. The founding Abbey sends a group of its own monks to start the new house. Ultimately they may sever their ties with the founding house and become monks of the new foundation.

Holy Trinity Abbey ~ the Benedictine monastery in Las Condes in Santiago. It was founded originally by French monks, then strengthened by Beuronese monks from Gernany. Now it is an independent member of the Cono Sur Congregation of South America.

Las Condes ~ this is a largely residential district in Santiago. It is on the edge of the lower mountains and on its outskirts is the Benedictine Monastery of the Holy Trinity, where José Manuel first learnt the meaning of *lectio divina*.

laudatio ~ the term used for a document of approval by the Pontifical Council for the Laity in Rome given to a new lay Movement like the Manquehue Movement.

lectio divina ~ this phrase is taken directly from St Benedict's Rule in the chapter where he speaks of the daily occupations of Benedictine

Communities. The day was split between *lectio divina* and manual work and normally the largest allocation of time was to *lectio divina*. It was primarily slow and meditative reading of the word of sacred scripture involving learning large sections - especially the Psalms - by heart. In modern times it is used for less demanding practices of meditative reading of the scripture. It is the primary daily practice of the Manquehue Movement and has been described in the text e.g. in chapters 3 and 16. *see also Appendix 1*

Leyda ~ this is the name of a small village and its surrounding district in the coastal hills some 80 miles west of Santiago. It is the district in which the farm belonging to the Eguiguren family and the old house of his grandmother, so familiar to him in his youth, were situated. In the same district is a community house built by the Oblates where they often go in groups for rest and retreats.

Liberation Theology ~ a term used rather loosely to refer to a tendency - rather than a school - of theology, which from the sixties onwards, particularly in South America, was concerned with the 'preferential option for the poor'. Their general aim of concern for the poor is widely shared by others but the appeal to violence and adoption of Marxist views alienated some of the liberation writers from orthodox Catholicism.

Liturgy of the Hours ~ see Divine Office above

Mallín Grande ~ the name of a small village on the banks of Lake General Carrera a few miles from the site of the Houses of the Manquehue Movement in Patagonia.

Manquehue ~ this is the name of a mountain (pronounced Man-kay-way), which is nearly 3,000 ft in height. It overlooks and dominates a district of Santiago which derives the name Manquehue from the mountain. In that district was the Manquehue School, which is still thriving, in which José Manuel completed High School education and where later he began his first teaching job with the Confirmation Class. Much closer to the mountain - in fact at its very feet - is the site of Colegio San Benito, the first school of the Manquehue Movement.

Minima Regla ~ this is the rule of life of the Manquehue Oblates. It is to a great extent inspired by St Benedict's Rule - a fact that is recognized by José Manuel's choice of a phrase from St Benedict's chapter 73. In that chapter St Benedict refers his monks to the scriptures and the great work of St Basil and others before describing his own Rule as something for beginners 'a very little rule' (minima regula for which the Spanish is Minima Regla)

misiones ~ a term used in Chile to refer to organized visits to poor and neglected areas of the Church to evangelize the people and bring them the sacraments. It is traditional in the Chilean Church but in the Manquehue Movement it relies principally on *lectio divina* and the development of personal relationships and support.

Movement ~ this is a commonly used term in the Catholic Church of today. It refers to any voluntary association of the faithful for mutual help and sanctification and for undertaking good works in the church and in the world. When such a Movement is recognized by the local bishop it becomes 'eccesial' and a recognized part of the local church. This recognition may be further strengthened (as it was with the Manquehue Movement) by receiving the approval or *'laudatio'* of the Pontifical Council for the Laity in Rome. *See also Chapter 14*

Neo-Catechumenate Way ~ The Neo Catecumenate Way is a world-wide organization within the Catholic Church which was founded in Madrid in 1968 by two Spaniards with the intention of bringing down to Catholics at ordinary parish level some of the inspiration of Vatican II. The two founders were lay but there are priests also in this Movement. They seek to revive in the Church today at parochial level the fervor and commitment of the early Church by centering their catechesis and evangelization on the the Word of God, the Eucharist and the Community. Their mission is to evangelize among Catholics in parochial life and to reach out also to those outside the Church. Their work has been successful both in renewal within the Church and in conversion of those outside.

Oblate ~ this word is derived from the Latin 'oblatus' which means offered or consecrated (in a general sense) to God. For centuries it has been used by Benedictines - both men and women - to describe a lay person who has sought and been granted a spiritual association centered on prayer with a particular Benedictine monastery. This association involved sharing the prayer of the monastery and often its good works. Over the ages there have been many different ways in which this type of association has been realized. Of particular interest and importance to the Manquehue Movement was St Frances of Rome's creation of an order of lay Oblates for demanding social work in the city. In the Manquehue Movement the Oblates are the inner core of the Movement. After a period of probation they have been accepted and have made their promises in a solemn ceremony. *see also chapter 14*

Providencia ~ a district - originally residential but less so now - near the center of Santiago. It is where Colegio San Benito began its existence in rented accommodation while awaiting the permanent buildings in Vitacura.

Puerto Guadal ~ the name of a small village on the banks of Lake General Carrera a few miles from the site of the Houses of the Manquehue Movement in Patagonia.

Punta de Tralca ~ a large complex of buildings suitable for residential retreats overlooking the Pacific 100 miles west of Santiago. It provides sleeping accommodation, refectories, lecture halls and a large church for groups (large and small) who make their own arrangements for retreats. It is owned and run by the archdiocese of Santiago. It has often been used by the Movement for their retreats

Responsable ~ as an adjective this word in Spanish is equivalent to the English adjective 'reponsible'. As a noun it is used for the person in charge of any undertaking. In the Manquehue Movement it is used for the Superior, who is in a comparable position to that of the Abbot in St Benedict's Rule. It is difficult to find a satisfactory English word and I think it is best to retain the Spanish name.

Secretary General ~ the title of an Oblate who has a co-ordinating responsibility for all the work and activities of the Movement. He works closely with José Manuel, the Responsable, and is in some respects like a Chief of Staff.

seminary ~ a college under the authority of the bishop to train candidates for the priesthood

St Louis Abbey ~ a Benedictine Abbey in St Louis, Missouri USA, which was founded 50 years ago by Ampleforth Abbey in England. It is now independent but has shared Ampleforth's interest and involvement in the Manquehue Movement. The Abbot of St Louis and one of the monks are members of the Cunaco group.

trabajo ~ refers to carefully prepared visits by groups of young people to poor areas to carry out work projects of repair and renovation.

tutoría ~ this is the Spanish word for which there is no exact English equvalent. In general it means 'guardianship'. In education it means the office of a tutor. It has a very special and precise meaning for the Manquehue Movement. For them it means the way in which older pupils meet younger ones in small groups for *lectio divina* so that they may share with them their own belief in the risen Christ and its effect in the shaping of their lives. The groups are organized and supervised by the Oblates and their assistants. The method is founded on José Manuel's perception of how much is lost in traditional catechesis through the enormous gap between the adult's and the child's mentality. He perceived how close older pupils are to the younger and what a powerful influence they have on the ways of thinking of younger pupils. In teaching them to convey their faith to the younger he also taught them how to deepen and value their own faith. In fact through *tutoría* he reversed the more normal pattern in the west through which younger children are commonly corrupted by elder teenagers and their gang leaders. With good reason he values *tutoría* as a necessary and precious instrument of Christian education in the Movement.

Vatican Council ~ also referred to as Vatican II was the pastoral Council called by Pope John XXIII 1962-1965.

Vitacura ~ a district in Santiago

Worth Abbey ~ a Benedictine monastery in England of the English Benedictine Congregation. José Manuel was invited to speak there in 1999 at an international conference of Benedictine educators. It was his

address on that occasion which inspired the creation of the Cunaco group
in the following year.

Appendix 1
Lectio Divina

José Manuel spoke and wrote many things about lectio divina during the course of his work with the Movement. The following is a translation of one short instruction which may help the reader to an initial understanding of it.

Lectio is a way of getting into touch daily in a personal and intimate way with the Father, the Son and the Holy Spirit; it is a way of getting into touch with Jesus Christ our Lord and our brother. It is a way of reading centerd on God and, if you do it with faith you will be able to hear what he has to say to you here at this moment. It is a way of reading which is slow so that the words are savored in meditation. It moves from the literal meaning to what only the Spirit can make clear to you. It calls for action by your involvement and for passive surrender as it draws you into the heart of God. It is disinterested; the text must be read for its own sake and not for the achievement of having read it.

Lectio is a way of experiencing Jesus Christ. You will encounter him personally in the sacred scriptures because he is there hidden in the pages of your Bible and you ought to believe in his presence with greater assurance than if you could see him with your eyes. He has the same power there as he revealed in the gospels and he cures you of your physical and moral ailments, brings his light to your everyday life and leads you to eternal life. Your encounter is with the Word who loves you unconditionally and is ever present and real in your life.

From all eternity God has had a plan for the whole course of your life, your personal fulfilment, your vocation, your happiness. You will surely stray from the right path and become alienated from your true self through serving other gods, if you do not allow him to reveal himself to you daily through his word. It is in your Bible that the true story of your life is written. If you don't at once understand what you read, then have confidence that the Lord will reveal it to you in his own time, because no word comes from the mouth of the Lord without achieving in you the work he intended. If your thoughts and imagination get in the way of your prayer, then fling them immediately before Christ. Make no attempt to master them by your own strength, but try to turn back to your prayer

You ought to do lectio every day, even if it is only on one single verse of the Bible, because "it is not on bread alone that man lives but on every word that comes from the mouth of God" (Mt. 4, 4) Your reading of the word of God should be deliberate, moving slowly from verse to verse, from word to word, watching for the context, paying close attention to each passage, looking out for the answers that are there in sacred scripture itself and the echoes they evoke, watching the notes and marginal references and always treasuring silence so as to make space to listen. You should know that the word you hear is directed to you personally and individually.

When you read the word of God, it speaks to you; when you pray, you speak to the word and so turn your prayer into conversation. Your prayer may be simply staying with the word in silence, or it may be a thanksgiving, or a petition, or praise, or blessing, or contrition, or intercession, or one single word on which you pause and then repeat it at will, or it may be a prayer of inspiration. If you are taking part in shared lectio the way to share what scripture has said to you is by means of a personal comment spoken in the first person singular and applied to your own life, or else it may be a prayer out loud offered directly to God.

CR

Appendix 2
Article from the Manquehue School Magazine
1979

see chapter 4

The following interview article by José Manuel Eguiguren, published in the Manquehue School Magazine in 1979, when he had already relinquished his job as Director of Christian Formation and was about to leave the Manquehue School, makes clear how developed his vision was and how ready he was for what was to come in the founding of his own schools

The Manquehue Apostolic Movement

During the last few years The Manquehue College of the Sacred Hearts has experienced a strong influence from the birth of a new spirit which has led to a lot of activity among the young. It is clear that the responsibility for this lies with the Manquehue Apostolic Movement from whose ranks have come four of the recent Presidents of the Students' Council, namely Gonzalo Loeser Bravo 1976, Recaredo Ossa Balmaceda 1977, Rodrigo Vial Fell 1978, and the current President - Juan Francisco Ossa Balmaceda.

The Movement's Governing Body includes among others: Alejandro Allende Marín, a student in Engineering; Carlos Figuera Guzmán, studying Law; Rodrigo Vial Fell, studying Agriculture; Jorge Baraona González, studying Law; José Antonio Navarro, studying Forestry; and Pablo Baraona Undurraga. The Founder of the Movement, who has given us this interview, is José Manuel Eguiguren Guzman, the former Director of the Department of Christian Formation which is the responsibility he bore when Mgr Alfonso Puelma Claro was Headmaster.

1   *What is the Manquehue Apostolic Movement trying to achieve?*
    It is a Christian Movement involving a vocation to serve the community. To this end it educates people to become leaders through a way of learning which relies on the Word of God as its source.

2 *In what does this way of learning consist?*

It is a way through which the Movement is inspired to realize a spirituality of friendship, centered on the Sacred Hearts, and the method of achieving this is threefold:

First of all there are the communities for the celebration of the Word, which rely on a way of meditation taught by the Benedictine monks of Las Condes. In these communities is to be found the primary source of all the Movement's action and they give it its true Christian character.

Then, secondly, come the organizations for education and service, which are groups for work set up in a spirit of co-responsibility for the assigning of jobs to be done. These organizations are designed to develop the many spiritual, intellectual, artistic and physical gifts of the members and to dedicate them to the service of others.

Thirdly there is the actual service which consists in all the activities of the Movement for the benefit of the community. This service in the third category is always understood to be the fruit of the first two.

3 *Could you name some of the services which the community provides?*

There are very many services performed by the Movement and it would take a long time to enumerate them all. Nevertheless, I must say that in practice there have been no activities in education, sport, spirituality or social action in which the presence of the Movement cannot be discerned. But among them all it is right to emphasize in their own special place the *tutorías* and the preparations for confirmation.

4 *How did the idea of the Movement arise?*

It was born out of necessity, it was the answer to a need for vocation, the young who joined the Movement found a new meaning in their lives through it, in a sense they created it and for many of them it has involved a change in their lives. This Movement began under Mgr Puelma as Headmaster and he lent all his support to this work and he had the vision to give it the breath of life even before it was properly formed. The Movement recognizes in him, Fr Puelma, and in Fr Carlos Schneider and Fr Gabriel Guarda its spiritual guides from the beginning.

Then, apart from that, Cardinal Silva in 1977 maintained that the Movement would achieve great good for the Church and above all he encouraged the young to continue their work for the good of the Manquehue College. Now, in 1979, under the headmastership of Fr Silva the Archbishop has recognized this Movement in the Church of Santiago.

5 *What sort of reception has the new Headmaster given the Movement?*
A very good reception. Fr Silva has recognized the Movement within the College in a ceremony in which the chief Governors of the College and of the Parents' Association as well as a large number of representatives and relations of the young men of the Movement took part.

Fr Luis Eugenio (Silva) has regularly supported meetings with the administration of the Movement as theological advisor, he has funded its office expenses and finally he has celebrated the weekly Eucharist for the Movement to which the whole community of pupils is invited.

6 *What do you mean by educating leaders?*
Fr Hurtado in an article published in the Review of St Ignatius' College maintains that the world lacks leaders capable of committing themselves radically to a cause and he writes that a leader should combine in himself idealism, organization and hard work. Thirty years have passed since then and we still lack leaders like that. The bishops of America in their meeting at Puebla have maintained that the education of leaders is a priority. In my opinion a leader is a man with the characteristics already mentioned but who also finds his nourishment in the Word of God, develops his personal qualities and devotes himself with all this wealth to the service of others.

7 *What role should the leavers play?*
The Leavers have been creating this Movement for more than two years with this aim in view. The Movement exists for them and it is through their perseverance in its communities, in its organizations, in its service and especially in its studies that the Movement lives, that is how the spirit is molded and how it learns how to give from the many gifts it has received. The sacrifice which the leavers make is surprising.

8 *Could belonging to the Movement be an obstacle to boys' studies?*
If God asks of us a special mission, that is not going to be at the cost of primary obligations which he himself has placed on us, like the obligations of our state. Among our members are the majority of the most successful pupils and some of the most successful former pupils of this College and of other Colleges. Then again, it is good students who are interested in the Movement. They may well turn out in the future to be good in their professional careers who because of their knowledge will be able to give of the best to those who follow them. Moreover, I know a number of pupils who have improved their performance from the time when they joined the Movement.

9 *What is the point of friendship with the Sacred Hearts?*

Friendship with the Sacred Hearts is a matter of spirituality. The Vicar for education, Mgr Gambino, has maintained that the original charism of the original founders of each congregation should be revived. The Movement, with the constant help of Fr Carlos Schneider, has succeeded in developing the spirituality of devotion to the Sacred Hearts in a form appropriately renewed for the laity and in a manner fitting for our times. Thus it has a style and a way of coming to life which fits our service and which could prove fruitful in another College.

10 *What is meant by tutoría?*

It is a bridge building institution through which the older pupils in a spirit of companionship take responsibility for the younger ones. They take an interest in their studies, join with them in sporting activities, join them in their days of celebration with children of their own age and promote good relationships with the whole College. The tutors in fact embody the role of a father in the scholastic education of their sons. Their presence has been particularly useful in cases where the father of a pupil has been involved in personal problems. This sort of care for the children on the part of the older pupils never existed before and is the special work of the Movement.

11 *How has the Movement managed in its withdrawal from the school?*

It has not been without difficulties, but there has been strong support from the student body, from the priests and representatives, from the administration of the College under the leadership of Don Henry Loeser and many of the professors who have in fact taken part in the activities of the Movement. And it is right that I should make special mention here of the Department of Physical Education and Don Manuel Solís and also the wise spiritual direction of the priests I have mentioned earlier.

CR

Appendix 3
Extracts from The Little Rule for the Oblates

No one can have greater love than to lay down his life for his friends
(Jn 15,13)

3 THE COMMUNITY AS A SCHOOL OF THE LORD'S SERVICE
Thanks to the help and guidance of many, they are now trained to
fight against the devil. (RB 1,4)

[1]The community of the Oblates is a school of the Lord`s service. (RB Prol45). [2]It is a school in which the brethren learn to live ever more fully their Christian vocation, the seed of which they received in their baptism. [3]Recognising that they are weak as individuals they need to be 'formed with the help of many` (RB 1,4) and 'are willing to be guided by an abbot` (RB 5,12). [4]That is why they are intent on finding everything they need within the community and the Movement: listening to the Word, celebrating the hours and doing their work. [5]In this school the brethren never cease to develop in their formation. [6]They receive all they need for this formation on various community occasions, [7]among which the following are the most important: the monthly meeting with a spiritual companion, [8]the weekly shared *lectio divina* , [9]the monthly *convivencia* , [10]the celebration in choir each week of at least one of the hours of the divine office [11]and community work. [12]The community itself is thus the school in which the brethren learn to serve Christ who 'brings us all together to eternal life` (RB 72,12)

6 THE RESPONSIBLE OF THE MOVEMENT AND
HIS SPIRITUAL COMPANIONSHIP
Therefore, drawing on this and other examples of discretion, the mother of virtues,
he must so arrange everything that the strong have something to yearn
for and the weak nothing to run from. (RB,64,19)

[1]The Manquehue Apostolic Movement is governed by a Responsible whose office is modeled on the role which St Benedict gives the Abbot in his Rule. [2]The Responsible is elected from among their number by all the Oblates, men and women, celibate and married. [3]Once elected he holds the office for

an indefinite period. [4]The Responsible is helped in the exercise of his office by the advice of the brethren according to the teaching of Chapter 3 of the Rule.

The most important office of the Responsible is the exercise of spiritual companionship; [6]that means being available to the brethren with encouragement, directing their attention to the word of God and guiding them lovingly towards Christ and towards becoming more truly the Church in the way of the Movement. [7]Following the guidance of what the Rule says in chapter 21 about the deans, the Responsible may select helpers to act as spiritual companions for the brethren (cf.Ex18,13-27). [8]Each Oblate has a spiritual companion with whom he meets every month in private. [9]Both of them bear a serious responsibility for making sure that the meeting takes place.

7   THE ACOGIDA - WELCOME AND AFFIRMATION IN CHRIST

It is this latter spirit that all who follow the monastic way of life should strive to cultivate, spurred on by fervent love.   (RB 72,3)

[1]The Oblates, like all other Christians, have by their baptism been united to Christ in his Paschal mystery. [2]This union and even identification with Christ himself is received as a potential which awaits development and it is through the exercise of love that it comes to be realized in its true fullness. [3]This is what Jesus teaches in a passage from St John`s gospel which has been a key text for the Movement since its beginning: "No-one can have greater love than to lay down his life for his friends." (Jn 15,13).

Thus the *acogida* - or making time to affirm and be available to others in the love of Christ - is an essential part of the Responsible´s work in the Movement, as it is also for those who share his work of spiritual companionship with the brethren. [5]The brethren themselves are to show the same warmth to each other [6]and also towards all others with whom they come into contact. It is just as St Paul said: "Accept one another, then, for the sake of God`s glory, as Christ accepted you." (Rom.15,7) [7]To offer such a welcome to another means to recognize and adore Christ himself in that person, [8]to open one's heart to the love of that other person, to make space in one's thinking and listen to another among all the preoccupations and tasks that absorb the mind, [10]to make every effort to meet others` needs from one's own resources whatever their requirements - whether material or spiritual. [11]In these relationships of the brethren there should always be room for the Word of God, just as St Benedict puts it: "The divine law is read to the guest for his instruction, and after that every kindness is shown to him" (RB 53,9)

8   LECTIO DIVINA - THE ATTENTIVE READING OF
SACRED SCRIPTURE

> *Let us get up, then, at long last, for the scriptures rouses us. Let us open our*
> *ears to the voice from heaven that every day calls out. (RB Prol,8-9)*

[1]*Lectio divina* is a special way of reading sacred scripture by which we meet personally with Jesus Christ through our reading. [2]It is a way of reading through which one moves slowly from verse to verse, from word to word, [3]reflecting on the context, examining each passage, [4]noting the answers given in sacred scripture itself and the other scriptural passages it evokes and the marginal comments and references, [5]cherishing also silence to leave room for listening [6]and responding to God in prayer. [7]Such a way of reading scripture is an essential pre-requisite for concentrating one's mind on the Divine Office. [8]For the Oblates *lectio divina* is a daily activity of radical importance because "to be ignorant of scripture is to be ignorant of Christ." (St Jerome)

[9]The Oblates should give themselves to *lectio divina* every day even though it be for no more than a single verse, because "Man lives not on bread alone but on every word that comes from the mouth of God." (Mt 4,4) [10]For this purpose they should select a book of the Bible which will usually be one of the gospels, as the Holy Rule says: "The gospel should be our guide in following the way of Christ" (RB.Prol,21) [11]Whenever they take up the Bible the Oblates should treat it with veneration as we know the Israelites did. (Ne.8,5-6)

[12]Once every week the Oblates meet together for shared *lectio divina*. [13]The purpose of these meetings is to listen to the Word and to respond to it through the *echoes* it evokes. [14]There are two ways of expressing the echo: the first is for each one to share with the brethren what the Word of God has expressed for him. In this case it is always expressed personally in the first person singular, that is: "For me this Word says...." [15]The second way is to pray aloud in a personal prayer offered directly to God, just as St John shows us that Jesus prayed aloud. (Jn.17,1-26) [16]Then the leader of the group may say some words of encouragement, if he thinks it appropriate.

[17]The meeting for shared *lectio divina* is a celebration of the Word of God. [18]Usually this celebration is included in the hour of the Divine Office which belongs to that time of day at which the brethren meet, although *lectio* can at

times stand on its own. [19]Last of all the brethren pray the *Our Father* together and conclude with an embrace or kiss of peace.

14   THE OBLATION

If after due reflection he promises to observe everything and to obey every command given him, let him then be received into the community. (RB.58,14)

[1]In baptism man receives the light of the Word of God; [2]all his sins are forgiven; [3]he dies to evil and rises again to a new life; [4]he comes to be a son of God and a member of the Church; [5]from then on he belongs to Christ. [6]Each one of these and all the aspects of baptismal grace that follow from them are received in the sacrament in an embryonic way like a potential that is called to gradual fulfilment throughout the course of life (CIC 1253ss). [7]The community of the Oblates is a way to achieve this fulfilment and the Lord in his goodness offers it to those who seek it. [8]The oblation is the acceptance of this offer.

[9]The Oblate in offering himself promises stability, [10]obedience and [11]Conversion of life [12]which are the promises proposed by St Benedict (cfRB.58,17) [13]and which in the Movement are given an interpretation appropriate to lay life. [14]As soon as he has made his promises the Oblate recites the verse: "Receive me, O Lord, according to your word and I shall live and do not allow my hope to come to nothing."(RB.58,21), because he knows that the fulfilment of the promise does not depend on himself alone but on the fidelity of God to his word.

[15]The promise is to last for an indefinite time. [16]Since it has reference to baptism, a sacrament which imprints on the soul a character which cannot be removed, it involves the intention of never coming to an end. [17]In spite of this it can be terminated by dismissal, if there should be a serious breach of the obligations of an Oblate, [18]or by a formal renunciation in writing of his commitment by the Oblate himself.

[19]The promise is not a vow, either public or private. It is not a religious profession because all the Oblates are lay [20]and the promise does not change this essential condition but only the way in which he lives his life as a layman.

19 THE CLOISTER OF THE OBLATES

The monastery should, if possible, be so constructed that within it all necessities are
contained, so that there will be no need for the monks to roam
outside because this is not good for their souls. (RB.66,6-7)

[1]St Benedict knew that the cloister is a great help to stability, Conversion of life and obedience. [2]The brethren are often inclined through weakness to evade the cross and look for an alternative way in their lives and in the different situations with which they are often faced. [3]The Oblates must not become idolaters who expect to find in the world solutions which are not to be found except in God and in his Son Jesus Christ. [4]Thanks to their cloister the Oblates can listen to God, who through his Word brings his light to bear on every circumstance [5]so that they can take up their cross and come to see it transformed in Christ into a cross of glory.

[6]The community of the Manquehue Oblates does not enjoy a physical cloister in the traditional sense. [7]Nevertheless they have two ways of bringing this principle home to themselves in their lives. They can achieve it in the first place by means of a certain degree of separation from the world, [8]and secondly by identifying the space in their lives which they need to carry out their activities, this space will for them be equivalent to a cloister.

[9]In the first place, then, separation from the world can be achieved by creating a private space in the home which is not accessible to anyone who does not live in the house. It will be the space reserved for family life whether for married or celibate Oblates. [10]This space should not be violated either through misplaced charity or through an inappropriate familiarity. [11]There is another form of cloistral space to be found in moments of the day or the week which are reserved for prayer or for special moments of family life, as for instance lunch on Sunday. [12]Finally the Oblates' instinct should guide their discretion in using the means of social communication like radio, television, periodicals, reviews, the telephone and computers. [13]That same instinct should be watchful also over the manner and frequency of the participation or involvement of the Oblates in shows in the theatre and cinema, in sporting events and in political and social occasions in general.

[14]In the second place the Oblates will discover that there does exist for them a space which, although it is not cut off by walls as in the monasteries, nevertheless has all the importance attached to the cloister by St Benedict in the Holy Rule. [15]This cloister is the normal round of the Oblate's life in which prayer, and work and family life and recreation and other activities take place. [16]The Oblates with the help of their spiritual companion will learn to distinguish the limits of their own cloister. [17]It is important that the

Oblates should help each other to avoid dissipation and not make comments to each other about events and news which they have heard about or seen" because this causes the greatest harm" (RB.67,5). [18]In the same way they should keep in mind that claustral space has different scope for different Oblates; that means that they should be careful not to bring another of the brethren where he should not be by enticing him from his duties and from his own appropriate space.

ജ

Appendix 4
Life in the Formation House in San José

Timetable

06:00   Get up. Light the fire. Prepare Breakfast. Each member of the community has a specific task for the day (eg. cooking, cleaning the bathroom or the rooms, chopping the wood for the stove or fire, etc.)

06:20   Lauds

06:50   Breakfast

07:20   Lectio Divina: Scrutinize a passage from Sacred Scripture. This involves 30 minutes of personal work, writing out the passage and its parallel passages and associated notes, then sharing a personal echo if they wish.

08:00   Clean the House (each person has an assigned task)

09:00   Spirituality: Spiritual conversation guided by an Oblate. Its objective is to enlighten the young persons experience in San Jose and focus on their life as a whole in the light of the presence of the Risen Christ.

10:40   Terce

11:00   Personal Reading. (Meanwhile the daily server cooks lunch).

12:15   Sext

12:30   Lunch (in silence with selected reading)
         None

13:30   Manual labour (in the green house or garden, sometimes with the cattle, generally outdoors.)

18:15   End of work, return to the formation house to shower

19:00   Vespers

19:30   Supper

20:30   Shared Lectio Divina in groups of two or three, reading the day's gospel verse by verse and with echoes in between.

21:00   Compline

At the weekends there are special moments for personal prayer and for community activities.

443

The Content of the Spirituality section:
(See the daily timetable above, from 09:00 until 10:40)

We take "El Camino Manquehuino" as a structure for subjects. As we go along we go into each subject deeply.

Subjects:

The Risen Christ; the Early Church; History of the Movement; Baptism; Communion; St. Benedict; Lectio Divina; Liturgy of the Hours; the organisation of the Movement, Oblates.

We use documents of the Movement (Minima Regla, Cristo Rey, El Qvaderno etc.), Bishops Letters, CELAM documents (Conferencia Episcopal de Latinoamérica), Vatican II, writings of selected Benedictine monks, the Catechism of the Catholic Church, Canon law. The young people get to know scripture very closely and also the Rule of St. Benedict. The Spirituality time is a space to welcome all their doubts. Our objectives for this time always have a pastoral focus, rather than an academic one.

Ecclesial Communion is a vital topic, in one of the most isolated geographical areas in the world. Although they are so distant, they are still very much a part of the Body of Christ and they realize, feel and live this.

Personal Reading : basic books

Searching for God. (Basil Hume)
Reading God (Garcia Columbás)
Life of St. Benedict (St. Gregory the Great.)
Spiritual Friendship (St. Aelred of Rievaulx
Colaciones II (Garcia Columbás) "El monje y el misterio Pascual".

Conclusión.

The formation given at San Jose is based on experiential knowledge, so all aspects of it become real facts, in their turn experienced by the young people while they are here. This means that they come to be able to say, with St John:

"Something which has existed since the beginning, which we have heard, and we have seen with our own eyes, that we have watched, and touched with our own hands, the Word, who is life, this is our subject. (1John 1:1)

For the Oblates that are part of the stable community in San Jose, each term a new community is founded at San Jose and there comes a new challenge to live deeply Manquehue´s charism, a new stage in the personal story that God is writing with each one.

All the life and work and the great fruits for the young of living in San Jose are the result of the life and communion of the Oblates' community and the

Movement and the whole Church. This is why we do our best to open our heart and mind and will to the Word and the Spirit.

Testimonies.

The Testimonies, from which extracts are given here, were written by young people of 19 to 23 years of age who study at University: Law, Engineering, Architecture, Design, Economics, Agriculture, History and Education.

Formation Programme for University Students in San José, Chilean Patagonia.
Mini testimonies:

General:

I don't know why I came here. The truth is that I didn't feel part of the Manquehue Movement. Here I have met the Oblates, who are now my friends; I have discovered the Movement's history, that is my own history, this breath of the Spirit, without planning, that gives rise to great things in little people- like me- who are just trying to give their whole lives to Christ and be able to live His love.

When I arrived I wanted to be out of the house as much as possible, to have long walks, climb hills, take photographs of this magnificent place, go fishing, etc... Now I still love living surrounded by nature but I prefer to stay at the house, talking with the others, singing, just being here now.

Lectio Divina:

When I arrived I used to talk a lot about love; with *lectio divina* I have learnt what love is in Christ. It is the most important activity, everything is born from it, it reflects my daily life, who is God for me. *Lectio* encourages me to go on, because it is where I have found god. I have advanced in the way of God, I have known God; there is much to advance. I want to go to God.

In shared *lectio* we build up community.

I have had to open myself to listen; a big effort to listen to the Word. Different situations have helped me: my echo, the echo of other members of the community. I'm not conscious of how the Word is building inside me. Sometimes it has been very difficult to start doing *lectio*, and afterwards I'm euphoric.

God speaks in *lectio divina*: I'm witness of that.

445

The best *lectio divina* were those that were difficult to do (because I was tired or in a bad mood). God speaks always to my personal situation, independent of my mood.

I want to do *lectio* with my girlfriend. I don't want to have relationships where Christ is not the center; I want to make them true and eternal.

I need perseverance; I'm afraid I'm going to fail doing *lectio* alone afterwards. I'm my own worst enemy.

Liturgy of the Hours

I didn't like it in Santiago, very boring. Now I feel a love for it. I feel full of the presence of God. The Psalms are about me; I'm praying with the whole church; it keeps me in the presence of God during the day; the bells bring me out of myself; the others' attitude in the oratory make me change mine (I'm not good at concentration). It's worth it.

It's very difficult for me, the most difficult thing

The Office makes me remember why I'm here, to live my baptism.

I'm offering to God every minute of my day.

"Always be joyful in the Lord". I may be sad because of a bad situation, or feel that someone, or the Lord Himself, is being unfair; maybe I'm even right to be feeling that way, but the liturgy brings me to the joy of God's presence in the world. He is the reason to be always joyful.

Shared Work:

It's amazing: we have eaten the potatoes we took out of the ground.

My point of view about work has changed radically. Now I understand that I'm building the kingdom, evangelizing; that is the reason to do it the best I can. How can we tell people in offices and companies this meaning of work?

I can see the work of people in the things I receive.

The more I work with the community, the more I feel part of it.

Community life based on the RB:

When I'm angry someone talks to me and he takes the demon away from me.

The Rule is a way of being Christian.

446

I have experienced humiliation: I'm loved just as I am, with my angers, my lack of patience with myself.

God is in the others. I don't have to be a hermit to discover Him.

Fights are great, because they take us to reconciliation.

Community is where I can live martyrdom.

Fraternal correction has helped me to discover that I'm not the owner of the truth, it makes me listen, open my eyes to reality - the presence of Christ in everything.

It is very important to have time together, to talk, to know each other.

I realize I'm not able to do things well; I'm weak.

I have discovered the spirit of the Rule by the Oblates' daily and living testimony.

Spirituality (Spiritual Conversations)

I feel part of the Movement, which is a base community. I know that it is not the only one, but it is my community.

I know what God has done with the Movement, how He acts, guiding, solving problems. It is a form of the Word of God; I feel full of ideals.

I feel a part of the Church. Now I understand what communion means.

 જી

Appendix 5
Santiago 20 June 2003
Friendship in Christ in the understanding of the Manquehue Movement

An extract from the document- Jesus Christ the King

Friendship in Christ in the Manquehue Apostolic Movement rests on five central principles:

1. The presence of Christ, because true friendship is never between two people since Christ is always present. This friendship is born in Christ, it grows in him and it reaches fulfillment in him. This presence of Christ is revealed by his own words, since he himself said: 'where two or three are united in my name, there am I in their midst.' (MT 18.20) He is present also through his dialogue with them by which he is made present to them in their reading of Sacred Scripture.

2. The expression of love. For friendship to be a reality love must be expressed, and the expression must be mutual, not on one side only. This love which is shared in friendship is always the same; it is the love of God. "This is what love is: not that we have loved God but that he loves us and sends his Son as a victim to expiate our sins." *(1 Jn. 4.10)* Jesus said: "I give you a new commandment: that you should love one another. That, just as I have loved you, so you should love one another. By this will everyone know that you are my disciples – if you have love for each other." *(Jn 13, 34-35)* By virtue of our baptism we have been enabled to love with the love with which Jesus Christ loves us, so as to put into practice the good spirit about which St Benedict speaks to us.[1]   St Paul speaks of it in the Romans: "because the love of God has been poured into our hearts by the Holy Spirit which has been given to us." *(Rom. 5,5)*

    This love is always the same. What changes is the way in which this love is expressed and the way in which this friendship in Christ is realized, for instance between husband and wife, parents and children, companions etc.

3.   Fraternal correction, which is encouraged by the creation of spaces in which friends are able between themselves: "to speak the truth with integrity of heart and tongue." (*Rule of St Benedict ch. 4, 28*) In doing this they seek the good of the other and not their own convenience. They take as their guides in such correction not personal criteria but the gospel and the Rule of St Benedict especially Chapter 4. They create spaces in their relationship to share the *agape*[2], the Our Father and the sign of peace[3], so that correction is followed by forgiveness and reconciliation.

4   Openness to the community. Although it is true that friendship should be seen as a sort of enclosure which is sacred, nevertheless, if it is healthy, friendship enriches the whole fabric of a community by radiating love. This point is given strong affirmation by St Paul: "may the Lord make you increase and abound in love to one another and to all men, as we do to you, [13] so that he may establish your hearts unblamable in holiness before our God and Father, at the coming of our Lord Jesus with all his saints." (*1Th 3, 12,13*) This shows that friendship in Christ is not founded on mutual satisfaction, because this would degenerate and be corrupted into a worldly and carnal form of friendship.

5   A shared mission. Although friendship is a good in itself and friendship is the fruit of friendship, nevertheless friendship in Christ disposes friends to give themselves to the community so as to live his Kingdom, to evangelize and to serve others.[4] In this way friendship becomes a realization of eternal life.

β

Notes for Appendix 5

[1] It is easy to recognize the bitter spirit of wickedness which creates a barrier to God's grace and opens the way to the evil of hell. But equally there is a good spirit which frees us from evil ways and brings us closer to God and eternal life. It is this latter spirit that all who follow the monastic way of life should strive to cultivate, spurred on by fervent love. By following this path they try to be first to show respect to one another with the greatest patience in tolerating weaknesses of body or character. They should even be ready to outdo each other in mutual obedience so that no one in the monastery aims at personal advantage but is rather concerned for the good of others. Thus the pure love of one another as belonging to one family should be their ideal. As for God they should fear him with deep reverence. They should love their abbot or abbess with sincere and unassuming affection. They should value nothing whatever above Christ himself, and may he bring us all together to eternal life. *Rule of St Bemedict chap 72*

[2] Agape among the first Christians was a fraternal meal of religious significance with the purpose of strengthening the bonds which united them.

[3] See the Rule of St Benedict: *Chap 13, 12 & 13:* "the celebration of Lauds and Vespers should never be concluded without the recitation by the superior of the whole of the Lord's Prayer so that all may hear and attend to it. This is because of the harm that is often done in a community by the thorns of conflict which can arise. The members of the community, bound by the very words of that prayer, "forgive us as we also forgive," will cleanse themselves from the stain of such evil."

Chap 53, 4&5: "First of all, they should pray together so as to seal their encounter in the peace of Christ. Prayer should come first and then the kiss of peace, in order to evade any delusions which the devil may contrive."

Chap 4, 25: "Don't pretend to be at peace with another when you are not."

Chap 4, 73: "seek reconciliation and peace before the sun goes down whenever we have a quarrel with another."

[4] *Rule of St Benedict chap 53, 9:* "Then some of God's teaching in scripture should be read for the spiritual encouragement it brings us, and after that every mark of kindness should be shown the guests."

451

Appendix 6
Pope John Paul II's call to Evangelize

<u>To Youth in Switzerland</u>
During a meeting June 5 2004 with Catholic youth in Bern, Switzerland, the Pope invited them not to be afraid to meet and listen to Jesus. "Do not be content with discussion; do not wait for opportunities that may never come, to do good," John Paul II urged them. "The time for action is now!"

The Pope added: "At the beginning of this third millennium, you too, young people, are called to proclaim the message of the Gospel with the testimony of your lives. The Church needs your energies, your enthusiasm, your youthful ideals to ensure that the Gospel permeates the fabric of society and inspires a civilization of authentic justice and love without discrimination."

In his homily at Mass the next day the Holy Father proclaimed: "The time has come for preparing young generations of apostles who are not afraid to proclaim the Gospel. It is essential for every baptized person to pass from a faith of habit to a mature faith that is expressed in clear, convinced and courageous personal choices."

This faith, he explained, will enable Christ's followers to build a missionary Church, "free from false fears because she is certain of the Father's love." John Paul II also reminded those present that the foundation of human dignity, and the source of "the greatness of man," comes from the image of God that "is mirrored in every human being."

<u>Spreading the Gospel</u>
A key theme in recent papal addresses centers on the dangers of a secular society that is increasingly hostile to Christian principles. This presents a double challenge: the need to defend the Church and the faithful against an undermining of Christianity; and the need to convince Christians to proclaim Christianity and convert society.

In his May 20 speech to participants in an assembly of Italian bishops, the Pope warned of "the penetrating influence that the media exercise today on mind-sets

453

and behavior, personal and collective, proposing a vision of life that unfortunately often tends to corrode basic ethical values, especially those that concern the family."

At the same time he pointed out to the bishops: "The media, however, also lend themselves to being used for and with very different purposes and results, making an important contribution to the affirmation of positive models of life and also to the spread of the Gospel."

The need for the new constitution of the European Union to contain a reference to the Christian heritage of the continent has been frequently mentioned by the Pope. In a May 6 letter written on the occasion of an ecumenical meeting in Germany, John Paul II also declared: "The Christian faith, however, also represents the present and future of Europe."

"Europe needs the commitment and enthusiasm of Christians, especially the youngest, if it is to receive the Good News of the Gospel of Jesus Christ," the Pope declared. At the beginning of this new millennium, he continued, believers must renew their efforts "to respond to the challenge of the new evangelization."

A witness to the truth

John Paul II explained in more detail what this new evangelization means, during his May 28 address to a group of U.S. bishops, present in Rome for their five-yearly visit.

Every Christian, he said, has a "responsibility for the truth" which has been handed down in the Tradition of the Church, and which in turn must be handed on faithfully. Proclaiming the message of the Gospel in contemporary society is not easy, noted the Pope, and requires a direct confrontation with "the widespread spirit of agnosticism and relativism which has cast doubt on reason's ability to know the truth which alone satisfies the human heart's restless quest for meaning."

The Pope also called for "a profound renewal of the missionary and prophetic sense of the whole People of God, and the conscious mobilization of the Church's resources in the work of an evangelization."

In part, noted John Paul II, this evangelization must be carried out through the network of educational and charitable institutions developed by the Church in the United States. But he also emphasized the role of the laity. "Now is above all the hour of the lay faithful, who, by their specific vocation to shape the secular world in accordance with the Gospel, are called to carry forward the Church's prophetic mission by evangelizing the various spheres of family, social, professional and cultural life."

Echoing his apostolic exhortation "Christifideles Laici," the Pope explained to the bishops that the Gospel's message is "the only fully valid response to the problems and hopes that life poses to every person and society."

Encounter with Jesus

In a June 4 speech to another group of U.S. bishops, the Pope explained in more detail what it means to proclaim the Gospel today. The underlying dynamic of Church's prophetic mission is to enable people "to be transformed by the power of the Gospel which permeates their way of thinking, standards of judgment, and norms of behavior."

To achieve this transformation the Pope urged the bishops that the center of their preaching of the Gospel be based on an encounter with Christ. "In fact, it is only by knowing, loving and imitating Christ that, with him, we can transform history by bringing Gospel values to bear in society and culture."

In a speech Thursday, to yet another group of visiting U.S. bishops, the Pope dealt with another aspect of evangelization. "Today creativity is especially needed in better shaping ecclesial institutions to fulfill their prophetic mission," he said.

He asked that they "embody a clear corporate testimony" to the saving truth of the Gospel. This means that they must be, "constantly re-examining their priorities in the light of their mission and offering a convincing witness, within a pluralistic society, to the Church's teaching."

The third millennium

The need for evangelization was a key theme in the Pope's apostolic letter "Novo Millennio Ineunte," issued in early 2001 at the close of the Jubilee year. John Paul II explained that from the celebration of the Jubilee "we must gain new impetus in Christian living, making it the force which inspires our journey of faith." In this journey we do not have to invent a new program. "The program already exists: it is the plan found in the Gospel and in the living Tradition, it is the same as ever" (No. 29).

He called upon the local churches to formulate pastoral plans that "will enable the proclamation of Christ to reach people, mold communities, and have a deep and incisive influence in bringing Gospel values to bear in society and culture."

He then went on with the following call to all Catholics:

40. To nourish ourselves with the word in order to be "servants of the word" in the work of evangelization: this is surely a priority for the Church at the dawn of the new millennium. Even in countries evangelized many centuries ago, the reality of a "Christian society" which, amid all the frailties which have always marked human life, measured itself explicitly on Gospel values, is now gone. Today we must courageously face a situation which is becoming increasingly diversified and demanding, in the context of "globalization" and of the consequent new and uncertain mingling of peoples and cultures. Over the years, I have often repeated the summons to the *new evangelization*. I do so again now, especially in order to insist that we must rekindle in ourselves the impetus of the beginnings and allow ourselves to be filled with the ardour of the apostolic preaching which followed Pentecost. We must revive in ourselves the burning conviction of Paul, who cried out: "Woe to me if I do not preach the Gospel" (*1 Cor* 9:16).

This passion will not fail to stir in the Church a new sense of mission, which cannot be left to a group of "specialists" but must involve the responsibility of all the members of the People of God. Those who have come into genuine contact with Christ cannot keep him for themselves, they must proclaim him. A new apostolic outreach is needed, which will be lived as *the everyday commitment of Christian communities and groups*. This should be done however with the respect due to the different paths of different people and with sensitivity to the diversity of cultures in which the Christian message must be planted, in such a way that the particular values of each people will not be rejected but purified and brought to their fullness.

In the Third Millennium, Christianity will have to respond ever more effectively to this *need for inculturation*. Christianity, while remaining completely true to itself, with unswerving fidelity to the proclamation of the Gospel and the tradition of the Church, will also reflect the different faces of the cultures and peoples in which it is received and takes root. In this Jubilee Year, we have rejoiced in a special way in the beauty of the Church's varied face. This is perhaps only a beginning, a barely sketched image of the future which the Spirit of God is preparing for us.

Christ must be presented to all people with confidence. We shall address adults, families, young people, children, without ever hiding the most radical demands

456

of the Gospel message, but taking into account each person's needs in regard to their sensitivity and language, after the example of Paul who declared: "I have become all things to all men, that I might by all means save some" (*1 Cor* 9:22). In making these recommendations, I am thinking especially of *the pastoral care of young people*. Precisely in regard to young people, as I said earlier, the Jubilee has given us an encouraging testimony of their generous availability. We must learn to interpret that heartening response, by investing that enthusiasm like a new talent (cf. *Mt* 25:15) which the Lord has put into our hands so that we can make it yield a rich return.

Texts from Zenit News Service and from Holy See Website.

SO